To,

Jan and Dave, (a wonderful couple),

May God bless you.

Binu

I AM WHO I AM

I AM WHO I AM

Unraveling the Mystery of God

Binu Edathumparambil

WIPF & STOCK · Eugene, Oregon

I AM WHO I AM
Unraveling the Mystery of God

Wipf & Stock
An Imprint of Wipf and Stock Publishers
199 W. 8th Ave., Suite 3
Eugene, OR 97401

www.wipfandstock.com

PAPERBACK ISBN: 978-1-5326-1297-8
HARDCOVER ISBN: 978-1-5326-1299-2
EBOOK ISBN: 978-1-5326-1298-5

Manufactured in the U.S.A.   JANUARY 20, 2017

Dedicated to all those who work to reduce conflicts
and promote peace and love in our world.

Contents

Introduction | ix

Part I: A Mystic-Scientist

1   Conservative or Liberal? | 3
2   A Humble Seeker | 10
3   The Tension Within | 15
4   Breaking the Barriers | 21

Part II: A Sense of the Sacred

5   Who Do You Say that I Am? | 29
6   The Evolution of the Experience of the Sacred | 33
7   Self-Driven or God-Driven Knowledge? | 40
8   Authenticating God's Revelations | 45
9   Images, Ambivalences, and Worldviews | 50

Part III: Judeo-Christian Understanding

10   Conventional Healthy Images | 57
11   Distorted and Unhelpful Images | 65
12   A Trinitarian God | 72
13   Unique and United | 82
14   God of the Temple and the Tent | 85
15   God of the Universe | 91
16   A God Who Hears Our Cry | 101
17   God is Love | 108

Part IV: Jesus: The Face of God

18   A Man of History and the Lord of Faith | 115
19   The Incarnation of Love | 119
20   Crazy in Love | 123
21   Why a Gruesome Path? | 130
22   Seeking Until He Finds | 135

CONTENTS

23   The Dialogical Triangle | 144
24   Love that Crosses the Border | 150
25   Jesus in Time and on the Move | 160
26   Moving Past the Temptations and the Tomb | 167

Part V: Living the Mystery

27   The Divine Dance | 173
28   The Christological Model | 179
29   Make Disciples of All Nations | 183
30   The Triangular Dialogue | 190
31   Dynamic and Positive Engagement | 204
32   Call to Communion | 209
33   Coming Home | 214
34   Loving as He Loves | 219
35   Forgiving Love | 228
36   Pilgrims on a Journey | 236
37   The Paradox | 246
38   Biblical Stories on the Paradox | 250
39   From Slaves to Sojourners | 265
40   A Species Hard to Tame | 271
41   Tilting to the Extremes | 277
42   Heaven, Hell, and Purgatory | 282
43   On Earth as It is in Heaven | 290
44   A New Heaven and a New Earth | 300

Conclusion | 315

Bibliography | 319

Introduction

I DOUBT MANY WOULD contest or deny that life is hard. With all the beautiful things we experience about life, we still struggle hard to push it through another day. The glimmer of hope is dangerously weak on many occasions. Most of us don't like the way life unfolds itself before us. It is fragile, stressful, and unpredictable. From the time we are born, we are constantly fighting hard to stay afloat. To begin with, at our birth, we find ourselves as one of the most fragile and feeblest of all animals roaming this earth. Many animals are ready to venture out into the world and be on their own after a few hours or days after their birth. But we, human beings, take months and years to become strong and stable. We are weak and vulnerable.

As we move forward in life, we experience the harshness and hard realities of life on many other fronts. Illnesses strike us without any warning. Emotional and psychological issues put our personal life and interpersonal relationships in turmoil. Marital and family relationships become strained and toxic. Financial instability and unsteady jobs create anxieties on top of everything else. Addictions and unhealthy habits hold us hostage, taking away our peace and joy. Feelings of loneliness and worthlessness darken our days, leaving us with a sense of helplessness and hopelessness. We get into problems with others ending up hurting them or getting hurt. Tensions in the community and society make us afraid and suspicious of each other. The unabated hatred and vengeance between individuals, communities, and nations make us wonder about what happened to the inherent goodness of human beings that we were made to believe in. Violence and wars people unleash on each other shake our faith in our systems and organizations. Death and disappearance of our loved ones make us question about the meaning and purpose of life.

And then there is a lot of unpredictability about even the simple affairs of our everyday life. We might have had a cup of coffee this morning, for example, but we don't know whether we would have one tomorrow. We might have spoken to our family and friends today, but we don't know whether they or we would be around to do it tomorrow. We might be feeling pretty healthy and happy today, but we don't know whether we would end up in the hospital or face something that would make us sad tomorrow.

We know when, where, and how we were born, but we don't know when, where, and how we would die. Even those who decide to take their life do not get to decide the exact moment and nature of their death. The departure of the last breath is not a choice. When the time comes, it simply leaves the person without his or her permission. Many things in our everyday life remain uncertain and open-ended. We ask questions, but we don't necessarily get answers. Even God seems to be silent on many occasions.

We could go to any country anywhere in the world, but I would think that the questions and problems we face in life are pretty much the same. But with all these going on in our life, it is amazing how we make it to another hour, another day, and another year. The mysteriousness and unpredictability of our lives might make us anxious, frustrated, and tired, but we keep moving. We live with hope and trust. We look forward to another day, another year, and another blessing.

We want to be happy about and grateful for what we have and what we are able to do. But the question is: Are we meant to live our lives in constant fights, frustrations, anxieties, and unpredictability? Or could we do better? Is there a better way to live our lives so that the moments of joy, peace, and love outnumber the moments of sadness, violence, and hatred? I tend to believe that there is a better way. That is what I suggest here. I suggest a roadmap or model of life, which, if implemented or lived well, would alter the quality and direction of our lives. It is called the *Christological Model*. It is a model of life built after the example of Christ. As Christ lived, we live our lives as a triangular dialogical relationship of love between God, others, and us, or God, the community, and the individual. The following is a pictorial illustration of the Christological Model.

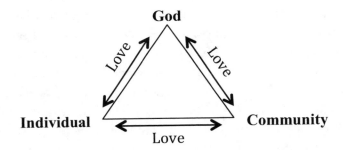

The Christological Model

As I see it, if we want to live our lives well, we have to be constantly in dialogue with God and others. The dialogue is more than mere verbal communication. It is a relationship, an uninterrupted relationship between God, the individual, and the community. And the basis and guiding force of that relationship is love. My life is incomplete without God. God is the source of my life, and to live my life well, I need to be constantly in dialogue or a loving relationship with him. My life is also incomplete without others. You are part of my life and I am part of your life. We need to be constantly in dialogue or a loving relationship with each other. We are not meant to be isolated beings. It is not just about my life or your life alone. It is about our life together. I cannot live without you, and you cannot live without me. When I refer to "you" or "others" I am not referring to just one particular individual or group. Others or the community refers to the whole creation that I am part of. I may be able to live without or separated from one individual or group, but I cannot live totally isolated from the rest of the creation. I shall elaborate on these components of the triangle in the later parts of the book. At this point what we need to remember is that our life is to be a triangular relationship between God, others, and us.

The primary focus of this book is the first component of the Christological Model, God. Although I make references to the other two components, most of the discussions in this book are on God and how our understanding and experience of God impact our lives. I hope to elaborate on the other two components of the Christological Model in separate works in the future.

God being the topic of this book, I envisage it somewhat as a journey into an unfathomable and yet a very tangible mystery. And that is what we call a mystery. A mystery is not something that is totally unknown. It is something about which we know a lot but we don't know everything. And since we don't know everything but are capable of knowing more and more, we keep unraveling it little by little.

The mystery of God has fascinated people of all generations. But he continues to remain as a great mystery. We know a lot but we don't know everything about him. Like everything else in life, we have to struggle hard to understand him and make sense of his presence in our lives and in our world. Hearing that some people might say that it is because we don't have sufficient or strong faith. But often it is not because of lack of faith. It is rather because of who God is and who we are. The infiniteness of God and finiteness of our being make it harder for us to comprehend that mystery. And it may be due to our shallow and weak faith too. Even the apostles who walked and lived with Jesus said to him, "Increase our faith" (Luke 17:5). Being weak and shallow in faith also becomes part of our struggle.

This struggle about not knowing or understanding the mystery of God as much as we would like to might make us frustrated and restless, but at the same time, it helps us to be hopeful and humble. The unknown dimensions of God make us humbly admit that we don't know everything about him but at the same time we remain hopeful of knowing him and experiencing him more and more.

Based on what has been revealed, people have tried to define, describe, and depict God in the way they deemed fit. But from what our ancestors and we have experienced, we realize that God has proved himself to be bigger than all human classifications and categorizations. He continues to reveal himself to us in ways that we sometimes least expect. He becomes so small that we can understand and experience him according to who we are and what capacity we have. But he is so big that he is beyond all our imaginations and fantasies. God remains as an unfathomable mystery, and we continue as insatiable seekers.

In the Judeo-Christian tradition, Jacob appears to be one of the first ones to seek a name for God (Gen 32:29). He wrestled with God a whole night at the end of which he asked God what his name was. Seeking God's name could be interpreted as trying to have some grasp of the mystery of God. But God did not give him a name. Jacob had an experience, but not an explanation. This has been repeated over and over again in human history. People have had an experience of God, but they could never come up with an accurate explanation of God because he is too big to be explained. Then we hear about Moses demanding a name from God. We hear the story of Moses in the book of Exodus, starting from Chapter 2. Although he was a Hebrew by birth, Moses grew up in the care of his biological family as well as the daughter of Pharaoh, the king of Egypt.

Having been raised partly in the palace of Pharaoh, we can assume that Moses was influenced by the customs and traditions of the Egyptians, including their religious beliefs and practices. He probably knew very little about the God of his compatriots, the Hebrews. But as he moved ahead in his life, his experiences and understanding of God seem to have gone through some significant changes. Once when he was shepherding the flock of his father-in-law, Jethro, Moses had an extraordinary experience of God (Exod 3:2). God revealed himself to Moses as the God of his father and his ancestors, the God of Abraham, the God of Isaac, and the God of Jacob. We could think of that experience as a new phase in the spiritual journey of Moses. He began to see and view God in a new way.

During that extraordinary experience, Moses asked God a very significant question, "If I come to the Israelites and say to them, 'The God of your ancestors has sent me to you,' and they ask me, 'What is his name?' what shall I say to them?" (Exod 3:13). On a peripheral level we could think of this as Moses wanting to know how he should introduce himself and God to his people, the Hebrews in Egypt. But on a deeper level, this could be looked at as Moses' struggle in his spiritual and religious journey. Maybe he wanted to know on a deeper level who this God was whom his family and ancestors worshipped. He needed to put a name and face to that God. We could also look at it as the need and spiritual struggle of the community. Moses must have been simply representing the collective voice of his community. Maybe the community wanted to know who this God was whom they and their ancestors revered and worshipped.

Whatever must have been the reason behind Moses' question, the response of God is very telling. God said, "I am who I am" (Exod 3:14). Wow! That's a change. This was the first time that God was revealing himself with some sort of definitive description. And it was not simply any description; it was very profound. It is possible that Moses' jaws dropped at this answer of God. The rest of his and his community's life was spent in deciphering what that description meant. I am who I am—what does that mean? And what are its implications for people's lives?

Moses got an answer for his question. God did not disappoint. But the description, "I am who I am" remained as an open-ended description. Moses and his community had to make sense of what that description meant for them. Who is this God who revealed himself, as "I am who I am?" The gradual unraveling of that mystery defined their life thenceforward.

That same God continued to make himself known to subsequent generations down through the ages. He revealed himself to each generation and peoples to the extent they could understand and experience him. They experienced God, but their explanation of him was always limited. Today, God continues to do the same in our lives as individuals and communities. We experience him in many ways. And we continue the path of our ancestors and past generations with no less effort or enthusiasm, asking the same question, "Who is this God who reveals himself as, 'I am who I am?'"

Often what and how much we understand of God depend on who we are, where we come from, what we have inherited, what we have been taught, and what we experience. Based on what and how much we have understood, we, as individuals and communities, have developed various images and ideas of God. Some of these ideas and images may be healthy and helpful while others may be distorted and destructive.

If we really want to understand and experience God as he reveals himself to us, we have to be open and willing to go beyond some of the images and ideas of God that we have inherited and developed. It is also important to go past some of those images and ideas of God because they have a significant influence on how we live our lives and relate to one another. This book is an attempt at seeking and unraveling this mystery of God. It is about what our forefathers experienced in the past and what we experience today. It is also about how our understandings and experiences of God shape our lives as individuals and communities.

In Part I of the book, I discuss the need for the mindset of a "mystic-scientist" to enter into our exploration and experience of the mystery of God. We remain as believers and yet we continue as insatiable seekers. In Part II, I talk about human beings' search for the sacred from time immemorial and how God has been revealing himself to people in various ages. I also talk about what it takes to authenticate our experiences of God's revelations. Part III focuses on the unique revelations and experiences of God in the Judeo-Christian traditions. I discuss the various images and representations of God, both positive and negative, present in these traditions. Part IV focuses on the person of Jesus who became the most tangible experience of God for human beings in history. It talks about how Jesus revolutionized our understanding and experience of God. It also discusses the model of the dialogical triangle that Jesus lived and exhorted us to implement in our lives. The final section of the book, Part V, is about living the mystery of God in our lives, which essentially involves living the dialogical triangle or the Christological Model. This is the model that fulfills the two commandments of the love of God and love of neighbor. This is the model that helps us to live our daily lives well and takes us into our life of communion with God and others in eternity.

Part I

A Mystic-Scientist

1

Conservative or Liberal?

WHEN I MOVED TO Saint Louis, Missouri, a few years back, someone invited me out one day to a restaurant for lunch. As I was new to the place, I was glad that this particular gentleman took some interest in getting to know me and introduce himself. But during our conversation, he asked me a question that took me by surprise, "Father, are you a conservative or liberal?" I couldn't say for sure why he asked me that question, and I had no idea whether he was one or the other. Not digging deep into his intentions or ideological affiliations, I simply replied him, "I am Catholic." He gave me a startled and inquisitive look.

When I said I was Catholic, I didn't think that there were any strings attached to my concept of my religious identity. I was a Catholic all my life, and that is how I thought of myself. The terminologies of conservatism or liberalism never crossed my mind as anything significant to my life or relationships. But I soon realized that that is not how many people in the United States viewed people's religiosity or viewpoints. In the United States, those terminologies are politically and religiously loaded, and they have many implications when it comes to people's lives and relationships.

This categorization of people in terms of conservatives and liberals may not relevant in every society and culture around the world, but groupings and clas tions of similar kind could be found everywhere. We congregate ourselves i camps as conservatives and liberals, Catholics and Protestants, capitalists ists, blacks and whites, Americans and Indians, rich and poor, man an caste and low caste, Jews and Muslims, and Buddhists and Hindus. S cally, politically, religiously, racially, and in many other ways we s regated classes and categories. On the one hand we are desper vision of a world wide web of relationships and global comm call ourselves the "www generation," while on the other insanely divided and disconnected. We feel different a We are often too caught up in how we look, where speak, what food we eat, what faith we profess, an

The classes and categories we find ourselves in are undeniable facts about us. We are either born into them or we pick them up as we move along. And many of us often stay tightly fastened to them. But the truth of the matter is that it is not only with us that we engage in this game of categorization but we apply it to God as well. People down through the centuries have attempted to put God into categories and classifications they deemed fit. God has been anthropomorphized so much that it is sometimes difficult to say whether there is anything more to God than what we often think of human beings. The Bible says that God created human beings in his own image and likeness (Gen 1:26), but we, human beings seem to have engaged in a counter-creative process, creating God in our own image and likeness. We give God names and faces. But God has proved himself to be much bigger than all these human fantasies and imaginations.

As mentioned, Moses, who was handpicked by God to redeem his people from slavery in Egypt, appears to be one of the first persons in the Judeo-Christian tradition to whom God seems to have said that he was much bigger than what human beings often conceived of. During the extraordinary experience of God that Moses had, he asked God what his name was (Exod 3:13). Although it appears to be a question out of Moses' curiosity, we could think of it as the result of his spiritual and religious inquiry. Maybe he was struggling for a while to understand who this God was whom his ancestors worshipped and who was now calling him to a great mission. The burning bush (Exod 3:2) might be referring to a burning desire in his heart to know and understand the great mystery of God. It is also possible that Moses was just voicing the deep desire of his community to know who this God was. It must have been an expression of the desire in the spiritual journey of the community.

some sort of grasp of the person or thing we are trying to describe.

nity must have been trying to have some sort of grasp of this erited and experienced. God did not disappoint that desire an answer. It was profound. There are three significant said to Moses, "I am who I am" (Exod 3:14). Sec- to the Israelites, 'The LORD, the God of your of Isaac, and the God of Jacob, has sent me this is my name forever, and this my title

4

very profound and telling in the of God. Moses wanted a name giving names and faces to ould understand and expe- ap of human categorization. to make God something that in human language was going ian language and categories are limited. God is incomprehensible and indescribable with our limited human mind. Just because we describe or depict God in some way, it doesn't mean that that is all what he is. The best we can think of God is that "He is who he is."

In saying, "I am who I am" God was letting Moses know that he was too big to be defined and described in any human terms and categories. We could also think of it as Moses and his community coming to the realization that God was someone that they could experience, but he was too big to be reduced to human descriptions, depictions, and definitions.

The experience of Moses and his community has been the experience of subsequent generations. People often tried and continue to try to define, describe, and depict God in many ways, but God continues to reveal that he is too big to be reduced to any of our categories and classes. But then the question is: What do we do with all the descriptions, depictions, and definitions of God we have? How do we make sense of God's revelations? Based on those revelations, we have inherited and developed many ideas and understandings of God. Are they all wrong or without any merit? To answer that question, it is good to think about how we understand ourselves. Our families and friends know us in many ways. If somebody asks them to describe us, they might say many things about us. But that doesn't mean that that is all what we are. We are much more than what they describe about us. Our families and friends know many things about us, most of which come from their external experience of us. But they do not know everything about us. They have only a partial knowledge. They may have very little knowledge about our internal self. Our best friends might know a little more about us. But even they do not and cannot know everything about us. At every moment of our life, we are different in many ways, and they do not have access to all that is going on with us. We ourselves sometimes do not understand fully who we are and what is going on with us. All the knowledge and descriptions about us out there are partial. But are all the descriptions that our families and friends give about us wrong and without any merit? No, not completely. There may be a lot of truth in what they describe. There may be also a lot of distortions in what they describe. Essentially what they have is a partial knowledge and experience. They don't have a complete picture of who we are.

We can say about ourselves the same thing that God said about himself. We can say, "I am who I am." That doesn't mean that we are equating ourselves with God. It simply means that we are much more than what people often think of us or describe about us. Today we are not what we were yesterday. And tomorrow we will not be what we are today. Everyday and at every moment of our life we are in some way the same but in many other ways different. Often people don't think of us that way. They may have already created certain images and ideas of us, and that is what they are holding on to. They see us from that perspective. We all create some sort of "schemas" in our mind about others, and it is with those schemas that we often operate in our relationships.

We do the same with God. We may have created our own schemas about him and we either try to fit him into those schemas or want to create new schemas about him. In saying to Moses "I am who I am," God was telling him and all of us that he was beyond all such schemas. If we say that we are the same and yet different yesterday, today, and tomorrow, how much truer it must be about God because he is far beyond our human comprehension. Hence we have to be very cautious about developing an idea that we have a complete grasp of him. Just because God reveals himself in certain ways or he has been depicted and represented in some way it doesn't mean that that is all what he is. He is the same and yet different everyday of our lives. He is who he is.

The second significant point in God's response to Moses was, "Thus you shall say to the Israelites, 'The LORD, the God of your ancestors, the God of Abraham, the God of Isaac, and the God of Jacob, has sent me to you.'" By listing Moses' ancestors, God was revealing to him a great truth. God was saying that he was not only God of the present but also of the past. It was the same God that was guiding and leading Moses' ancestors. God was in his and his people's history. It is not a God who just popped up from somewhere. Such gods and goddesses often pop up in human cultures and societies. People create their own gods and goddesses. Some win favor with people for sometime and then they lose out to others. People create new ones discarding the old ones. But the God who revealed himself to Moses was the God who was from the beginning. This is not a God who disappears from the scene. He is always present.

God was telling Moses and his people that they were connecting links in a long chain of history of God's salvific work. They were not isolated individuals and community. That truth has a lot of significance for our life. God is reminding us that we are not isolated individuals and communities. We are connecting links in the long chain of God's salvific plan. We may have gone into slavery of different kinds like the Israelites, we may have lived scattered and disconnected from others, and we may have felt that we are abandoned and forsaken, but with all that, God says that we are still part of his divine plan. We never go off his radar. And as part of God's plan, we are all connected with one another. We are not meant to be isolated beings.

The third point in God's response to Moses was, "This is my name forever, and this my title for all generations." This is also very telling about who God was and what Moses and his people recognized about God. God reminds Moses and the future generations that his name will be the same always—that is, "He is who he is." He is not only the God of the past and the present but also of the future. God knew that even the future generations would try to give him names and faces and limit him to their categories and concepts. But he was not going to fall into that trap. He would always remain, as "I am who I am." Just as he revealed himself to Moses and his people in specific ways, God continues to reveal himself to people of different ages in ways that are uniquely appropriate and understandable for them. But he is always who he is. We dare not limit him to this or that.

And then God said that his title would be the same for all gen« be known as our God and the God of our ancestors. He would b« ham, the God of Isaac, and the God of Jacob. And in that title we « names. He is the God of Moses, the God of David, the God of Isaia the God of John the Baptist, the God of Peter, Matthew, James,] and so forth. We can add the names of our own ancestors in our individual ... histories, such as he is the God of Frank, the God of Theresa, the God of Bob, the God of Pat, the God of Maria, etc. God is the God of all these people who have gone before us. He is the God of all the people living today. And he would be the God of the future generations. So we can add our names to that list. And we can add the names of our children, grandchildren, and future generations. In other words, our God is the God of the past, the God of the present, and the God of the future. He is the almighty and eternal God, who was, who is, and who will be, the Alpha and the Omega, the beginning and the end (Rev 1:8).

In that revelation to Moses, God was essentially saying that all of us are included in the realm of the divine. If all of us are included, it means that God does not exclude anyone. The exclusions in our life happen because of the classes and categories we create or inherit in our human communities and societies. But God being beyond all those classes and categories, everyone has a place in his divine realm. Every one of us is precious and important to him. Saint Paul, in his letter to the Romans, asks: "Is God the God of Jews only? Is he not the God of Gentiles also? Yes, of Gentiles also, since God is one" (Rom 3:29–30). The God who revealed himself to Moses and subsequent generations reveals himself to us in our present times, and he will continue to reveal himself to future generations. All of us—the dead, the living, and those yet to come— have a place in his divine plan.

However, taking this idea of Saint Paul that God is one and God belongs to everyone, some people could fall into a grave danger of thinking that we all worship the same God. And they might say that since we all worship the same God there should be no reason for us to fight over our religions and spirituality. I wish the issue were so easy as it seems. The fact is that we all have a place in the plan of God, but it is not the same God that we all are worshipping. We all have created our own schemas or ideas and images of God, and that is what we are often worshipping. Even within the same religion people create different images and ideas of God. Some worship a God who kills and annihilates his enemies while others worship a God who loves his enemies. Some worship a God who hates sinners and fallen away people, while others worship a God who loves everyone and goes in search of sinners. Some worship a God who scares us with hell and punishments while others worship a God who comes to us with mercy and grace. Some worship a God who has no names or faces while others worship a God with many names and faces.

The God we worship is different depending on who we are, where we come from, what we have been taught or how we have been indoctrinated, and what we have ilated. In many ways, we are not any different from the Israelites who created golden calf and worshipped (Exod 32:4). We create our own golden calves and call them God. We may have created or inherited many images of God over the years. And we might tend to think that those images capture the reality of God. But we should not forget that our ancestors also were like us, creating schemas, ideas, and images of God, and not all of them were necessarily healthy and true. There are many people who think that they have an absolutely accurate idea of God and they try to monopolize him. They come across as unquestionable authorities over God. They act as if they know better than God does.

If we really want to know and experience God we have to remain open and go beyond the schemas, ideas, and images of God that we have created. To the Samaritan woman Jesus said, "Woman, believe me, the hour is coming when you will worship the Father neither on this mountain nor in Jerusalem. You worship what you do not know; we worship what we know, for salvation is from the Jews. But the hour is coming, and is now here, when the true worshipers will worship the Father in spirit and truth, for the Father seeks such as these to worship him. God is spirit, and those who worship him must worship in spirit and truth" (John 4:21–24). This is the God that we want to understand and experience. And to understand and experience that God, sometimes we have to go beyond the ideas, images, descriptions, and depictions of God that we have inherited or developed.

When we understand and experience this God more and more we will understand ourselves better and better because we are created in the image and likeness of this God (Gen 1:26). We may have created or inherited certain labels for ourselves, and we might think that that is who we are. Just as my lunch host asked me whether I was a conservative or liberal, all of us may have developed many ideas and images about ourselves. Even after I said I was Catholic, I had to wonder whether that simply denoted my denominational identity or it meant what it is supposed to mean—that is, universal. I may not have thought of myself as a conservative or liberal, but my association as a Catholic itself could be a narrow understanding of myself. My Catholicism could simply be a group identity that I have inherited and maintained rather than understanding it as what Jesus truly envisioned for his disciples and the humanity.

If my Catholicism is to be something that Jesus envisioned for his disciples and the humanity, then I have to go beyond my ritual and denominational identity. If my humanity has to be something that God envisioned for the world, then I have to go beyond my ethnic, racial, linguistic, and national identity. So it is imperative for me to ask: How catholic is my Catholicism, how Christian is my Christianity, and how human is my humanity? The same thing should happen with all the other labels I have given myself or others have given me. I should ask myself whether I am something more than all the labels and descriptions people give me or I give myself. Such reflections will help me to be more and more who I truly am instead of trying to fit into the schemas or categories people have given me or I have given myself.

When we understand God and ourselves better it will make a qualitative differ-ence in the way we live our lives. We will begin to live, as God wants us to live. It will also make a difference in the way we relate to others. It will help us to reflect on and review our perception of others. We may have created our own schemas, ideas, and images about others. Some of them may be true and some of them may be distorted. But all of them put together still give us only a partial understanding of others. The fact is that there is something more to them than what we often see and think of.

The ultimate goal of revisiting and examining our schemas, beliefs, ideas, and thoughts is to go beyond our usual ways of seeing God, others, and ourselves. It is to get to the vision of life and way of being where God, others, and we will have our due places. In that vision and way of being, we will preserve our individual dignity and uniqueness and at the same time maintain an inseparable union with God and others. It is a vision of life and way of being where we would see and relate to everything and everyone as God sees and relates.

2

A Humble Seeker

USHERING IN A NEW vision of life and a new way of being has to happen both on the individual and communal levels. God told Prophet Jeremiah: "Today I appoint you over nations and over kingdoms, to pluck up and to pull down, to destroy and to overthrow, to build and to plant" (Jer 1:10). Jeremiah was commissioned to bring about a transformation in his community. He had to pull down structures and systems that had become unhealthy and ungodly. His people had moved away from God and begun to live unhealthy lives. He had to help them change their distorted schemas about God and themselves and put in place a new standard of living whereby they would walk in God's ways and care for each other as brothers and sisters united in one heart. But before Jeremiah plucked up and pulled down systems and structures in the external world, he had to go through that process internally. The narrative says that Jeremiah found himself inadequate for God's mission, "Ah, Lord God! Truly I do not know how to speak, for I am only a boy" (Jer 1:6).

Jeremiah's admission that he was only a boy and that he didn't know how to speak could refer to the fact that he himself had to first rise up to the new standard of life before he set it before his people. He had to change his schemas and develop a new vision of life and way of being. He couldn't ask his people to follow the new path until he himself had begun to walk on it. His recognition of his inadequacy could refer to the elements in his own life that had to be changed or reformed. He had to be transformed first before he could take up the mission of transforming the community. And God helped him engage in that self-purification and setting his ways rights (Jer 1:9). Cleansed and purified he was ready to take up the mission of transforming his community.

This transforming work of God continues in our world. We are called by God to pull down structures and systems that have become unhealthy and toxic in our world. We have to put in place a new vision of life and a new way of being that is healthy. But before we pluck up and pull down anything to rebuild and replant in the external world, we have to be willing to execute that task in our own personal lives. There may be many things in us that we may have to pluck up and pull down. There may be a need to review and reform many of our schemas, thoughts, attitudes, ideas, and beliefs that we have created about God, others, and ourselves over the years. Plucking up and pulling down some of them may not be easy, as we may have held on to them as sacrosanct for the most part of our lives. But remaining open to God and with firm resolve and determination in our heart, we can hope to reenact in our lives the story of Prophet Jeremiah and his community.

To begin this new vision of life and way of being the best position we can take is that of a humble seeker. We want to begin with all humility that we don't know everything. And we want to be insatiable seekers wanting to unravel the mystery of God and the mystery of our lives. We may not get to all of it, but we will get to some, and we can continue to seek and hope to find the rest. And to those who seek, Jesus said, the mysteries of life will be revealed, "Ask, and it will be given you; search, and you will find; knock, and the door will be opened for you. For everyone who asks receives, and everyone who searches finds, and for everyone who knocks, the door will be opened" (Matt 7:7–8).

In this effort to be humble seekers, there are two pathways that I suggest that we take for our reflections and discussions. The first is a *scientist-practitioner* approach and the second is to go beyond the surface level meanings of things, which in psychology is often known as differentiating between the *manifest content* and the *latent content*.

In the field of psychology, a new model of training called the scientist-practitioner model, also referred to as the "Boulder model," was introduced from the late 1940s. It was felt that "psychologists should be trained as both scientists and practitioners" (Jones & Mehr, 2007). To have the best outcome both in providing services to patients as well as in advancing knowledge in the field, it was found important to have both research and practice to mutually inform and complement each other. Researchers who were not involved in clinical practice and clinical practitioners who were not current with the latest developments and research findings in the field were found to be less effective if not outdated in their respective areas. The scientist-practitioner model of training was meant to integrate science and practice, giving the best to both practitioners and scientists.

Not only in psychology but also in many other fields this model of training and learning has been implemented more and more over the years. Today few people would appreciate a teacher who teaches outdated theories and ideas or a doctor who treats a patient with medicines that were already proved harmful and prohibited many years back.

In trying to unravel and understand the mystery of God and the mystery of our lives, we want to take the same approach, the scientist-practitioner approach. We want to try to unravel and understand the ontological or metaphysical dimension of God. But we also want to take stock of the experiential parts of our God-experience in our lives. We want to engage in theological discussions, but we also want to take into consideration the everyday life experiences of people. We want to answer both "Who is God?" and "How do I make sense of what I experience in my life?" We want to understand who God is in his transcendental dimension, but we also want to pay attention to his immanence. If we simply remain on the ontological, metaphysical, or transcendental level, we will be out of touch with the reality of our experience of him in our everyday lives. But if we focus only on our everyday experiences and the immanence of God, then we will end up limiting him to our schemas, ideas, and images. We will also remain very subjective in our discussions and may not be able to find any commonality or connecting link with others. We need to be able to see some connection between who God is independent of who we are and how we experience him in our lives. We need both the subjective and objective truths about God.

There is another reason why we need to take this scientist-practitioner approach in our reflections and discussions on God and our lives. It is to make our discussions and deliberations comprehensible and available to the non-academic and ordinary folks and to remain open to the wisdom that they have to offer. The reflections and discussions about God and our lives are often pictured as the monopoly of "the learned," and the ordinary folks are considered less worthy to attempt to do anything of that sort. They are often meant to be receivers of the lofty wisdom poured out to them by the intellectuals. And they are also often kept out of the decision-making processes of the community.

One of the major issues that we often find in many religious traditions is the disconnectedness between the theology and spirituality of the theologians or leaders and the rest of the community. The theological reflections often remain on the intellectual level of the select few who hold leadership positions within the community and make decisions. Even if all the theologians do not hold leadership positions, many of them influence the deliberations and decisions of the leaders. Their reflections and thoughts often do not find their way down to the ordinary members of the community. But the ordinary members also experience God and engage in reflections and thoughts in their everyday life. Sometimes some of them are better theologians and more learned than those in the official category. However, they often have no avenues available to share those experiences and thoughts with the theologians and leaders. Both groups remain in their own camps and do not find ways to mutually help refine each other's theology and spirituality. Such disconnectedness, if not reduced, will gradually lead to the indifference of the members and the disintegration of the community. The community needs to get back to the dialogical process and allow God to be bigger than their little quarters or camps.

Even this book, I am aware, is going to be available only to a privileged few, those who can read and those who have money to buy it. That would mean that these reflections on God and our lives are going to remain unavailable to the less privileged unless the privileged few find some ways to share it with them, and I hope they do.

Otherwise, we will continue to be a less cohesive community, keeping God to our own quarters.

Jesus warns those who insist on theological and spiritual monopoly: "Woe to you, scribes and Pharisees, hypocrites! For you lock people out of the kingdom of heaven" (Matt 23:13). Theologians and leaders are called to open the door of wisdom and knowledge of God to the ordinary members of the community and remain open to the wisdom and experience of the latter.

People who live ordinary lives have great wisdom to offer us, and so do those in the academia. We need the wisdom and experience of both the intellectuals as well as the commoners. The scientist-practitioner model in religion and spirituality is about having regular interactions or dialogue between the leaders and the ordinary members.

The second pathway we want to follow in our reflections and discussions is the need to go beyond the superficial or surface level meanings of things or differentiate between the manifest content and the latent content of the "wisdom nuggets" presented to us through the stories of individuals and communities. I call them wisdom nuggets because they come in small portions or packages. But they are treasure troves of meaning. These wisdom nuggets are found in various forms in all communities and cultures. They are presented to us by way of revelations, stories, legends, proverbs, teachings, and the real everyday life experiences of people. The sacred texts in the Bible, for example, could be considered a collection of wisdom nuggets. Each of the stories or verses in it contains profound truths and meaning. They are stories of individuals or communities experiencing the mystery of God. Each of those stories has its historical or particular context. But they also carry a deeper message for people of all generations.

An event or story from the everyday life of an individual in the present times also could be considered as a wisdom nugget presented to us. Although the story might apply directly to the individual person, it may have a wider application and significance for a whole lot of other people. Whatever may be the shape or form in which they are presented to us, when we encounter such wisdom nuggets, we have to see and understand them on two levels: the actual and the symbolic, the physical and the spiritual, the peripheral and the deeper, the manifest and the latent. We have to understand what may have actually happened or is happening in its historical and cultural context, and we have to also see what deeper meaning it holds for us.

In common language, we would call it reading between the lines. The deeper meaning may not be immediately available and obvious. We have to reflect on it and discover it. We have to enter into the life context of those concerned and see what the story really signifies.

In psychology or psychotherapy, we would call these different layers of meanings the manifest content and the latent content of the patient's story. The manifest content is what is immediately presented and available, the facts or storyline that the patient presents. But it is only the tip of the iceberg. The true thought, meaning, or story is hidden under and is referred to as the latent content. The job of therapy is to unravel this latent and hidden content as well.

In unraveling the mystery of God and the mystery of our lives, we have to look at the manifest content and latent content of what we experience and what has been presented to us. If we focus only on the surface level or manifest content of the wisdom nuggets, we will miss their deeper meaning. And if we focus only on the deeper meaning or latent content, then we will end up denying or ignoring the immediate, tangible, and here-and-now experience that we have of the divine.

It is almost like talking about what makes a river. Is it the water on the top or the ground beneath the water that makes the river? Can there be a river without water? No. But does the water alone make the river? That's not possible either. It needs a ground or platform beneath it or on which it can flow. But sometimes our focus can be so much on the water on the surface that we forget about the ground beneath. A river consists of both the water and the ground, what's on the surface as well as what is deep beneath. To understand the river fully, we have to look at both the water and the ground beneath it.

Being humble seekers with a scientist-practitioner mindset and an openness to look at both the manifest and latent contents of what we experience and what has been revealed to us, we explore the mystery of God and the mystery of our lives.

3

The Tension Within

TRYING TO UNRAVEL THE mystery of God and the mystery of our lives by taking the position of humble seekers takes us to an issue that has been debated and discussed in many cultures and societies. The issue is about being scientific and yet religious or spiritual at the same time. Can science and religion go together? Can one be a true seeker and scientist if he or she is religious or spiritual? Can one question and debate and yet be a believer at the same time?

Some might say that if we are truly scientific, we cannot be religious or spiritual, and vice versa. I tend to differ on that. In my opinion, science and our religiosity are not and do not need to be irreconcilable archrivals. Both fields could be more complementary than conflicted in their relationship. Both fields have provided us with answers and affirmations beyond our imagination.

I use the terms "religious" and "spiritual" interchangeably. They don't refer to any particular religion or religious group but rather to the religious or spiritual dimension in us. And I use the gender specificity of He/Him when I refer to God. It has nothing to do with my understanding of God. It is only for the easy use of language. God, as I understand, is beyond genders and categories. But as we try to understand God in our human language, we have to also use the language that is most relatable and familiar to us.

Being scientific does not mean that one has to be doing tests or experiments in laboratories or do research in the traditional sense of the term. Being scientific here simply means that one is open to leaning more, challenging one's own of beliefs and thoughts, testing new hypotheses, and acknowledging that he or she doesn't know everything about everything. It is about not being afraid of or shy about examining one's own beliefs and practices so that unfounded, unhealthy, and archaic elements in them can be changed or refined. It is about being a humble seeker rather than being an all-knowing fanatic.

In fact, both these fields of science and religion are the results of our seeking. We believe and yet we want to know more. If we see a tension, it is to be seen not as a tension between two fields of study or inquiry that are independent of us but rather as a tension within each one of us, a tension between the scientific and the spiritual realms of our being. Some of us might focus more on one realm than the other. But both have to be seen as part of our being and seeking.

The results of the scientific search may be more externally manifested while the results of the religious or spiritual search may be more of an internal experience. Our beliefs or faith may be prominently manifested, but that doesn't mean that we are not scientific. Or the scientist in us may be more visible to others, but that doesn't mean that we are not religious or spiritual.

It is interesting to note how we sometimes try to avoid this tension in us by employing a sort of defense mechanism of externalizing the problem. Externalization, according to Léon Wurmser, "is the defensive effort to resort to external action in order to support the denial of inner conflict" (Wurmser, 1981). Being unable to handle the inner conflict between our scientific curiosity and religiosity, we might make it look like we are focused only on one of these realms and have nothing to do with the other, as if the other realm is external to us. We might shut out one realm completely to avoid any of that tension. We may not want to go into or deal with religion or spirituality at all and might claim that we are all scientific. But that doesn't mean that the religious or spiritual realm of our being doesn't exist. It might lay dormant in us since we don't want to wake it up. Or we may not want to do anything with science because of the fear of it contaminating our religious or spiritual beliefs. But that doesn't mean that we don't have the capacity to be scientific.

Thus a scientist might try hard to ward off the "evil of religion" and a religious fanatic might try to ward off the "evil of scientific inquiry." When we shut out one realm and focus only on the other, it is possible that we become so absorbed in our chosen path and don't even think about the other. Gradually we might think of the other realm as totally alien to us. I can shut out the scientific part of me to a great extent by being overly absorbed in the religious or spiritual realm of my being. And the same can happen vice versa, shutting out the religious or spiritual part of my being by being overly absorbed in the scientific realm of my being. But in a split second, hardcore scientists can all of a sudden become religious and spiritual, and hardcore religious fanatics can become scientific and even irreligious all of a sudden.

Getting absorbed in one realm, we might think that the other realm is someone else's problem. And as long as we think of the other realm as alien and someone else's problem, we might feel uncontaminated, safe, and secure. This might work fine to a great extent from the perspective of an individual's life. One could be a fanatic religious person having nothing to do with science or one could be an absolutist scientist claiming to have nothing to do with the spiritual dimension. Although such a fanatic and absolutist position goes against who we truly are, it may not be hard to stick to one or the other position till the end of one's life. After all, an individual's lifespan is short and limited. But when it comes to our life as a human community, such avoidance is not possible, because first of all it goes against who we truly are, and secondly humanity's lifespan is not limited to one or two generations or centuries. We have been around for a long time and hopefully we are going to be around for a very long time.

We have seen religion trying to shut out science and science trying to shut out religion. It might work for sometime. But it is destructive and counter-productive. The majority in such groups and communities might surrender to that pressure and indoctrination, and one or two generations might pass by with that one-sided position. But that doesn't mean that everyone would buy into that forever. Someday, a dissenting voice will come up and the unquestionable doctrine and beliefs or ideologies and theories will be questioned.

Every now and then in human history we see certain groups and communities taking on a false idea that they can tutor all people into one or the other positions. They assume that they can indoctrinate everyone into certain ways of thinking and believing and everything will be in perfect order. It has happened with politics and ideologies, and theologies and philosophies. Whenever people try to indoctrinate others into certain ways of thinking and believing, and deny them the freedom to question and think what they believe in, someday it is all going to fall apart. Indoctrination is not necessarily education and growth, and blind and forced obedience do not lead to true beliefs and convictions. There is a lot of wisdom in the ancient saying that is often attributed to the Greek philosopher, Socrates: "The unexamined life is not worth living." Often indoctrination and rigid and dictatorial enforcement of obedience are signs of fear of losing control. But God as I understand is not concerned about or afraid of losing control and does not engage in forcing people into something.

Hence when it comes to the tension between science and religion, we have to simply admit the fact that we cannot do away with one or the other. As individuals we might do that, but as a human community, we will see both these realms actively present in different communities and cultures in one way or the other.

We have to also accept the fact that these are all not anything new. These debates and differences have been present in human history for a long time. We can assume that for so long as intelligent, logical minded, and curious human beings have been around, there were tensions between science and religion. They believed in certain things, and they also asked questions about what they believed in. We may not have any proof for this tension existing in human communities if all the relics and remnants of those individuals and communities have been totally destroyed or buried beyond excavation.

Therefore, the first thing for us to do as humble seekers and scientist-practitioners is to admit that we know some things but we don't have an absolute answer for everything. As Saint Paul tells us in his letter to the Corinthians: "For now we see in a mirror, dimly, but then we will see face to face. Now I know only in part; then I will know fully" (1 Cor 13:12). In this world, all our knowledge is partial and limited. Some people may not like to think that way and accept that fact. They might live with the belief that they have an absolute idea about and answer for everything. But in reality, they don't. There is nothing absolute in this world. We believe and we question. Even with all the near absolute answers provided to us by scriptures and sages, we still ask those questions. Even with all the scientific discoveries and proofs provided to us, we still believe in things that are beyond what science can provide. Sometimes we are not satisfied with the answers given to us; we want to find out for ourselves. We seek and explore. We question, we doubt, and we debate. We question our own questions and we doubt our own doubts. We study and yet we surrender. It is a struggle that has been there, and I believe it will continue to be there as long as human beings roam this earth. This is all part of who we are.

We question and doubt not because we are bad people, but that is how our mind and our being function. Depending on our personality, culture, and how we have been indoctrinated into certain beliefs or ideas, we might stick to one or the other of the positions and vehemently oppose the other. But the question is not about whether we totally buy into what science and religion says, but rather whether we can handle that tension without getting overwhelmed or becoming dismissive.

Even Jesus had moments when he questioned, doubted, and examined his own beliefs. In the temptation narrative, we hear the devil saying to Jesus, "If you are the Son of God, tell this stone to become bread . . . If you are the Son of God, throw yourself down from here" (Luke 4:3, 9). This could be understood as a voice coming from outside or inside. It could indicate that there was an internal voice that created a self-doubt for Jesus where he questioned or doubted his own identity. Or it could have been an external voice coming from outside making him to doubt his own identity. But the question or doubt did not mean that he was not the Son of God. He was fully human and fully divine. But being fully human, we have to assume that he had also questions and doubts like any other human being has.

The Bible says that we are all children of God created in his image and like-ness, and we believe that God deeply loves each one of us. But there could be mo-ments when we doubt about this identity and God's love for us. When we are faced with some difficult situations or challenges in our life, we might doubt and question whether God truly loves us. But that doubt and question do not cancel out our identity as God's children and God's love for us. Hanging on the cross in excruciating pain, Jesus cried out, "My God, my God, why have your forsaken me" (Matt 27:46). Hav-ing been abandoned by everyone and hanging between the earth and the sky in that agony and pain, Jesus had a moment of doubt and question whether even his heavenly Father had abandoned him. But that doubt and question didn't mean that Jesus did not believe in his Father's love.

Most of the time our questions, doubts, and debates can lead us to some deeper reflections, discoveries, and convictions. If we can stay on the path of reflections, dis-coveries, and forming convictions, then they will lead us to some significant growth and development. That doesn't mean that we will not ask questions or stop our curiosity about the mystery of God, the wonder of our being, and the magnificence of this universe. We will continue to explore and seek answers for our million questions.

As I understand, those who vehemently oppose everything about science and scientific enquiry do that because of their fear and lack of exposure to avenues of learning. Rightly understood, there is nothing to fear and fret about God. God is capable of taking care of himself. If God is God, nothing of what we do can threaten his existence. His existence does not depend on us; we rather depend on him. However, some of the developments in science might shake up some of our beliefs.

These days, people talk about the possibilities of finding forms of life on other planets. We haven't succeeded yet in exploring the depths of other planets. But Mike Wall, a senior writer on Space matters reports that the scientists at NASA are talking about the possibility of sending a manned mission to Planet Mars in the next fifteen or twenty years. Looking at the pace in which our science and technology moves forward, I wouldn't be surprised if our scientists land on many planets in the next two hundred or three hundred years. We don't have any proof for it yet, but the future scientists and explorers might also even discover that there are forms of life existing on some other planets. Some even speculate that there could be beings more intelligent than human beings.

Some people might panic at the prospects of such happenings because their beliefs and thoughts about God and the world might be severely affected by that. Some people might even wonder whether God, religion, and spirituality would even be relevant then. But if we rightly understand it, there is no reason to panic. If it is God who created us with all this intelligence to explore and discover many things in the vast universe then that God is not going to be threatened by all such happenings. God would continue to be God. He would rejoice in the heights of growth and development that we are making just as a parent rejoices in the growth and accomplishments of his or her child. Sometimes because of the growth and accomplishments he or she has obtained, the child might think and act like he or she is better and stronger than the parent. But that is more out of ignorance than what is factual. However much the child grows and develops he or she still cannot take the place of the parent. When it comes to being a parent, it is not only about doing or accomplishing many things but also about being a parent. In a parent-child relationship, each holds a unique position that one or the other cannot undo or negate.

A similar dynamic plays out in our relationship with God. Our advancements and accomplishments are not going to put God out of work. God is going to be God and he might just laugh if we ever think that we are about to unseat him from his position. It is not God who is threatened by our accomplishments but rather we who are threatened because we may be afraid of getting our systems and structures destabilized. We may be afraid of moving out of our comfort zones. Often we are resistant to any change in our beliefs, thoughts, and attitudes even if they are distorted and unhealthy. We may have held on to them as unquestionable and sacrosanct for many years. It is possible that some of our discoveries and developments might force us to challenge and change some of them. It is good if that happens because God constantly invites us to go beyond our small thinking and perceptions. He and the world are much bigger than what we often think and imagine of. If we think that our new discoveries and findings have made God irrelevant or got him unseated from his position, we have to simply think that what has been unseated or become irrelevant are our distorted images and ideas of God. And that will not be the first time that such challenges and changes have come up in our faith history. As people move from age to age, their understanding and ideas of God and the world continue to be refined and renewed.

Hence if some of the developments in science help us to correct some of our distorted beliefs and thoughts, then it is good. But God will continue to be God, and as I believe he is capable of taking care of himself. Our job is not to be his defenders but rather to be his beloved children and partners in his mission. In this context, I believe that many of those who claim to be atheists are not really unbelievers in God in the true sense. What they don't believe are the gods and goddesses that are often presented to them or the thoughts and beliefs about God that are distorted and unconvincing. Given a chance to experience the true God, many of them would not be unbelievers.

We also need to understand that science also does not have answers for everything. There are assumptions, speculations, and beliefs in science as well. Science also has to learn from mistakes and change what needs to be changed. It is a journey for both scientists and mystics.

Given all these factors about the nature of our being, the position that we can take is that of a humble seeker and believer, a mystic-scientist who loves, desires, and tries to unravel the mystery of God, the mystery of our being, and the mystery of the creation. We become humble seekers of truth. And that is a life-long process. We may have to change many of our strongly held ideas and views and remain open to the ever-revealing mystery of God. This position of being a humble seeker of truth is very different from the position of an arrogant religious fanatic or an absolutist scientist or atheist who thinks that he or she knows everything and is eager to show to the world that he or she got it all figured out.

4

Breaking the Barriers

UNRAVELING THE MYSTERY OF God and the mystery of our lives as mystic-scientists calls for an openness and willingness to break the barriers and walls that we build around ourselves. We cannot understand and experience God if we think that we already know everything about him. We have to remain open to the million ways in which he reveals himself to us. The same thing applies to our lives. Life presents itself to us in so many new ways every day. We need to remain open to its novelties with the mindset of a learner rather than an expert. Such openness sometimes calls for challenging and changing certain of our attitudes, beliefs, ideas, and practices.

As we grow up, all of us develop certain attitudes, beliefs, thoughts, and ideas about God, others, and ourselves. Because of how we have been raised and what we have experienced in our life, it is possible that some of those attitudes, beliefs, thoughts, and ideas are narrow or distorted. But because they often influence our actions and relationships it is important to review them to see if they are accurate, healthy, and helpful. Jesus often found it hard to break the negative attitudes, thoughts, and beliefs of certain people. They were so set in their ways that they did not want to change.

I would like to use an example from my own life to explain why it is important to revisit and examine our attitudes, beliefs, thoughts, and ideas. By birth I am an Indian, born in the state of Kerala and raised as a member of the Syro-Malabar Catholic community. Kerala is considered one of the most advanced states in India with regard to education, life expectancy, gender equality, social development, and the overall human-development index. The scenic beauty of Kerala due to its sprawling backwaters, lush green vegetation, coconuts and palms, the long coastal line created by the Arabian Sea, and the long range of mountains known as the Western Ghats give the state a unique name, "God's own country." The state has been an attractive destination for tourists, spice traders, and those seeking rest and restoration through the ancient Indian medical system of Ayurveda. Being home to rubber plantations, waterways, and many centers of learning, Kerala is sometimes known as the land of latex, lakes, and letters.

These characteristics of the state have created an inflated sense of self-pride for most Keralites (a native of the state of Kerala). Someone from Texas recently told me that there is no need to ask Texans where they are from. They will tell you they are from Texas even before you ask. My guess is that the same is true of people from Kerala. They will tell you that they are from Kerala even before you ask them. Such an affinity to one's own state may not be very peculiar to Keralites alone. India being a very multicultural and heterogeneous country, it wouldn't be a surprise if people's loyalty were often more to their own state or ethnic group than to the country as a whole.

Growing up in Kerala, my world was Kerala. I didn't know anything more than that. Even within Kerala, my world, in fact, was my little town that I grew up in. I never knew that India was a large heterogeneous country. I still don't have a good grasp of how diverse India is. There are hundreds of languages with many of them having their own alphabets. Each state represents one or more distinct ethnic groups. They eat different kinds of food, dress differently, and follow different customs and traditions. Such diversity and peculiarities of each state or region make people remain secluded in their little worlds. Moving out of Kerala in later years was an eye-opener for me. I experienced a much larger world outside of Kerala.

Added to the sense of pride in my ethnic and cultural background as a Keralite, I inherited another dose of pride and exclusive status as a "Syro-Malabar Catholic." It may not mean much for others, but for a Keralite who belongs to the Syro-Malabar Catholic rite, it is an identity that carries many meanings.

Many Catholics and others may not be aware of it, but the Catholic Church is a communion of several individual Churches, approximately 23 of them, with the Pope or the Bishop of Rome as their universal head. Sometimes these individual Churches are referred to as different *Rites*, indicating their individual uniqueness and differences in ecclesiastical traditions. These rites are grouped into two categories, the Western and the Eastern or Oriental Churches. The largest of these rites is the Latin rite. All these individual Churches vary in their heritage, emphasis on theology, liturgy, canon law, celebration of sacraments, etc. Many of these Churches have married clergy.

The Syro-Malabar Church is one of these rites within the Catholic communion primarily located in the state of Kerala in India. This Church has its own unique history and traditions. Sometimes referred to as the Saint Thomas Christians, the Syro-Malabar Catholics in Kerala trace back their history to the first century AD/CE. According to the tradition, Saint Thomas, one of the apostles of Jesus, arrived in Kerala in 52 AD/CE and introduced the Christian faith to the natives. At the time of Christ and even before, it is established that there were trade links between the Malabar Coast or Kerala and the kingdoms in the Middle East, Greece, Persia, and the Roman Empire. The merchant ships going back and forth between Kerala and other ports presumably helped Saint Thomas to travel to Kerala. It is also believed that due to the trade relationships, there were people in Kerala who spoke Aramaic and Hebrew in those days. They were not necessarily Jews but the business relationships introduced those languages to the natives. But there were also people of Jewish origin who settled in Kerala. Having people who spoke his language in Kerala might have helped Thomas' initial introduction to the people of the land and his work of spreading the gospel. Thomas also might have stopped at other places on his way to Kerala and established Christian communities.

In any case, the Syro-Malabar Christians hold Thomas, the Apostle, as the "father" of their faith. The number may be disputable, but some say that there were seven high caste Hindu families that embraced the Christian faith as a result of Thomas' evangelization. The Syro-Malabar Catholics appear to trace their origin back to these seven families. Because of this lineage, the Syro-Malabar community maintains a distinct identity as opposed to other Christians in India most of whom inherited their Christian faith either from the European colonizers or other Christian missionaries from the West fifteen hundred years later. Interestingly, Kerala, specifically the city of Calicut (now Kozhikode), was the first entry point for the Portuguese in 1498, which then led to the colonization of India by them and other European powers. Hence we could say that Kerala was the entry point for even the second wave of evangelization and spread of Christianity in India.

When it is looked at from outside, the Catholic Church or Christians in India might look like a homogenous group. But only a closer look at each of the individual Churches or rites in India would tell us how different they are and how embedded is people's faith in their culture, history, and traditions. I come across people in the United States who think that the rest of the Catholics all over the world belong to the Latin rite or celebrate the liturgy and practice their faith just the same way they do. Growing up in Kerala, I was not much different in my thinking. I thought that the rest of the Christian world was Syro-Malabar! Little did I know that there were Christians within and outside Kerala who belonged to other traditions. My world was all "Syro-Malabar," and I had little knowledge of anything other than that. And if there was anything else, it, in my perception, was not "real" Christian or Catholic.

In the religious circles in India and outside, the Syro-Malabar Catholics would often like to highlight their two-thousand-year-old Christian tradition going to back to Saint Thomas, the Apostle. They stand out as distinct from other Christians or Catholics in Kerala and other parts of India.

Besides these differences in the origin and traditions, the "high caste" stature of the Syro-Malabar community sets it apart from most other Christian and Catholic communities in Kerala, which do not claim to have the same lineage. Amali Philips (2004), a researcher on marriages in Kerala, found that the Syro-Malabar community continues to maintain its elite and exclusive identity by remaining as endogamous (marrying within one's own group, caste, or clan) and hypergamous (marrying into an equal or more prestigious social group, caste, or clan) in their marital alliances. For example, a marriage with Latin Catholics (*Paraya* Christians, *Pulaya* Christians,

Nadar Christians), who are generally new converts from lower castes, is often discouraged in the Syro-Malabar community.

Nilufer Medora (2007), a researcher, commenting on the influence of caste system in India, suggests that although the Indian government declared the caste system unconstitutional in 1950, it continues to influence the life and relationships of Indians even to this day. Besides determining people's occupations, friendship circles, marital alliances, and associations, caste puts people into endogamous groups making them exclusive and isolated. The caste system has been around for a few thousand years and it has so long been practiced that it seems to have been ingrained in people's psyche making it difficult to erase. Although the Syro-Malabar Catholic community does not promote or adhere to the dictates of the caste system, its lineage as a high caste group and continuation as an endogamous group appear to have kept it as an exclusive and dominant group for a long time. Coupled with that historical background is its claim to the apostolic tradition going back to Saint Thomas, the Apostle, which leads to the maintenance of its exclusivity within the Christian and Catholic communities in Kerala and India.

The Syro-Malabar community has done a great amount of good for the social, economic, educational, and spiritual development of people in Kerala and India. The community has maintained a peaceful and respectful co-existence with other castes and communities. It has also raised many men and women who dedicated their lives as missionaries to go all over the world to bring God's love to others. However, looking back at this community that I grew up in, I realize that our community was not without its pitfalls. Although the community could take great pride in its rich and long tradition, its charitable and outreach programs, and its tolerant and peaceful co-existence with other communities, it is to be admitted that by and large this community has remained as an elite and exclusive community within Kerala. Its claim to the apostolic tradition and the high caste status consciously or unconsciously alienating people of other castes and communities for centuries cannot be completely ruled out.

Growing up, I didn't even think that my faith was so embedded in this exclusive and elite culture and traditions of my community. Even today, many in the Syro-Malabar community may not be aware and admit that they were and are an exclusive and dominant group in the society. After I stepped out of Kerala and started encountering and experiencing other cultures and communities in a larger way, I began to realize how secluded and small my world was. Joining a missionary order that was primarily Latin rite in its heritage and practices, I began to learn more about other traditions within the Christian community.

Reflecting on the person of Jesus and his message and weighing that against my own Christian identity that I was carrying, I began to realize that I was far from what Jesus envisaged for his disciples. I was almost like Saint Paul who boasted about his past and then realized that it was all a waste: "If anyone else has reason to be confident in the flesh, I have more: circumcised on the eighth day, a member of the people of

Israel, of the tribe of Benjamin, a Hebrew born of Hebrews; as to the law, a Pharisee; as to zeal, a persecutor of the church; as to righteousness under the law, blameless. Yet whatever gains I had, these I have come to regard as loss because of Christ" (Phil 3:4–8). Paul broke with his past and exclusivism because he discovered a larger world and larger truth. He realized how small his world and understanding was until then. The call of Jesus was to break down his exclusivism and embrace a larger world. Being struck down on his way to Damascus could be indicating a transition from his exclusive and elevated position to becoming a more open and all-embracing disciple of Christ. The early Christian community in Jerusalem was no different. They did not want anything to do with the gentile Christians first. We read about both these in the Acts of the Apostles. I was in the same boat. My psyche had developed beliefs, thoughts, and ideas about God and people that were so small and limited. My world was very exclusive and secluded. I didn't know anything more than what I was used to.

When the person who invited me out to lunch asked me whether I was a conservative or liberal, I responded that I was a Catholic. But I realized that my Catholic identity for a long time was not all that Catholic. It was exclusive, narrow, and elite. I had to break out of those barriers to see the larger world outside. The mission is not completed yet; everyday I have to work on it. My Catholic tradition and ethnic background are only two of the things that contribute to such exclusivism and seclusion. There are many other barriers that I need to break down to see and embrace the larger world that God presents before me.

This is not an isolated phenomenon with one individual or community. We see that all across the world. We sometimes do not think of the world or ourselves anything more than what we inherit or are taught. Our societies and communities are often structured that way. We are born into a particular nation, community, race, religion, and language, and we often grow up as exclusive groups and communities. We get into certain exclusive groups by occupation, beliefs, ideology, or interests, and we stay there isolated from everyone else. We often tend to make friends with those who like us and those who are like us. Our history, lineage, affiliations, beliefs, and practices sometimes take the center stage and they make us build walls around us. Those factors sometimes create a tunnel vision for us. Although the Christian way of life was meant to break down all walls and barriers of exclusivism and narrow-mindedness, Christians themselves have become creators of such walls in many places. Sometimes we turn into the very same things that Jesus stood against. Jesus tried to break down such barriers and small worlds, but sometimes his own disciples end up going back to the very same things he tried to undo. Any new movement or way of life that begins with a novel vision has an inherent danger of getting institutionalized, becoming exclusive, and turning out to be the opposite of what it was meant to be in the first place.

We are all part of such systems and structures. There may be many unhealthy, exclusive, and narrow-minded thoughts, beliefs, ideas, and practices that have been ingrained in our psyche or we have inherited or developed over the years. We may hold on to the idea that we have got it all right. Such rigidity needs to be challenged and changed for God to break into us. Religion is to be a dynamic relationship in which God continues to reveal himself to us rather than seeing it as a rigid system or structure where God has no freedom to influence or work with us whatsoever.

Part II

A Sense of the Sacred

5

Who Do You Say that I Am?

REMAINING AS MYSTIC-SCIENTISTS AND being open to go beyond our exclusivist and narrow beliefs, ideas, and thoughts, we continue our exploration of the mystery of God and the mystery of our lives. Jesus asked his disciples, "Who do people say that the Son of Man is" (Matt 16:13). The general population had their own ideas and opinions about who Jesus was. For most of them, Jesus was either a prophet, the reincarnation of one of the ancient prophets, or a great teacher and reformer. They probably didn't think anything more than that. And then Jesus asked his disciples a very personal question, "But who do you say that I am" (Matt 16:15). They were not like other people. They were his close companions. They lived with him, they followed him wherever he went, they saw all his miracles, they heard him preach and teach, and they lived as a close-knit community. Their understanding of him was not the same as that of the general public. But to answer that question they all probably had to take some time to think about it. Even if they gave an instant answer, like Peter did, it must have taken some time for this very personal question to sink in. Maybe they pondered over that question everyday. Everyday they were discovering something new about him.

This question could be also seen as the one question that the early Christian community was trying to answer. Jesus was so powerful and yet so simple, so divine and yet so human, so calm and peaceful and yet so full of passion and power. "Who is this Jesus?" they appeared to have asked over and over again.

It took several years and centuries for the Christians to answer this question. The results of those theological and Christological reflections and thoughts are often reflected in some of the titles given to Jesus. Jesus is often referred to as Son of Man, Son of God, Son of David, Lamb of God, Christ, Lord, Logos (the Word), New Adam, Second Adam, Last Adam, King of the Jews, Rabbi, Light of the World, so on and so forth. After many centuries of discussions and debates, the Church definitively defined the nature of Jesus as divine and human, true God and true man (Catechism of the Catholic Church, 422–483), and put a cap on all other speculations. The whole book of the Catechism of the Catholic Church codifies the Church's beliefs about the mystery of God as it has been revealed to humanity. And yet, that same question continues to be put to all of us everyday, "Who do you say that I am?" Everyday we unravel the mystery of God, or everyday he reveals himself to us in new ways.

The struggle to have some grasp of the mystery of God is not limited to one community or generation. Those who are born and raised in communities or families that have some sort of religiosity or spiritual base know that their families and caregivers plant in them seeds of faith and present them with some images of God that might or might not make sense at that time. But as we grow up, we try to make sense of what we were presented with. For some people, it is not a struggle or big deal. They just believe in what they were presented with and they continue the beliefs and practices of their parents or past generations. But not all are completely settled with what has been presented to them. Not that everything that was presented to them was bad or negative, but rather, being insatiable seekers, they attempt to unravel more and more the mystery that has been presented to them. Thousands and thousands of pages of literature on God, hundreds and thousands of talks and sermons delivered to them about God, and numerous icons, images, pictures, and other depictions of God they have come across still do not stop them from this seeking.

It is not only the theologians in centers of learning who are engaged in this endeavor of understanding better the mystery of God, but also the unassuming and ordinary people we come across in everyday life situations. They also dwell on and deal with this mystery. After the birth of Jesus, a group of shepherds, who reportedly received a message from the angels, came to pay homage to him. They searched for the mystery that was said to have been born in their midst. And when they found him, they rejoiced. They narrated to Mary, Joseph, and others all that had been revealed to them. Mary seems to have taken in that mystery reverently but at the same time she pondered over it. The gospel states: "Mary treasured all these words and pondered them in her heart" (Luke 2:19). As she rejoiced at all that had been revealed about her son, Mary also seems to have wondered about what all that meant. She had to understand and make sense of all that mystery gradually.

We have been presented with different images and ideas of God, but many of us keep pondering in our heart what all that means. Many of us ask the same question that Saint Paul asked, "Who are you, Lord?" (Acts 9:5). Pondering and seeking do not make one an unbeliever. It is simply part of our spiritual growth. God never stops revealing himself. Before he ascended to heaven, Jesus said to his disciples, "I still have many things to say to you, but you cannot bear them now. When the Spirit of truth comes, he will guide you into all the truth" (John 16:12–13). We cannot take all of the information at once. It has to be taken little by little. I could wish that when I was five or ten years old I had all the information and knowledge I have now. But that is a futile and unrealistic wish. When I was five or ten years old I was not ready to take all these information and knowledge. I had to grow physically, emotionally, psychologically, spiritually, and in many other ways to get to all of that. My brain was not ready to take in all the information. Today when I look back, I realize that twenty years back I did not read and understand the Bible as I do today. Thirty or forty years back, I did not understand and think of God as I do today. This truth about my gradual growth applies not only to the Bible and my understanding of God but also to every other aspect of my life. I had to grow up to get to all the knowledge and understanding I have today. I could also wish that I had the wisdom and understanding of a ninety-year-old person. But that is also a futile wish because I am not ninety years old yet. I cannot have all of the experience and wisdom that a ninety-year-old has. I need to make my own journey to those ninety years or whatever is going to be my life span to get to all the wisdom and knowledge that those years would bring.

Parents might like to tell their children a lot of things and might wish that they grasped and digested all of that. But it doesn't happen that way. Everything has to be given in small dosages. Children cannot chew and digest everything at once. Children learn and grow little by little. It is the same with our spiritual growth. Jesus had many more things to tell and teach his disciples, but he knew that they were not ready for that yet. It had to be given little by little, step by step. Even Jesus had to wait until he was thirty years old before he could enter into public life and ministry. Seeing what and how much he accomplished in three years, we could wonder why he couldn't start his public ministry when he was fifteen or twenty years old. But that was not meant to be. He had to be ready for that. Although we don't have any details about his life between the infancy narrative and his public life, we can assume that Jesus was growing in wisdom and knowledge.

We cannot understand the mystery of God in one sitting. It is a life long process where God reveals himself to us gradually. We have to also admit that with our limited mind we cannot understand fully the mystery of God. I will be a fool to think that I can understand the unlimited God with my limited mind. That does not fit well with logic. As a created being I am limited in the possibility of knowing my creator. A son can grow into the stature of his father but can never replace or substitute the father. Jesus said, "Very truly, I tell you, servants are not greater than their master, nor are messengers greater than the one who sent them" (John 13:16). The creator brings the creatures and the creation into being which necessarily leaves the creatures and the creation subject to the creator.

Although it is illogical to think of knowing and understanding this unlimited Creator God with our limited mind, it is highly proper to think that it is he who planted in us that seed of curiosity and desire to seek, explore, and understand. The Catechism of the Catholic Church states: "The desire for God is written in the human heart" (27). God keeps nurturing and promoting that desire in us just as a parent would keep teaching and coaching a child step by step. As the child grows older and older he or she gets to know things more and more. Having been planted with this seed of curiosity and desire, human beings have been making this search from time immemorial. Being part of this same history and long chain of seekers we too make an attempt in the same direction without claiming to be either the first or the last in this endeavor.

We also engage in this pursuit of understanding God with the awareness that he is an inexhaustible reality, and we will know him fully only when we are united with him in eternity. Saint John speaks of this limited understanding that we have in this world and our hope to know everything fully in eternity, "Beloved, we are God's children now; what we will be has not yet been revealed. What we do know is this: when he is revealed, we will be like him, for we will see him as he is" (1 John 3:2).

6

The Evolution of the Experience of the Sacred

JUST AS JESUS TOLD his disciples that he would reveal everything to them gradually, it appears that the humanity as a whole has been making baby steps in unraveling the mystery of God, or God has been revealing himself gradually to the humanity from time immemorial. When we consider our understanding and experience of God and faith, we have to always take into consideration our history and how and from where we got here. If we think that what we believe in and practice now have always been what people believed and practiced from ancient times on, that may be a little too much of a stretch. Like everything else in our human history, our understanding of God and faith also had a gradual growth and development, and it continues to be so.

It will be interesting to see what our own ancestors in our individual family history must have believed in some five or ten thousand years back. Maybe they were nature worshippers. Maybe they believed in some celestial beings. Some of them may not have believed in anything celestial or divine. Maybe we would call them "pagans" in comparison with what we believe now. But with all that, it is still a fact that they were our ancestors and God was working in their lives as he does in ours now. We are a connecting link in that long history of humanity. They lived in a different age and we live in a different age.

If we wonder why people of the ancient times did not believe in God as we do now, it will be the same as asking why a five-year-old child cannot behave like a fifty-year-old person. The simple fact is that the five-year-old cannot but be like the five-year-old because its brain and all the faculties are not developed enough to understand things, as an adult or fifty-year-old would do. The cosmology, theology, philosophy, and other areas of knowledge and experience available to the ancient people were much different from what we have today. Their experience was limited and we speculate that their imaginations and thoughts were not sophisticated and developed. They communicated with each other with sounds and sign languages but we have Emails, Instagram, Google, Facebook, Pinterest, Tumblr, Twitter, and all other kinds of networks and media for communication. They and their children looked at the stars in the sky and wondered what they were. We have explored the universe and have made extensive strides in understanding the nature of many stars. They watched the winds and seas with horror and awe. We have befriended the seas and winds to do kayaking, snorkeling, parasailing, and all other ways of navigating the waters and the air. The people of ancient times and we are not on the same page when it comes to experience, expertise, and making sense of things. They tried to make sense of everything with what they had, and we try to make sense of everything with what we have now.

To see this difference, we don't need to go as far back as the ancient times but rather look at how things are viewed by the older and younger generations today. Seeing the big gap, sometimes people refer to the two generations as the "old school" and the "new school." The older generation and the younger generation have what I called in my previous book, their own "accents." Just as differences in linguistic accents sometimes make people wonder whether they are speaking the same language, our individual and generational differences might sometimes make us feel like we are from two different planets. The older generation comes from a particular era and they were not exposed to all the novelties and developments of the present day. While growing up they were pretty much secluded in their own community, ethnic group, or race. Their interactions were limited to their own people. The science and technology they had were still in their early stages of development in comparison with what we have today. Their theology, spirituality, and understanding of God were very different from what many young people have today. What and how they were taught is much different from what and how the present day generation is taught. The older people are still very much limited to their homes and immediate surroundings. They are not much exposed to the diversity of the current society. Many of them being retired and mostly homebound, they don't associate too much with people of other age groups, cultures, and backgrounds. Based on what they have experienced and been exposed to, they are somewhat set in their ways and they find it difficult to understand the ways of the younger generation that is growing up in a very different era.

The younger generation today is exposed to a much different world. They are born into an advanced scientific and technological world. They deal with a diverse and multicultural population wherever they go, whether it is at school, work place, or the larger community. Their spirituality and sense of community are much different from what the older generation has. The society they interact with today is much different from the one the older generation interacted with some years ago. Their ways and means of communication, such as those through the social media, are unfamiliar and even irreverent to many of the older folks. In short, the older and younger generations have their own particular "accents," and sometimes they don't match. This is not an isolated problem with our times alone. This, I believe, is how two different generations feel at any given time in our human history.

But these differences are not peculiar to people of different generations alone. It happens in any context of life. In a family, the parents and children have different accents. The siblings themselves have different accents. People have different accents when it comes to different races, religions, classes, and castes. Women and men have different accents. People of different nationalities, political affiliations, and ideals and ideologies have different accents. When our accents are different, there are all kinds of mismatching thoughts and feelings that are exchanged between us externally and internally. The fact is that all of us have our own accents depending on where we come from, what we have been exposed to, and how we look at the world, others, and ourselves.

When we think of the people of the ancient times and their difference with us regarding how things are perceived and understood it is something similar to this difference between people in the present times because of their accentual differences. The people of ancient times lived as exclusive groups and their interactions were within the group. Their exposure to other groups and communities were nil or limited. They were still in the early stages of development with regard to the use of their faculties, intelligence, and scientific inquiry, although some of the things that we excavate or discover about them today make us amazed about their intelligence and abilities. They were not so primitive as we often think of them. A sense of the sacred seems to have existed in most of such ancient communities. Because it was not based on any advanced theological inquiries or contemplation, we might consider their sense of the sacred or understanding of God rudimentary and unrefined. But presumably given their situation that is the best they had.

Just like a child making baby steps, humanity had to go through various such steps to get to where we are now. The understanding of God continues to grow, and as different generations come and go, the revelation and unraveling of the mystery of God will continue to happen in so many different ways. Just because what we have today is much different from what they had before, we don't just throw away the old completely or find fault with everything that is new. We have to see it as a process of growth, valuing both the old and the new, and at the same time refining what is distorted and unhealthy.

To get anything accomplished, we often work with the available materials. We don't wait for everything to be perfect to start working. Similarly, God works with the available material. If we are primitive, he works at the level that we can understand and experience him. If we are advanced, then he works with us at that level. That is the difference between the ancient people and us. He worked with them at their level, and he works with us at our level. And in our own depiction or presentation of our understanding and experience of God, we use languages and media that are specific to our times and culture in history. To later generations those languages and media might look less advanced and bizarre, but in the present times, they make perfect sense.

In comparison with the people of the past generations we have an added advantage of looking back and taking stock of what they had so that what we come up with is not just a repetition of what they had but a refinement of and addition to what they had. That does not mean that we are much better than them or have figured out everything about God. When we think of our advanced theologies and technologies today we have to remember that the foundation for them were laid by the past generations. What we have today is built upon what has been present before our arrival. We don't come up with anything totally new. In this post-modern age, we may have a temptation to think that what we have achieved today is solely by our own effort. It is not so. Whatever we accomplish today has been possible only because the people who went before us had created an environment for us to do that. Today when children start their education and learning, they are presented with an environment that promotes their advancement and quick learning. They would not have been able to be on that path of advancement if the past generations did not create that environment for them.

The accomplishments of the past generations might look crude, crazy, and less advanced, but what they accomplished becomes the stepping-stones or foundation for the accomplishments of later generations. No researcher is completely novel in his or her findings. Researchers always build upon what others have done before, or they are able to come up with something new because others had prepared the ground or environment for them to do that. The only one who can claim to be an originator of anything that is totally new is God. Of course, God's revelations are unique to individuals and communities, and yet when we think of the development of our faith and understanding of God we need to acknowledge that we build on what has been done before.

Even in our own present age we know that we all are not on the same page when it comes to our sense of the sacred or understanding of God. Even with all the developments in every area of science and religion that we have today, a person in a society or culture in Asia or Africa has a different theology and understanding of God in comparison with a person in Europe or the Americas. A person in the Christian tradition has a different experience and understanding of God in comparison with a person in the Islamic, Hindu, or Jewish tradition.

We grow up and live at the same time, but we don't carry or develop the same understanding of God. What we have grown up with or been presented with are different depending on who we are and where we come from. When we think of our sense of the sacred or understanding of God, it is important to keep these things in mind.

Having said all that, let us take a quick look at what has been the experience of the past generations. We don't have access to all that existed at all times in our human history since most of our information about the prehistoric and ancient people is very much dependent on the available archeological findings, written materials, and oral traditions. Many of our conclusions based on these available resources are speculative. But except through these limited sources that have been unearthed we don't have access to those people in any other way. It would have been great if we had those people around so that we could hear them and ask them questions.

Human history is often traced back only to some of the early human societies which gradually developed into civilizations. Human beings abandoned their nomadic and hunter-gatherer lifestyle and began to settle down as civilizations. With them began what the historians usually refer to as the "Pre-Axial" age (Gorski, 2008). A civilization, according to Eugene Gorski "is the coming together of a large group of people to achieve feats or projects impossible at the family or small tribal scale" (Gorski, 2008, p.5). As major projects, civilizations built cities, constructed irrigation systems, organized themselves into unified societies, developed written languages and writing tools, and developed their own unique cultures, religion, and other structures and systems. Many of these civilizations had religious beliefs and practices as an integral part of their everyday life. They built temples in honor of their deities. It must have taken hundreds of years even for these unique features to develop in these civilizations. The prominent of these civilizations that we know of are the Sumerian or Mesopotamian, Egyptian, Indus Valley, Mayan, Chinese or Yellow River Valley, Ancient Greek, Roman, Persian, the Aztecs, and the Incas.

Although we have been able to trace back to these civilizations because of what has been unearthed or left behind, we can assume that many human communities and societies had come and gone even prior to the pre-axial age without leaving behind any trace of their existence. But from what we know it is clear that people of ancient times believed in the existence of certain spirits, gods, or supernatural powers. They were considered as superior in power to human beings, and they were looked upon with fear, wonder, and awe. While some cultures and communities believed that human beings were meant to be at the service of these gods and spirits and were to fear them, others thought of these gods as benevolent and kind to human beings. They had rituals and worships to placate and appease these gods and spirits. The rituals and practices were mainly to ensure a good life for people while they lived in this world. The gods and spirits had to make sure that the human beings had fertile grounds, fruitful crops, protection from scary forces of nature or their enemies, and an overall happy life. And the human beings in turn would be obedient and reverent toward these gods. It was mostly about people's life on this earth and there was no concept of them joining or moving to the world of gods after their life in this world. By and large, we could consider the religious beliefs of these ancient people as rudimentary and rustic. They were not highly organized or sophisticated.

Most of the civilizations were polytheistic, believing in the existence of multiple gods and goddesses. Just as the society was organized into various classes and levels, the gods and goddesses also were thought to be belonging to different sections and levels. Some deities were believed to be superior to others. Some deities had assigned roles and functions. In some communities it was a female deity that was supreme while in others it was a male deity who occupied the prime spot. Most of their images and ideas of these gods and goddesses were anthropomorphic. In some communities, the forces of nature got deified and people began to think of everything that was superior to them in power as a deity. Thus the sun, the moon, the wind, the earth, and all such objects and forces were deified. There were deities of peace and war, and restoration and destruction. Some deities were assigned the role of an aggressor or warrior and were pitted as allies of the men or groups who took to fighting and aggression with other groups. However, with all these developments, these religions still remained as tribal or ethnic religions. They didn't have any specific names or universal appeal. As time passed, most of these religions seem to have disappeared or given way to new religions, beliefs, and practices.

As the early civilizations declined some groups and communities migrated to different parts of the world, while others continued to stay put. Those who migrated to new places came into contact with other communities and tribes that inhabited those lands. Some groups integrated or coexisted with the natives while others conquered and established their supremacy over the people of the occupied land. Some continued some elements of their old religious beliefs and practices while others developed new ones integrating what they encountered in the new places. For example, in the *Vedic* times, which began in around 1500 BCE, it is believed that the Aryans from Central Asia migrated to India. Of course, the India of those days was not the same as the India of today. The Aryans appear to have conquered or settled alongside the native Dravidians and other inhabitants of the land. The Aryans spoke an Indo-European language, which gradually evolved into a specific language called Sanskrit. The Aryans also brought with them the polytheistic religion they had practiced in Central Asia. Having encountered the natives of India and having been influenced by the already existing religions and beliefs in the land, the religion of the Aryans seems to have gone through some changes. The changed beliefs and practices seem to have gradually given rise to a distinctive religion called "Hinduism."

Similarly, there were other groups and communities rising and making their presence felt in other parts of the world. And they also were fertile grounds for the rise of certain religious founders and distinctive religions that still stand the test of time to the present day. Thus besides Hinduism, we have Zoroastrianism, Buddhism, Jainism, Confucianism, Daoism, Shintoism, Judaism, Christianity, Islam, and Sikhism. Some of these religions were offshoots of other existing religions. Although many of these religions began as tribal or ethnic religions, they spread out and grew large giving them a universal appeal. Today they are counted as "world religions."

Many of these religions still carry elements from their parent religions, but they also have their own unique creed (what they believe), code (how they live), cult (how they worship), and community (who follow the specific way). These religions became more organized, structured, and sophisticated. They developed unique and advanced theologies. They connected the physical and the metaphysical. There are similarities among many of these religions, but all of them claim their own uniqueness as well.

Among the religions that acquired a universal appeal, the birth of Abrahamic or Judeo-Christian-Islamic faith traditions marked a significant departure from polytheism to monotheism. Many religions that existed before and after them believed in the existence of multiple gods or deities. Each of these deities was believed to be supreme or powerful over certain worlds or realms of the universe and certain periods of time. Moving from the belief of many gods or deities controlling different worlds or realms of the universe and certain periods of time to the belief in one God having authority over the whole world or universe and over all times and seasons was a significant change in people's understanding in not only about God but also the world. If one God was the creator and in-charge of the whole world or universe that would mean that all human beings and all beings of the world or universe belonged to one family under one God. Such a concept of God and the world we would think should have helped people to come out of their exclusivist and isolationist attitudes and behaviors, but unfortunately that hasn't happened yet. Our diversity and attachment to exclusivism are such that even a changed concept of God or new theology doesn't seem to be enough to bridge the gap. Even the monotheistic religions themselves do not agree on the understanding of God and the world.

Some of the world religions have declined or splintered into smaller sects or groups over the last few centuries. But most of them continue to occupy a prime spot in people's life and spirituality today. We could say that the sense of the sacred and the understanding of God have gone through a sea change from the prehistoric times to the present day. The beliefs and practices of people today have become much diverse, complex, and sophisticated in comparison with the religious beliefs and practices of the people of the prehistoric times. The sense of the sacred seems to have been present from early on and continues to be present in almost all cultures and communities around the world today. God continues to occupy a prime spot in most communities today. But the way God is perceived in all these cultures and communities is immensely diverse.

7

Self-Driven or God-Driven Knowledge?

ALTHOUGH THE IMMENSE DIVERSITY in our beliefs and practices today could make us question what is true and what is not true, one thing that our history shows us is that the development of our religions and understanding of God were a step-by-step process. What we have today has a history behind it. We are part of a long chain of people who have been unraveling the mystery of God. Just like a child is unique in him or herself but is never completely independent of the parents, no religion of the present day has had an origin totally independent of what the past generations believed in. The founders or the faith traditions grew out of something that already existed. The new faith or tradition might have had many new and novel things, but they always carry something of the parent religion or faith, or they are influenced by other faiths or traditions.

Now looking at all these historical developments of people's faith and religions, the question is whether these developments were all a fantasy and creation of human beings, or they were a result of God's active working in those people and cultures. In other words, were these developments in which we see human beings and the divine connected a self-driven or God-driven development? Was it an initiative of human beings to reach out to God or was it God's initiative to reach out to human beings? I would think that it was essentially God's initiative or God-driven. I could think that human beings have a spiritual dimension in them that helps them to reach out to God, which would make us think that it could be an initiative of human beings or self-driven rather than God-driven. However, believing that it is God who created us and planted in us that spiritual dimension, I would give God the credit for taking the initiative and stirring up the desire in us to know and experience him. Saint John says that it is not we who loved God but God who loved us first (1 John 4:10). So when we look at our history of faith and evolution in the understanding of God, I would consider that it was all a God-moment. However rudimentary and rustic they might have been, God was present in them. If God is the creator of all human beings and the whole creation, which I believe is the truth, all the historical developments were also part of the plan of God. If all of us are children of God, our ancestors and all people of prehistoric and other times were and are also children of the same God. No one is kept out of that divine realm.

That doesn't mean that all of us have inherited or developed the same understanding of God. All the children in a family do not think of their parents in the same way. The parents are the same, but the way the children perceive and experience them is different. Because we assume that the life of our ancestors was not as advanced as our life today, we have to also assume that their faith and understanding of God also were not advanced with high theology or concepts. But there is no reason for us to think that their faith was completely invalid and untrue. God was working in their lives and cultures as he is working today in our lives and cultures. It was God who was leading them and guiding them. It was God who planted in them the desire to connect with him. When God said to Moses, "I am the God of your father, the God of Abraham, the God of Isaac, and the God of Jacob" he made it clear that he was present in the history of Moses' ancestors. Moses' ancestors were much more primitive than him, but he believed that it was the same God who was working in them. It was and it is God who was and who is actively present at every step of our human history, whether it is pre-axial, axial, post-axial, or present age.

But at the same time, at various times in our human history God has been inviting people to refine their understanding of him. God asked Abraham to leave his country and kindred and go to the place that God was going to show him (Gen 12). This call of Abraham could be seen as an invitation to break with his past and develop a new vision of and relationship with God. Abraham's ancestors could stand for those who believed in and practiced a rustic and rudimentary religion as those of the pre-axial age. But Abraham stands for those who developed a refined understanding of God and religion. Abraham marks the beginning of a shift from polytheism to monotheism. Abraham had to go through different phases in his understanding of God. It took time. In his early years, Abraham also was unrefined in his religion and spirituality. But as he grew older, God helped him to refine it. This refinement of faith and religion and growth in the understanding of God continued down through the centuries.

Even today with all our advancement in theology, philosophy, science, technology, and cosmology, we know that we cannot have an absolutely accurate idea or understanding of God because only an absolute being can have anything in the absolute sense. We are limited beings with limited intelligence and understanding. We cannot reduce the reality of God to our little minds. Besides, it is impossible to know even our own self completely. We surprise ourselves in many ways with the way we think, feel, and do things. When we are not experts even on ourselves, or when we struggle to understand our own self fully, how do we claim to understand the omnipotent and omniscient God? We cannot reduce the reality of God into our little concepts and ideas.

So if our understanding of God is not self-driven and we cannot have an absolutely accurate understanding of the unlimited God with our limited minds, how can we understand him and how much can we understand him? I tend to believe that we can know and experience him only to the extent he reveals himself and only to the extent our human mind and intelligence is able to grasp and comprehend him. Just as Mary, the mother of Jesus, pondered over what had been revealed to her, and just as many others who have gone before us had reflected and contemplated over what had been revealed to them, we engage in an exploratory, reflective, and contemplative process over what has been and what is being revealed to us over the course of time.

We don't get it all in one day or as one piece not because God does not want to reveal himself to us completely but because we are not capable of taking it in just like that. It is almost like babies being fed with liquid and soft food first and then gradually given more solid food that they can chew and digest. It could be also thought of as something similar to the gradual adjustment of our eyes to bright lights when we wake up in the morning or when we go out of a dark room into the bright daylight. It takes a little time for our eyes to adjust and see everything clearly.

In the gospel of Mark, there is a narrative about Jesus restoring sight to a blind man at Bethsaida (Mark 8:22–26). It was a step-by-step-process. First Jesus put saliva on his eyes and laid hands on him, and the man gained some sight. He said that he could see people but they looked like trees. His sight was blurred. Jesus laid his hands on him again and prayed, and then the man gained complete sight. He could see everything clearly. This story could be seen as indicating a gradual development in our spiritual life and understanding of God. We don't see everything clearly at once. We gain that clarity, understanding, and wisdom only gradually. We come to know and experience God more and more as we move along in our faith journey. Nobody has got it all completely. And if somebody claims to have it all, it simply needs to be taken as a wish fulfillment and grandiose idea rather than anything close to the truth.

Even as I pen these thoughts and reflections on the mystery of God and the mystery of our lives, I am aware that my understanding and experience of God may be different when I turn seventy or eighty years old (If I live that long), depending on how much God reveals himself to me and how much I can absorb and comprehend.

It is not only that we are limited in our comprehension and ability but also that we all differ as individuals and communities in what and how much we understand and experience. The way I am able to comprehend is not the same as what my friend or neighbor is capable of. The way my community understands God is not same as how another community understands God. Even in our capacity to understand we differ. My mind and intelligence may not be as good or sharp as that of another person, and hence my capacity to understand God may be different from how and how much that person can understand. Besides, what we have been presented with, what we have been taught, the culture and community in which we are raised, the times and historical contexts in which we grow up, and all such factors influence how and how much we can understand. And none of us, as individuals or communities, can fully understand God during this earthly life because of our limitation by space and time.

When we hear the stories of great prophets and saints, we are awed at the level of holiness and intimacy with God that they had attained. But when we look closely at their lives, we realize that the roads they traveled on were not easy and smooth. Although the contexts and details were different, we also realize that their lives were not much different from what we experience today. Many of them had to recognize God's presence and voice in ways that they least expected of. God surprised them in many ways. And they had to grow in their understanding and experience of God gradually.

One of the persons who experienced God in such varied and sometimes in the most unconventional ways was Prophet Elijah. Elijah is pictured as one of the greatest prophets that Israel ever had. He was fierce in his speech and actions. Hoping that his people would repent of their sins and turn back to God he invoked God's name and withheld rain for three and a half years causing a terrible drought and famine in the land (1 Kgs 17:1). On another occasion, enraged by the apostasy of his people who followed the practices of the corrupt and wicked king, Ahab and his pagan wife, Jezebel, Elijah ordered the slaughtering of the four hundred and fifty prophets of the pagan god, Baal (1 Kgs 18:20).

Even Elijah with such a fierce and powerful personality and prophetic power had to go through a gradual growth in his understanding of God. Generally, it appears that Elijah was used to God's revelations in the most extraordinary ways and he was least prepared for anything less than that. But there is one occasion where we find him totally baffled by the way God revealed himself. The experience is in the context of Elijah infuriating King Ahab and his pagan wife, Jezebel, and they in turn seeking to kill him (1 Kgs 19:1). Elijah flees from the land and ends up in the desert. Exhausted and broken in spirit, Elijah lay down under a tree. Desiring that he would die rather than continuing to face his hardships, he cries out to the Lord, "It is enough; now, O Lord, take away my life, for I am no better than my ancestors" (1 Kgs 19:4). But God sends him an angel and feeds him, and asks him to continue his journey. Elijah continues his journey for another forty days and forty nights and reaches Mount Horeb. He found refuge in a cave there. While being in the cave, he has an unusual experience of God. God told him to go out of the cave and stand on the mountain so that he could experience him as he was passing by.

Elijah seems to have waited for the Lord expecting to see him in some extraordinary ways. First there was a very strong wind and Elijah expected that God would be in the wind, but God was not in it. Then there was an earthquake and Elijah expected that God would be in the earthquake, but God was not in it. Then there was fire and Elijah expected God to be in it, but God was not in it. Then there was a sound of sheer silence, a gentle whispering sound, and Elijah covered his face in his mantle. And then he heard the voice of the Lord. Elijah had least expected God to come in such a quiet and simple way as a gentle breeze, a whispering sound. He was used to having God's revelations in the extraordinary events and forces of nature, and he didn't expect him in any other way. But God came to him in the most unexpected way. That was yet another way that God revealed himself to Elijah.

Elijah's experience could be our experience. We could be caught up in some idea of God that we have created in our mind and then all of a sudden we might recognize him in a totally new way. Like Elijah we could be looking for God through powerful miracles and manifestations. We seek him in such extraordinary ways especially when we experience trials and turmoil of life. In such moments we want God to manifest himself in extraordinary ways. But through Elijah God reveals that he could be coming to us in many unexpected and ordinary ways in our everyday life.

Another person who experienced God in an unusual way is Mary Magdalene. Mary Magdalene is a very intriguing character in the gospels. People have made all kinds of speculations about her. One thing that simply stands out in the gospels is that she deeply loved Jesus. She probably was someone who knew Jesus more than many of his family members and disciples. She was probably the best disciple and friend that Jesus had. Maybe she was a true friend with whom Jesus could share his joys and sorrows. She was there for him in his life and death. She was there at the foot of the cross. She was there at the tomb early in the morning. Maybe the other disciples did not really measure up to her. They all ran away and abandoned him. She was in so much grief when Jesus was killed and taken away from her life, and she was so over-joyed when he appeared to her after the resurrection. But even with all her love and understanding of Jesus, the resurrection experience took her by surprise. She went to the tomb expecting to pray at the tomb, hoping that the body of Jesus was inside (John 20:1). She seems to have not expected Jesus in any other way. But Jesus surprised her by appearing to her. She first did not recognize him because she did not expect him in any other way than being dead and in the tomb. She had a personal and deep love for him but she expected him to be in a certain way. The risen Christ was a surprise to her. She had to rise above her expectations and images of Jesus she had. She had to see him in a new way.

As individuals and communities, we keep growing in our understanding and experience of God. God surprises us in many ways. If we all can look back at the history of religion and faith in our individual families in the last several centuries or thousands of years, we would realize that we have come a long way in our understanding and experience of God. Our forefathers some thousands of years back did not believe in and experience what we believe in and experience today. But we share in their history. God reveals himself in unique ways to all of us at all times. It is God who has been working in our history, and he is working in our lives today. Our knowledge, understanding, and experience of him are his initiative. Hence we keep remaining open to that revelation.

8

Authenticating God's Revelations

WE BELIEVE THAT GOD has revealed himself in many ways in our human and faith history. But how do we know that something is really God's revelation and not simply some imagination or fantasy of some individuals or groups? The best way to authenticate it, I believe, is to engage in a process of dialogue and discernment with the community. The community provides objectivity and authenticity to people's claims of visions, revelations, and other extraordinary interventions of God. Just as in a scientific method, the community would engage in listening to the experiences and systematically observe, verify, and test and retest the individual or group's claims. The individual or group, in turn, listens to and dialogues with the community. Such dialogue and discernment in the community would help us to understand the purpose and the implications of the revelation, and it becomes a shared experience or knowledge. The process of dialogue and discernment with the community helps to weed out baseless and inaccurate claims of individuals and groups who might be imagining and hallucinating rather than really receiving any revelation of God.

We shall look at some stories in the Judeo-Christian traditions that highlight this process of authenticating God's revelations and its importance. Even though in some of these stories, the individual revelations seem to get more emphasis than those of the community as a whole, the purpose of these revelations and their implications for the community are always highlighted.

God spoke to Noah and made known his plan about how he was going to renew the earth after human beings had grown wicked and evil beyond redemption. The purpose of the revelation was the formation of a new community under the leadership of Noah, the righteous man. God called Abraham to begin a new phase in his life, and the purpose of the revelation was again the formation of a new community. Moses had a very personal experience of the revelation of God in which God commissioned him to go and rescue his people from slavery in Egypt. The purpose of that revelation was to free the people from all kinds of slavery and to form a new community. Among the prophets who received God's revelation and call to renew and reform the community, some of the prominent names are Hosea, Jeremiah, Isaiah, and Ezekiel. In the New

Testament, some of the prominent stories of God's revelation to individuals are that of Zechariah, John the Baptist, Mary, all the Apostles, and Saint Paul. The revelations to all of them involved a new understanding of and relationship with God, and they were all called individually for some special mission in the community and the world.

Although it is not specifically mentioned, we can assume that all these individuals had to dialogue with their families or others in the community to confirm that their calls and revelations were really coming from God, and not simply some imagination or fantasy. We can assume that when Abraham felt called by God to embark on a new journey, he had to dialogue and confirm with his wife Sarah and many others that it was really a call from God. Moses probably consulted with his father-in-law, Jethro and many others in the community before he could be sure that his call was truly from God. We can think of that process of dialogue and discernment with the community happening in the lives of all other individuals who were called by God. Many of these individuals experienced miraculous signs along with God's revelations, and yet we can assume that they still had to dialogue with some people in their families and communities to authenticate their experience as a God-experience.

We hear about false prophets and leaders in the Bible who falsely claimed God's revelations and authorizations, and misled people. The community did not authenticate their claims. Jesus warned his people about such prophets, "Beware of false prophets, who come to you in sheep's clothing but inwardly are ravenous wolves" (Matt 7:15).

There are also stories in the Bible about God revealing himself to the community as a whole. In the book of Exodus, there is a reference to God's presence being revealed to the whole Israelite community in the shape of clouds and fire. Again God made his presence known to the whole Israelite community by raining manna or bread from heaven as they were travelling through the desert and had no food. God revealed his glory to a group of shepherds and announced to them the news about the birth of Jesus. Jesus revealed his glory to a group of disciples at the transfiguration. After his resurrection, Jesus appeared to his disciples as they were gathered together. Jesus ascended to heaven as the disciples watched. When the disciples were gathered together, the Holy Spirit descended upon them at Pentecost. In these group or community experiences also we can assume that they had to dialogue with each other about their experience to confirm that it was truly from God.

We could argue that when it comes to the revelations to the group or community, it is still personal. Even if God reveals himself to a crowd, it still comes down to each individual person in the crowd experiencing that revelation in his or her own way. The objective knowledge includes the subjective experience of people. It is very rare that we experience God in the form of clouds and fire as the Israelites did. But even if we do, we have to dialogue with each other to ensure that what we are experiencing is truly from God.

Even the Bible, which Christians believe as God's Word and revelation, is a God-inspired work of individual persons, but authenticated as God's Word by a process of dialogue and discernment in the community. Christians don't think of the Bible as something dropped down from heaven but rather as the Word of God written by God-inspired individuals. Saint Paul makes reference to this idea in his letter to Timothy: "All scripture is inspired by God and is useful for teaching, for reproof, for correction, and for training in righteousness, so that everyone who belongs to God may be proficient, equipped for every good work" (2 Tim 3:16–17). Christians know that the four gospels and other books in the New Testament were written a few decades after the resurrection of Jesus. Until they were written down, the early Christian communities passed on the words and message of Jesus and everything associated with him through oral tradition.

We can assume that while passing on the original experiences through oral tradition a lot of details were lost. Probably as a result of looking back and reflecting on all that had happened a lot of new details were also added. Even today from our own experience we know that when the words and messages of people are passed on orally, a lot of additions and deletions occur. What I remember from what people did or said thirty or forty years back are only remnants of what actually occurred. Many things from the original script have been lost over the years. The memories have faded. When I talk about them today, it is possible that a lot of original details are lost and a lot of new details might be added.

Those who are involved in the exegeses of the scriptural texts can tell us how much of what we read in the gospels might be original texts going back to the time of Jesus. But even with all those changes happening over the years, we believe that God inspired the evangelists and other authors to pen down what they experienced and what has been handed down to them. And in writing them down, these authors had to dialogue with the community to authenticate that it was truly God's Word and not simply their own imaginations. Even after these books were written, the Christian community went through a long process of dialogue and discernment to determine which books should be and should not be included in the canon of the Bible.

We see this process of authenticating individual experiences through a process of dialogue and discernment with the community being played out in the life of Saint Paul. First we hear of Paul's claim to God's revelation and inspiring work in his life, "For I want you to know, brothers and sisters, that the gospel that was proclaimed by me is not of human origin; for I did not receive it from a human source, nor was I taught it, but I received it through a revelation of Jesus Christ" (Gal 1:11–12). Saul who became Paul would appear to be two different persons before and after his conversion. The violent persecutor of Christians became a zealous follower of Christ. He knew that it was God who intervened in his life and brought about the change. The inspiration, he believed, was of divine origin and not of human origin. But given his background before his conversion we can assume that it was not easy for other Apostles and Christians to accept his claim just like that.

It looks like Paul stayed with his personal convictions for sometime without checking with anybody whether what he claimed to have been God's revelations and inspirations were really coming from God. Maybe he got tired of trying to convince them and decided to keep to himself. In the same chapter of his letter to the Galatians he says, "But when God, who had set me apart before I was born and called me through his grace, was pleased to reveal his Son to me, so that I might proclaim him among the Gentiles, I did not confer with any human being, nor did I go up to Jerusalem to those who were already apostles before me, but I went away at once into Arabia, and afterwards I returned to Damascus" (Gal 1:15–17). But then he seems to have realized that he had to authenticate his experience of the divine revelation or the inspiration he received. For that he had to involve the community in the process. So he says, "Then after three years I did go up to Jerusalem to visit Cephas and stayed with him fifteen days; but I did not see any other apostle except James the Lord's brother" (Gal 1:18–19). It appears that by the time Paul went to Jerusalem to meet with the community, only two of the apostles, Peter and James, were left there. All the other apostles might have left Jerusalem to preach the gospel in other parts of the world, as Saint Thomas went to India. Again after fourteen years, Paul went back to Jerusalem and conferred with Peter, James, and John about his revelations and the gospel he was preaching, and they, on behalf of the community, seem to have authenticated his experience (Gal 2:1–2, 7–9). In Chapter 15 of the Acts of the Apostles we hear again about Peter and James authenticating Paul's missionary work.

To authenticate God's revelations or to understand God as he reveals himself to us, we thus need to take into consideration both the individual and communal experiences and engage in a dialogical process. If we take into consideration only the personal or individual revelations, we might run into the danger of being very subjective and lacking objectivity and legitimacy. Anybody can claim to have received revelations, visions, and apparitions from God but there might be little evidence to show that the claim is true. And being personal experience and claim, it is very difficult to test whether the claim is true or not. All that we may have may be the self-report. Taking the self-report alone might run into the problem of lacking authenticity. That is where the community becomes very important in authenticating such personal revelations. We are not isolated individual human beings. We are also a community of people amidst whom God lives and works.

But if we insist only on the group or communal experience and disregard personal experiences of individuals, we might run into the danger of absolutism, dogmatism, and rigidity as well. The community needs to listen and take into consideration the experiences of its individual members. We need a process of dialogue that takes into consideration both the individual and communal experiences and claims.

We see this combination of the experience of the individuals and the community being taken into consideration to authenticate the post-resurrection experiences of the disciples of Jesus. After Jesus was raised he first appeared to Mary Magdalene and a few other women who had gone to the tomb to pray and pay respects. Jesus asked them to communicate the message to his apostles, the eleven disciples, but when they did, the disciples refused to believe that Jesus was alive. They did not believe the women because it was a self-report and the group consisted only of a few women who were not part of the inner circle of the apostles. There was no way to verify that report. They probably thought that the women were hallucinating or imagining things.

And then Jesus appeared to two other disciples who were walking into the country, supposedly Emmaus. They reported their experience to the rest of the apostles, and still they refused to believe. Again, they probably found it hard to believe because it was personal experience, and there was no way to test or verify it. And then Jesus appeared to the eleven disciples when they were gathered together and rebuked them for their lack of faith. According to John's gospel, even after all these, there was one, Thomas, who refused to believe when his companions told him that Jesus had appeared to them. And then Jesus appeared again when Thomas was with them, and he was satisfied, and his doubts were cleared.

The individual revelations or the revelations in small groups were authentic but it took several attempts from Jesus to convince the larger community that it was he who had revealed himself to each of those individuals. And then the community as a whole experienced him. The community had to share their experiences, test and retest, and verify it from different sources, including their own experience as a group before they accepted the claims as true. In the case of Thomas, the community's experience alone was not enough for him to believe. He wanted to experience it himself.

This process of dialogue and discernment, and balancing the individual and communal experiences of God's revelations have been an indispensable pillar of the Christian community down through the centuries. Whenever there was a denial or disregard for any of these components, the community experienced divisions or distress of indescribable nature. God continues to reveal himself to us individually and communally, but it is important to authenticate our claims through a dialogical process to ensure that they are truly God's revelations and not just imaginations and hallucinations.

9

Images, Ambivalences, and Worldviews

IN TRYING TO UNDERSTAND God as he has revealed himself in our human and faith history, it is also important to look at the images and ideas of him that we create, the philosophical and theological ambivalences that we struggle with, and the worldviews with which we operate.

Images and their Implications

Based on what has been presented to us and what we have experienced, we create or develop certain images, ideas, visions, and understandings of God. These images, visions, and ideas of God were and are important because we often try to connect our knowledge with our personal and tangible experiences. Without these media many of us find it hard to relate to God. Even if we say we can relate to God without a picture or image, we need to have some idea or understanding about him.

Some might say that they don't want to have any such idea or image of God because it would reduce God to our human concepts and categories. There are others who would avoid making any comments about God because none of the comments or concepts can capture the reality of God. For them the best answer about God would be to say, "I don't know" or "Not that and not this." Although such positions would be a safe way to avoid making any wrong statements about God, I tend to think that it is impossible to avoid all pronouncements or ideas about God. Even those who avoid images and depictions of God do have some sort of idea about God when they think of him. They may not convert that idea into any visible image or concept but they still hold some ideas about God. It is through that idea that they communicate with or about God. It is highly improbable that one can communicate about and relate with God without some sort of idea or understanding. It is difficult to relate to a reality in vacuum. Even when I say that I think of God, reflect on God, or communicate with God it automatically refers to some kind of idea, image, or vision of God that I am holding within myself. Even the word "God" or "divine" refers to an idea or concept.

An absolute vacuum is a non-starter for any discussion on knowing or experiencing God.

Given that fact, we can think that over the years everyone has developed certain ideas, images, or visions of God. It is important to examine them, because they often determine our relationship with God.

Let me explain it with an example. Water buffalos were supposedly domesticated in the Indian subcontinent around five thousand years back and they are very commonly found in many Asian countries today. People view and assess the usefulness of this animal in several different ways. Depending on the view they have, their approach or relationship towards this animal differs. If it is viewed as a good animal providing them with milk and other dairy products people will make sure that it is fed and taken care of well. If they view it as a violent animal they will be afraid of it and hesitate to go close to it. If people look at it as an animal useful for meat, hide, and other products, they will kill it and get what they want. If they view it as a sacred animal as the *Todas* of the Nilgiris mountain range in South India do, they will worship and honor it. The Todas are one of the original tribes inhabiting the highest regions of the Nilgiris mountain range in South India. According to the Todas, the goddess *Teikirshy* and her brother first created the sacred buffalo and then the first Toda man. They worship their water buffaloes. The same thing could be said of cows. Different people perceive cows differently. Some view them as animals that provide milk and other dairy products. Others see them as violent animals. Some others look at them as useful for meat, hide, and other products. And still others, like some Hindus in India, consider them as sacred.

Depending on the view or image of the water buffalo or cow, people's relationship and approach to the animal change. The animal, buffalo or cow, is the same and it does not change. But the way people look at it is different, and accordingly, their approach is different. Similarly, the reality behind everyone's faith could be God, but the way he is viewed or conceptualized is different. This difference can occur among people who follow different religious faiths and traditions or even the same religious faith and tradition. It can happen among people who affiliate themselves to the same denomination or sect within the larger religion. It can happen even among the members of the same family living under the same roof. So differentiated are our images or understandings of God that even the person sitting next to us reciting the same prayer that we are reciting could be very different in his or her understanding of God from that of ours.

Often it is the different images and ideas of God that we have created that we are worshipping, and many of them may not be representing the true God. It is possible that we all have created God "in our own image and likeness." I am not minimizing the personal experiences of God that all of us might have had, nor am I saying that all these images, ideas, and visions that we have inherited or developed are wrong and misleading. What I am suggesting is to simply become aware of what we are carrying within ourselves so that we can ensure that our beliefs are healthy and helpful, born out of convictions and authenticated experiences. If we realize that some of these images and ideas that we carry are distorted and not healthy we can review them and change them.

A wrong and distorted vision of God leads to an unhealthy spirituality and religiosity. A healthy vision of God leads to a healthy relationship with God and consequently a healthy spirituality and religiosity.

Our Philosophical and Theological Ambivalence

In taking stock of our understanding of God, it is important to be aware of the ambivalence that we come across in the philosophical and theological circles, the ambivalence concerning the transcendent and immanent dimensions of God. Since God is an unlimited and absolute being, he is thought of as transcendent, beyond all descriptions and limitations of space and time. He is the creator and not a creature. There is nothing or no one that he can be compared with. Any comparison or description will be an attempt to limit him and put him in a category. God cannot be reduced to any concepts or category. But at the same time God is also thought of as an immanent being. Everything and everyone in the creation is permeated by his divine presence. He is everywhere, in everyone, and in everything. There is no place, where God is not present, and there is no time when God is not present. The Psalmist says, "Where can I go from your spirit? Or where can I flee from your presence? If I ascend to heaven, you are there; if I make my bed in Sheol, you are there. If I take the wings of the morning and settle at the farthest limits of the sea, even there your hand shall lead me, and your right hand shall hold me fast. If I say, 'Surely the darkness shall cover me, and the light around me become night,' even the darkness is not dark to you; the night is as bright as the day" (Ps 139:7–12). God is as close to me as my breath. I cannot escape his presence anywhere anytime.

Some faith communities and schools of philosophy and theology stress on the transcendent character of God while others focus on the immanence of God. Sometimes there is a tension between these two understandings of God. Depending on which of these tracks of thinking they take, individuals and communities form their spirituality and religiosity around it. The problem with too much stress on transcendence is that it leads to an understanding of God as an impersonal God who is far separated from human beings to the extend that we cannot know him and understand him at all. He will be presented as someone far out somewhere, distant from us, and remaining as an observer. He watches over us and takes care of us but he is inaccessible and unapproachable. Some people like that idea of God. They like to have a God who is close enough to watch over them but far enough that they don't need to deal with him all the time. If he is perceived as someone within and very close then we will have to be open to him and be present to him all the time. If he is within us and within everybody else, then we will also have to see his presence in everyone, which means that we will have to treat everyone with awe and respect. To disrespect and abuse others or the creation would mean that we are disrespecting and abusing God himself because he is present in everyone and in the creation. Hence excessive stress on the transcendence of God has the danger of distancing him from us and perceiving him as a distant and inaccessible reality.

If the idea of the immanence of God is excessively stressed it can lead to God being reduced to or equated with the created world and everything in it. That would deny God any greater dimensions than what is assigned to the creation, and God would be conceptualized as too anthropomorphic. And there is also a danger of engaging in idol worship. If God is present in me, I could begin to equate myself with God and think of myself as God. Equating myself with God I might start worshipping myself, or make others view me as an object of worship. Being aware of the presence of the divine in me or seeing myself as a child of God is different from seeing myself as God. I am not God. I am a human being created in the image and likeness of God. I am a child of God with God being always present in me. I could also engage in idol worship with other created beings. Since God is present in everything, I might engage in equating everything with God. That would be pantheism. God being present in everything doesn't mean that everything is God. The father and the mother being present in the son or daughter does not mean that the son or daughter is the same as the father and the mother. The creatures or the creation is not the same as the creator. Hence too much emphasis on the immanence of God can lead to all kinds of idol worship and reduction of God to what we see and experience in the creation. I cannot say how big God is but he must be much bigger than what I think or conceptualize of him. If he is the creator, he must be bigger than the creation.

The images and ideas of God that we develop are often influenced by these philosophical and theological viewpoints about the transcendence and immanence of God. For some of us, our ideas and images of God may be leaning more toward his transcendental dimension, while for others, they may be leaning more toward the dimension of immanence.

Our Operational Cosmology and Worldview

When we try to understand God, another factor that is important to take note of is the cosmological standpoint from which we operate. The cosmology and the worldview that many of us must have been holding for a long time or still continuing to hold may be geocentric where we think that the earth is the center of the universe. A good many of us, save those who are well informed in this area of knowledge, might not be concerned about anything more than the earth, the sun, and the moon. What really counts for many of us in this cosmos are these three—the sun, the moon, and the earth. These three have an immediate impact on our lives, and hence we often think about them. The little twinkling stars up in the sky are nothing more than the illuminations in the ceiling of the sky for many of us. They don't mean much to us except that they are pleasant to the eyes. We don't care much about the solar systems, galaxies, milky ways, so on and so forth. If I tell someone that this universe is said to be ever expanding or our understanding of it is expanding, and that there are millions and millions of planets, solar systems, and galaxies in this universe their eyes might twinkle for a moment at the mind-boggling information and express their awe by a deep "wow" expression. They are all nice information to hear and good stuff to read about. But when it comes to our everyday life and our faith they don't count much. We don't care much about their existence or non-existence, whether they are big or small, and whether they are expanding or shrinking except when we hear about some meteoroids entering the earth's surface.

Even if we are well informed in the area of cosmology and science, when it comes to our faith, what many of us often really care about is whatever comes above the ceiling of the sky, what is under the sky, and what is below the earth. What is above the ceiling of the sky is often thought of as the realm of God, the heaven to be precise. What is below the earth is the nether world, the underworld, or the world of the devil, which we call hell. And what comes in between is the earth, the realm of the human beings. For many Christians, there is one more realm that matters, the Purgatory. But no space or location is usually assigned to it. The most desirable realm is the realm above the ceiling in the sky, heaven or the realm of God, and the least desirable place is the underworld, the hell. The realm of the human beings, the realm of the earth, is sometimes perceived as desirable and sometimes as undesirable.

As we know today, this is a distorted worldview because our universe is not geo-centric. The sky is not a dome or net above which God dwells. And it is very difficult to say where the bottom of the earth is because it depends on who is talking and from where he or she is talking. And wherever it may be, we know that the earth is sur-rounded by space and not any underworld or netherworld. But many people operate with this worldview or cosmology. And it has a significant impact on their image of God and spirituality. This worldview creates three clearly defined realms—the realm of God up above, realm of human beings in the middle, and the realm of the devil or evil one down below. These three realms are conceived as three clear spaces of existence for these three kinds of beings. For people who work with this worldview, their cosmology or concept of the universe is still rudimentary and distorted, and consequently, their understanding and ideas of God remain somewhat distorted too.

Part III

Judeo-Christian Understanding

10

Conventional Healthy Images

EVEN WHEN WE BELIEVE that God has been revealing himself to our ancestors and others in our human and faith history, we still look at specific contexts and ways in which he has revealed himself. The common belief is that he has revealed himself in the creation, in general, and in different cultures and traditions, in particular. In those particular revelations to cultures and traditions, the hand of God is believed to have been at work in the formation of their communities, writing of their scriptures, and continuation of their faith life over decades and centuries. God is also believed to have been especially present and at work in certain individuals who either held leadership roles in those communities or became the voice of God at certain significant moments in their history.

It would be wonderful if we could look into all of these specific contexts and ways in which God has revealed himself. But that is a daunting and unrealistic task, and it is beyond the scope of this book. Hence from this point on, I am going to narrow our discussions down to just one of those contexts of God's revelations, specifically, the Judeo-Christian traditions. Even within these traditions, my focus will be primarily on the Christian experience of God's revelations. I believe that the God who has revealed himself in the Judeo-Christian traditions is the God who has been revealing himself throughout our human and faith history from the beginning of creation. My hesitation to make much comments or references about other faith traditions is mainly because it is, first of all, an unimaginably vast area to cover, and secondly, my knowledge about other traditions is mostly academic rather than experiential. But when it comes to the Christian revelation and understanding, I can relate to both the academic and experiential aspects of this revelation, and I feel rather confident in sharing that with others. I have not only inherited and learned about God but also experienced God in my personal life.

Learning about and living the faith is different from simply learning about a faith. Even about the Christian understanding and experience of God, I don't find myself adequate to make an exhaustive presentation or thesis on it. I am no expert on God or Godly matters. I shall leave all such lofty discussions to theologians and other experts and shall simply focus on presenting a few of my thoughts and reflections. What I discuss here does not cover the entirety of the Judeo-Christian understanding of God. I focus only on a few aspects of the understanding of God in these traditions. I don't claim to have a faith, understanding, or God experience any stronger than that of an ordinary Christian either. Many of them, I believe, carry a much stronger faith and they experience God in a much deeper way than I do. However, it is my hope that they and the people of other faith traditions would be able to relate to most of what I discuss here.

In narrowing down our discussions to the Judeo-Christian traditions, the first thing that we want to look at is how God has been perceived in these traditions. As mentioned before, based on God's revelations and our experiences, we, as individuals and communities, develop many images and ideas of God. Although we believe that the revelations of God and our core beliefs in the Judeo-Christian traditions are authentic because of the long process of dialogue and discernment that we have engaged in, we have to admit that not all the images and ideas of God that we have developed or been presented with are necessarily healthy and helpful. To understand and experience God better, we need to examine some of these images and ideas that we carry. If some of them are distorted and unhealthy, God would want us to correct and refine them, which once again involves a process of dialogue and discernment with others in the community.

For Christians, much of our ideas and images of God come from the Bible, our parents, teachers, friends, books, talks, worship celebrations of the community, traditions, various kinds of media, icons, pictures, so on and so forth. We shall first discuss a few of the healthy and helpful images of God that are commonly held by Christians in general.

Father

One of the most popular images of God that we come across in the Bible and that has been presented to us by others is that of a "Father." People's experience of father varies. For some, their experience of their father, whether they are biological, foster, or adoptive, is very healthy and happy. They experience their father as loving and caring, providing them with what they need, both physically and emotionally. For such people, "father" represents someone that is very loving and caring. They long to be with their father. They miss their father when he is away. But that is not everyone's experience. Some experience their fathers as cruel and hateful. They are the opposite of anything that is good. They are punitive, abusive, destructively angry, profoundly neglectful, and scary. They are self-absorbed men who don't care about their children or family. They are not to be bothered. Thinking of such fathers, some people shudder and shiver. They experience a rush of hateful and scary feelings at the thought of their fathers.

There are other fathers who are not punitive, abusive, or neglectful, but just cold and distanced. Their children cannot connect with such men because they are elusive. They take care of the material needs of their children and family. They don't abuse or scare their children. But they are emotionally distanced and are not available to their children and family. And then there are fathers who are fathers only in name and records—that is, they give birth to their children and then they vanish. They are not present in the life of their children physically or emotionally.

When the Bible presents God as the "Father," it is not an image of just any kind of father, but a loving and caring father. It is a father who is deeply involved in the day-to-day lives of his children. In the book of Hosea we hear of God being presented as such a father who helps his people to learn and grow just like a father who helps a child or toddler to walk: "When Israel was a child, I loved him, and out of Egypt I called my son . . . It was I who taught Ephraim to walk, I took them up in my arms" (Hos 11:1, 3). When a father or mother holds the hand of the child or carries the child in his or her arms, the journey becomes easier for the child. God presents himself as a father who holds our hand and carries us in his arms, making it easier for us to move ahead. In the prayer that Jesus taught his disciples, God is presented as, "Our Father" (Matt 6:9–15). This is a father who loves, cares, forgives, protects, and provides. In Paul's letter to the Corinthians we again see God being presented as a caring father, "I will be your father and you shall be my sons and daughters, says the Lord almighty" (2 Cor 6:18). God says that he would live in us and walk among us. It is an image of a loving and caring father who is intimately part of our life.

A loving father corrects and disciplines his children so that the children can grow up well. If the father does not tell his children what is right and what is wrong and guide them in the right path, he is largely responsible for ruining their life. Jesus says that as a loving Father, God prunes us or corrects and disciplines us so that we bear more fruit (John 15:1–2). Pruning or disciplining does not mean that he is engaging in punishments and harm. Disciplining or correcting is not same as punishing or harming children. Loving fathers or parents who correct and discipline their children do not intend any harm for their children. But it is the responsibility of a loving and caring father to make sure that his children are guided in the right path of growth and development. For that he may have to discipline, correct, and set restrictions and boundaries. Jesus himself rebuked and corrected his disciples on several occasions, but he never harmed them. Leaving children to do what they want and failing to set boundaries and limits can lead to children engaging in destructive behaviors and ruining their life. Children may not like boundaries, disciplines, and restrictions, but they are necessary for their growth and development.

For those who don't experience their biological, foster, and adoptive fathers as loving, caring, forgiving, and protecting, it may be hard to relate to the "father" image of God. When they pray the prayer, "Our Father," it may not create any loving feelings for them if they had a cruel and uncaring father in their life. When the Bible presents

God as a father, it is in the sense of a most loving and caring father who would do anything for his children.

Mother

God has been presented as a "mother" or someone with motherly qualities. The same reference to God as a loving parent in the book of Hosea could be seen as a reference to God's motherly qualities. Just as a mother holds the hand of her child or carries the child in her arms, God holds our hands and carries us in his arms. In the book of Isaiah, God presents his love as going beyond that of a mother. He says, "Can a woman forget her nursing child, or show no compassion for the child of her womb? Even these may forget, yet I will not forget you" (Isa 49:15). In the normal circumstances of a loving relationship, a child is a great blessing for a couple. In such a family, it is unthinkable of parents, especially, a mother to forget their or her own child. A mother has a personal and intimate connection with her child. The child is her flesh and blood. She carries the child in her womb for several months. She nurses and nurtures the child. The child is one with her, and that connection is something very special.

In a loving mother-child relationship, it is not likely that the mother would forget her child. Even if a mother is not loving and caring, and even if she abandons or neglects her child, it is still most unlikely that she would forget her child. Even though it is near impossible and unlikely for such things to happen, God does not rule out such possibilities. God knows that such things happen in human relationships. There are cases where mothers abandon and forget their children. God says that even if such things happen, he will not forget us. He will not and cannot forget us because we belong to him. Referring to God as a loving mother, the book of Isaiah again says, "As a mother comforts her child, so I will comfort you" (Isa 66:13).

Just as in the case of fathers, not everyone experiences his or her mother as loving and caring. Some mothers are cruel, punitive, abusive, destructively angry, and profoundly neglectful. Some mothers abandon their children. Some mothers hurt and kill their children. Some mothers are cold and distanced. Those who experience their mothers in such ways may have a great difficulty in connecting with the image of God as a mother. But when the Bible presents God as a mother, it is in the sense of a most loving and caring mother who would die or do anything for her children.

Shepherd

"Shepherd" is another image that is often attributed to God in the Bible. The Psalmist says, "The Lord is my shepherd, I shall not want. He makes me lie down in green pastures; he leads me beside still waters; he restores my soul. He leads me in right paths" (Ps 23:1–3). Jesus calls himself the good shepherd, "I am the good shepherd. The good shepherd lays down his life for the sheep . . . And I lay down my life for the sheep".

(John 10:11, 15). There are all kinds of shepherds—good, bad, neglectful, and greedy. Jesus says that some shepherds are hired hands and they don't know the sheep and they don't really care about their sheep. They are focused on the financial benefit. And then there are shepherds who are thieves. Their intention is to steal, kill, and destroy.

The good shepherd cares about the sheep. There is a personal connection between the sheep and the shepherd. The sheep know the voice of the shepherd and the shepherd knows each sheep by name. When the sheep are out in the field grazing, there is always the danger of wolves or some wild animals attacking the sheep. Jesus says that a good shepherd will lay down his life for his sheep. He will be willing to risk his own life to protect the sheep. Jesus calls himself such a shepherd. God is presented as such a shepherd in many places in the Bible. He is willing to take any risk to save us and to show us how much he loves us. The very incarnation of Jesus, his life, and his crucifixion and death bear testimony to God as a good shepherd who lays down his life for his sheep, for us, his children.

In his conversation with the Pharisee, Nicodemus, Jesus reiterates this point, "For God so loved the world that he gave his only Son, so that everyone who believes in him may not perish but may have eternal life" (John 3:16). Saint Paul captures this aspect of the self-giving love of God in his letter to the Philippians, " . . . though he was in the form of God, did not regard equality with God as something to be exploited, but emptied himself, taking the form of a slave, being born in human likeness. And being found in human form, he humbled himself and became obedient to the point of death-even death on a cross" (Phil 2:6–8).

Although this is a beautiful image used for God, shepherd is an image that many people may not be able to connect with. People who have never lived on a farm or been exposed to sheep or other livestock may not have much idea about the life of sheep and shepherds. Hence it is hard to say how much people can relate to this image of God.

Spouse and Lover

Two other noticeable images that are closely associated and used for God in the Bible are that of a "spouse" and a "lover." Both these images point to a very intimate, personal, and passionate love that God has for his people. In the book of Hosea, God presents himself as a lover and husband to his people, "Therefore, I will now allure her . . . and speak tenderly to her . . . On that day, says the Lord, you will call me, 'My husband' . . . And I will take you for my wife forever; I will take you for my wife in righteousness and in justice, in steadfast love, and in mercy. I will take you for my wife in faithfulness; and you shall know the Lord" (Hos 2:14–16). God laments that his people have been unfaithful to him like an unfaithful wife, but he does not turn his back on them. He comes in search of them like a faithful and passionate lover and husband. In the book of Isaiah we hear a similar account of this intimate love of God for his people, "See, I have inscribed you on the palms of my hands" (Isa 49:16). Usually tattooing and inscribing someone's name or picture on one's palm or other parts of the body is a sign of a very personal and intimate connection with that person. It is almost like saying to the person, "You are as close to me as my flesh and skin." As an intimate and passionate lover, God has tattooed us in his heart. Again in the book of Isaiah, we hear about God's personal love for us, "I have called you by name, you are mine" (Isa 43:1). To say to somebody "you are mine" and calling somebody by name, make it very personal. God has put his seal on us. Nobody and nothing else can claim us. We are his beloved and chosen people.

There is a whole book in the Bible about this intimate and passionate love that God has for his people. The book of Song of Songs is a love poem, with a very detailed narration of an intimate and passionate love between a lover and his beloved. The narration is God's love story. It is about God's faithful, eternal, and unconditional love for his people.

God presents himself as a loving and caring husband who rejoices over his bride. In the book of Isaiah, we read, "For as a young man marries a young woman, so shall your builder marry you, and as the bridegroom rejoices over the bride, so shall your God rejoice over you" (Isa 62:5). Applying this image of God as a husband to himself, we see Jesus presenting himself as the bridegroom, "The wedding guests cannot mourn as long as the bridegroom is with them, can they? The days will come when the bridegroom is taken away from them, and then they will fast" (Matt 9:15). Jesus used many parables about wedding feasts where God is presented as the bridegroom and human beings are presented as the bride. Just as a loving and faithful husband rejoices over his wife, God rejoices over us, his people.

The images of God as spouse and lover are helpful to those who have experienced the love and care of their spouses and lovers. But not all spouses and those who fall in love experience such intimate and passionate love. Some partners in such relationships are abusive and violent. For those who have been exposed to such experiences, it may not be easy to relate to these images of God.

Friend

God has been presented as a "Friend." Jesus says to his disciples, "I do not call you servants any longer, because the servant does not know what the master is doing; but I have called you friends, because I have made known to you everything that I have heard from my Father" (John 15:15). Friendship is something that helps us to be who we are with another person. In good friendships, there is a freedom for each of the friends to be vulnerable and yet not be afraid and ashamed. A good friend desires only the best for us and helps us to build our lives. A good friend is willing to make sacrifices for us, make time to spend with us, would feel our pains and joys, and would feel our absence when we are away. In good friendships, there is no place for hatred, jealousy, envy, or selfishness.

Jesus in presenting himself as a good friend wants us to know that we can be who we are with him. He loves and cares about us and wishes the best for us. We can be vulnerable and yet not be afraid or ashamed. Jesus walked with his disciples in their successes and failures. He never abandoned them even when they abandoned him. Jesus also talks about what a good friendship would involve, "No one has greater love than this, to lay down one's life for one's friends" (John 15:13). And that is what Jesus did. He laid down his life for us. Of course, not everyone experiences the kind of friendship that Jesus is talking about. There are friendships where people end up hurting each other. People who have had such experiences in friendship might not be able to understand fully what Jesus is talking about.

King

God has been presented as a "King" who loves and cares for his people. The Psalmist addresses God as king and calls out to him for help, "Listen to the sound of my cry, my King and my God" (Ps 5:2). In his response to Samuel's complaint and displeasure with his people, God tells him that his people had rejected him from being their king. The Lord said to Samuel, "Listen to the voice of the people in all that they say to you; for they have not rejected you, but they have rejected me from being king over them" (1 Sam 8:7). When presented before Pontius Pilate before his crucifixion and death, Jesus presents himself as the king, not as a king according to the earthly understanding but as the king and Lord of the universe (John 8:36–37).

Good kings care for their people. But that is not everyone's experience. People have experienced some of their kings as cruel, brutal, murderous, dictatorial, sadistic, vicious, and suppressive. They were concerned only about their power and position. Although God could be thought of as the ideal king, people who have been under the reign of unjust and brutal kings may have a hard time relating to this image of God.

Other Images

There are other images that have been used for God in the Bible and presented to us by others such as "gardener," "vine," "rock," "judge," "ruler," "fortress," "shield," etc. As a gardener cares for his garden, God cares for his people. Jesus is united with us as a vine is united with its branches. Jesus presents himself as the just judge. The Psalmist has several titles for God, "I love you, O Lord, my strength. The Lord is my rock, my fortress, and my deliverer, my God, my rock in whom I take refuge, my shield, and the horn of my salvation, my stronghold" (Ps 18:1–2). Although most of these images are good, some of them could remain on the poetic level rather than having much application in our relationship with God.

God as Love

Finally, summing up all these images of God, Saint John presents God as "Love" itself. John says, "Beloved, let us love one another, because love is from God; everyone who loves is born of God and knows God. Whoever does not love does not know God, for God is love" (1 John 4:7–8). All the other images listed above are all about God manifesting his love to his people. Therefore, in John's understanding, wherever there is love, there is God, and God can be understood as Love itself. This is an image or idea that almost all people can relate to. And this is an idea that is more open and universal than the other ones. All the other images are restrictive. The image of the father, for example, is very restrictive. Although it could be a good and positive image, it is limited to a male figure who holds a position or role in the family. And if a person had a negative experience of his or her father, this image of God as a father may not carry a good and positive feeling. The same thing applies to other images that are role or position-based. But when it comes to "love" it does not limit its application to anyone group or section of humanity. There is love in the father, mother, friend, spouse, king, shepherd, etc. It applies to everyone. It is something that everyone can relate to. It is not only an idea or concept but also something experiential. People everywhere know and experience what it means to love and be loved. I shall elaborate on this idea of God in later chapters.

11

Distorted and Unhelpful Images

WHILE WE REALIZE THAT most of the images of God that we have been presented with or have developed are positive and healthy, it is possible that we have been presented with or have developed in our minds some images of God that are distorted and not so healthy and helpful. Some of these distorted images could be a development from certain stories presented in the Bible or they were created in the minds of our parents or others who presented them to us.

Angry and Wrathful

Sometimes God is depicted as an angry, wrathful, vengeful, murderous, and destructive person. Some of the references for such images of God in the Bible are: "Even at Horeb you provoked the Lord to wrath, and the Lord was so angry with you that he was ready to destroy you" (Deut 9:8). "In the greatness of your majesty you overthrew your adversaries; you sent out your fury, it consumed them like stubble" (Exod 15:7). "Now let me alone, so that my wrath may burn hot against them and I may consume them" (Exod 32:10). "And the Lord's anger was kindled against Israel, and he made them wander in the wilderness for forty years, until all the generation that had done evil in the sight of the Lord had disappeared" (Num 32:13). "But by your hard and impenitent heart you are storing up wrath for yourself on the day of wrath, when God's righteous judgment will be revealed" (Rom 2:5).

God is sometimes presented as a warrior or fighter who acts out of fury: "The Lord is a warrior" (Exod 15:3). "The Lord goes forth like a soldier, like a warrior he stirs up his fury; he cries out, he shouts aloud, he shows himself mighty against his foes" (Isa 42:13).

John the Baptist makes references to the wrath of God, "But when he saw many Pharisees and Sadducees coming for baptism, he said to them, 'You brood of vipers! Who warned you to flee from the wrath to come?'" (Matt 3:7).

Such presentations of God are not helpful in developing much of a positive or healthy image of God in our mind. Anyone who tends to focus on these passages in the Bible and fails to look at the overall picture of the salvation history can easily be duped into creating very negative and unhelpful images of God. They lead to the development of a spirituality that is negative, narrow, and hateful. In addition to these direct references to such negative images of God in the Bible, there are many other unhealthy images of God that are presented to us as we grow up.

Grandfather in the Sky

One of the images of God that many children develop or is presented to them from their childhood is that of a pious and yet serious-looking grandfather or father with a long beard sitting somewhere in the sky surrounded by clouds and looking on us his children. This is how God is sometimes depicted in pictures and icons. This of course is not a completely bad image, and many people can relate to it. It is a nice thought to have God as sitting in the clouds or in the sky and watching over us. However, this may not be the best image that we should have. The fact that he is up in the sky some-where means that there is a distance between him and us, and such an image lacks an intimate and close relationship. A God who sits in the sky pitying our helpless and hapless situation down below is not a very comforting image. Besides, everyone is not necessarily close to his or her grandfathers or grandmothers. Not in every family the grandparents are actively involved in the life of the grandchildren. Some grandfathers are strict taskmasters and authoritarian figures, and such a personality keeps grand-children away from them. And some grandparents are distant and cold, and they don't like to be bothered.

Sometimes parents present the grandparents as people to be feared and revered. And when the children misbehave, it is not rare in families to hear references to fa-thers or grandparents to bring a sense of fear. The mother might say things like, "I am just waiting for your father to come home and then you will learn to behave." Recently a woman was telling me about how things have changed in families with regard to conversations between parents and children. Talking about her daughter who was supposedly a little disrespectful and rebellious, the woman said, "She uses words that she would never use before her grandma." It appeared like the daughter was scared of her grandmother. Maybe it was a combination of respect and fear. It was good that the daughter was respectful around her grandma. But the question would be whether fear or respect was dominant in the daughter's mind when it came to her relationship with her grandma.

Because God has often been portrayed as a male figure it is the image of a grand-father and not a grandmother that many have developed. So if we have been carrying this grandfather image of God, and if our relationship with our own grandparents has not been very positive, it is possible that our relationship with God is one of fear, dislike, and distance. Some people go to their grandparents not because they love it or enjoy being with them but rather their parents ask them to do it. Sometimes we could be relating to God not because we have developed a loving relationship but because the voice of our parents, teachers, or others is still ringing in our ears. We might be going to church or keeping our faith and religion not so much out of conviction and love for God but rather out of habit and compulsion. If we don't keep the faith or religion we might feel that we would be disappointing our parents or others who wanted us to practice our religion. In a true friendship or love relationship, we can't wait to see or spend time with our friend. If we feel forced to visit or spend time with someone because we think the person will otherwise be angry or upset, then we may not really enjoy or look forward to the visit. We might do it out of obligation or guilt feeling, and if we had a choice we would rather stay home or do something else.

The grandfather image of God sitting in the sky can lead to the development of a top-down spirituality that sees God as someone who talks down on us and sends us messages and commands "from on high." It is a spirituality of passivity. It is the spirituality of the rich grandpa in the sky. If we are good and follow his directions, he will give us the goodies we want. Such spirituality has many implications in our decision-making processes and execution of things. It takes away personal involvement. People could develop an idea that if they are told what to do all the time they don't need to take personal responsibilities and initiatives in the discernment process.

Some people might apply this image of the grandfather God sitting in the sky and looking down at us to people who have died and gone away from us. They develop an idea of those departed souls sitting somewhere in the sky with God and looking down at us. For some people it may be a comforting image but for others it is not. They probably would have liked to have those persons stay with them rather than going up in the sky and looking down at them.

Judge and Policeman

Another distorted and unhealthy image of God that people develop from their childhood or later is that of a law-enforcement officer such as a policeman, a strict judge, a taskmaster, or a disciplinarian. Policemen, judges, disciplinarians, and taskmasters are all symbols of authority as well as punishment. Their job is to make sure that everyone abides by the law and if anyone were found guilty of violating the law they would be handed down some punishment. Unless one is a friend or relative, usually very few people associate with a policeman. They are often good people, but because they carry this mantle of crime and punishment, they are kept at a distance. It is interesting to note how people drive when they notice a police car. They might have been over-speeding for a while, but the moment they notice a police car they slow down and begin to drag. At the sight of the police car, a rush of fear and anxiety kicks in.

Some view God as a policeman or a strict judge who waits to see who is breaking the law or commandments. If we commit a sin or does something wrong, he would punish us. And when it comes to God, the thought of the punishment is not only about what we are going to suffer here on earth but also in eternity. Many people carry the burden of fear of being condemned to hell. This image of God creates a spirituality of fear and avoidance. It might make people avoid wrong doings and sins out of fear and not out of love and out of the realization that they are unhealthy. The question would be whether they are moved to do good more out of love for God or fear of the punishment. If it is out of fear of God and punishment, then it does not create a close, intimate, and loving relationship with God. It only generates fear and hatred. That is not the God whom the Bible presents.

Businessperson

Some people think of God as a businessperson or salesperson with whom we enter into a contract, trying to make the best deal out of the bargain. We consider ourselves as customers or consumers. The relationship might involve business practices like bargaining, negotiations, and setting terms and conditions. We try to get the best deal. In business relationships, usually there is no intimacy or love. As long as the amount is paid and the product is delivered, there is no reason for any hard feelings between the customer and the businessperson. They reconnect with each other only when they enter into another deal or contract for another product or transaction. It is purely a business relationship.

When God is viewed as a businessperson and we consider ourselves as customers or consumers, there is no intimacy in the relationship. We approach God only when and because we need something. We pray not because we have an intimate relationship with God but because we want to receive some favors. We make sacrifices and make offerings to God as if we have to appease him to make his face shine on us. And if the demands or the terms and conditions are not met, the contract or the deal might be broken, and God and us may not be on talking terms. In a business-like understanding of God, he might be also viewed as the "problem-fixer." If he fixes the problems, he will be worthy of our praise and honor. If not, he will be blamed and questioned. In such an image of God, we don't see God as someone in whom "We live and move and have our being" (Acts 17:28). Trying to rectify this businessperson image of God, Paul says to the people of Athens, "The God who made the world and everything in it, he who is Lord of heaven and earth, does not live in shrines made by human hands, nor is he served by human hands, as though he needed anything, since he himself gives to all mortals life and breath and all things" (Acts 17:24–25).

The image of God as a businessman leads to the development of a spirituality of consumerism. God is not a provider in the sense of a businessman or benefactor with whom we have to be on good terms. In a business relationship the businessperson needs customers or consumers to keep his or her business going. But when it comes to God, his existence does not depend on us. If we think God's existence depends on us, then we have a distorted image of God. God is God without needing us to be around.

It is almost like the relationship between parents and children. Parents' existence does not depend on the children. But children's existence depends on the parents. Parents were around before children came around. But children would not have been around if parents were not around. But once the children are born, parents need children to cooperate with them to keep the family together. Even if the children do not cooperate, parents will continue to exist. But if they do not cooperate the family will be in disarray. It will not be a healthy and happy family. Children don't need to appease the parents or each other. They just need to genuinely love the parents and love each other.

So to keep the family healthy and happy, parents and children need to be together, love each other, and work together. It is the same principle that applies to our relationship with God. God will continue to be God even if we do not stay close to him. We are not the only beings in God's creation so as to make his relevance and existence depend on us. But the family of God, which consists of God and us and everything in the creation, will be in disarray if we stay away from him or from each other. God is not a businessperson. We are not consumers and customers. We are God's children, part of the family of God.

Sadist and Puppeteer

There are other people who think of God as a sadist and murderer who makes us suffer, takes pleasure in our suffering, and annihilates the infidels. He is a perpetrator of and accomplice in acts of violence unleashed on humanity. He is like a puppeteer who holds the puppets by strings and makes them dance by pulling the strings. God makes us to dance (suffer) as and when he wants. He is viewed as a warmonger and annihilator of infidels. When we hold such images of God, our sufferings, our wars and violence, our diseases and deaths, our injustice and evils that we perpetrate on each other, and all such things will be seen through that filter. We would justify and even glorify injustice and evils in our world attributing it to God's will or blaming God for it. It creates a spirituality of aggression and war. Some people might become allies of God and take on themselves the task of "defending" God and getting rid of the infidels, or those who disagree with their ideas, beliefs, and practices. They become a terror, and they will present themselves as agents of God directly authorized by him to do away with his enemies.

Masochist and Patron of Pain

Some view God as someone who enjoys and glorifies suffering and inflicts pain on himself. Jesus dying on the cross could be seen as a perfect example of a sadist-masochist God. The heavenly Father makes his son suffer and the son himself appears to be glorifying suffering through his gruesome death. Viewed from that perspective all sufferings are presented or looked at as God's will. Such an image of God creates a spirituality of masochism, hatred, helplessness, and anger. God is presented as the God of the poor and the suffering who rejoices in the poverty and sufferings of his people. Heaven is presented as a reward for those who suffer and live in poverty. It is a bottom-up spirituality.

Of course, God is the God of the poor, but presenting God as someone who desires his people to live in poverty and suffering is a negative and distorted representation of God. Such an image of God leads not only to the continued thriving of the perpetrators of evils but also masochism, fatalism, and discouragement among victims and sufferers. Promotion of such images of God would make systems, structures, and evil-minded people to continue to keep people suppressed, oppressed, and abused. And the victimized would either consider their situation as willed by God and surrender to those evils and injustice to "please" God or they would be angry and totally give up on God. If they are angry, they might ask why they should relate to a God who makes them suffer. They would have no interest in a God who does not listen to their pain and cry. They would rather surrender to their fate than to God. They would ask: If God is good and loving, why should he allow us to suffer, why should he allow the evil people to thrive, why would he allow so many wars and violence, and why would he be silent when innocents suffer and die?

These images of God are simply results of our ignorance of who God is and who we are. The God who has revealed himself in our human and faith history is not a God who takes pleasure in our sufferings and pains. He is not a God who inflicts pain on us. He is not a God who glorifies pain and suffering. He is a God who abhors injustice, evils, pains, and sufferings. He is a God who desires our well-being and happiness. He is a God who desires that we live in peace and harmony with each other. He is a God who loves us and wants us to love one another. He is a God who suffers when we suffer. There are many reasons why we suffer and die. There are many reasons why evils and injustice are perpetrated in our world. And there are many things in our life for which we don't have answers. God may be an easy target for blame for all our unanswered questions and evil doings. But that is not the God we encounter in the Bible and in our faith history.

There could be many more of such distorted images of God that have been presented to us or we have developed over the years. But this is not the God who has revealed himself to us down through the ages. The God who has revealed himself to us is a God who hears our cry, knows our sufferings, and comes to deliver us. God said to Moses, "I have observed the misery of my people who are in Egypt; I have heard their cry on account of their taskmasters. Indeed, I know their sufferings, and I have come down to deliver them" (Exod 3:7–8). In the book of Revelations, God says, "I know your afflictions and your poverty" (Rev 2:9). He is not a warmonger or hateful God but a God who tells us: "Love your enemies and pray for those who persecute you" (Matt 5:44). This is a God who invites us to come to him when we feel burdened by the problems and anxieties of life, "Come to me, all you that are weary and are carrying heavy burdens, and I will give you rest" (Matt 11:28). He is a God who strengthens us when we are afraid and weak, "Do not fear, for I am with you, do not be afraid, for I am your God; I will strengthen you, I will help you, I will uphold you with my victorious right hand" (Isa 41:10). The God who has been revealed to us is not a God who needs to be appeased, coaxed, and be kept in good cheer. He is not a heartless and cruel God who thirsts for our blood.

Maybe our parents, teachers, religious leaders, and others communicated some of the distorted images of God to us. Maybe they thought that these were the ways to create in us a holy fear and reverence for God. They themselves might have received these images from their parents and others. But now as we realize how distorted and misleading some of these images could be, we take some time to review and rectify some of our own ideas or images of God that we carry.

If we don't rectify and transform we would continue to make the mistake of the past generations, blindly carrying the wrong or distorted images of God. If we don't change those distorted ideas and images, we would also transmit them to our children, our friends, our neighbors, our students, and all others whom we encounter and influence. The book of Genesis tells us what such wrong images of God can do to us. Adam and Eve are presented as having a distorted idea of God. They thought that God was a selfish and narcissistic God, forbidding them from eating of the tree in the middle of the garden so that they don't become like Him. Hence to become like God, they defied God's commandment and ate the fruit. Then they realized that they were duped. They were ashamed and afraid. They covered themselves with fig leaves and hid themselves. They started blaming each other and hiding from God. They recognized their vulnerability. Their distorted idea of God and themselves had taken them to all kinds of troubles.

A wrong or distorted image can impair our relationship with God. If we have been holding on to such unhealthy and distorted images of God, we have to move on to a mature faith and healthy understanding of God. We have to follow the example of Saint Paul who said, "When I was a child, I spoke like a child, I thought like a child, I reasoned like a child; when I became an adult, I put an end to childish ways" (1 Cor 13:11). We need to put away our childish, unhealthy, and infantile images of God. We are people who can think and reflect about what we believe in, and correct them if need be. By doing that not only that we will develop a new and healthy relationship with God but also help others to do the same.

12

A Trinitarian God

THE CONVENTIONAL IMAGES OF God, both positive and negative, that we discussed are those that are often held by those in the Judeo-Christian traditions. If we turn to other religions and cultures around the world, we might learn of many more of such images and ideas of God. God might be viewed in as many ways as we are split as human beings.

Although there are all these multiple images and ideas of God in the Bible and traditions, God has also been revealed as someone much bigger than the usual anthropomorphic images attributed to him. One of those revelations is that of him as a Holy Trinity. This is an image that obtained a prime place in the Christian proclamation of faith. In fact, Christians sometimes refer to this faith in the Holy Trinity as something unique to them. There may be some sort of Trinitarian ideas of God in some other traditions too, but they are not the same. In Hinduism, for example, there is a concept called *Trimūrtis* or Trinity referring to the three supreme gods, *Brahma*, *Vishnu*, and *Shiva*. Brahma is the creator, Shiva is the destroyer, and Vishnu is the preserver. It is possible that some people mistake the concept of these three gods in Hinduism with the idea of the Holy Trinity in the Christian faith. They are not the same. The two faiths are not talking about the same thing when they refer to the Trinity.

In the Christian proclamation of faith, the creed, whether it is the Apostles' Creed or the Nicene Creed that the Catholics and a few other Christian denominations recite during their liturgical celebrations, summarizes their faith in the Trinitarian Godhead. The Catechism of the Catholic Church dedicates almost half of its articles to elaborate on this core faith of the Christian community. Sometimes the terminologies and statements in these creeds and faith documents can be so overwhelming and difficult to understand that people often think of this idea of God as something too abstract, complex, and complicated, and they think that it is better to leave it alone rather than trying to wrap their heads around it.

I do not wish to make it complicated any further, but I would like to share some of my thoughts on what this mystery means for us. The Christian community believes that God has revealed himself as a Trinitarian God—Father, Son, and Holy Spirit

(Catechism of the Catholic Church, 261–267). It is one and the same God, but consists of three persons. The three persons are unique in themselves and yet inseparable and one in substance and glory. These three divine persons are inseparable in what they do, but each does it in the way that is proper to him. This is an image or idea of God that is different from the other anthropomorphic images attributed to God. When we think of God as a father, mother, or friend, we can usually associate that with human beings. We know what it means to be a father, mother, or friend. But when we say God is a Trinity, it is more than the human categories. We don't think of a human being as consisting of three persons. Human beings are single or individual persons. I am not a union of three persons; I am one person. Of course, I believe that I am created in the image and likeness of the Trinitarian God. I also believe that I am united with God and others. And yet, when I think of myself, I see myself as one person, not three. But God is a Trinity or one in being with three persons inseparably united with each other. That is more than what we conceive of in human beings.

These faith statements might sound like high theology, and they are. But they are the result of our experience too. What we proclaim as our faith is what we experience in our daily lives. I could ask a question to all the Christians or Catholics who pray: When you pray, whom do you pray to? Do you pray to the Father, do you pray to Jesus, or do you pray to the Holy Spirit? Or do you pray to all three of them? Maybe sometimes you simply pray to God? I believe you do all these. Sometimes we address our prayers to the Father. Sometimes we address our prayers to the Son, Jesus. Sometimes we address our prayers to the Father through the Son, as the Son is our intercessor, friend, and brother. And sometimes we pray to the Holy Spirit. Sometimes we pray with Jesus and the Holy Spirit. Sometimes we address our prayer simply to God. But at the same time, with all these, we believe that it is the same God that we are praying to, one God but three persons. We also believe that all the three persons of the Holy Trinity are present in us. The Father lives in us, and journeys with us; the Son lives in us, and journeys with us; and the Holy Spirit dwells in us, and journeys with us. At the same time, we believe that it is the same God who lives and is present in us.

In the book of Genesis, we read: "God said, 'Let us make humankind in our image, according to our likeness'" (Gen 1:26). There are several things to understand from this verse. One of the things that is important to note is the reference to God as "Us," a plural pronoun. God said, "Let 'us' make humankind." The immediate question about this Biblical revelation of God as "us" would be: Is God one or more than one? The Christian faith holds that God is one but it is a Trinity or triune God consisting of three persons, the Father, the Son, and the Holy Spirit. We believe that God created us. We are sons and daughters of the creator God. We believe that the same God came to save us in Jesus Christ. He is our redeemer. We also believe that the same God continues to lead us and sanctify us through the Holy Spirit. It is the same God but it is a Trinity. That would mean that the Trinitarian God is the creator God, with all the three persons being actively present and involved in the creative work. The Trinitarian

God is the redeemer or savior God, with all the three persons being actively present and involved in the redeeming or saving work. And the Trinitarian God is the sanctifier God, with all the three persons being actively present and involved in the sanctifying work. Each of the persons in this Trinitarian Godhead has a specific role and great significance in our lives, but it is the same God. Let us look at each of these persons of the Holy Trinity in a little more detail.

God, the Father

The God who reveals himself to us as our creator also reveals himself as a "Father" who deeply cares about us, provides for us, and sustains us. Although we all have our own particular experiences of our own earthly fathers, when we think of God as the Father, we think of him as the most loving, kind, compassionate, and forgiving father. He is the epitome of who a loving father can be. Jesus invites us to see God as "Our Father" (Matt 6:9–15), who provides for us, forgives us, and protects us from temptations and trials.

This is not simply any high theology; this has been the personal experience of many of us. We believe that God created us. We didn't create ourselves. We could say that our parents created us, but they didn't create themselves. They received their life from their parents. But their parents didn't create themselves; they received it from their parents. If we go back to all the past generations, we know that none of them created themselves. They all received life from somebody, which ultimately goes back to the author of life, God. There are all kinds of debates and discussions going on about how life began. I don't think I can engage in a detailed discussion on that topic in this book, except to say that according to the Judeo-Christian faith, everything began with God. He is the creator of all that is, in whatever form they must have begun. Hence, our life is a gift from God. But God is not just a creator of life. He is also our sustainer and provider. We believe that God has been providing for and taking care of us throughout our life. Maybe on many occasions life was not easy, and maybe there were many things that were difficult in our life, but God has been sustaining us, giving us grace and strength, and helping us to overcome all those challenges.

If we look into our own personal stories, we would see how and when we have experienced the powerful presence of God as a loving father, parent, or caregiver. Just like a father or mother holds the hand of the child to keep him or her from falling or stumbling, God has been holding our hands. Just like a parent helping the child to get up when he or she falls, God has been helping us to rise from our falls and failures. Just like a parent carries the child when the child finds it hard to walk or when there are dangerous and deadly things on the road, God has been carrying us when we were finding it hard to carry on. All of us can relate to times or moments in our lives when we felt drained out of energy and strength and felt that we couldn't go on any longer or wondered how we would go on. But at all those times, we found a renewed strength and grace to overcome those problems and challenges. After those trying times passed we might have wondered how we did it. Some people might attribute it to the inner strength that people have. Their drive to survive helps them to bounce back. But for a believer in God, the source of that drive to bounce back or that inner strength is God himself.

A person who believes in this loving Father God knows that it was none other than him who was holding our hands and helping us to pass through those difficult situations. This is the Father God whom the Israelites experienced at the various significant moments in their salvation history. He led them out of slavery in Egypt when they were at the point of giving up. He led them through the Red Sea when they felt that they were going to perish in the waters. He led them through the desert when they thought that they were going to starve and die. He led them out of exiles and foreign oppressions when they felt that they were going to be decimated as a group or nation. All these Biblical events may not be necessarily referring to historical events but could be seen as representative of the hardships and difficulties they faced and God helping them to move on. The Israelites had an enormous amount of bad things happening in their life. Being in slavery, being in exile, ruled by foreign rules, and badly ruled by their own kings, they had a lot of instability and suffering in their life. On many occasions they were at a point where they thought that even God had forgotten and abandoned them. But through prophet Isaiah, God says, "But Zion said, 'The Lord has forsaken me, my Lord has forgotten me.' Can a woman forget her nursing child, or show no compassion for the child of her womb? Even these may forget, yet I will not forget you" (Isa 49:14–15). I believe that it is not only the Israelites but also all the human communities who can recount the constant experience of the fatherly and providential care of God in their lives and history.

The creator God who is the Father of us all continues to care for his children generation after generation. He knows us. He knows our strengths and limitations. He knows where we are at this moment in our life. He knows what has happened in our life journey. He knows what is going on in our life right now. And with all that, he simply says: "Do not fear, for I have redeemed you; I have called you by name, you are mine" (Isa 43:1). He is a God who has been with us from the beginning, and he will continue to be with us always. As he journeyed with those people before, during, and after their slavery in Egypt, he journeys with you and me today. He has been a father to all, beginning from creation to this moment. He has journeyed with the people of all ages and cultures. After creating the universe he did not stay away or take a break from our lives for a period of time. He has been with his creation all throughout. And he will continue to be with us in the ages to come. God wants us to rejoice and be strong not because everything is perfect but because he is with us always. He will never abandon us because we are his own.

In the Book of Revelations we read: "'I am the Alpha and the Omega,' says the Lord God, who is and who was and who is to come, the Almighty" (Rev 1:8).

Referring to this everlasting love of the heavenly Father, Saint Francis de Sales says that we should always remember and believe that the everlasting Father who took care of us yesterday will take care of us today and tomorrow. We know that is our experience. No matter what our struggles and problems in life might have been, God took care of us yesterday and until this moment. And we believe that he will continue to take care of us today and in the days to come. When we think of God taking care of us, we have to always remember that it is not necessarily referring to God insulating us from all the limitations of this physical world or death but rather to the constant grace and strength that he would give us during this earthly life and the assurance of our union with him in eternity. This Father God is with us at every moment of our life. He is magnificent and majestic, transcendent and almighty. But he is also immanent. He knows us through and through. He lives in us and walks with us in our life journey.

God, the Son

The God who had been revealing himself as a Father through the beautiful creation, through traditions, cultures, and peoples, through scriptures, through prophets and leaders, and through various life events in our human history revealed himself in a very concrete and tangible way through the person of Jesus, the Son of God, the second person of the Trinity. The creator triune God incarnated in our midst as our redeemer and savior. He came down to our level and lived with us. Affirming this truth about Jesus being the same God who created us and provides for us, Saint John begins his gospel by saying, "In the beginning was the Word, and the Word was with God, and the Word was God. He was in the beginning with God. All things came into being through him, and without him not one thing came into being. What has come into being in him was life, and the life was the light of all people" (John 1:1–4). The "Word" refers to Jesus, the second person of the Holy Trinity. Identifying himself with the same creator Father God, Jesus said, "I and the Father are one" (John 10:30).

Reiterating this truth about the divine identity of Jesus, Saint Paul says, "He is the image of the invisible God, the firstborn of all creation; for in him all things in heaven and on earth were created, things visible and invisible, whether thrones or dominions or rulers or powers—all things have been created through him and for him. He himself is before all things, and in him all things hold together" (Col 1:15–17). In Jesus, the redeemer and savior, the Father and the Holy Spirit were fully present. The Father was loving and saving us through the Son who was being led by the Holy Spirit.

In the book of Deuteronomy, we hear Moses assuring the people that the transcendent God whom they were experiencing would become tangible and relatable: "The Lord your God will raise up for you a prophet like me from among your own people; you shall heed such a prophet. This is what you requested of the Lord your God at Horeb on the day of the assembly when you said: 'If I hear the voice of the Lord my God any more, or ever again see this great fire, I will die.' Then the Lord replied to me: 'They are right in what they have said. I will raise up for them a prophet like you from among their own people'" (Deut 18:15–18).

This reference to the prophet that God was going to raise is often believed to be a reference to the Son of God, the second person of the Holy Trinity. People fearing the voice of God and the reference to God's appearance as the blazing fire seem to be references to God's transcendence which people found difficult to relate to. People pleaded with God to not show himself in all his glory lest they die.

We know newborn babies and the grown ups differ in their tolerance and resistance power. A newborn baby is very feeble and weak, and its tolerance and resistance power is much less than that of an adult. An adult may be able to withstand a high decibel sound without much damage to his or her ears but that same sound may be highly damaging for a newborn baby. Human beings are on a completely different realm of life and being in comparison with the realm of God. God in his full power and glory is incomprehensible and overwhelming for us. We need a God who is relatable and understandable. The answer to that desire is Jesus Christ, God who became man. He is the Emmanuel, God with us (Matt 1:23).

Saint John speaks about why God became man, "For God so loved the world that he gave his only Son, so that everyone who believes in him may not perish but may have eternal life" (John 3:16). If Moses had saved his people from slavery in Egypt, God's Son, Jesus Christ, was going to save us, his people, from our slavery to evils, sins, unhealthy habits and behaviors, broken relationships, and all other kinds of things that we have been enslaved to. Referencing Saint Athanasius, the Catechism of the Catholic Church says, "For the Son of God became man so that we might become God" (460). And the path he chose to do that saving work was becoming one of us. He became our brother, our friend, and our traveling companion.

When referring to the incarnation of God in Jesus, some people tend to have a false idea that God existed in some mysterious world and then one day decided to enter into our world. Sometimes the language used for such references itself could be giving such an idea. Expressions such as, "He 'came down' from heaven" might give an idea that heaven is somewhere up in the sky where God dwells and one day he decided to come down to our world, the earth. That is a distorted idea of God. God was not away from our world before the incarnation of Jesus. God was and God is always with us. This world, our mother earth, belongs to God, and we belong to him. He has been present in the life of our ancestors. He was present in the life of the Patriarchs and prophets. The incarnation of God in Jesus was a unique way for God to be with us, to bring us back to our true identity as children of God and to show us how he willed our life to be. And that redeeming act of God is not ended; it continues through all generations. "Coming down" to our level simply refers to God revealing himself to us in a very unique way as a human being. Becoming a human being was the best way for God to identify himself with us to show us that he was one with us, as companion and friend, walking hand in hand with us in our life journey. But in incarnating and becoming a human being, God was taking a great risk. The unlimited God had to enter into the realm of limitations and weaknesses as we experience. Human life on earth is limited by space and time. In becoming one of us, God had to be prepared for this limitation. His physical presence and mobility were limited to certain geographical areas. His relationships were limited to a limited number of people. He felt hunger and thirst like anyone of us. He was rejected, abandoned, criticized, misunderstood, and mocked by others. He was tempted and tested many times. He felt angry and tired like anyone of us. He felt pain and sorrow on many occasions. He was reviled and ridiculed by his family, friends, and others.

Many people took him for granted, giving him importance no more than that of a fellow human being. And finally, his life on this earth was cut short at a young age by conspiracy and betrayal. Being a human being he could not live unendingly on this earth because no human being lives on earth unendingly. Of course, as God he could have lived unendingly if he chose to. But that would not have brought him at par with human beings. If he had to completely identify himself with human beings he had to also die one day. And the manner of his death was even more tragic. His community excommunicated and condemned him. He was put to a shameful death like a criminal. It is not something that any human being would like to see or experience. So it is not only the matter of death but also the manner of death that was risky.

Many people wondered and still continue to wonder: What kind of God is this that he becomes a human being? God should remain as God and shouldn't switch roles with human beings. That was the great risk he was taking. When human beings are often trying to become masters and super heroes God becomes a servant and weakling. God allows himself for a self-ridicule. But God was willing to take that risk to show us how much he loves us and cares about us. Saint Paul in his letter to the Philippians speaks to this humbling act of God: " . . . though he was in the form of God, did not regard equality with God as something to be exploited, but emptied himself, taking the form of a slave, being born in human likeness" (Phil 2:6–7).

Jesus is someone we can relate to. He knows what we are going through. When we suffer, when we struggle, when we are tested and tempted, and when we are rejected and condemned, he knows what we are going through because he has been there. In Jesus, we have a God who understands what we experience. People experienced his love and compassion in a tangible way. The gospels are full of stories of people who experienced this love of Jesus in a very personal way. Saint John speaks of this personal experience he and the people had with Jesus, "We declare to you what was from the beginning, what we have heard, what we have seen with our eyes, what we have looked at and touched with our hands, concerning the word of life—this life was revealed, and we have seen it and testify to it, and declare to you the eternal life that was with the Father and was revealed to us" (1 John 1:1–2). This same Jesus walks with us in our life journey.

As he often said to his disciples and others he says to each one of us, "Do not be afraid, I am with you." He is with us. He shows us how to live well. When we fall, when we are disappointed, and when we are broken and finding it hard to go on, he lifts us up and tells us to not be afraid. As he stood in the midst of those apostles who were terrified and said to them, "Peace be with you" (John 20:19), he stands in our midst and extends his peace to all of us. He holds our hand. He is our friend, our brother, and our savior. He comes to save us and redeem us. Referring to the unfailing love of this loving God, the author of the letter to the Hebrews says, " . . . he has said, 'I will never leave you or forsake you'" (Heb 13:5). He will never abandon us. The God who created us and sustains us came to live with us and redeem us, and he continues to live with us and redeem us. He is always our Emmanuel, the God with us.

God, the Holy Spirit

The creator triune God who is a father to all of us and who came to live with us and save us, continues to dwell with us and within us as the Holy Spirit. Before Jesus ascended to heaven he said to his disciples, "I still have many things to say to you, but you cannot bear them now. When the Spirit of truth comes, he will guide you into all the truth" (John 16:12–13). It is believed that the apostles spent about three years with Jesus. Jesus was with them to guide them and lead them. He was there to instruct them. He would tell them what to do, what not to do, how to do things better, so on and so forth. They didn't have to worry about who would guide them and instruct them. But as Jesus was ascending, he was not going to abandon them or leave them without guidance. Jesus wished that he could teach and tell his disciples a lot more. There was so much that he wanted to tell them or teach them. But they were not ready yet. Their minds and hearts were not ready to receive those teachings. They couldn't take all of that. It had to be given gradually, step by step. So for all that, Jesus was going to give them the gift of the Holy Spirit. It was the Holy Spirit who was going to teach them and guide them. They were going to be taught everything gradually. Jesus was going to teach them through the Holy Spirit about the love of the Father and the importance of loving one another as the Holy Trinity does.

Those who are parents know how much they would like their children to know everything. They have so much to tell them and teach them. They want them to learn and do so many things. But the parents also know that the children cannot take all that altogether. They are not ready yet. Their minds are not developed for that yet. So what do the parents do? They give them the guidance in small dosages. And step-by-step the children grow. This is what happens in our spiritual life too. We grow and make progress gradually. We cannot have all of the wisdom at once. We cannot understand everything just like that. It takes time. God's revelation comes to us little by little. We don't grow in God's love in one sitting. It is a gradual process. The saving and sanctifying work is a gradual process.

When Jesus told his disciples that they were not ready yet to take in all what he wanted to teach them, he was not just referring it to those individual disciples alone. He was referring it to the human race as well. Even with his incarnation, God knew that the human race was not going to grasp everything about him just like that. The unraveling of the mystery of God had to continue. In every age, God's revelation was going to continue and human beings were going to unravel that mystery according to their capacity and context. The Holy Spirit is the one who makes that unraveling possible.

It is not because God does not want to give himself completely to us but rather because we are not able to grasp and take in all of that mystery. The Holy Spirit teaches us all that gradually. For that we have to remain open to the Spirit. We are learners all the time. If we think that we know everything, and we have all wisdom and knowledge, then God cannot teach us anything anymore. We will not grow anymore. If we don't remain open to the voice and inspirations of the Holy Spirit, we might hear only our voice and follow only our desires and wishes. God can speak to us in many ways. Everyday he reveals to us his plans and will in many ways. Everyday we discover him in many ways. The spirit of God directs us to his voice coming to us through scripture, our friends, our family, our colleagues, our cultures, the strangers that we meet on the way, through various life events, through the creation, through our life contexts, and in so many other ways.

It is not that the Holy Spirit was inactive or absent before Jesus ascended into heaven. The Holy Spirit has been actively present like the Father and Son throughout the salvation history. The Holy Spirit was present at creation. The creation account in the book of Genesis says: " . . . while a wind from God swept over the face of the waters" (Gen 1:2). "The wind from God" refers to the Holy Spirit. The Holy Spirit was present in the prophets and kings. The Spirit of God came upon David when he was anointed king, "Then Samuel took the horn of oil, and anointed him in the presence of his brothers; and the spirit of the Lord came mightily upon David from that day forward" (1 Sam 16:13).

Prophet Ezekiel was filled with the power of the Holy Spirit: "The spirit entered into me, and set me on my feet; and he spoke with me and said to me: Go, shut yourself inside your house" (Ezek 3:24). We see the presence and activity of the Holy Spirit more prominently in the New Testament. The Holy Spirit came upon Mary and brought forth Jesus into this world, "The angel said to her, 'The Holy Spirit will come upon you, and the power of the Most High will overshadow you; therefore the child to be born will be holy; he will be called Son of God'" (Luke 1:35). Elizabeth and Zechariah were filled with the Holy Spirit. The Holy Spirit descended upon Jesus in bodily form like a dove (Luke 3:22). Promising the Holy Spirit, Jesus says to his disciples, "And I will ask the Father, and he will give you another Advocate, to be with you forever. This is the Spirit of truth, whom the world cannot receive, because it neither sees him nor knows him. You know him, because he abides with you, and he will be in you" (John 14:16–17). Jesus breathed on his disciples and said, "Receive the Holy Spirit" (John 20:22).

All of us are filled with this same Holy Spirit. Saint Paul says that we are the temples of the Holy Spirit (1 Cor 6:19). The Holy Spirit, God, dwells within us. It means that God is not confined to a building or structure like temple or church but is active and alive in us. God is in his people. Jesus speaks of this living presence of God in us in his conversation with the Samaritan woman, "But the hour is coming, and is now here, when the true worshipers will worship the Father in spirit and truth, for the Father seeks such as these to worship him. God is spirit, and those who worship him must worship in spirit and truth" (John 4:23–24).

Seeing ourselves as the temples of the Holy Spirit is a significant change from the understanding of many people. Many people think of God as confined to a worship place or building and do not think of his presence permeating the whole creation, including themselves. Consequently, too much emphasis is sometimes given to the architectural beauty and magnificence of temples, churches, and other worship places over God's living presence in people. Our focus has to be more on God's presence in us. We thank God for our artists and architects who are bestowed with enormous gifts, and they need to be given opportunities to bring those talents to their utmost expression. But if we have to choose between beautifying the external structures and the internal beautification of our lives and the lives of others, we have to choose the latter. God is more present and alive in his people than in man-made structures and monuments. Building our lives and the lives of others in a healthy and godly way needs to have priority over the elaborate external expressions of our religiosity and spirituality.

If we are the dwelling places of God it means that we have to live our lives worthy of that dignity. We should put away all that is against God's will and live holy lives. In the book of Leviticus we read about this call to holiness, "You shall be holy to me; for I the Lord am holy" (Lev 20:26). We see Jesus being upset and angry with those who were doing business in Jerusalem temple. Quoting the scripture he says to them: "Is it not written, 'My house shall be called a house of prayer for all the nations?' But you have made it a den of robbers" (Mark 11:17). The temple that was meant to be a place of prayer, experience of God, and gathering of the community had become a place of business. God's dwelling place is not to be turned into a market place. Sacrifice of animals and birds and other external expressions of their religiosity had taken priority over their internal sanctity. Jesus cleansing the temple and restoring it to its original purpose was indicative of his call to free our lives from all kinds of ungodliness and sins.

We being the temples of God has a great significance for our interpersonal relationships too. If we are the temples of God's Spirit, it calls for mutual respect and love. If I am God's temple, I should accept that others also are God's temples. And if they are God's temples I should approach them and treat them as I would approach or treat God—that is, with reverence, love, and wonder.

The Trinitarian image of God as it is understood and experienced by Christians has been a core element of Christian faith and life. Our whole life and being as human beings are patterned after this Trinitarian God. Our creator God lives with us and sustains us as our father, lives with as our redeemer and savior, and lives with us as our sanctifier and guide.

13

Unique and United

METAPHORS OFTEN DO NOT capture and communicate the whole reality that we are trying to understand but at the same time they can be great tools to give us a pretty good idea of what we are trying to understand. There are many metaphors that people use to explain the mystery of the Holy Trinity. One of them is the metaphor of the sun, the star at the center of our solar system. I would like to look at this metaphor in somewhat a detailed manner. This is not to be taken as equivalent to the reality of the Trinitarian God that we are trying to understand, but this metaphor might help us to understand the reality better.

The sun is a massive and gigantic star that emanates unimaginable amount of energy and heat. At the center of the sun it is believed that the temperature reaches 27 million degrees Fahrenheit. That is something unfathomable. When the temperature in the summer in Saint Louis, Missouri crosses the three digits or gets to eighties and nineties, people already get too upset and agitated. Thank God, the full effect of the sun's heat and light do not get to us. If they did we wouldn't be able to survive. That could once again make us think of the providential care of God who planned everything so beautifully and meticulously that we have an environment that is conducive for our health and well being. But even though the sun is placed far away from us, we know that the sun is so much part of our life. We cannot live without it. Its light and energy sustains our life on earth.

When we think of the sun, we can think of three main aspects of it—the sun itself, its light, and its heat. We know that the sun is there and it sustains our life, but with our naked eyes we cannot see it as it is. Our eyes are not powerful enough to withstand the energy and radiation from it. We cannot comprehend it completely. But we can see the light that emanates from the sun. The light from the sun that gets to us is more conducive and compatible for our eyes. So we cannot see the sun, but we can see the light that comes from the sun. But even the light itself is very bright and strong that sometimes our eyes cannot stand it. If we keep looking at it, our eyes get strained and we get blinded. We can take the light only as much as our eyes are able to absorb and withstand. We also experience the warmth or the heat of the sun. But we don't see the warmth. We can only feel it or experience it. If we stand in the sun we feel warm. We feel it, but we cannot see it. We say, "I feel the warmth" or "I feel the heat." We don't say, "I see the warmth" or "I see the heat." Again, we cannot take in the whole warmth or heat of the sun, because our body is not able to absorb its full effect. If we stay too long in the sun, it becomes too warm or hot and our body gets tired or heated up. When the temperatures go up too high in some places, people die of sunstroke or extreme heat.

So we know that the sun is there, but we cannot really see the sun as it is. We can only see the light coming from the sun. Now, is the light different from the sun? In one sense, yes, it is different. But in another sense, it is not different from the sun. It is one and the same. They both are one, but they are different. Similarly, we can feel the warmth or heat but we cannot see it. Is the warmth or heat different from the sun? In one sense, yes, it is different form the sun. But in another sense, it is not different from the sun. The sun and the heat are the same. The warmth or heat comes from the sun. Can we say that the light and the warmth are two different things? In one sense, yes, they are different. But in another sense, they are not different. They are one and the same. It is the light that brings us the warmth or heat. It is the sun that brings us the light and the warmth. But without that light and warmth the sun will not be sun. They all are one, but they all are unique in themselves. There is an inseparable unity, but there is also an undeniable uniqueness.

If we use this analogy to understand the Holy Trinity, the Father is like the sun, Jesus is like the light from the sun, and the Holy Spirit is like the warmth or heat of the sun. We know that God who is a Father to all of us sustains us and takes care of us. But we cannot see him as he is. He is like the sun. Just as our physical life on this earth will become impossible without the sun, our life in its totality will be impossible without God, our loving father. He is our creator and the one who provides for us and sustains us. But that God manifests himself in Jesus. Jesus is the face of our loving God. We see God in Jesus. To one of his disciples, Philip, Jesus said: "Whoever has seen me has seen the Father . . . Believe me that I am in the Father and the Father is in me" (John 14:9, 11). In his letter to the Colossians, Paul wrote about Jesus, "He is the image of the invisible God" (Col 1:15). Jesus is like the light of the sun. We can see him, but he is one and the same God with the Father. But just as we cannot absorb the light of the sun completely, we cannot comprehend the person of Jesus completely. Everyday we experience him and discover him little by little.

And the same God who incarnated in Jesus continues to be with us through the Holy Spirit. The Holy Spirit brings us energy and strength. He guides us and leads us in the path that Jesus has traced for us. Referring to this guidance of the Holy Spirit, Jesus said, "When the Spirit of truth comes, he will guide you into all the truth" (John 16:13). The Holy Spirit is like the warmth or heat coming from the sun and its light, giving us energy and strength.

Thus it is all the same God, but three persons. There is an inseparable unity within the Trinity, but there is an undeniable uniqueness to each of the persons. It is an intimate relationship. And the uniting force or glue that makes that relationship possible is love.

The almighty God who manifested himself as the creator and providential Father, incarnated himself as the redeemer and savior in the person of Jesus, and continues to love and live in the creation and in each one of us as the sanctifier through the person of the Holy Spirit. It does not mean that the three persons of this Trinitarian God have separate and isolated characteristics and functions. They also do not withdraw from the scene after the completion of their tasks.

The whole Trinity works in unison, and they are constantly at work. The Father continues his work of creation in the world bringing into being each one of us and other beings. He continues his creative work through each one of us. We are not finished products. We grow and develop step by step. We begin our life as tiny zygotes in our mothers' wombs. God's creative work continues in us throughout our lives. The beauty of our being is constantly unfolding. He continues to love and care for his creation, including us, his children. He is ever active and involved in our lives and in our world as he was in the beginning. He is not sitting somewhere idle and inactive. He is constantly at work. The Son is not done with his act of redemption. He continues his redemptive act in each one of us. He continues to transform and renew the world and us. He continues to love and live with us. He continues to call us to a life of repentance and renunciation of sins. The Holy Spirit continues to work in each one of us as our sanctifier, counselor, and advocate. He makes us remain open to the love of the Father and the Son. He helps us to cooperate with the saving work of the Father in Jesus. The Holy Trinity works in unison. There is absolute harmony, unity, and oneness in the Trinity.

14

God of the Temple and the Tent

ANOTHER DIMENSION OF GOD who has revealed himself in the Judeo-Christian tradition is that he is a God of the temple and the tent. He lives in the historical contexts of his people, but he is also a God who keeps moving forward. He is the God of stability and uniqueness, but he is also the God of dynamism and universality. Let us look at these two aspects concerning God.

God of the Temple

A temple stands for the permanence and particularity or uniqueness of a faith community. Every community may not call it a temple. They may call it a church, mosque, or something else. Christians build churches and chapels wherever they form a community. Jews build synagogues and dream of rebuilding their temple in Jerusalem. Hindus build temples. Muslims build mosques. Sikhs build gurdwaras. Other religious communities or faith traditions build their own worship places.

Temples, churches, and other worship places are locations or spaces where communities gather and worship. They are conceived as the dwelling places of God. They represent God's presence in the midst of his people not only for one generation but also for many generations to come. If one temple or church is demolished or destroyed they build another one. The physical structure of a temple or church gives the community a sense of permanence and stability. It points to their history and physical existence in time and space. God being in the temple or church means that he is with his people in their history in time and space.

Temples, churches, and other places of worship point to particularity or uniqueness. Each community has its own understanding of God and way of worship, and their worship places manifest their uniqueness. By looking at a place of worship we can often make out what community or group gathers in there. The worship places of all communities do not look alike. They also do not worship the same God or in the same way. They all have different understandings and images of God.

God in the temple also indicates our call to a life of holiness. Temples are believed to be dwelling places of God, and everyone who comes to the temple is called to remain close to God. In the Christian tradition, a temple or church represents us, human beings, who are the real temples or dwelling places of God (1 Cor 6:19). More than being present in the temples made of bricks and mortar, God is present in us. As a temple or church is considered a holy place, we are called to be holy, manifesting the presence of God. As God dwells with and in his people, he invites everyone to dwell with and in him. God is always with us, but the question is whether we are with him. It is one thing for God to be with us and another thing for us to be with God. And we know that we are not always necessarily with God. Sometimes we are focused solely on ourselves or other things that are not godly and holy. Sometimes we are in our own world. Even in our ordinary conversations, when people are trying to communicate or get some message across to others, we hear them asking, "Are you with me?" That question is to make sure that the other person is present not only physically but also emotionally and psychologically. It is about a mindful presence, or being completely present. We can be physically present with people but psychologically absent. Our mind may be in another world. Our thoughts and feelings may be with something else.

Being temples of the Holy Spirit means being fully present to God. It is a mindful presence with God. We remain aware of God's presence in us and around us, and remain attuned to him. God desires that love and presence are mutual. As he is fully with us, he wants us to be fully with him. And that is what we call holiness. Holiness means being united with God and others in love at all times. It is about being fully or mindfully present to God and others. It means keeping away from everything that distances us from God and others psychologically and spiritually. It is about getting rid of all the unhealthy and evil things in our life. It is about keeping away from everything that is self-destructive. Ultimately, it is to live the two commandments of loving God and loving our neighbor as ourselves. God calls us to do that individually and communally.

Although temples, churches, and other worship places evoke a sense of the divine and remind us of our call to holiness, they could also turn out to be symbols of restrictiveness and exclusivism. They are built where the particular community has a significant presence, but the community could remain exclusive and distanced from other faith communities in the area. Often people of one faith tradition do not go to the worship places of other faith traditions. They remain within their community and use their own worship places for their prayer and gathering. Going to other communities and their places of worship are often uncomfortable because of the differences in their understanding of God and way of worship. Going to somebody else's worship services and places would be also unwelcome and frowned upon by other community members.

A temple, church, or other places of worship could speak about God's presence among his people in their historical context and their uniqueness, but those structures and specificities have an inherent danger of presenting God as exclusive and small. Sometimes even within the Judeo-Christian tradition that is how God has been perceived and presented. God has been perceived as the God of the "chosen people." He was seen and some still do see him as the God of a select group in terms of ethnicity, tribe, and race. In some way we could blame it on God himself. He loves us so personally and treats us as very special as if we are the most important individual or group in the whole world that we begin to think of ourselves as the only individual or group that God loves and cares about. But as I understand, that is not what chosen people means. It simply means that we are chosen to be holy or to be with him. It is about being united with God and others. But that call is extended to everyone in the world. All of us are chosen for or called to a life of holiness. It is not restricted to one group of people. It is unfortunate that the idea of the chosen people led to the perception of God as exclusive and small. The idea of God as one dwelling in the temple and dwelling among his people is primarily about his ever-abiding presence and union with the humanity. He was in the history and everyday life of his people. But he being uniquely present to one individual or group did not mean that he was not present to anybody else. He is not a tribal God. He is the God of the universe.

God of the Tent

The idea of God as one present to all humanity is brought out more powerfully in the image of God as one who lives in a tent. A tent stands for movement, universality, and open-endedness. The Ark of the Covenant containing the two tablets of commandments that Moses received from God (2 Chr 5:10) remained in a tent. God is pictured as being in a tent and moving with his people during their journey to the Promised Land. After he built his palace, King David wanted to build a majestic temple and transfer the Ark of the Covenant from the tent to the temple. He was not happy about the Ark being in a tent. He said to Prophet Nathan, "See now, I am living in a house of cedar, but the ark of God stays in a tent" (2 Sam 7:2). God does not grant David's wish. He continued to remain in the tent.

God being in a tent has many meanings. A tent is movable or transferable. People pitch their tent anywhere, and it can be moved from place to place. People can take it with them wherever they go. The Ark of God being in the tent could indicate that God was on the move. He was moving with his people wherever they went, generation after generation. He dwells with his people in unique ways and lives in their history, but he also keeps moving forward. He cannot be confined to certain structures, places, and times. He is not a God who gets stuck with man-made structures and systems. Sometimes our focus can be so much on the temples, churches, and other worship places that we lose our sense of God living in and with us. God living in the tent meant God living within and amidst his people. When the focus is too much on the structures, it is also possible that we lose our sense of community. We are a people of the tent moving forward as one community with God and each other. When the sense of community is lost, we become splintered groups and individuals.

In every age and in every community we see people being very eager to "house" God in magnificent buildings and structures. And God keeps reminding us that he cannot be housed or restricted to those structures. Those structures and buildings get demolished or destroyed. He lives in and with his people.

King David wanting to build a temple for God could be seen as he and his people wanting to restrict God to a permanent dwelling place. Although God does not grant David's wish, his son, Solomon, ends up building a magnificent temple for God. But God was not going to make that his permanent place. King Nebuchadnezzar of Babylon destroyed the magnificent temple built by Solomon. The temple was again rebuilt after the Israelites returned from Babylon during the reign of King Cyrus of Persia. But the Romans destroyed this second temple as well, and Jesus had prophesied its destruction.

People continue to limit God to a temple, church, or other structures. But God continues to show that he is a God of the tent, a God who lives in and with his people, and a God who keeps moving. He is not a God who can be limited to a structure made of stones and mortar. He wants to live in and with his people. But that is not how people often perceive God. Building a temple for him is probably a way to see him as someone whom they can look upon and worship rather than someone in whom they have to live and have their being. For many of us, relating to a God out there may be easier than having him within us. Being aware of God within us would mean that we have to be constantly attentive and present to him. If he is out there in a temple or church, then we might think that we don't need to relate to him too often except when his intervention becomes really necessary or when we go to those places to fulfill our obligations. It will not be a surprise if we realize how reverent we are toward churches, temples, or other worship places but very irreverent toward others and ourselves who are the living temples of God. We bow to those external and material houses or dwelling places of God, but we irreverently treat each other who are the real dwelling places of God. It is not that God is not present in the temples, churches, and other worship places, but that he cannot be restricted to those inanimate structures alone. When it comes to our life and relationship with him, his real dwelling place is each one of us. We are his tents and temples that carry him and house him.

God being in the tent also means that God is not a God who gets stuck with particular times and seasons. He is in time and space but he also goes beyond time and space. He is journeying with us at all times and in all places. He is the God of the past, the present, and the future. He is a God whom Saint Augustine of Hippo referred to as "ancient yet ever new." As God is moving forward, he wants us, his children, to keep moving forward with him. We are not to get stuck anywhere or with anything.

God being in the tent also indicates that God cannot be confined to and contained by one group or community of people. He pitches his tent anywhere and everywhere. A tent is not restrictive like a temple or church. It can be moved. It can be folded up and taken anywhere. It can be pitched anywhere. God lives with his people in their particular contexts but he is not stuck anywhere. He is omnipresent or everywhere. He is a God of all peoples. He belongs to everyone, and everyone belongs to God. He has no favorites, although we may think that we are his favorite. We could also say that we are his favorites, but with the admission that others are also his favorites. That is the difference between him and us. He has a heart large enough to hold all of us, making us feel that we are his favorite. In our case, we may be very selective about whom we want to hold in our heart. It might take years and years to enlarge our heart to invite more people into it. God's love is present to everyone. He reveals himself to us in unique ways according to our uniqueness but he is the God of the Universe. He has been present to our forefathers in various cultures, and he is present to us today. We all are his children. I shall elaborate on this universality of God in the next chapter.

God being in the tent also could be representing the psychological and spiritual changes and transformation that we are called to engage in. It is not just about moving forward physically. To keep the momentum in our growth and development we need to be willing to make psychological and spiritual changes from time to time. We have to be willing to change some of our thoughts, ideas, opinions, and viewpoints. We have to engage in constant dialogue and discernment with the community instead of getting stuck in our ways. We have to be willing to change the way we see people, the world, and ourselves. We have to be open to the new ways in which God reveals himself to us, which means that we have to change some of our ideas and images we have of him. We have to be like Saint Paul who said that he had moved from speaking, thinking, and reasoning like a child to an adult who had begun to speak, think, reason, and act like an adult (1 Cor 13:11). Moving forward with God would mean letting God cleanse us and purify us as Jesus cleansed the Jerusalem temple.

So looking at all these, there are many things that stand out about this Judeo-Christian image of God as the God of the temple and the tent, and it has many implications for our life. First, God dwells with us, his children, in our particular contexts and life situations. He is present to each one of us in our own unique ways. He is immanent, present in our lives and in our creation. God wants us to live with that awareness of his ever-abiding presence. Second, as God dwells with us, he desires that we dwell with him. He wants us to grow in holiness everyday. He wants us to change things that are unhealthy and ungodly in our personal and community lives. He is not someone who desires to be reduced to some inanimate places and structures. He wants to be alive and actively present in each one of us. Third, God is universal. He is the God of all peoples. He is not limited to one select group of people, culture, or context. We all are his children. He is bigger than the created world and bigger than human conceptions. We have to see God as someone more than all the conventional and anthropomorphic attributes and images that we give to him. Fourth, God calls us to live as one universal family. Many of us see ourselves in terms of our particular context and background. We may have reduced ourselves to some labels and categories based on our ethnicity, race, religion, caste, class, ideology, so on and so forth. We need to rise above those classifications and categories and become universal like God. Fifth, God is on the move. He does not get stuck with times and places. He keeps moving forward and invites us to move with him. Our life is a journey. We need to keep moving forward physically, psychologically, and spiritually. Sometimes we get stuck or go backward. When we don't move forward with God we stifle and become stagnant, and we don't grow and bring the best out of ourselves.

15

God of the Universe

ALTHOUGH THE CONVENTIONAL BELIEF may be that the Judeo-Christian God is a God of a select group of people, the actual understanding of God in these traditions is that he is present with his people in their particular historical contexts and at the same time universally present to everyone everywhere. This image of God as the God of the universe is highlighted throughout the Bible. We shall look at a few of those stories.

Abraham

Abraham is one of the persons whose story powerfully brings out the understanding of God as the God of the universe. We hear his story starting from Chapter 12 of the book of Genesis. God asked Abraham to leave his country and kindred and embark on a journey. Abraham was probably planning to settle down and make a secure life for himself and his wife, Sarai in the safe environment of his family and tribe in Ur. But God asked him to go to a land that he was going to show him. Asking him to leave his country and kindred could mean inviting him to see God as someone bigger than what he usually thought of.

Responding to God's call, Abraham begins his journey. Although Abraham stands out as the leading figure in the story, there was a whole group of people going along with him, which means that God was calling all of them to a new phase in their spiritual growth. Abraham takes with him his wife, Sarah, his nephew, Lot, and many other men and women who were either workers or slaves. In those days it was not uncommon for rich landlords and tribal leaders to have slaves and servants. It is possible that Abraham, Sara, and Lot had many slaves. We hear of Hagar as the slave girl through whom Abraham had his son, Ishmael. The group must have included other relatives of Abraham as well. In the story, Abraham stands as the leader for all of them. But that doesn't mean that God was calling only Abraham. He was calling all those who went with him. And on a larger scale, Abraham stands for all of us, the whole humanity, whom God is calling to be on the journey with him.

On his journey, Abraham stops in many places and in some of those places he appears to have settled down for a while. Wherever Abraham went he built an altar to the Lord, which could indicate that God was going with him wherever he went. He experienced God as someone very personally present in his life. He felt that he was someone special to God.

The story of Abraham doesn't have to be seen only from the physical perspective. It was not just about leaving one territory and going to another in the physical sense. It could be seen from the spiritual perspective where Abraham is telling the story about God and human life. Asking Abraham to leave his country and kindred could be seen as God calling him to a life of holiness and new understanding of God. It was an invitation to leave all the distorted conventional images he had about God. He was invited to experience God in a new way. Maybe it took many years for Abraham to grow in that holiness and new understanding of God. But he was on the journey, growing closer to God everyday and understanding him in new ways.

Abraham's encounter with King Melchizedek of Salem and his short stay in the kingdom of Gerar are interesting pieces of the larger story that speak more in depth about the spiritual journey that he was engaged in. When his nephew, Lot was taken captive by the kings who were attacking the kingdom where Lot settled in, Abraham went into battle with those kings to rescue his nephew. The kings who fought with and against Abraham appear to have looked at him as someone specially blessed by God. When the battle was over and the enemies were defeated, King Melchizedek of Salem came to congratulate and celebrate with Abraham for his victory (Gen 14:18). The story also tells us that King Melchizedek blessed Abraham because he was also the priest of God Most High. Some scripture scholars equate Melchizedek with Christ himself since the name, King Melchizedek of Salem could mean "king of righteousness and peace," and Jesus himself is the king of righteousness and peace. Melchizedek being portrayed as the priest of the Most High and placing before Abraham bread and wine could also be a reference to Jesus, because Jesus himself is the High Priest and he becomes the new bread and wine for his people, sharing his body and blood with us. But if we want to look at Melchizedek as a priest of God in the usual sense and see his encounter with Abraham from the perspective of God revealing his universality, we could think that this was a new revelation and experience for Abraham.

It is believed that Abraham's family and ancestors were polytheists, which would mean that he was only used to tribal gods who were concerned only about a small tribe or group. But now he was experiencing God in a larger way, as one working in the life of other tribes and people. Melchizedek did not belong to Abraham's tribe or family. He was a stranger that Abraham met, but God was present in his life too. That realization must have been life changing for Abraham because that would mean that God was not only his and his tribe's God but also the God of the whole universe, all tribes and all peoples. That would mean that all the people all over the world were God's children and were special as Abraham was special. If Abraham was special to

God so was Melchizedek. So Abraham was a brother to all other human beings. He was being made aware that he was part of the universal family of God. That must have been a new revelation for Abraham. Encountering Melchizedek who was the priest of the "Most High" must have made Abraham see God as someone bigger than a tribal God.

By asking him to leave his country and kindred God was asking Abraham to come out of his exclusive and tribal mentality and see the world and God in a new way. He was no more a tribal man but a man of the universe, and man of God's family. Unless he came out of his little world he could not experience the larger world out there. He was not meant to remain in that small world and little tribe. He was meant to be like God himself, universal and all embracing. That transformation had to happen more in the psychological and spiritual terms than in the physical sense. Of course, his tribal feeling and attitudes were not going to change overnight. He had to constantly work on coming out of them and becoming a man of universality and inclusivism. As I mentioned about my realization of the need to come out of my ritual and ethnic mentality as a Syro-Malabar Catholic and Keralite respectively, all of us are called to come out of our own small worlds and see God as someone bigger than we usually think of.

Abraham's encounter with King Abimelech of Gerar was another occasion when he experienced God as someone bigger than a tribal God. King Abimelech had decided to take Sarah as his concubine because Abraham had lied to him about her saying that she was his sister. God spoke to Abimelech and said that he was going to punish him for keeping Sarah. When Abimelech found out the truth about Sarah he gave up his plan of keeping her. But God speaking to King Abimelech tells us about the new understanding of God that Abraham must have attained in his spiritual journey. Abimelech is presented as an honest and truthful man. He remained faithful to God, the same God who was leading Abraham. So it was the same God who was speaking to Abraham and Abimelech. Abimelech was not part of Abraham's tribe or family, but the same God was working in his life too.

Sometimes people might develop an idea in their mind that God was working only in the life of Abraham, which creates an idea of God as an exclusive and tribal god. But God was also working in the life of Melchizedek, Abimelech, and many others. It once again reveals to us that the God whom Abraham was encountering was not a tribal god but the God of the universe. The way he was working in Abraham's life was probably not the way he was working in Melchizedek or Abimelech's life. God works in everyone's life uniquely according to his or her unique situations. God is everyone's God, and he is on the journey with everyone. Abraham was growing in this understanding of God.

There were also other occasions when Abraham experienced God as the God of the universe who loved everyone. One of those experiences involved his slave girl, Hagar through whom he had his son, Ishmael. Sarah and Hagar had gotten into fights, which led to the expulsion of Hagar and Ishmael from the household. That must have been a very distressing time for Abraham, and he must have grieved thinking of Hagar and Ishmael's plight. But God revealed to Abraham that he was concerned about Ishmael and Hagar as much as he was concerned about him and his wife, Sarah. God was not going to forsake Hagar and Ishmael just because Hagar was a slave girl and Sarah had disliked her. God was going to lead Hagar and Ishmael in a different direction. Abraham was happy, but the experience must have once again helped him to recognize God as someone bigger than he thought.

Another experience that made Abraham recognize something new and bigger about God was when God asked him to sacrifice his son, Isaac. After waiting for a long time, Abraham and Sarah had their son, Isaac in their old age. But then God takes Abraham by surprise by asking him to sacrifice Isaac. We could imagine how distressing it must have been for Abraham. Of course, God did not make Abraham do the dreadful act of killing his son; Isaac was safe and Abraham was happy. But the story speaks of another level of spiritual growth that Abraham attained. Abraham learned once again that God was not a tribal God but the God of the universe beyond human imaginations. Animal and human sacrifices to appease gods and goddesses were not an uncommon thing in various tribes and communities in the ancient world. Some of such rituals and sacrifices happen in many communities even today. The story of Isaac's sacrifice could be understood as a change from such kind of spirituality and religiosity to something new.

Abraham must have conceived of God as a tribal god who needed to be pleased by animal and human sacrifices. But God was revealing himself as someone bigger. God revealed to Abraham that he was not a blood thirsty God but a God of love. He did not need to be appeased or kept in good cheer. God was entering into a covenantal relationship with Abraham in which the glue that sealed the covenant was not any animal or human sacrifice but unconditional and total love from each other. The only thing that he desired from Abraham was that he reciprocates God's love. Abraham's willingness to sacrifice his son was indicative of his willingness to go to any extent in expressing his love for God. God and Abraham had entered into an eternal covenant of love. Abraham had moved into another stage in his spiritual growth and understanding of God. God is the God of the whole universe. The whole creation belongs to him. His pleasure is not in some human beings doing some animal and human sacrifices to please him. He doesn't need all that. What really pleases him is human beings, his children, responding to his love.

Abraham experienced God as someone who lived with him in his personal history, revealing himself to him in unique ways, but this God was also moving through times and tribes, revealing his universality and all-embracing love. He is big and transcendent, but he also becomes small and personal to come to our level. He does not get stuck in one place or time. He is the "I am who I am," a God who he is present at all times and in all places.

Abraham stands for all of us who are invited to trust in this transcendent and yet immanent God. He is personally present to each one of us, but he is also universally present to everyone everywhere. Every human being is precious and dear to him. As he did with Abraham, God does the same in our lives. He wants to take us out of our small and tribal mentality and open us up to the larger world of experience and wisdom. He reveals himself to us as someone bigger than what we usually think of him. He is our God but he is also everyone's God, the God of the universe.

Moses

Moses is another prominent character in the Judeo-Christian tradition who brings us the image of God as someone uniquely present to us but also universally present to everyone. We hear Moses' story starting from Chapter 1 of the book of Exodus.

Although a Hebrew, Moses was adopted by Pharaoh's daughter and grew up in the palace of Pharaoh. He was probably influenced by the customs and traditions of the Egyptians including their religious beliefs and practices. He must have had very little idea of who God was to begin with. But as he grew more and more aware of his Hebrew identity he not only matured as a great leader for the community but also grew in his understanding of God.

Moses began to notice the slavery his fellowmen were subjected to in Egypt. When he saw an Egyptian ill-treating a Hebrew he was full of rage and came to the rescue of his defenseless kinsmen and even ended up murdering the Egyptian. But the news about him killing the Egyptian reached the ears of Pharaoh and the latter was seeking to kill him.

Fearing the retaliation of Pharaoh, Moses flees to the land of Midian and ends up staying with the priest of Midian, Reuel and his daughters. But even before he went to stay with them, he is again pictured as a person who abhors injustice and stands up for the weak and the defenseless. When Reuel's daughters came to the well to draw water for their father's flock Moses saw some shepherds coming to boss over the women, trying to drive them away. Moses intervened and defended the women against the ruthless men. The women returned home and gave an account to their father about their newfound defender. Reuel ends up hosting Moses and gave one of his daughters in marriage to him. It is also possible that one of the daughters or all of them were so impressed by his concern for them that they desired to have him as their husband.

We don't know what God or deity Reuel and his family worshipped. Maybe they worshipped the same God who was revealing himself to Moses. Moses going and staying with Reuel probably was God's way of providing him with a spiritual guide and refuge. Moses was running away from Pharaoh. He needed a place of refuge. And God appears to have prepared Reuel and his family as Moses' refuge. Being with them and married to Reuel's daughter we can assume that Moses shared in their beliefs and participated in their worship services. Reuel and his family don't appear to be Hebrews.

They must have been belonging to another culture and ethnic group. If Reuel and his family worshipped the same God who was revealing himself to Moses, this experience of staying with this family and participating in their religious ceremonies must have been another stage in Moses' understanding of God. He was gradually learning that God was not a God of a small tribe or group but rather the God of the universe.

And then Moses has an extraordinary experience of God that confirmed for him that God was the God of the universe. As we discussed before, it happened when Moses was tending the flock of his father-in-law. Here we have a confusing account of Moses' father-in-law. The father-in-law is named, Jethro, and he is described as the priest of Midian. But in Chapter 2, the father-in-law is named Reuel, and he is also described as the priest of Midian. In the book of Judges, there is another person named Hobab who is mentioned as the father-in-law of Moses (Judg 4:11). These contradictory descriptions seem to be because of the different sources such as "Yahwist" and "Elohist" traditions that contributed to the texts of the Bible. Each scribe or author who recorded or copied down the oral and written traditions inherited from others might have changed or added names and details as they found fit according to their times and history. It is also possible that Moses had more than one wife and had more than one father-in-law, as polygamy was not unusual in those days.

As he was tending the flock, Moses had an intense personal experience of God in a flame of fire in the burning bush. It first of all changed Moses' understanding of God. God revealed himself as the God of Moses' ancestors, the God of Abraham, Isaac, and Jacob. And then he revealed himself as "I am who I am." He also told Moses that this would be his name forever and for all generations. This must have been a significant turning point in Moses' life and spiritually. Moses experienced God as someone very close to him personally in his life and personal history. He experienced God as someone who has been present in the history of his ancestors, connecting him with people who have shared and lived the same faith and beliefs before him. He also experienced God as someone who keeps moving forward through times and tribes revealing himself to all people of all times and generations, indicating that he was the God of the universe.

As Most took up his mission and continued his journey God continued to journey with him in multiple ways. Until God called him for the great mission, Moses probably did not think of himself as anything more than an ordinary man tending the sheep. When God gives him the greater mission, he probably realized that God was calling him to be a man of the universe like God himself. At one point, Moses is pictured as God's friend who spoke to him face to face, which simply indicates that he had advanced much in his spiritual journey and grown very close to God. Before Moses no one ever dared to see or speak to God face to face lest they die. Moses had grown very deep in his relationship with and understanding of God. Moses had moved through many stages in his spiritual development and relationship with God. He also encountered many cultures and peoples during his journey, which also must have revealed to him that God was present in the lives of all those people in their own unique ways.

There are many other stories of individuals and groups in the Old Testament that echo this idea of God as the God of the universe. Although the main focus of all the texts are on God's presence and working in the lives of the Israelites who claimed to be the "chosen" people, there are many instances where God reveals himself as the God of all peoples, the God of the universe.

The New Testament

More than anybody else, it is Jesus who reveals to us the universality of God. He was born for all people. One of the stories that powerfully brings out this message is the visit of the magi in the infancy narrative in the gospel of Matthew (Matt 2). According to the story, when Jesus was born in Bethlehem, wise men, known as magi, came to pay him homage and offer him gifts. The magi represented the non-Jewish world. There is no information about where they came from, what race or language they belonged to, and what God or religion they followed. Their arrival simply indicates that God was working in their lives too. Their presence revealed that Jesus was born not just for one group or community of people but for all peoples all over the world. He was a Savior for all.

Through his life and ministry Jesus revealed to the world that he was a God of all peoples. His ministry to the tax collectors, sinners, and other outcasts in the society, his love for the Samaritans and people of other non-Jewish territories, his concern for the Jews and the gentiles and the rich and the poor, and his ultimate sacrifice on the cross for the whole humanity speak to his all-embracing love and universality. And then he sent his own disciples to the ends of the earth to let everyone know that he was everyone's God.

When the Samarian woman engaged in a conversation with Jesus about the Jews and Samaritans worshipping in their own temples, Jesus made it clear to her that God couldn't be contained in or limited to a specific place like temple, specific times in history, or specific groups and communities in the world (John 4:21–24). Jesus was inviting her and all of us to see God beyond the small worlds that we have created for him. Jesus said to Nicodemus, "The wind blows where it chooses, and you hear the sound of it, but you do not know where it comes from or where it goes. So it is with everyone who is born of the Spirit" (John 3:8).

As Spirit, God moves wherever and whenever he wants. But we may have a temptation and tendency to contain and control this Spirit. We might try to reduce him to our conventional concepts and ideas, and our structures and worship places. We might like to claim monopoly or "copyright" over him. We might want God to stand with our group and our community and fight against other groups and communities.

But Jesus kept reminding his people that they could not domesticate and reduce God to their small thinking and ideas. God was everyone's God.

The idea of God as someone bigger than our usual human conceptions is evident in the conversation between Mary Magdalene and the risen Christ. When Mary Magdalene encountered the risen Christ, she was so overjoyed that she wanted to cling to him. She probably wanted to hold on to him and did not want to let him go. Jesus said to her, "Do not hold on to me, because I have not yet ascended to the Father. But go to my brothers and say to them, 'I am ascending to my Father and your Father, to my God and your God'" (John 20:17). She was so grief-stricken when he was crucified and killed. Having found him again, she probably did not want to let him go. She wanted to put her arms around Jesus and cling to him.

Although this reaction of Mary Magdalene could be seen as an innocent reaction of a true friend, it could be also seen from a deeper level of her understanding of Jesus. It was a significant moment in her spiritual journey when she discovered something new about Jesus. Maybe like everybody else she also had developed certain ideas and images of who Jesus was. She probably did not want to let go off those images and understanding. She wanted to continue to cling to them. She wanted to keep him to her level. But Jesus was revealing himself to her as someone bigger. He was not meant to remain only on the physical and earthly level. He was already ascending. Yes, he came down to our level, but it is a mistake to think that that is all what he is. He is much more than his physical and human nature. He also belongs to the non-physical or divine level. He is in time and space but he is also beyond space and time. When Jesus told Mary Magdalene that he had to ascend to the Father he must have been telling her to begin to think of him in a new way.

Ascending to the Father must have also meant that he was rising to wider circles of presence and relationship. He was not the God of only a small group or small territory; he was a God for all people. Maybe he was telling her that life was a journey into that universality, and we all are meant to move and ascend like him. He had come down to our level to take us to his level, the level of God (Catechism of the Catholic Church, 460). As he abides within us and in our world, he wants us to abide with him, becoming people of the universe.

When Jesus commissioned his disciple to go to the ends of the earth to spread the good news of God's love, they were being reminded that God was not a God of a select group of people. He was the God of the universe. When Jesus confronted Saint Paul on his way to Damascus, he was reminding him that God was not the God of only Jewish people but also all people of the world, which ultimately made Saint Paul to become an apostle to the gentiles.

As God is inclusive and universal, he wants us to be the same. All of us are his children, brothers and sisters forming one family with God. As individuals and communities, it is possible that we have become exclusive and restrictive in our dealings and interactions. That needs to change.

These days there is a lot of conversation going on in many societies about being inclusive, and people may have all kinds of ideas about what that means. Some people might think that being inclusive means becoming accepting of every new development in the society or approving everything that people do. Some others might think that being inclusive is about living without any distinctiveness or uniqueness. When God asks us to be inclusive and universal, I don't believe that it is about approving everything that everybody does or everything that is going on in our societies. Societies or communities cannot function without certain commonly accepted norms and behaviors. If everybody begins to do what he or she wants, social and communal life becomes difficult. Life becomes difficult also when the community or society becomes too restrictive. It will be also a fantasy if we think that we will be completely free from all our particularities and uniqueness. As individuals, group, and communities we are unique, and that uniqueness is going to stay in some way.

Being inclusive and universal is to be respectful of each other as God's children. It is to treat everyone with dignity and consider that God is everyone's God. He is not the God of one individual or community alone. He lives in everyone and journeys with everyone. That does not mean that he approves and accepts everything that we do or what is going on in every society. He is sad when we make unhealthy and bad choices that destroy our personal or communal lives. He wants us to be responsible children making healthy choices for our own individual lives as well as for our life as communities and societies. Jesus welcomed and included the tax collectors and sinners in his company, but that does not mean that he was approving all what they were doing. He loved them and valued them, but he also wanted them to make better choices and change their ways. He accepted and forgave the sinner woman, but he told her not to sin anymore. He wanted her to choose healthy ways of living. That love and respect he showed them changed their lives. Being inclusive and universal is about loving and valuing everyone as God's children and as our brothers and sisters and at the same time all of us making efforts to make healthy choices for our own good and the good of others.

We are also going to have our unique characteristics and particularities as groups and communities. Racially, ethnically, linguistically, religiously, socially, and in many other ways, we are different. Many of those differences are going to continue as long as we live in this physical world. Being inclusive or universal does not mean living with the fantasy that those differences don't exist. It will be too unrealistic to think that soon all of us would belong to one race or one religion, or speak one language. Being inclusive is about being aware of our differences and yet living as brothers and sisters, united in the Lord. We respect and love each other without discriminating and demeaning.

Inclusiveness and universality are about gradually getting rid of the unhealthy feelings and attitudes that may have grown in our minds because of our differences. In a family, everyone is different, but when they all love and respect each other, they are able to have a loving family. As individuals and communities, we all are different. When we all love and respect each other, we will be God's family.

God reveals himself to people in their particular cultural and historical contexts, but he is also the God of the universe. No group can monopolize him. Groups and communities might make us think that God has his favorites and he loves only a certain group of people. But the God who has been revealing himself in our human and faith history, particularly in the Judeo-Christian traditions is a God of the universe.

16

A God Who Hears Our Cry

ANOTHER IMAGE OF GOD that is prominent in the Judeo-Christian traditions is that of one who hears our cry. God's heart goes out especially to those who suffer and are in pain. He is close to those who are hurt and are crying. He is close not only to those who are physically hurting but also those who are in distress emotionally and spiritually. The Psalmist sees God as someone very near to the broken hearted (Ps 34:18). This image of God is present throughout the Bible, especially in the person and ministry of Jesus.

In the book of Exodus we hear about God listening to the cry of a whole community. God tells Moses, "I have observed the misery of my people who are in Egypt; I have heard their cry on account of their taskmasters. Indeed, I know their sufferings, and I have come down to deliver them from the Egyptians" (Exod 3:7–8). Slavery is an inhuman act a human being commits against his or her fellow human being. Whether it was in Egypt, Israel, Europe, or America, slavery has been a bad mark on the societies where it has been practiced and perpetrated. It has done irreparable damage to not just one individual or generation but to a whole lot of people and their subsequent generations. Suppressing and denying the basic and God-given human rights and dignity affects not only the everyday physical lives of the slaves but also alters their individual and group psyche. They are tortured physically and mentally. Their brain and mind get altered in such a way that they begin to think and believe that they are meant to be slaves and that even God intended that for them. And their owners or taskmasters often ignore and suppress their cry.

The people of Israel living in slavery in Egypt must have given up their hope of ever being freed from their hapless condition. Many of them must have died of torture and starvation. And many of them must have felt that their God had abandoned them. The slavery must have done a great damage to their faith in God. But through Moses, God comes to them and says that he had not forgotten or abandoned them. He wanted them to know that he had not intended it for them or for anyone. He wanted his children, all human beings, to love and care for each other. The Egyptians also were his children and he wanted them to realize what they were doing to their fellow human beings, the Israelites. Even though the Egyptians ignored, God heard the cry of the Israelites, and he saw their suffering. He comes to rescue them from their misery through Moses.

The slavery in Egypt was not the only time when the people of Israel felt that God had abandoned or forgotten them. We have several references to their sense of abandonment in the Bible. In the book of Isaiah, we read, "But Zion said, 'The Lord has forsaken me, my Lord has forgotten me'" (Isa 49:14). Again in chapter 62 of the same book we hear about God telling his people that they shall never be forsaken or forgotten. The Israelites had much misfortune and bad things happening in their life. They were in exile many times. Driven away from their own land and held captives in exile, life must have been very tough. We can assume that many of them gave up the hope of ever returning to their own land.

Today we hear about refugees seeking asylum in many countries. They are driven away from their own land. There are a lot of debates and discussions going on about giving an asylum to these refugees. We can assume that many of these refugees give up the hope of ever returning to their homes and their land. It is pretty hard to go through such moments and we can assume that it brings a sense of despair and discouragement. Often the leaders, out of their craze for power and control, make decisions and engage in actions that bring misery to the ordinary folks. Sometimes groups and communities, driven by their narrow, fanatic, and exclusivist mentality, attack and try to annihilate each other. Caught in the middle of the conflict, many people lose their lands and loved ones. Driven out of their land, they seek refuge in other places, but they are not welcome in all places. Many societies and communities do not have healthy ways and systems of integrating them into their societies. And the refugees themselves are not adequately prepared to integrate themselves in the communities or societies that welcome them. The Israelites were going through something similar. They had foreign rulers occupying their land and ruling over them on several occasions. Their own rulers and governments had badly ruled them for centuries. They were affected by famine and other natural calamities. They were driven out or forced out of their land many times. They were refugees on many occasions.

But God sent his prophets and messengers to rescue them and assure them that he would never abandon them. His love for them was so much that he would never forget or abandon them. We hear God's voice coming to them through Prophet Baruch, "Take off the garment of your sorrow and affliction, O Jerusalem, and put on forever the beauty of the glory from God . . . see your children gathered from west and east at the word of the Holy One, rejoicing that God has remembered them. For they went out from you on foot, led away by their enemies; but God will bring them back to you, carried in glory, as on a royal throne" (Bar 1:1–6). The Lord had not abandoned them. He had heard their cry and seen their sufferings. He was going to rescue them. God wanted them to continue in faith and not give up. The Psalmist reminds the people about God's never-failing love, "For the Lord is good; his steadfast love endures forever, and his faithfulness to all generations" (Ps 100:5).

It is not only the community that felt abandoned and helpless but also several prominent individuals who felt all alone and broken. Prophet Elijah, as we discussed, was a powerful prophet in the history of Israel. Many revered him but he created many enemies for himself by his speech and actions. The murder of the prophets of Baal infuriated the queen, Jezebel, and she sought to kill him (1 Kgs 19:1–3). Fearing for his life, Elijah flees from the country. He travels a long distance going through desert and difficult terrains. Exhausted and worn out, Elijah appears to be almost giving up. Maybe he felt lonely and abandoned. Maybe there were moments when he felt that even God for whom he did everything and spent his life and energy had abandoned him. As he lay down under a tree to rest, we hear Elijah's groaning, "It is enough; now, O Lord, take away my life, for I am no better than my ancestors" (1 Kgs 19:4). God hears his cry and sends an angel to bring him strength and comfort. Refreshed and renewed, Elijah continues his journey.

Prophet Jeremiah is another individual who had a hard life as a prophet and yet remained faithful to his commitment to the Lord. God chose him as a prophet. Jeremiah did not want to take up the role of a prophet. He probably knew that the life of a prophet was often hard. They had to speak against injustice and evils and criticize rulers and religious leaders who moved away from God's ways. Jeremiah tried to make many excuses to escape God's call. He said he was only a boy and did not know how to speak. But God would not leave him; he was chosen. And God promised him that he would be with him. But as Jeremiah began his ministry, there were times when he felt that he was all alone and even God had abandoned him. Crying out to the Lord, Jeremiah said that the Lord had duped him. He believed in the Lord's promises and started working for him, but instead of being helped and protected he felt cheated and abandoned. People mocked and derided him. Jeremiah was obviously angry and disappointed with God. On one occasion his enemies plotted against him and threw him into a well hoping to kill him. Since there was no water in the well he didn't drown and die. There was mud and he sank into the mud. But God did not let him die there. A eunuch who served the king in his palace rescued him, and Jeremiah continued his prophetic life.

As we move into the New Testament times we again hear a message of love and comfort. God listened to the cry of his people and reached out to them with kindness and compassion. John the Baptist appeared on the scene with a message of hope for his people. Announcing the salvation of the Lord, his preaching echoed the words of Prophet Isaiah, "Every valley shall be filled, and every mountain and hill shall be made low, and the crooked shall be made straight, and the rough ways made smooth; and all flesh shall see the salvation of God" (Luke 3:5–6). The valley could mean a valley of despair and darkness. John tells his people that all such valleys will be filled with hope and joy. The mountains and hills could mean different things. It could mean a mountain of pride and arrogance in the world; God will bring it down. It could mean mountains of hardships and hurdles we experience in our lives. There may be things in our life that look like huge mountains that we find difficult to climb or overcome. But God says, it will become better. They will be leveled. We will be able to climb or overcome those mountains. The crooked paths will be straightened and the rough roads will be made smooth. If the road that we are treading is rough and tough it will become better and smooth. John's message was that God would make things better. But until then he wanted his people to remain strong in faith.

The God who hears the cry of his people becomes very personal in the mission and ministry of Jesus. He became the tangible experience of that redeeming love of God that has been promised. In him people found their God who listened to their cry and saw their sufferings. He was so close to them that they could hear him, look at him, see him, and touch him (1 John 1:1). From him we hear one of the kindest and most comforting words, "Come to me, all you that are weary and are carrying heavy burdens, and I will give you rest" (Matt 11:28). And he often told his disciples and others to not be afraid.

Jesus heard the cry of his people and felt their pain. One of the stories in the gospels that relates to the compassion and kindness of Jesus toward those who were suffering is that of the widow of Nain. In the Bible we hear about widows and orphans mentioned together. Theirs was a sad, lonely, and hopeless situation. For widows, losing their husbands in a patriarchal society meant life becoming very hard and challenging economically, emotionally, and socially. And then to lose their children was even worse. They would become destitute. They had nobody. Their future became uncertain. It wouldn't be surprising if they felt that even God had abandoned them or he had punished them for their sins. And the society would sometimes blame them for the death of their husbands and children. They would be branded as sinners. Even today, the situation of widows in many cultures is not any better. They experience neglect, loneliness, and destitution.

As Jesus journeyed to the town of Nain he came across a widow whose dead son was being carried out for burial. Jesus had a large crowd following him. He was busy. But he took time to see the tears and hear the cry of the widow. He stopped and coming closer to her he said tenderly, "Do not weep" (Luke 7:13). Seeing her pain, Jesus does not just walk by. He stops and attends to her need. He gave her hope, courage, and strength to move on in her life. Her grief and sorrow turned into joy.

We see Jesus doing the same thing for his own mother, Mary on Calvary. As he was dying on the cross, his heart went to his grieving mother. Since we don't hear any account about Joseph being around at the time of Jesus' death, it is assumable that Mary had already become a widow. And Jesus being her only son, she would become a destitute after his death. Recognizing that, he entrusts his mother to John, his beloved disciple, saying, "Here is your mother" (John 19:27). And entrusting his disciple, John to his mother, he tells her, "Woman, here is your son" (John 19:26). Although these words of Jesus could be interpreted as Jesus entrusting his Church and each one of us to the motherly care and intercession of his beloved mother and asking Mary to be a model and mother to all of us, in the context of Mary's life thereafter it could be seen as Jesus ensuring a safe and supportive environment for his mother. He wanted to make sure that his mother was not a destitute and that she did not spend the rest of her life lonely and desolate. Just because Mary was Jesus' mother she was not going to be insulated from the struggles and problems widows and destitute women suffered in the society in those days.

Another story in the gospels that demonstrates the compassion of Jesus toward those who are grieving and in pain is that of raising Lazarus from death. Lazarus and his two sisters, Martha, and Mary were among the best friends of Jesus. Maybe they were all young like him, in their twenties or thirties. Their home, according to the gospel accounts, was a place where Jesus could freely walk in and be himself. But when Lazarus was ill and dying Jesus was not around. Martha and Mary appear to have really felt his absence. If they were all young as Jesus was, it was too hard for them to lose a brother so young. Again, in a patriarchal society, losing their brother was almost like becoming destitute. He was their strength.

Martha and Mary must have even felt abandoned by Jesus when he did not go to them for a few days even after hearing of Lazarus' death. When he finally went Martha expressed her frustration, "Lord, if you had been here, my brother would not have died" (John 11:21). And later her sister, Mary said the same to him, "Lord, if you had been here, my brother would not have died" (John 11:32). What they really meant must have been a complaint like, "Where were you when we most needed you?" But Jesus does not argue and justify. He simply shares in their pain. He was greatly distressed and disturbed. And the gospel says that he "began to weep" (John 11:35). He shares in their sorrow and weeps with them. Being friends with Jesus did not stop Lazarus from dying. But Jesus proved to Martha and Mary that they were not alone in suffering and death. He was with them, weeping with them and sharing in their pain. And he turned their sorrow into joy by raising Lazarus.

We experience all kinds of pains and sufferings in our life. They could be physical, emotional, spiritual, or psychological in nature. Sometimes we are struck by physical illnesses of serious nature, some of which even lead to death or lasting debilitation. We are subjected to many kinds of losses and deprivations. Death of loved ones causes enormous grief and pain. Many are afflicted by loneliness, sadness, depression, anger, and other kinds of psychological problems some of which make them hurt or kill themselves or others. Many parents find it difficult to understand and manage their children triggering all kinds of negative emotions in them. Many children turn into problematic behaviors. Many children find it hard to understand their parents and their ways. They rarely receive love and kindness from their parents. Many marriages are ridden with conflicts and lack of love. Many of them end up in separations and divorces. Many individuals and families face financial difficulties, unemployment, and poverty. Many individuals and families are subjected to violence, discrimination, and exclusion from their community or society. Many people are suppressed and oppressed denying them freedom and basic human rights. Many are burdened by sins and evils experiencing a kind of darkness of the soul. Many people carry burdens of addictions, shame, and other evils. Many people are anxious and worried about their past, present, and future. Many feel that even God has abandoned and forgotten them.

Sometimes life gets really hard and difficult. We experience its weight internally and externally. We all are pushing a "wheelbarrow" of sufferings, pains, and burdens of life. How much and what is in our wheelbarrow differs from person to person. When we are overwhelmed by our sadness and grief, we may feel all alone. Even God may seem to be far away from us. Burdened by these sufferings, many of us have tears rolling down our cheeks. And when we cry, one of the things that we hope for is that somebody sees our tears and would come to help. We look for some relief. We wish that we had some relief from our daily struggles and anxieties. Some people have their tears suppressed internally. They don't have anyone to see it or share it with.

As a priest and psychotherapist I get to see and hear some of the most painful moments in people's lives. People share some of the most intimate stories of their lives. I see lives that are broken and shattered, individuals who have been abused and traumatized, and people who have been offenders and offended. Both in the therapy room and in the confessional, it is the pain of people that I often see and hear. But even with all that I still don't know everything about them. Only God knows everything. And that God who knows everything about us says that he hears our cry and sees our sufferings.

I may not know everything that is going on with even my best friend. I only see things partially. My observations, intuitions, thoughts, and ideas are all limited. I may know some things but I don't know everything. The sorrows, the pains, the anxieties, the hopes, the dreams, the shame, the guilt, the anger, the frustrations, the disappointments, the fears, the sadness, and all such things that we experience and go through may not be known to our friends, spouses, colleagues, parents, children, neighbors, or others. But God knows everything. He knows what our struggles and troubles are. He knows what the desires and longings of our hearts are. He knows our disappointments and distress, and our anxieties and fears. He knows our joys and sorrows. He knows what we treasure in our hearts as our deepest secrets. He knows us through and through. That God tells us that he loves us no matter what.

God assures us that he does not remain silent in our afflictions. He hears our cry. He sees our suffering, and when we suffer he suffers. He walks with us even in the darkest moment of our lives. Our story may be a story of disappointment, anger, frustration, and sadness like that of the Israelites in Egypt. There may be moments when we feel like the Israelites in exile. There may be moments when we are driven to situations where we don't want to be. There may be situations where we feel like we are away from our true home, where we really want to be. It could be an illness, some problems in the family, financial crisis, unemployment, and death of loved ones, or some of our own sinful habits that we are trying to break free from. These are all situations where we may not want to be in. Just like the Israelites who did not want to be in exile, who wanted to be home, we want to be home where we feel healthy and happy.

Sometimes we might feel like Prophet Elijah, abandoned and lonely, and tired and broken by the problems and cares of life. With a lot of faith we make commitment to God and follow his ways. But we are not insulated from sufferings and crosses in our life. When they come, we might feel angry, afraid, disappointed, and deceived. We might tell the Lord that we cannot go on any longer. And the Lord tells us that he hears our cry and does not abandon us. He comes to rescue us. Sometimes we might feel like Prophet Jeremiah, sinking deep into the mud. We may not die, but we sink deeper and deeper into the mud, almost to the neck level, not being able to lift ourselves up. We feel abandoned and all alone.

Our story may be one of a silent cry like that of the widow of Nain or Mary at the foot of the cross. Our story may be one of complaint and grumbling like that of Martha and Mary. Our lives may be filled with valleys of darkness and mountains of hardships. The road that we travel on may be rough and uneven. But he sees and listens to all that we experience. He feels our pain and comes to comfort us. Just as he said to the Israelites God says to each one of us, "I know your afflictions; I have heard your cry; and I have come to deliver you." When things are going bad or we find ourselves in situations where we don't want to be, it is possible that we give into despair and fear. But God wants us to hold on to our faith and continue to live with hope and courage.

When we come across somebody who is going through some difficult times, one of the things we say is, "hang in there." That is what God says to each one of us, "hang in there." To the young Christian community in Philippi, Saint Paul wrote a letter of encouragement, "I am confident of this, that the one who began a good work among you will bring it to completion by the day of Jesus Christ" (Phil 1:6). Probably the letter was written in the background of persecutions and problems in the community as the new community was trying to grow and live their faith. They needed a word of encouragement and hope, and that is what Paul offers them. He tells them to hang in there. That is what we need to hold on to. God will give us strength. He has been the one leading us and guiding us until this moment and he will continue to do that. He wants us to hang in there.

17

God is Love

GOD HAS BEEN EXPERIENCED and presented in so many ways in the Judeo-Christian traditions. He has been experienced and presented as a father, mother, friend, spouse, lover, shepherd, gardener, king, etc. He has been experienced as the God of the temple and the tent. He has been experienced as one who hears our cry and sees our pain. He has been experienced as a Trinitarian God, which gained prominence in the Christian proclamation of faith. The Evangelist, John, looks at all these images and revelations of God and sums them up in one word, "Love." God is love. In his first letter he says, "Beloved, let us love one another, because love is from God; everyone who loves is born of God and knows God. Whoever does not love does not know God, for God is love" (1 John 4:7–8). As a father, mother, shepherd, lover, spouse, king, or friend God comes across to us as love. It is love that glues and holds together the three persons of the Holy Trinity, the Father, the Son, and the Holy Spirit. Love is the force that holds them inseparably united with each other. It is love that makes God cry when we cry.

Human beings experience love in many different ways. John says that God is the source of all these dimensions of love. We know that there is nothing in human language that can adequately describe who God is. Nothing can exhaust the reality of God. God is non-definable. The moment we define him we are trying to limit him to our own concepts and categories. In the faith statements of the Catholic Church we can see how carefully the Church has tried to choose words or terms to refer to God or mysteries that are actually indescribable in human language. The Church is aware that even the chosen words are imperfect or limited. But because we have to have some way of describing them in our language we choose the most appropriate terms. When Saint John says that God is Love he means that there is no better word in human language than this to describe God. This is the noblest attribute that we can think of in human language. Anyone who has true love has all other noble qualities that we can think of. All the other virtues and noble qualities are rooted in love. It is the perfection of all virtues. So if love is the perfection of all virtues it first and foremost belongs to God because he is the perfection of all perfections.

Love is a universal theme. No matter in what century we live or what community or culture we come from, love is a language that everyone understands. Love is the force that connects us. It connects us with each other, and connects us with God. Love is the force that brings lovers, spouses, and friends together. Love is the force that connects a mother and child or a parent and child. Love is the force that keeps a family together. But all these loves are different. The love of a father or mother is different from the love of a friend or lover. The love of a spouse is different from the love of a teacher or spiritual guide. The love of a king is different form the love of a coworker or fellow citizen. People down through the centuries experienced God in all these dimensions of love, and Saint John does not find a more appropriate term to describe God. God is love.

We realize that this attribute of God as love is what explains the reason for our being as human beings. When we think of our lives, one of the questions that we might ask is, "Why did God create us?" Saint Francis de Sales, in his book, *Treatise on the Love of God*, gives us an idea about why God created us. He says, "God in creating man in his image and likeness wills that just as in Himself so too in the human person everything must be regulated by love and for love" (De Sales, 2005). The reason for God to create us, according to the saint, is love. He created us out of love. He beholds us through the eyes of love. And he desires that we live in and for love.

An analogy might make clearer this idea of God's love as the reason for our creation. We know children are born in all kinds of ways and for all kinds of reasons. Children are born through conjugal or loving sexual unions, casual and promiscuous sexual relationships, rapes, in-vitro-fertilization, etc. But if we really look at good, healthy, and truly loving relationships, we understand how and why children are born. When we look at those relationships we will understand why parents bring children into this world. In truly loving relationships of couples or lovers, sexual union is the expression and experience of their deepest love and intimacy toward each other. The partners in such relationships give themselves totally to each other. They fully give and they fully receive. There is no holding back, there is no regret, and there is no other thought than the love for the partner. A child is the result or fruit of that loving union. So the reason for the child's origin is love. People might say that children are procreated to continue the family line or take care of the parents. But the real reason for the child's life and birth in a loving relationship is love itself. The child is the result of the parents' love. The child is born out of love or love gives birth to the child. And ideally that is how children are to be born. Children are to be the result of the loving union of their parents. Children are to be born in and out of love. But unfortunately many children are not born in and out of love, but rather out of domination, abuse, and violation of people's dignity and rights.

If children are born in and out of the love of the parents, then in the bigger picture of our lives, we have to believe that we are born in and out of God's love. The reason for God to create us is his love, because he is love itself and he is the source of all love.

And love is creative and life giving. This love of God goes much beyond the physical and temporary. It is eternal and beyond measure. When God works in space and time, he works in and through his creation. Thus in the birth of a child, God works through his or her parents. When loving parents give birth to their children through their loving union, they are bringing to birth God's love. So our lives are a result of God's love manifested through the loving union of our parents. But we also know that not all parents give birth to their children out of love. Many children are born out of abuse and as unwanted. That is why God tells us through Prophet Jeremiah that even before our parents knew us, he knew us, "Before I formed you in the womb I knew you" (Jer 1:5). Even the love that the parents share with us is an extension of God's love because he is the source of all love. Therefore, even if our parents deprived us of their love or we were not born out of their love that still does not deprive us of God's love. His love always remains strong and steady for us.

We may think that it is our parents who planned our life and they are the people who should love us first before anybody else does. But God shows us a bigger picture of our lives. Yes, it is true that our parents are the immediate source of our life and they are or they should be our first and immediate connection with any experience of love. But they are only channels or agents through whom God brings us into being in this world. That doesn't mean that parents are passive tools in the hand of God. Instead, they are active cocreators with God. They cooperate with God and his plan to bring us into being. They cooperate with God's love in sharing their love for each other. Hence ultimately it is God who plans our life. It is God who is the source of our life.

Saint John says that God is the originator of love and that our love has its source in him, "In this is love, not that we loved God but that he loved us and sent his Son to be the atoning sacrifice for our sins. Beloved, since God loved us so much, we also ought to love one another" (1 John 4:10–12). Saint Paul reiterates the same point when he says that God pours his love into our hearts through the Holy Spirit (Rom 5:5).

Being the source of love, it is God who planted love in our parents or created them as loving and loveable people. In that respect, no human being is independent by him or herself. Even in the biological sense, our parents received their life from their parents, and their parents received their life from their parents. Our life is a continuation of the life of our parents, grandparents, great grandparents, and all the generations before that. We are part of a long chain of people in our history, and our life is intimately connected with them. This chain goes back to generations and generations until it reaches God who is the source of all life. Similarly, our love is a continuation of love that goes back to generations and generations in our history and ultimately it all goes back to God who is the source of all love or who is love itself. Hence even if our parents didn't love us or welcome our life, God had already planned it and welcomed us.

Being aware that in human communities love and life are denied and deprived, God says that we are not to worry and be sad because he is the real source of life and love. Through Prophet Isaiah God reminds us that no child or individual is forgotten in his sight, "Can a woman forget her nursing child, or show no compassion for the child of her womb? Even these may forget, yet I will not forget you" (Isa 49:15). God's love is never deprived to anyone. Our parents may not have wanted us or may not have been happy when we were born. The world may not have welcomed us with open arms. But God does. God welcomes each one of us with open arms. God rejoices over us. It is not only we but also the whole creation who are the result of God's love. God created this world out of love and his love permeates the whole creation.

People in our faith history experienced this love of God in different human dimensions, as father, mother, friend, lover, spouse, king, shepherd, etc. It was not like any father, mother, king, or spouse that we come across in our lives. God was like a loving and caring father or mother who loves and cares for his children and family, a loving spouse who cares for his or her loved one, and a loving and caring king who cares for his people. When God said to Moses, "I am the God of your father, the God of Abraham, the God of Isaac, and the God of Jacob" (Exod 3:6) God was probably telling him that if he had been with his forefathers, he would continue to be with him and his people now. It is the same God that was leading them and guiding them down through the centuries. So Moses was in fact being assured by God that he didn't have to fear or worry about how things would go. It was God who was guiding him. Moses and his people were another connecting link in the long chain of God's love and life.

That is our experience too. We inherit a faith history that has shown us how much God has been part of our life down through the centuries. We carry on the faith of our forefathers. We continue with confidence that the same God who took care of our forefathers will continue to take care of us. In Psalm 100 we read, "For the Lord is good; his steadfast love endures forever, and his faithfulness to all generations" (Ps 100:5). Through Prophet Jeremiah, God assures his people that in his larger plan for them, everything is for their welfare, "For surely I know the plans I have for you, says the Lord, plans for your welfare and not for harm, to give you a future with hope" (Jer 29:11). God assures us the same. In the bigger picture of our lives, God has a plan and that plan is for our welfare and not destruction.

God's love has been presented as everlasting and faithful. Through Prophet Jeremiah, God says to his people, "I have loved you with an everlasting love; therefore I have continued my faithfulness to you" (Jer 31:3). Echoing this same sentiment about the faithfulness of God, the Psalmist says, "But you, O Lord, are a God merciful and gracious, slow to anger and abounding in steadfast love and faithfulness" (Ps 86:15). The Psalmist again says, "O give thanks to the God of heaven, for his steadfast love endures forever" (Ps 136:26). In Psalm 103, the Psalmist says that God is slow to anger and abounding in steadfast love. Many of us are quick to anger, but God is slow to anger. God's primary nature is love.

Referring to this faithfulness of God, Moses said to his people, "It was because the Lord loved you and kept the oath that he swore to your ancestors, that the Lord has brought you out with a mighty hand, and redeemed you from the house of slavery, from the hand of Pharaoh king of Egypt. Know therefore that the Lord your God is God, the faithful God who maintains covenant loyalty with those who love him and keep his commandments, to a thousand generations" (Deut 7:8–9). In his letter to the Ephesians, Paul desires that we all come to know the breadth and depth of God's love, "I pray that you may have the power to comprehend, with all the saints, what is the breadth and length and height and depth, and to know the love of Christ that surpasses knowledge, so that you may be filled with all the fullness of God" (Eph 3:18–19). In sharing this love with us, God shows no partiality. The book of Job says, " . . . who shows no partiality to nobles, nor regards the rich more than the poor, for they are all the work of his hands?" (Job 34:19).

This faithful love of God is not withdrawn from us even when we commit sin and turn away from him. Saint Paul says: "But God proves his love for us in that while we still were sinners Christ died for us" (Rom 5:8). Citing his own life as an example, Paul says that he had experienced the abundance God's love and mercy (1 Tim 1:12–15). For that reason, he says, he gave his life completely to Christ, "I have been crucified with Christ; and it is no longer I who live, but it is Christ who lives in me. And the life I now live in the flesh I live by faith in the Son of God, who loved me and gave himself for me" (Gal 2:19–20).

Jesus himself said that he had come to seek the lost and the lonely (Luke 5:32; 19:10). His love flows out to saints and sinners, " . . . he makes his sun rise on the evil and on the good, and sends rain on the righteous and on the unrighteous" (Matt 5:45).

God as love sums up all the other images of God that have been presented to us. This loving God has poured his love into our hearts (Rom 5:5) by creating us in his image and likeness (Gen 1:26). And he calls us to a life of love, inviting us to gradually grow in love until we reach that stage where we totally identify ourselves with him who is Love itself.

Part IV

Jesus: The Face of God

18

A Man of History and the Lord of Faith

OUR HUMAN AND FAITH history, particularly, the Judeo-Christian traditions, demonstrate that our God is a God of love. The most tangible experience of that love of God was the person of Jesus Christ, God who became man. In the letter to the Hebrews we read, "Long ago God spoke to our ancestors in many and various ways by the prophets, but in these last days he has spoken to us by a Son" (Heb 1:1–2). God who has been revealing himself as love took a concrete shape and form in the person of Jesus. In him, the love of God became visible for us (Col 1:15). He is the Emmanuel, God with us (Matt 1:23).

As the Emmanuel, he is with us not only in time and space but also beyond time and space. He is our brother and friend, but he is also our creator and redeemer. Although the previous sections have made many references to Jesus and his love, we shall discuss a little more in detail how he became and continues to be the face of God.

The person of Jesus is not easy to discuss and understand because he is both a man of history and the Lord of faith. He has been a topic of everyone's imagination. The people of his time as well as later generations have developed different ideas about him and attempted to fit him into categories and labels they found most suitable. The people of his hometown, Nazareth, took offense at him because he appeared to be someone different from and bigger than they thought: "'Where did this man get this wisdom and these deeds of power? Is not this the carpenter's son? Is not his mother called Mary? And are not his brothers James and Joseph and Simon and Judas? And are not all his sisters with us? Where then did this man get all this?' And they took offense at him" (Matt 13:54–58).

The historical person of Jesus surprised and fascinated many people and continues to do so. People had all kinds of ideas and opinions about him. They all wondered who this man was. He looked like anyone of us. He was weak and vulnerable like any one of us. He worked hard and experienced fatigue. He was hungry and thirsty, and he ate and drank. There were moments when he was angry and upset, but there were also times when he was full of joy and laughter. He experienced temptations and trials like anyone of us. He doubted and questioned, but he also prayed and trusted.

He abhorred injustice and cruelty, but he suffered injustice and death. He spoke and taught with authority and went right to the heart of the matter. The Jewish people had many teachers. They had the scribes, the Pharisees, and many others. But Jesus was a different kind of teacher. There was something special in him that they could not find in others.

But there was something more than human in him. People had healers in Palestine at that time. But Jesus was a different kind of healer. Even the evil sprits obeyed him. They trembled before him. There was something special about this healer. He liberated people from their physical, emotional, and spiritual ailments. He freed them from their sins. He forgave them. The Jewish leaders questioned and were even angry that he forgave people's sins. He appeared to be blasphemous to them. But he continued his liberating work.

He obeyed Mary and Joseph at Nazareth, but the winds and waves obeyed him. The God who takes care of us allows himself to be taken care of by us. He was the master and Lord. But he was also a servant. He bent down and washed the feet of his disciples, an act which no master or leader would normally do. He asked the Samaritan woman for a drink of water, but he changed water into wine and satisfied everyone. He was hungry but he fed the multitude. He walked through the streets and alleys of Galilee and Jerusalem but he also walked on water. He was the sacrificial lamb who suffered and died on the cross for us. But he was also victorious over suffering and death. He rose from death. Jesus was all of these, but Jesus was more than all these.

The political and religious leaders of the time wondered who this man was who had captivated the people that they wanted to make him a king. Herod wondered whether he was the reincarnation of John the Baptist and even feared that he would be overthrown. The chief priests, the scribes, and the Pharisees found that there was something special about him, but in many ways he did not seem to fit into their idea of the Messiah. They all wondered who this man was who went around doing good, healing the sick, cleansing lepers, forgiving sinners, and raising the dead to life.

Based on bits and pieces of information and experience they had about him, people today and in the ages past have made conclusions about who Jesus is. Christians and non-Christians, Catholics and Protestants, blacks and whites, capitalists and socialists, conservatives and liberals, and all others have found Jesus a perfect ally to fit into the boxes and categories they have created for him. He is conservative to some and liberal to others. He is religious to some and spiritual to others. He is a Jew to some and a gentile to others. He is God to some and man to others. But to everyone's surprise, he still escapes all human classifications and imaginations. No labels that we give can fully capture who he is.

We don't even know how Jesus looked physically. Many of us still hold on to a picture or idea of Jesus as a light-skinned, brown or light-haired, well-built, handsome-looking man as painted by the Western or European artists centuries later. Artists in other continents have done similar works, depicting Jesus according to their imagination. Not wanting to reduce him to a male figure alone, some have pictured him as a woman. But we know that these are all imaginations of artists. Even picturing him as a man of Palestinian or Jewish looks we know that there was no photography or painting in those days. Nobody knew how Mary or Joseph looked. But we have pictures of all of them registered in our mind. And how easily do we get stuck with the idea that that is how they really looked! Even if we want to think of the physical features of Palestinian or Jewish people at the time of Jesus and apply it to him, we should still remember that Jesus was both divine and human. He must have had some resemblance to Mary, his mother, but not to Joseph because he was not his biological father. But even if we want to assume that he had some resemblance to Mary, we don't know how Mary looked. The Mary that we see in pictures and statues is not the Mary we encounter in the Bible. Besides although we want to think of Jesus as a regular man of Palestinian or Jewish looks, it is still difficult to say how he looked because he was also God.

It is not only the historical person of Jesus who has been a topic of discussions, debates, and fascinations but also Jesus of faith. There have been many theologies and varied types of spirituality that have been developed based on the person of Jesus. The way Saint Paul perceived Jesus was not the same as how Peter, James, or other apostles saw him. We have a lot of information about Saint Paul's missionary journeys and his epistles form a good part of the New Testament. But we don't have much information about many of the apostles. We have some details about Peter, James, John, and a couple of other apostles, where they went and what they did, but others seem to have disappeared into near obscurity. They all went to different parts of the world, preached the gospel, and established Christian communities. Some of those communities grew large over the centuries while others dwindled in their numbers. Many of the individual churches within the Catholic Church and other Christian denominations today trace their origin back to those apostolic traditions. As these traditions developed, they also gave rise to their own unique theologies. While some focus on the crucified Christ others focus more on the risen Christ. Some look at Jesus as an acetic and contemplative while others look at him as a person of active ministry. Some concentrate more on the transcendental dimension of Jesus while others focus more on his immanence.

Although the Christian community as a whole has come to a certain consensus about who the person of Jesus is, we haven't come to a point where we can get everybody agree on everything about Jesus. And the main reason is that we don't know everything about Jesus. We continue to grow in our understanding and experience of him. Even all the members of the same family practicing the same religion and faith may have a different take on Jesus. We never stop knowing and experiencing Jesus. If we ever think that we know Jesus fully, we stop growing spiritually. Our whole life is a journey of growing closer to Christ, knowing and experiencing him more and more everyday. Everyday he amazes and surprises us. He is a God bigger than we think, but he is also a God who is small enough to come to our level to be with us. And that is how the experience of God has been throughout our human history. God keeps encountering us in many ways and we keep encountering him in our own unique ways.

Often Jesus has been presented in ways that are not proper to who he is. The person and message of Jesus have been often misinterpreted and misrepresented. He may be misunderstood and monopolized by some and portrayed as a leader or deity of a select group of people. But in truth, Jesus goes beyond religions, politics, races, castes, classes, and all such human categories and imaginations. He is a Savior for all people. He is a friend and a father to a non-Christian as much as to a Christian. If we want to see him the way we want, we might find him a perfect fit for the labels we create for him. But if we want to get at least a glimpse of who he truly is, we have to go beyond the labels that we often give him.

19

The Incarnation of Love

THE EVANGELIST, JOHN SUGGESTS that it was love that resulted in the incarnation of Jesus, "For God so loved the world that he gave his only Son, so that everyone who believes in him may not perish but may have eternal life" (John 3:16). Jesus was the incarnation of love. He became the face of the loving and merciful God. In him people experienced and continue to experience a love that is unfathomable. In him was the Psalmist's proclamation fulfilled, "The Lord is merciful and gracious, slow to anger and abounding in steadfast love" (Ps 103:8). Jesus challenged and changed people's idea of God as a vengeful, murderous, and destroyer God. He reminded the people over and over again that they had gotten the image of God distorted and vilified.

Inaugurating a new era in people's understanding of God, Jesus began his public ministry itself by announcing a time of God's love and favor as prophesied by Prophet Isaiah, "The Spirit of the Lord is upon me, because he has anointed me to bring glad tidings to the poor. He has sent me to proclaim liberty to captives and recovery of sight to the blind, to let the oppressed go free, and to proclaim a year acceptable to the Lord" (Luke 4:16–21). He wanted his people to know that God was truly loving and caring and that he was going to demonstrate it by his own life. Jesus was not only announcing glad tidings to the people but also making it an experiential reality for them. The whole life and ministry of Jesus speak to this unconditional love of God revealed to us in and through him. Wherever he went, people experienced God's love and favor.

There are several stories in the gospels where people experienced the love and mercy of God flowing out to them through Jesus. He touched and healed those who were afflicted with illnesses and pains. He was the face of the kind and compassionate God. In the gospel of Mark, there is a story of a blind man named Bartimaeus (Mark 10:46–52). Besides being blind, Bartimaeus was a beggar. As the gospels relate, blindness and many such physical deprivations were considered a curse and result of sin in those days. Their families and the society often rejected them, and many of them might have taken to begging. Given this background, Bartimaeus' perspective about himself, God, others, and the world must have been pretty negative and sad. He was desperate for redemption from that situation. And so he cries out to Jesus, "Jesus, Son of David, have mercy on me . . . let me see again" (Mark 10:47–51).

It was not just the physical healing alone that Bartimaeus was asking for. Of course he needed physical healing; he needed freedom from his blindness. But there was much more than the physical healing that he needed. He was deprived of many things in life. He was deprived of emotional support. His family, community, and society had despised and rejected him. He was cut off from everybody else, and he needed to reconnect again. He was a beggar; he didn't have much support from anybody financially or economically. He needed a change in that. He also probably thought that even God had abandoned him and that his blindness was a punishment for his sins or the sins of his parents as the rest of the community believed. He needed a spiritual healing. So he was asking for a total change, a new life.

Bartimaeus had to overcome many obstacles and discouraging elements to get to Jesus and experience the healing. The crowd tried to shut him up. They told him to be quiet. But his faith, desire, and the determination to get healed and experience a new life were much stronger than any of those discouraging elements.

It is important to note the question Jesus asked Bartimeus and the answer the blind man gave. Jesus asked, "What do you want me to do for you?" (Mark 10:51). And Bartimeus answered, "My teacher, let me see again" (Mark 10:51). In the normal circumstances, the blind beggar would have asked for some money or for some help for his immediate needs. But that is not what he asked Jesus for. If he had asked for money, it would have probably satisfied him in some way or taken care of his immediate needs. But the problem would have been that he would have continued to stay as a beggar, sitting on the roadside. His life would not have changed much qualitatively. He instead asked for something more than his immediate needs, something that would last for a long time. He did not want to sit on the roadside anymore. He did not want to just keep maintaining what he was doing. He wanted to be different. And Jesus granted him his wish. Once his wish was granted, he was no more sitting on the roadside begging. He was on the move, following Jesus.

Jesus consoled and comforted those who were ashamed and broken. He was the face of the loving and merciful God. In the gospel of John, there is a story of a woman caught in adultery that points to the skewed justice system in a patriarchal and hierarchical society (John 8:1–11). The scribes and the Pharisees brought to Jesus a woman caught in adultery. According to the law as they presented, she had no right to live. She was to be condemned and stoned to death. She was made to stand in front of everyone as an object of ridicule and shame. Some of them probably had humiliating looks and comments directed at her. The story says that their intention was to trap Jesus because he often denounced their hypocrisy. If he let her go without being condemned and stoned they could accuse him of having no respect for the law and customs. If he allowed her to be condemned and stoned to death they could accuse him of not being kind and compassionate as everyone considered. But Jesus could read what was hidden behind their stony and vicious faces. His answer made them swallow their own words, "Let anyone among you who is without sin be the first to throw a stone at her" (John 8:7). He saw the corruption in their heart and forced them to confront their own conscience.

The story says that Jesus bent down and wrote on the ground. What he wrote on the ground is anyone's speculation. It could be that he was writing down the sins of the men who had brought the woman. It could have been that he was writing the question, "Where is the man who committed adultery with her?" meaning that their judgment and justice system was partial, favoring men and might. They told Jesus that they caught her in the very act of committing adultery. So the immediate question would have been, "Where is the man?" But being a male-dominated society, they would not even consider such questions. The woman had no power and privilege as that of men. It is also possible that he was writing the word "love" all over the ground. Maybe he was telling them by his writing that love was the only way to transform themselves and the woman. Being made to confront their own consciences and aware that they had lost their face, the men left the scene one by one.

It is incredible to see how Jesus responded to the woman. He does not condone her act but neither does he condemn her. He said, "Neither do I condemn you. Go your way, and from now on do not sin again" (John 8:11). Including her in his company did not mean that he was approving her lifestyle. He asked her not to sin again. But he does that in a respectful way. Even though she was a sinner, she was still a child of God. She was already humiliated and disrespected by the crowd and he does not humiliate her any further. He gives her an opportunity to try and make her life better. With regard to her rights, he levels the ground and puts her on the same level of the man who committed adultery with her. With those few words, he questions and seeks to straighten the skewed societal system. He brought back love and mutual respect as the only way to transform the world and human hearts.

Jesus consoled and comforted those who were grief-stricken and sorrowful. He was the face of the God who stands with us in our sufferings and pain. Tragedies, illnesses, death, and other difficulties leave us feeling helpless and hopeless. In the gospel of Mark we hear the story of a synagogue official and a woman both of whom were grief-stricken and at the point of giving up. The synagogue official, Jairus pleads with Jesus to rescue his daughter from impending death. As Jesus was on his way to Jairus' house, a woman who had been suffering from hemorrhage for twelve years comes to Jesus with the hope of getting healed and touches his cloak. In both these cases, the concerned parties seem to be very desperate for some relief and help and they must have reached the point of giving up hope. Probably the synagogue official had gone to all the doctors in the area seeking help for his daughter. But none of them could help him or give him any hope. Jesus comes to his rescue and raises his daughter from death. The woman with hemorrhage according to the story, had gone to many doctors, but instead of helping her they made her condition worse. In the story, the evangelist, Mark has some warning for doctors and others who misuse their positions and professional status to exploit and take advantage of those who depend on them. Having been made to suffer by many physicians, the woman comes to Jesus at the point of hopelessness. And Jesus does not disappoint her.

Jesus took time to be personally present with these people. He took time to go to the Synagogue official's house and restore his daughter to life. As we understand, Jesus was often busy. There were too many people to help and too many things to attend to. There were crowds waiting for him in many places. He could have told Jairus that he was busy and didn't have time to go to his house. But that is not what he did. He found time to be with the grief-stricken man and his family. He heard the cry and helplessness of this man and attended to him. Jesus took time to speak to the woman with hemorrhage and reassured her. In the Jewish society, a woman with bleeding was considered impure and was not allowed to be with others in public because she would make everyone defiled. Jesus, having been considered a Rabbi, was taking a great risk in allowing this woman to touch him because no rabbi would ordinarily go anywhere close to such impure women. He would be defiled. But Jesus took time to be with this woman who was hurting. He heard her cry and pain. Jesus was willing to be defiled for the sake of love.

There are many events in the gospels where we see Jesus doing things that would have defiled him. He touched lepers, he interacted with Samaritans, he allowed the sinner woman to touch him, he touched the coffin of the dead son of the widow of Nain, and he ate and drank with tax collectors and sinners. For Jesus, these were not the things that defiled people. These were things that discriminated people and he was determined to change them.

As in the case of Jairus and the woman with hemorrhage, there are many things and situations in our life that take us to the point of hopelessness and helplessness. Jesus assures us that he does not simply walk by ignoring our pain and cry. He listens to our story and comes to help. He cannot but love us because he is love itself. He is willing to take any risk in showing us how much he loves us. The very incarnation of Jesus was a great risk. By becoming man, he was taking the risk of being ridiculed and rejected by human beings. But he took that risk to come down to our level to show us the face of God that was kind, compassionate, and loving.

20

Crazy in Love

GOD'S WAYS ARE SOMETIMES mysterious and perplexing. He surprises us in ways that we least expect of. He is sometimes found in the most unexpected places, people, situations, and experiences. That is what the person of Jesus reveals to us. In Jesus we find a God who is crazy in love with us, human beings.

No one expected God to be born in a stable in Bethlehem. Today the nativity scenes laid out in stores and churches might look pretty and adorable. We might feel like touching or kissing the little statues and the artwork in those scenes. But that is not how it was when Jesus was born. It was most probably a smelly, cold, and dirty stable that no one wanted to be born in or even be close to. Although the gospels talk about the angels singing alleluias and the shepherds visiting the baby Jesus, it is appropriate to think that the birth of Christ was a very low-key event happening in the darkness and obscurity of that stable. There was no crowd or big family present except Mary and Joseph who might have been still trying to make sense of everything and wondering what God was calling them to. The gospels don't say that Mary and Joseph heard any angels singing. They were there with the baby Jesus in that cold and darkness and God was right there with them in that cold and darkness. God must be really crazy to be born first of all as a human being and then to be born in such an undesirable environment.

No one expected God to die on the cross on Calvary. There were many other ways that he could have chosen to show us his love. To look at a cross or crucifix and feel sorrow for Jesus or admire his self-sacrifice may be a nice and pious thing to do today. But when he was really hanging on that cross as a criminal on Calvary, there was nothing nice or pious about it for the passers-by. He was an object of ridicule and shame. He was a criminal, renegade, blasphemer, and scandal for the vast majority of people. Why did he have to go through such a sad end and die such a gruesome death?

No one expected God to share a meal with the most hated people, the tax collectors and sinners. Why did he have to be an object of criticism and anger before the religious and political authorities and give up on his good fortunes and name in the society? No one expected God to forgive the dreaded criminals and hateful men who persecuted and killed him. Why did he have to bow down before the madness of those wretched men and be humiliated by them?

In the normal circumstances, all these don't make any sense. But God did all these because of one thing—Love. It all makes sense when we understand God as one who is crazy in love with everyone, from the least to the highest, from the poorest to the richest, from the most innocent and vulnerable to the most hated and sinful. The power and depth of God's love is unfathomable.

The whole public life of Jesus was a manifestation of that crazy love of God. He was busy from the get go. The gospel of Mark says that Jesus and his disciples were so busy ministering to the people that they didn't have even time to eat and rest (Mark 6:31). He touched and healed those who were afflicted with illnesses and pains. He welcomed and included those who were rejected and excluded. He consoled and comforted those who were grief-stricken and broken. And he spoke with kindness and compassion to those who came to him disheartened and distraught. His heart went out to his people whom he found as a "sheep without a shepherd" (Mark 6:34). Jesus truly brought a time of God's love and favor to his people.

But the best in Jesus was not in all his miracles, preaching, and teaching. It was in his final act of love on the cross. That is where he was at his best. Jesus said, "No one has greater love than this, to lay down one's life for one's friends" (John 15:13). On the cross he proved to be our best friend.

In many cultures and religions, people had developed an idea that they had to appease and keep in good cheer an angry God for them to live a happy life. And sometimes appeasing God involved sacrifices, both animal and human. Human beings had to spill blood of the animals and birds or their own to get to God. And there are still many people in the world who believe that. They believe in a God who needs to be appeased by spilling blood. But Jesus put an end to all such misconceptions of God. Instead of making us sacrifice and suffer, he suffers and sacrifices himself. Instead of we spilling our blood for him, he spills his blood for us.

In Jesus we see a God who spills his blood to get to us, human beings. The death of Jesus was not to pay God some price to make him feel good or please him. Instead it was a price that God paid to show us how much he loves us. The passion, crucifixion, and death of Jesus changed the whole dynamic of our relationship with God. It is no more an angry God whom we had to fear, but rather a loving God who would do anything for us. It was no more a distant and untouchable God, but a God who was so close to us, to whom we could relate. The sacrifice of Jesus on the cross was a turning point in how we understand God and relate to God.

For many people, there is nothing good about "Good Friday." It is a bad Friday. It is a day of defeat and deception. But for many, it is a day of Salvation. It is the day when Jesus gave us his best. When we say to someone, "I will do my best for you," the best we often offer and mean is very limited. But when God gave himself he gave us his best in all sense. Jesus, in giving himself, gives totally. He becomes the wounded healer that

Prophet Isaiah speaks of (Isa 53:5). In the process of healing us he got wounded. In the process of saving us he got killed. If someone wants to save another from a burning house, there is the risk of getting burned and killed. Jesus took the risk of getting hurt and killed in loving us. He did not hold back anything in expressing his love. He showed us that real love involves real sacrifice. The story of Christ's passion and death is a story of love—God's love for us. If for the last two thousand plus years Christ has been a force to reckon with, it was not because of any military or money power, any intimidation or indoctrination, but simply the power of love. Jesus shows us that love can do incredible things in our life. Jesus with his outstretched arms on the cross is a reminder of God embracing the whole world with his love.

One has to be insane to love to the extent Jesus loved. He gave everything, to the point of his last drop of blood. He did not count the cost in showing how much he loved us. But that crazy love changed the world. The world may not have become perfect, but with the ultimate sacrifice of Jesus on the cross on Calvary, the world has not been the same anymore. The word, "Love" received a new meaning. The understanding of God was turned upside down. The relationship between God and human beings has not been the same anymore.

The story of the suffering and death of Jesus on Good Friday is a story of injustice and evil reigning over justice and truth. Jesus was falsely charged of crimes he did not commit, and he was unjustly sentenced to a death he did not deserve. One of his companions betrayed him, another one denied him, and all the rest deserted him. He stands alone, rejected, misunderstood, defeated, abandoned, betrayed, arrested, and nailed to the cross. The people he loved demanded his crucifixion. One day they were singing Hosanna to him. Within a few days, they jeered at him and shouted, "crucify him," "crucify him." Dragged and spat upon, he endures the passion to the very end. Finally, he was nailed to a cross and stood hanging continuing to be an object of ridicule and mockery for his persecutors and passers-by. And when he finally died, he was hastily buried in a tomb. It is a story of betrayal and lies, dishonesty and meanness, and unfaithfulness and wicked violence directed against an innocent person.

We can assume that it was not easy to wash the feet of Judas who was going to betray him or Peter who was going to deny him, or all the disciples who were going to run away from him. How many of us would share a meal with somebody who is going to betray us? Even after he knew what was going to happen, Jesus had a place for Judas at his table. Jesus didn't turn Judas away telling him that he was dishonest and unworthy to sit at his table. He didn't excommunicate or exclude him. How many of us would continue to include in our company someone who has denied us? Jesus continued to trust and love Peter even after he denied him. He didn't turn Peter away accusing him of lack of commitment and weak spirit. We can imagine that Jesus had to have a tremendous amount of patience and perseverance to love them even after knowing that they would betray him and deny him. We can assume that it was not easy to love the crowd who shouted, "Crucify him" or forgive those who persecuted and crucified him. But that is what Jesus did. He still loved them.

We have to wonder what makes Jesus special. Is it the betrayal, denial, and even the cross? That is not what makes Jesus special. There are thousands of people who die as victims of violence and hatred. There are thousands of people who are falsely accused, betrayed, denied, and abandoned. Some of them are even crucified. What makes Jesus special is that in all those experiences that he went through there was only one thing that stood out—love. It was not out of force or because he had no choice that he suffered and died. He could have very well escaped cross and death if he wanted to and if he was willing to bow down to the powers of evil. He could have suffered and died with hatred and anger in his heart. He could have asked his heavenly Father to take revenge on the evil men who had plotted against him, persecuted him, and killed him. He could have asked his companions to take revenge on the perpetrators of those crimes. He could have simply annihilated them by a single word. He could have been depressed and scared when excruciating pain was inflicted upon him. But we don't see any of these in Jesus. There was only one thing—love. Yes, he suffered, and the pain was excruciating. But there was no hatred in his heart. He loved even the least loveable of those people. He loved and stood for love until the end. If Jesus focused on what those people did to him, he would not have been able to love them. He instead looked at them as his children who did not know what they were doing (Luke 23:34).

How often do we give up on people? Being tired of trying to love and show compassion to their wayward children we see some parents giving up on their children. They show love and compassion again and again. But some of them come to a point where they say that they cannot do it anymore. There is a limit to their love. There is a limit to their compassion. There is a limit to their patience and perseverance. And they give up. Sometimes communities and societies give up on some of their members. They try to love and show compassion. But they come to a point when they feel that they cannot do it anymore. They reject them and exclude them. They don't have a place for such people at their table as Jesus had for Judas, Peter, and others. They take revenge and inflict the same amount or more of pain on the offender or perpetrator of the crime. They brutally kill the brutal killer, paying back in the same measure. But God in Jesus shows us that he does not give up on even the worst criminal. His love has no limit.

We could wonder why he loves us that way. It is to fulfill the one mission of bringing us all together as one family. Evils and sins make us scattered. We spill each other's blood. We go away from God and from one another. The mission of Jesus was to bring us all together as one family, one community under God. If he rejected or gave up on Judas or Peter or anybody else, that mission would have stayed unfulfilled. Even when he was torn within, he kept them together. Probably no one understood the anguish and anxiety that he was going through when everybody abandoned him and treated him like a criminal, but he still kept them together. He loved them to the end. He was the wounded healer.

Jesus did not allow evils and negativity to take over him. He did not allow temptations and trials to distract him from his mission of manifesting love. It was love that reigned from the beginning to the end. He was willing to suffer anything for the sake of love. He was not suffering and making sacrifices to glorify suffering or pain. He knew that suffering and pain were bad and evil, and he reached out to people in many ways to alleviate their sufferings. It is not for the sake of suffering that he suffered. He suffered for the sake of love. Not all sufferings are the result of love. Many people suffer not because of love but because of imprudence and bad choices of their own or of others. Many people suffer because they have no other choice. Some people suffer with vengeance, hatred, and anger in their heart. For Jesus, his suffering and sacrifices were a result of his great love. He was willing to lay down his life for the sake of love. If he had to still love the disciple who betrayed him, love the one who denied him, love those who abandoned him, love those who demanded his crucifixion and death, and love those who mercilessly persecuted and killed him, his love had to be unimaginably great. Genuine love calls for sacrifice and sufferings. If one truly loves, he or she has to be willing to make sacrifices and suffer. It is not necessary that suffering should happen, but one who loves has to be always prepared to suffer and make sacrifices.

Being the wounded healer, his heart went out to others even when he himself was suffering. In the gospel of Matthew, there is a miracle of Jesus feeding a great crowd, about five thousand men besides women and children (Matt 14:13–21). If they counted the women and children, it must have been ten thousand or more. Prior to this story, the evangelist mentions that Jesus heard about the beheading of John the Baptist and he withdrew to a deserted place by himself. Withdrawing and going to a deserted place could be interpreted as him going to pray. But there must have been something more than praying. Maybe he needed a break from everything. Maybe he was grieving and wanted to be by himself. John the Baptist was his cousin. Hearing about his gruesome killing, Jesus must have been intensely shaken, shocked, and sad. He must have been grieving. John the Baptist was not only his cousin but also his precursor, the one who prepared the way for him. So if his cousin and precursor was killed, the natural thinking must have been that the next in line to be killed would be Jesus himself.

Given his nature and style, there is no reason for us to think that Jesus was afraid. He was not afraid of Herod or death. Some Pharisees, probably those who were friends with Jesus, had told him to be careful and stay away from Herod because Herod was planning to kill him (Luke 13:31). Jesus replied them that he was not going to run away for fear of Herod or death (Luke 13:32–33). But that doesn't mean that Jesus was not upset and disturbed when he heard about the beheading of John the Baptist. Overwhelmed by all kinds of emotions he probably wanted some time and space for himself. Maybe he wanted to stay away from everybody and his usual work. But did the people allow him to have that time for himself? No. They found out that he was in the area and they came in large numbers. They were in need of help. They needed healing and comfort. And seeing that great need, Jesus keeps aside his own needs, and reaches out to them.

It is not that Jesus was not aware of the importance of self-care. More than anyone else Jesus knew that self-care was important. When his disciples returned after their missionary work, Jesus told them, "Come away to a deserted place all by yourselves and rest a while" (Mark 6:31). But there were times when he had to keep aside his self-care and care for those who were hurting more. The situations were such that the needs of the people around him were much more than his own needs. And so he keeps aside his needs and goes to help them. He heals and comforts them and finally feeds them. He once again becomes the wounded healer. Within himself he was going through so much of suffering and grief at the loss of his cousin and thinking about what was awaiting him. He was wounded. But seeing the greater need of the people he goes out to heal and help them.

There may be moments when we are going through difficult times physically, emotionally, and spiritually, and we might want to have some time and space for ourselves. We want to be away from everybody and everything, a little time for self-care. But often we are not able to do that because the needs of people around us are much greater. We once again love and serve. I hear some parents talking about this great desire they have to have some time for themselves. Sometimes the demands of caring for their children and their families are so much that they feel exhausted. Some of them have children who demand a lot of patience and energy from them. Being exhausted they wish that they could be away from their children, away from their spouse, and away from everything for a little while. But very rarely they get that opportunity. The demands and needs of their children and families are so much and sometimes greater than their own needs that they once again return back to loving and serving. They become wounded healers. Even while they are wounded, they continue to heal other people. It is not only parents but also many others who become such wounded healers.

Jesus was a wounded healer not just once, but throughout his life. Even while he was in excruciating pain and agony, he brought healing and comfort to others. While he was carrying the cross to Calvary he consoled the women who were weeping. Even while he was hanging on the cross and dying, his heart went out to his mother and the disciple standing at the foot of the cross. He entrusted them to each other's care. Even while he was dying, he was compassionate to the good thief and forgiving to his persecutors. He continued to be the wounded healer until the end. It was all because of love.

Even to the last moment of his life, he sought the will of his heavenly father. We know that he was tempted many times to deviate from his path. He prayed that the cup might be taken away from him. Even on the cross he was tempted by his executioners to come down and show his power. But it was not about him. It was about us and about showing us how much he loved us. It was about fulfilling his Father's will. He lived and died in and for love. That love was totally self-giving.

There was no greater love in human history that we know of than that of Jesus. We have stories of saints and others who have lived heroic lives and died a martyr's death. But they all go back to Jesus as the source and model of that love.

What makes the love of Jesus different from the love of all others is that it is not only unconditional and total but also unlimited in space and time. He loves us as much as he loved those people in Palestine, Jerusalem, and the surrounding regions two thousand years back. He loves an American as much as he loves an Indian, Chinese, Mexican, Russian, or someone from Africa, Europe, or any other part of the world. His love is not limited to a certain period in history or people of a certain culture and color. His love is all embracing and everlasting.

21

Why a Gruesome Path?

We could wonder why Jesus suffered and died the way he did. Why did he choose a gruesome path to suffer and die? If he was God, why couldn't he stop Peter from denying him and Judas from betraying him? By allowing Peter and Judas to do what they did, was he allowing them to give into their passions and engage in criminal activities? We could wonder why he couldn't stop his persecutors from committing the heinous crime. We could also wonder why he allowed himself to be tortured and crucified. Couldn't he die in some other way, which was less painful and heinous? So by allowing all these, was he suicidal, killing himself even though he could have saved himself from all these trouble?

All these are legitimate questions, and the answers are not easy. But at the same time, we are not totally clueless either. First of all, even before we think about Jesus' suffering and death, we could wonder whether it was necessary for God to come down to our level and become a human being. Weren't there other ways that he could find to save us or make us realize that we had to live healthy lives and live in communion with God and one another? Couldn't he simply say, "Let all human beings live healthy and happy lives, free from all evils, sins, and sufferings?" If he were omnipotent, wouldn't such an order or command work?

The answer to these questions is, no. The God who has revealed himself to us in our human and faith history is not a magician or dictator although he sometimes seems to be depicted that way in the Bible or by some people. He is not a God who threatens and makes us do things against our will and freedom. He is not a God who wants us to be passive recipients or compliers of his commands. He is neither a micromanager nor a macro manager. The God who has revealed himself in the Judeo-Christian traditions and who incarnated in the person of Jesus is a God of love. The only reason why God has done what he has done is love. The very reason for our creation is God's love. As we discussed, we were born out of love or we are the result of God's love, just as children are the result of the loving union of loving parents. Although many things in the Bible are presented as a command or magical pronouncement of God, they are to be seen in the context of the times and people who tried to communicate about God in their own language.

Because of all the hardships and struggles they have to face in life, children could ask their parents why they conceived them and gave them birth in the first place. The only answer loving parents could give to those children would be that they were born out of love and that they would continue to love them and do everything possible for them. They may not be able to take away their children's sufferings altogether, but they can continue to love them and help them to live healthy lives. And if there are still some sufferings that the children cannot do away with or the parents cannot take away, the parents can suffer with them so that their sufferings ease up a little bit. That is exactly what God does in our life. The only answer that God gives for our creation is his love. We were born out of his love. And he assures us that he continues to love us and would do anything to show us that love.

And that is the very same reason for which he suffered and died. He suffered and died for the sake of love. God does not assure us that he would take away all of our sufferings. He would help us to do away with unnecessary sufferings that we bring upon ourselves by our bad choices and decisions. He shows us how to make healthy choices and live happy lives. He alleviates our sufferings in many ways. But that does not mean that we are going to be completely insulated from sufferings. There are sufferings that come to us because of who we are as human beings. By the fact that we are human beings we are limited by space and time. Our body and mind have their own limitations. Our body is prone to diseases, death, and decay. Our mind is prone to thoughts and imaginations that are negative and unhealthy. Even as we walk around looking healthy and happy, our body might be in the process of developing some ailments that are going to cause us some sufferings. We age and our health deteriorates. Our muscles and joints are not going to stay strong for all eternity. Even if we are not alcoholics, heavy smokers, and substance abusers, we still eat and inhale many things that are toxic and unhealthy for our body. All the food that we eat, all the air that we breathe, and all the water that we drink are not the healthiest all the time. We inherit many unhealthy things from our past generations. We share in the degeneration, death, and decay of the physical realities of this world.

We are subject to the forces and elements of the universe and environment in which we live. We are not the most physically powerful beings in the universe. We are tiny creatures in comparison with many other animals and creatures. We have intelligence to find ways to protect ourselves from many forces in the nurture and the universe. But we are not completely free from all dangers and calamities. We can be blown away in an instant by a strong wind or storm. We can be swallowed up into the belly of the ocean or the earth without any warning by a tsunami or earthquake. We can be scorched by heat waves and frozen to death by cold spells.

Of course, we don't like any of these misfortunes and sufferings. But unfortunately they are inevitable parts of our human life in this world. The pleasures and the pains of this world come as one package. We could either call it the limitations of space and time or the actual components of our life in space and time. This is what life on this earth or life in space and time involves. Given all that, we might ask why God could not create us without those limitations. That would have been great, but then we would not be human beings. To be human is to live partly in space and time, subject to all the limitations that come with the physical realities of the world. If we expect or ask God to take away all our sufferings or wanted him to create us without our limitations that would mean that we are asking him to make us something other than being human beings. That would be something similar to a dog or cat asking God to turn it into a human being or something other than being a dog or cat. The dog or cat may be tired of human beings bossing over them or unhappy about their short span of life. They may not like those limitations. But the truth is that they are cats and dogs and not human beings.

We could also think of angels or other heavenly beings asking God to turn them into human beings because they like the beauties and wonders of human life. And we don't know what their limitations are. But the truth is that they are angels or heavenly beings and not human beings. Each of God's creation has its own beauty, specificity, and uniqueness, and it appears that all of God's creation has some limitations. Again, we can look at it as limitations or as part of our being. What God desires is that all of his creation live true to their being. We are human beings and our call is to be human beings. When we forget that, we will end up with the same mistake of Adam and Eve who wanted to be something other than who they truly were. They wanted to be God. We are not God and we are not anything else. And being human, we are going to face sufferings and pains at some time or the other in this physical world.

Part of that suffering or our being in the physical world is our final death. Although for some extraordinary reasons unbeknownst to us God could carry us into eternity or the non-physical realm without making us go through physical death, in the ordinary circumstances we need to face physical death before we can enter into the realm of eternity. We may not want to face that death, but that too is an inevitable part of our human life on this earth. In all of these, the only thing that God assures us of is that we are not alone in those moments of sufferings and that our life is not ended with the physical death. Even though he may not take away all of our sufferings, he would stand with us in those moments and suffer with us so that his presence and love ease up our sufferings a little bit. He cannot but be part of our sufferings because we are part of him. The struggles, sufferings, and death that Jesus went through were a way to tell us that he knows what we are going through, and that he is with us when we go through them. His incarnation, his life with us, and his suffering and death were a way to tell us that he is with us at all times. He is the Emmanuel, the God with us.

If we are his children and if we share in his life, then our sufferings are his sufferings and our death is his death. By his suffering and death, Jesus was simply telling us that our God is not someone who makes us suffer but someone who suffers with us. When my hand or leg is hurt, the rest of the body cannot disown my hand and leg and say, "we have nothing to do with that hand or leg." When my hand or leg hurts my whole body hurts. When anyone of us suffers, God suffers. We are parts of his body. We are his. He does not disown or distance from us.

But Jesus also assures us that death does not stop our life. We resurrect because we continue to live in him. His resurrection was an assurance that we are also going to resurrect with him. Being part of him, we cannot but resurrect. Our physical sufferings and limitations will end with death, and we will rise to the non-physical realm of peace and joy. But we also know that while we live on earth, our sufferings are not only physical in nature. They can be also emotional and spiritual because of the evils, sins, and the unhealthy life-styles we become slaves to. Jesus wants us to be free from all those sufferings while we live on earth and in eternity. If we continue to be slaves of sins and evils even to the point of death, we might continue to be the hurting members of the body of Christ in eternity just as a hurting hand or leg hurts the whole body. I shall discuss more about this under the topics of heaven, hell, and purgatory in the last few chapters of the book, but at this point what we need to remember is that when we are hurting or suffering, Jesus is hurting or suffering.

The sufferings and death of Jesus were a result of God's respect for human freedom and will. Jesus could have stopped Peter from denying him, Judas from betraying him, and his persecutors from torturing and crucifying him. But that would go against God's respect for our human freedom and will. He does not force anything on us against our will and freedom. True love has to be mutual and reciprocal without either of the parties forcing the other into anything. Jesus warned Peter, Judas, and others about the dangerous path they were treading and where they were heading. But Peter appeared to be overconfident about his capacity to resist temptations and Judas and others appeared to be dismissive about Jesus' warnings. God warns us in many ways about the dangerous and sinful paths that we sometimes take, but he does not force us into something. He respects our freedom and will. If he forces us into something, then it becomes a master-slave relationship. But that is not how God or Jesus relates to us. In fact, he becomes a servant for us. Forcing us into something is against true love. God does not treat us as puppets in his hands. We are his children, friends, co-creators, and partners in love.

Allowing himself to be tortured and crucified was also a way to join himself to us. It is not that he was suicidal or intentionally killing himself but rather he was willing to go to any extent of sacrifice for the sake of love. He was prepared to face the worst kind of death prevalent in those days. He was prepared to die for what he stood for, not only justice and truth but also unconditional and forgiving love. He chose to die rather than running away to save his life or surrendering to the powers of evil. He probably knew how he was going to be tortured and killed and that could be one of the reasons why he sweated blood in the garden of Gethsemane. But he did not run away from it.

I also believe that there were other reasons why Jesus died the way he did. It was to show to the world how human beings could be inhuman and cruel to the maximum possible level. Human beings who are created in God's image and likeness could sometimes turn out to be the images and likeness of the devil. Jesus wanted us to realize how evil we could turn out to be if we let our negative passions and emotions take over us. We have seen the best and the worst of human beings in our human history. We have seen human beings turning out to be godly and devilish. Human beings engage in gruesome acts of terror, torture, and murder. If such dastardly acts were done against God himself, how much more could we expect them to be done to each other?

Jesus' torture, crucifixion, and death were also God's way of telling the most ill-treated and tortured people in our world that he knows what they are going through and that they are not alone in their suffering and death. There are many people who are tortured, ill treated, and killed in the cruelest way, and some of them are the most innocent of all. In their suffering and death, they might feel that even God has abandoned them. But God's answer to that desperation and suffering is his own sacrifice and death on the cross. When they cry, he cries; when they suffer, he suffers; when they are tortured, he is tortured; and when they die, he dies. Again, some people might ask, "instead of crying and suffering with them, why doesn't he do something to alleviate their suffering and destroy their torturers?" But again, God is not someone who fights evil with evil. He fights evil with love. He is not someone who twists our arms and forces us to do something. He is someone who wants us to recognize what we are doing and take responsibility for our actions. He wants us to fight evil with good. He cries and suffers with the sufferer and waits for the repentance and return of the sinner. If he has to punish and force all sinners, then he has to do that with all of us because all of us are sinners and all of us make bad choices. Some of us may be greater sinners than others, but who can judge but God alone. Love and love alone is the weapon that Jesus uses to win us back. And love can do incredible things.

22

Seeking Until He Finds

MANY PEOPLE THINK OF God as someone who waits for his devotees or worshippers to come to him, but in Jesus we find a God who goes out to his people. He comes down to our level rather than expecting us to come to him. He entered our human realm, becoming even like a slave (Phil 2:6–8). He became the Emmanuel, God with us. And in coming down to our level he wanted to gather us all together as one family and community. So we see him going after the lost and the lonely, those who had distanced themselves or kept away from God and others. He knew that his kingdom would not be built or God's family would not be complete until everyone came together as one sheep under one shepherd (John 10:16).

People sometimes forget and leave things behind. In many places these days there are what is often referred to as "Lost and found" boxes or bags. Many churches and stores have such facilities. Whatever people forget and leave behind are put in those boxes so that if the people come back to look for what they lost, they can get it back. When people find and receive back what they lost, they are often excited and relieved. And if they don't find it, they continue to look for it. They don't easily give up. They keep searching and searching with hope until they find it. If the lost item was of small value or significance, they might give up on it after a while. But if it is of some great significance or value they keep looking for it.

When it comes to God's love for us that is how he searches for us. If we are lost and gone away, he will keep waiting and searching until he finds us. His love for us is so much that he will never abandon us or give up on us. He will never give up on us because there is nothing in this world for him as valuable as we are. We are his children, his beloved sons and daughters.

Jesus uses many parables and stories to tell us about this abounding and faithful love of God. Three of those parables, the parable of the lost son(s), lost sheep, and lost coin (Luke 15) stand out as some of the prominent ones demonstrating God's unceasing love. He seeks until he finds us.

The Lost Son(s)

Although the parable of the prodigal or lost son is often thought of as referring to one son, the story is about both sons taking the negative route and the father inviting both sons back home. Both sons were lost in their own way. So I would call it the parable of the prodigal or lost sons.

The younger son took his inheritance from the father, went to a far away country, and squandered his property, leading to his own destruction. He separated himself from his father and brother, and lived a totally self-focused life. He abandoned his home and family. He spent his money on drunkenness and debauchery, physical and sensual pleasures. He got addicted to many things. He became wasteful and ignorant of the consequences of his actions. Asking the father for his share of property when the father was still alive was like considering his father as dead. It was most disrespectful and unkind. He seems to have developed a high sense of entitlement as though he had a right to everything. The story says that he went to a distant country which means that he was far away from "home." He was far away from his father and brother. He was not "at home" any more. He was disconnected and distanced.

When all his money and resources were spent, he started living a miserable life. His pleasurable days and fun-loving friends were gone. He was all alone, desperate and desolate. He hired himself to the citizens of the foreign country, people who were not his own, which once again indicates that he was disconnected and far away from "home." And the job he received was feeding the pigs, which for the Jewish people would be the most despicable job. No Jew would want anything to do with a pig because pigs were the dirtiest and most unclean of all animals. It would defile a Jew if he or she associated with a pig like the younger son did. He not only fed the pigs but also started feeding himself with what the pigs ate. It simply means that he sank to lowest and most despicable level that a human being could sink into. He had become totally unclean and disconnected.

The elder son stayed with the father, but he was full of rage and held a grudge. He remained as dutiful and faithful to the father and family but he was angry with the father and brother. He did not truly love his father and brother. He also seems to have developed a high sense of entitlement as though somebody owed him something. He wanted to see his brother being punished. He suppressed his anger and did not show it out for a long time. He allowed the negative emotions to grow in him. He was passive-aggressive. But then he blows up one day. His anger burst out when the father welcomed the younger son back into the house. His suppressed anger and disappointment came into the open when he saw his father forgiving his younger brother.

Both sons lived negatively, but each one had his own way of doing it. They were cut off from the father and from each other. They did not really live healthy and happy lives. Their negative living left the family divided and the father distraught. One was narcissistic and wasteful, and the other was passive-aggressive. Both were destructive for themselves and their family. One went away and one was in the house, but both were unhappy and away from "home".

We could think about all kinds of reasons for the younger son's wayward behavior. Perhaps he was duped by wealth, power, sense of entitlement, desire for adventure, and other attractive things. Perhaps he felt controlled, bullied, and criticized by his elder brother and he didn't want to stay with him anymore. Sibling rivalry is not anything uncommon in many families. Maybe he misunderstood his father's love and did not like his directions and discipline.

The elder son also must have had many reasons for his behavior. He seems to have looked at his father as a taskmaster. He seems to have built up negative emotions, thoughts, and judgments over the years. He must have looked at his younger brother as the favorite of the father, which happens in many families. Being the first-born, he must have taken upon himself a "parent" role, which happens with many first-borns in many families. He must have expected obedience and loyalty from his younger brother and approval of his behaviors from the father. Maybe he wanted to control the family affairs. He did not find ways to address and change his negative thoughts and emotions.

To both sons, the father was loving and kind. He didn't have any favorites. He loved them both. He grieved for his younger son who had gone away. He never gave up on him. He waited and waited, until the younger son returned. He forgave all his doings. Many people would have told the father to forget about the younger son, that he was lost and beyond redemption. But he never gave up or shut the door against him. When he returned the Father was overjoyed. He arranged a great feast to celebrate his return. He reinstated the son to his former status. He did not dig up the son's past doings and start blaming or shaming him. He simply welcomed him back with open arms. The son was given new sandals or shoes, new clothes, and a ring on his finger, all of which meant that the father was not only accepting the son back but also helping him to regain his lost status. He was not going to continue to live in filth; he was renewed and refined. The father wanted him to start anew, making healthy choices, just as Jesus told the adulterous woman to go and not sin anymore.

The father did not give up on his elder son either. He grieved for him as well. He loved him just as he loved his younger son. When the elder son was angry and upset and stayed outside the house refusing to come in, the father went out to invite him in. Many people would have told the father to forget about the elder son and leave him in his anger and stubbornness. But the father does not give up on him. He goes out to him as well. He wanted his son to forgive and be free of his anger and negative emotions. The father wanted him home.

The family was not going to be complete when either of the sons stayed away. The father wanted both sons to be home, to be at home with the father and with each other as brothers. Both sons had to find their rightful place in the family. They didn't need to take the role of the father or parent or be envious of each other. They just had to be who they were, as sons and brothers.

Jesus uses the parable to show how God is loving and forgiving to all of us. Perhaps some of us are like the younger son, narcissistic and wasteful, abandoning God and the community. We leave our "home." We seek adventures. We think that we are entitled to something. We sometimes don't like directions and discipline. We stay away from God and others. We make bad choices and waste away our gifts and talents. We end up with unhealthy and despicable behaviors, addictions, and miserable situations of life. Sometimes we sink to the lowest and dirtiest levels of living. We find ourselves far away from "home," not necessarily in the physical sense but psychologically and spiritually.

Maybe some of us are like the elder son, angry and disappointed with God and others. We remain as dutiful and faithful members but we grumble and complain. We think that the whole world is against us and we are angry. We remain stubbornly sad and angry, and that takes away our joy in life. We are like saints with sad or sour faces. We feel entitled as though someone owes us something. We are home but not happy. Sometimes we suppress our anger, disappointments, and frustrations, but one day we blow up. They come out through our words and actions.

There could be many reasons for what we do and how we live our lives. Maybe like the younger son some of us are duped by wealth, power, sense of entitlement, desire for adventure, sensual pleasures, and other attractive things. Some of us may be finding our families as uncaring and bereft of love. Maybe we have developed negative and unhealthy images of God and others. Some of us may have been abused, mistreated, bullied, and uncared for in our early years of life or we continue to experience them in our present life. Maybe we find our community and society too controlling and rigid. Our communities and societies may be just the opposite, without any structure and boundaries for healthy life. Maybe some of us were taught and trained to engage in unhealthy activities.

Maybe like the elder son, we feel entitled. We might like to take the role of the father or God and be in control of everything. We may be expecting everybody to consider us as important and worthy of praise and adulation. We may have built up negative emotions, thoughts, and judgments over the years. We may have allowed those negative thoughts and emotions to control us. We may be angry and upset when we see our rivals and enemies thriving. We may be asking why God is allowing such people to thrive. We might like God to punish them. We may be angry with God when we don't see him doing that.

Like both sons, we may have forgotten about our rightful place in God's family. Jesus loves all of us, the lost ones and the angry ones, those who live in sin and evils and live away from the church or community, and those who remain in the Church or community but are angry and unhappy. He wants all of us. He wants us to recognize our rightful place. We are God's children, sons and daughters and brothers and sisters.

Jesus comes to restore us to our rightful place, to bring us back "home" so that we can be with our father, God, and our brothers and sisters.

Jesus was kind and compassionate to both sinners and the self-righteous. He went out to seek the lost and the least, the sinners and prostitutes, those who were "outside" the house or community like the prodigal son. He also loved the scribes and Pharisees, those who were "inside" the house or community like the elder son. The scribes and the Pharisees were angry and judgmental. They wanted to see all the sinners and renegades punished. Jesus called them also to conversion. He dined and conversed with them as well. Jesus knows how we are often lost and far away from home. He wants to bring us back home, to healthy and happy living.

In the parable, the story ends with the younger son returning home and everyone celebrating it. We don't hear much more about him than that. We also don't hear anything more about the elder son. We don't know whether he really listened to his father and came into the house or he stayed with his anger and disappointment. Jesus left it open-ended. Of course, this parable could be looked at from the perspective of our final redemption when we are finally "home," united with God and our brothers and sisters for all eternity. But the parable doesn't have to be simply about our life in eternity alone. It could be about our life on this earth as well. While we are on this earth, the story of the younger son and elder son might keep repeating over and over again. We could wonder whether the prodigal son stayed home for the rest of his life. Perhaps he left the father and brother again and went away wasting his life. And the father must have waited for his return again and again. It happens in our own families and communities. Sometimes children go into unhealthy and destructive ways of living. The parents wait for them and are so overjoyed when they make changes and return back to healthy choices. But sometimes they go away again. The parents wait for their return again. In communities and societies, some members engage in unhealthy behaviors. When they turn away from their negativity and destructiveness the community or society breathes a sigh of relief. But sometimes, these members go back to their old ways again.

The same thing happens in our relationship with God. We commit sin and engage in evils, turning away from God and others. But then we repent and return back to God and the community. However, we engage in evils and sins again. We distance ourselves from God and others. And God waits for us again. He waits for us unceasingly. The story of our life is filled with this dynamic of going away and returning back. Being tired of this drama others might give up on us, but God never gives up on us.

We also see the story of the elder son being played out in our lives. Sometimes some of us hold on to our anger and disappointments and refuse to come into the house—that is, return to a healthy relationship with God and others. For some people it is very difficult to forgive and let go of what others have done. They hold on to their anger and disappointment. Sometimes we forgive and return but then again we go back to our anger and disappointments. It might keep repeating over and over again.

And the father keeps calling us to come into the house or return to healthy relationships and life.

Sometimes it is the parents who go into unhealthy ways, and children wait for their return. In many families, children are grieving the waywardness of the parents and they hope and pray that their parents would return to healthy living. Sometimes it is the community or society that goes weird and unhealthy, and the members hope for its return to healthy ways of functioning. All these are possible in our human relationships.

In my mother tongue, Malayalam, there is a saying, "*Pukanja kolli purathu*," meaning, "The damp and smoldering log is out of the hearth." Before the modern kitchen stove and oven took over the culinary traditions at homes, hearth cooking was the art of the ancient people. Every house had an open hearth in which people used dry logs of wood to create a fire to cook. The drier the wood, the easier it is to light the fire. And people often collected these logs of wood from their own trees on the farm or nearby forests. However, my home state, Kerala experiences heavy rainfall in the monsoon seasons, which mainly occurs twice a year, in June and October. During those monsoon seasons, it is not easy to find any dry logs of wood around. So sometimes people have no choice but to try to light the fire in the hearth with wet or damp logs. Unfortunately, some of such logs never produce any fire. They only smolder or create smoke. Being frustrated and tired of blowing into the hearth and trying to get the fire started, the person might take the damp log out of the hearth and throw it away. The expression, *pukanja kolli purathu* literally refers to such an act of throwing away or discarding the smoldering log out of frustration. But what it actually refers to is a person who hasn't lived up to the expectations of the family or society and has been causing problems and difficulties by his or her behaviors. As a result the family or society decides to reject or keep that person out of their lives considering him or her as an alien or outcast.

Both the sons in the parable of the prodigal sons were like the smoldering log. They were not producing healthy results. They both seem to have misunderstood their father's love. But the father does not abandon or give up on them. He does not throw them out. He was compassionate and loving toward both of them. Maybe some of us have been or still are like the smoldering log in our families and communities. God does not give up on us. He wants us to return back "home" and begin healthy life again. Some of us may be frustrated with others because they refuse to return to healthy living, and we may be at the point of giving up on them. But like the loving Father, God asks us to be patient and loving toward those smoldering logs in our lives.

The Lost Sheep

The parable of the lost sheep is similar in its message as that of the prodigal sons. The sheep was disconnected from the shepherd and the rest of the flock. The shepherd leaves the ninety-nine sheep and goes in search of the one lost sheep. We could wonder what made the sheep wander away. There could have been many reasons. The sheep must have lost its path. Maybe it was rebellious, narcissistic, and selfish. It may have hated the rest of the group. The rest of the group may have bullied it. Maybe it hated, was angry with, or afraid of the shepherd himself. The sheep may have been sick and weak. Perhaps the sheep was dumb, foolish, and careless. Whatever must have been the reason, the sheep was lost and the shepherd was worried.

The shepherd leaves all the other sheep and goes in search of the lost one. The sheep is feeble and weak. A bear, lion, or wolf could attack it and tear it into pieces. The sheep is unaware of it, but the shepherd is. The shepherd is concerned about the safety and welfare of the sheep. He would not be happy until he found the sheep.

Sometimes we are lost and disconnected from God and others like the sheep. Sometime we may not be aware how far away we have gone from healthy life and relationships with God and others. There could be many reasons why we do what we do. Perhaps we are narcissistic and selfish. Maybe we have been mistreated and not cared for by our family and community. We may have been misled and ill informed. Maybe we are dumb, careless, and clueless, and make bad choices. We may have developed a negative and unhealthy image of God and others. Those who simply look at us from outside may not know all that. But God does. That is why he is concerned.

The evils and troubles of this world put us into great danger. God is concerned about us. As a father or mother who is distressed about his or her lost or sick child, God is distressed about us when we are lost and broken or sick and tired of all the things going on in our life. He searches for us until he finds us. He does not stop. He keeps searching. We may reject him once, twice, or thrice, but he still seeks us. Jesus came in search of all the lost and the lonely. He steps into our brokenness, to lift us up. He does not reject us even if we reject him. The shepherd rejoices when he finds the sheep. God rejoices when he finds us, when we return to healthy ways of living.

We see that it is the shepherd that went to the sheep and not the other way around. The sheep was not able to come to the shepherd by itself. It must have been resistant, afraid, ashamed, and unsure. A sinner who lives in sin or a person who is going through a difficult situation is like that. He or she is unable to come back to the Lord or to the family and community by himself or herself either because the person is completely given into evil ways or he or she is overwhelmed by what is going on in his or her life. The person may be ashamed and afraid. The person may be stuck in anger and resentment. He or she needs God's grace and the support of the community to return to healthy living.

Many people would have told the shepherd to stop worrying about the dumb and wayward sheep. But he does not give up. That is how God is. Many people might give up on us, but God never does. He continues to look for us because he knows that when we are far away from him or the community, we are not living healthy and happy lives. We may have many things, but our life may be deprived of real peace and joy. When the sheep was away, the shepherd's flock was incomplete. It may not have mattered much to the other ninety-nine, but it did matter to the shepherd. He needed all of them together. When we are lost and lonely, it may not matter much to others, but it does matter to God. He wants all of his children together. The parable does not need to be seen only from the perspective of two categories of people, the righteous and the lost. It could be also seen as two dimensions of life within us, the parts that are holy and healthy and the parts that are unholy and unhealthy. The percentage of these two dimensions might alter from time to time. Jesus wants to redeem those areas in us that are lost, lonely, and hidden. He is not going to rest until our whole self is healthy, happy, and holy, and is united with him.

The shepherd carries the sheep on his shoulders. We could wonder whether the sheep was sitting still and quiet. Some sheep try to wriggle out and want to run away. We could also wonder whether the sheep stayed with the flock for the rest of its life. Maybe it strayed again several times. And the shepherd must have gone in search of it again. Sometimes God tries to bring us back, but some of us try to wriggle out and escape. Sometimes we return to healthy ways of living for sometime, and then we fall back into unhealthy ways again. We get into problems and conflicts again. We give into our anger, hatred, frustrations, selfishness, and all such negative emotions and unhealthy ways of living again and again. But God calls us back over and over again.

The Lost Coin

The parable of the lost coin also carries a similar message about God's unceasing love. It is the story of a woman losing one of her ten silver coins. She searches for it until she finds it. As the woman frantically searches for the lost coin, God is frantically searching for us when we are living in sin or gone into unhealthy ways. The coin was of a very small value. But it appears that for the woman it was of great value. For others we may not matter much. It may not matter much to others whether we live or die, whether we are lost and broken. Others may consider that we are of not much worth or value especially if we are not as good as others or we have been a problem in the family or community. But for God we are of great value. We may not be very gifted and talented like others; we may not be rich and influential like some; we may not be powerful and noticed in the community like some; and we may have done things in the past that have reduced our value in the eyes of the community or world. But for God we are still precious and special. We still have the same value that he bestowed on us when he created us. Many patients that I treat in my clinical practice feel that their families and the world would be better off without them. They have been abused and maltreated and they have come to a sense that they don't really matter much for the rest of the world. But that is not how God sees us. We do matter for God. No matter what may have happened to us, for God we are still precious and immensely valuable.

To celebrate and share her joy with her friends and neighbors about finding the coin, the woman seems a little illogical and irrational in her spending. She spends a whole lot more than the value of the coin. Some might call her "crazy." But Jesus wants us to know that that is how God is. He is "crazy" in love with us. He would do anything for us. However small or insignificant we may be in the eyes of the world, we are important to God. God would celebrate our return. Some people would think of Jesus dying on the cross as craziness. But that is the crazy love of God. He would go to any extent to save and love us. The cross simply tells us that he would go even to the point of giving his last drop of blood and breath of life for us. Even in death Jesus was life giving. And nothing could stop that love.

Many people would have told the woman to forget about the coin because it was insignificant. But the woman does not forget. However insignificant we may be in the eyes of the world, God does not forget or ignore us. There are a lot of us who feel insignificant, little, or unimportant in the society, community, or family. Many feel like being swept under the carpet by others. But to all such people God says, "You are special and valuable beyond measure."

A twenty or fifty dollar bill or currency note might look crumbled, dirty, and worn out, but its value does not change. It is still a twenty or fifty dollar bill. Whether it is in a poor man's hand or rich man's hand, the dollar bill has the same value. We may be sinful, stumbling, hurting, poor, unrecognized, not as intelligent and capable as many others, not rich and powerful as others, and not holding any position or power in the society or community, but we are still God's special creation, deeply loved by him. Left to itself, the coin may have been of very little value, but when it was together with other coins, its value was much greater. Left to ourselves, we may be weak and helpless, but when we remain united with others, our strength and what we can accomplish are much greater. God wants us to live and work in communion so that we can bring the best out of ourselves and be a blessing to others.

23

The Dialogical Triangle

THE FACE OF GOD that Jesus manifests is that of one who is in dialogue. He was constantly in dialogue with his heavenly Father and the Holy Spirit. And he was constantly in dialogue with his community or others. A healthy life is one that ensures a triangular dialogical relationship of love between God, self, and others or the community. As the source and sustainer of our life, God needs to be an integral part of our life. Without him our life is incomplete. Our life is also incomplete without others. We need the community or others because we are not meant to live in isolation. And in reality it is impossible to live without others. Jesus models this triangular relationship by his own life. He built his life, mission, and ministry around this dialogical triad involving God, the community, and himself, and he calls us to do the same.

Being one of the persons of the Holy Trinity, Jesus always remained united with his heavenly Father and the Holy Spirit. United with the Father and the Holy Spirit, he identified himself with the God who has been revealing himself in human history. He said, "Very truly, I tell you, before Abraham was, I am" (John 8:58). Throughout his life and ministry, we see Jesus dialoguing with his heavenly Father and being led by the Spirit. Demonstrating what his priority was, Jesus said, "My food is to do the will of him who sent me and to complete his work" (John 4:34). Very rarely we find Jesus glorifying himself or making himself as the focus of all that he was doing. He was always giving glory to his heavenly Father and directing the people to the love of his Father. Confirming his union with his father, he said, "The Father and I are one" (John 10:30). Jesus allowed himself to be led by the Holy Spirit (Luke 4:1). And he promised his disciples of the guidance of the Holy Spirit, "But the Advocate, the Holy Spirit, whom the Father will send in my name, will teach you everything, and remind you of all that I have said to you" (John 14:26).

Rejoicing over the successful mission of his disciples, we find Jesus totally united with his Father and the Holy Spirit, "At that same hour Jesus rejoiced in the Holy Spirit and said, 'I thank you, Father, Lord of heaven and earth, because you have hidden these things from the wise and the intelligent and have revealed them to infants'" (Luke 10:21).

Amidst the busyness of his life and ministry, Jesus found time to pray and be in union with his Father and the Spirit. The evangelist, Mark says that Jesus did that at the beginning of the day before he started the ministry, "In the morning, while it was still very dark, he got up and went out to a deserted place, and there he prayed" (Mark 1:35). Matthew talks about Jesus ending the day with prayer and communion with the Father, "And after he had dismissed the crowds, he went up the mountain by himself to pray" (Matt 14:23). If we think of prayer as our dialogue with God, Jesus spending time in prayer would indicate that he was in dialogue with the heavenly Father and the Holy Spirit.

The gospels also narrate about Jesus spending time in prayer before he took some significant decisions or did something special. Before choosing his apostles, Jesus spent dialoguing with the Father and the Spirit, "Now during those days he went out to the mountain to pray; and he spent the night in prayer to God" (Luke 6:12). Before facing his final hours of crucifixion and death, Jesus prayed in agony, "Then he withdrew from them about a stone's throw, knelt down, and prayed, 'Father, if you are willing, remove this cup from me; yet, not my will but yours be done'" (Luke 22:41–42).

He prayed for his disciples, especially, for unity among them, "Holy Father, protect them in your name that you have given me, so that they may be one, as we are one. While I was with them, I protected them in your name that you have given me" (John 17:11–12). Jesus allowed himself to be influenced and led by his heavenly Father and the Holy Spirit. He was united with the Father and the Holy Spirit not only in his active ministry but also during his final hours and death. In his agony the whole Trinity was in agony. If the Trinitarian God is inseparable, they were inseparable on the cross as well. When Jesus died, we can say, the whole Trinity died. When Jesus rose, the whole Trinity rose.

However, in his humanity, there were times when Jesus was tempted to doubt the love of the Father and the Holy Spirit. The temptations of Jesus narrated in the gospels speak to those moments. The devil tempted him several times with the question, "If you are the Son of God . . . " (Luke 4:1–13). Those temptations must have returned to him several times later, especially when he was going through some difficult moments. While hanging on the cross in excruciating pain, he was tempted to ask, "My God, my God, why have you forsaken me?" (Matt 27:46). But in spite of those moments of doubts and temptations, Jesus continued to remain in communion with his heavenly Father and the Holy Spirit. He did not allow these temptations and doubts to cause any interruption or break in the dialogical process. The dialogue and the journey continued, and love was victorious again.

But Jesus' communication was not just with his heavenly Father and the Holy Spirit alone. He constantly interacted with others or his community as well. He was in communion with the whole creation. In his immediate context, he respected and followed many ideals and practices of his Jewish community, and at the same time he tried to change the unhealthy elements that had crept into their community life.

He was not a fanatic or extremist, rigid in his ways and thoughts. He was not a loose cannon or extremely liberal person disrespectful and avoidant of everything of his community either. He was open, flexible, grounded, and balanced in his thinking and doing. He had high respect for the laws and commandments. He said, "Do not think that I have come to abolish the law or the prophets; I have come not to abolish but to fulfill. For truly I tell you, until heaven and earth pass away, not one letter, not one stroke of a letter, will pass from the law until all is accomplished" (Matt 5:17–18). And he warned and corrected those who thought that he had come to abolish all the laws and regulations, "Therefore, whoever breaks one of the least of these commandments, and teaches others to do the same, will be called least in the kingdom of heaven; but whoever does them and teaches them will be called great in the kingdom of heaven" (Matt 5:19). However, he wanted his people to understand the law in its right spirit instead of being caught up in their own rigid interpretations and thoughts, which was often seen in the practices of the scribes and Pharisees, "For I tell you, unless your righteousness exceeds that of the scribes and Pharisees, you will never enter the kingdom of heaven" (Matt 5:20).

On a day-to-day basis, Jesus also interacted with his community. As a good Jew, he spent time with his people in synagogues praying, teaching, discussing, and debating. Luke mentions that it was Jesus' custom to go to synagogues: "When he came to Nazareth, where he had been brought up, he went to the synagogue on the Sabbath day, as was his custom . . . After leaving the synagogue he entered Simon's house . . . So he continued proclaiming the message in the synagogues of Judea" (Luke 4:16, 38, 44). Even as a young boy Jesus engaged in learning from and discussing with teachers and others in the community. When Jesus was lost for three days at the age of twelve, his parents, Mary and Joseph found him in the Jerusalem temple, sitting with the teachers, listening to them and asking them questions. In all of these instances of him being associated with the temple and synagogues, we can assume that he was not only praying with the community but also dialoguing with the community. That dialogue presumably influenced his thoughts and ideas in many ways and helped him to gain more clarity about his mission and ministry.

Jesus had many disciples, and he spent a lot of time with them. His interactions with them must have influenced his thoughts, beliefs, and ideas, giving him opportunities to gain more clarity about things. When we think of his disciples, we understand that they fall into different levels of discipleship. He had his twelve apostles who were probably the closest to him. He had other disciples like the seventy or seventy-two he sent on a mission, which must have included the twelve apostles too. It is not clear whether this group consisted of only men or included both men and women. Maybe it consisted of both. There were many women who accompanied him and provided for him and his disciples with their resources. All these people were part of the community that Jesus was dialoguing with.

With his twelve apostles, he had a very close and personal connection. They were not like master and servants. They were friends. They shared their life in common. He said, " I do not call you servants any longer, because the servant does not know what the master is doing; but I have called you friends, because I have made known to you everything that I have heard from my Father" (John 15:15). Although Jesus is often seen as teaching and guiding the disciples, it is appropriate to think that he learned many things from them as well.

To understand how they and the general public perceived him, he asked them, "Who do people say that I am?" (Mark 8:27). It looks like it was important for Jesus to know what other people thought about him. People had all kinds of ideas about him, but most probably very few of them told him what they thought of him. But they must have told his disciples about what they thought of their master. And the disciples told him what the general public thought of him. He then asked them, "But who do you say that I am?" (Mark 8:29). It looks like Jesus found it important to understand what his closest companions thought of him. They were not like other people. They knew him more than others. Peter answered him, "You are the Messiah" (Mark 8:29). All these were probably important things that shaped his ministry. These were part of his dialogue with the community. We may have some idea about who we are. But sometimes it is important to find out what others think of us and how they perceive us. The general population may have their own ideas about us, and our close friends and families have their ideas about us. We often may not know how we come across to others. Knowing what others think of us can help shape better our behaviors and relationships in some way.

Jesus must have had a lot of other good friends who also influenced his thoughts and ideas. Jesus is believed to have been friends with Martha, Mary, and Lazarus. He must have spent a lot of time with them, sharing his joys and sorrows, receiving their hospitality, and listening to what they thought of him.

Another of the prominent names mentioned as a close disciple or friend of Jesus is Mary Magdalene. People have made all kinds of conclusions about her relationship with Jesus, portraying her as a gravely sinful woman or adulteress, or even as a secret lover of Jesus. Scripture scholars suggest that Mary Magdalene was not the sinful woman mentioned in the gospel of Luke or any secret lover of Jesus. She was a true friend and disciple. Mary was believed to be a woman of wealth and resources who must have provided for Jesus and his disciples. As an itinerant preacher we know that Jesus did not have a permanent abode or much resources. He and his disciples needed help in terms of money, food, and other necessities. Mary Magdalene is believed to be one of those persons who provided for them. But as a good friend she was probably one of the few persons who really knew the sorrows and struggles of Jesus. As a human being, we can assume that Jesus also needed somebody who could listen to him, understand him, and provide him with love and comforting presence. Mary Magdalene must have been one of the persons who provided him with that.

She was there for him at some of those moments when he most needed support and encouragement. She was at the foot of the cross when he was dying. She was at his tomb before anybody else. She became the first missionary announcing the good news of resurrection. It is appropriate to think that it was not just a one-way traffic where Jesus influenced and changed her life, but that she also must have influenced him in many ways. She was not only a friend but also a devout disciple.

We don't hear too many details about it, but we can also assume that Jesus spent a lot of time with Mary and Joseph at home discussing and dialoguing with them. Luke says that after Mary and Joseph found Jesus in the temple, they all returned to Nazareth and Jesus was obedient to them. Being obedient to Joseph and Mary could mean that he allowed them to instruct him, guide him, influence him, and clarify his questions and doubts. As a child and young teenager, he must have learned many things from Mary and Joseph.

These disciples, friends, and family were all part of the community, and Jesus must have learned many things from them. His discussions and conversations with them must have helped him to clarify many of his thoughts and ideas.

It is believed that Jesus began his public ministry when he was around thirty years old. We can assume that during those thirty years before he entered the public arena he must have spent a lot of time dialoguing with many people in the community, such as rabbis, people of high scholarship, and men and women who lived ordinary lives. Jesus included the young and the old, the learned and the ordinary, the rich and the poor, the sick and the healthy, the likeable and the unlikeable in his ministry. He welcomed children and made others aware of the dignity and importance of children. He was kind and compassionate to widows and the poor. He took time to be with them. The general idea in the society was that children, the widows, and the poor were not important to be considered or valued. But Jesus by his actions and interactions made known to his people that they had to be in communion with others irrespective of who they were and what class or category they belonged to.

Jesus was in communion not only with human beings but also with the nature and the whole creation. Jesus being born in a stable amidst animals indicates his one-ness with the non-human parts of the creation. He spoke about the heavenly Father caring for the birds of the sky and the lilies of the field. He spent a lot of time on the lakes and the waters. He calmed the seas and the winds when they appeared to be rough and dangerous. He walked on the water. He spent time in the desert. He spent time in prayer on the mountaintops and other natural settings. Luke says that when Jesus was dying on the cross, darkness came over the whole land and the sun's light failed (Luke 23:45). It could indicate that the whole creation was sad and weeping at the death of Jesus. Jesus was in communion with the angels and the saints in his ancestry. Angles sang at his birth and ministered to him during his agony in Gethsemane. At the transfiguration, we see him conversing with Moses and Elijah.

But we also see that Jesus was not simply a passive receiver and executor of the will of his heavenly Father and the Holy Spirit. He was also not a blind follower of the expectations and dictates of the community. He was an active participant in the decision-making processes and their execution. In fact, at the transfiguration, the heavenly Father directed the disciples to listen to Jesus and follow his directions, "This is my Son, my Chosen; listen to him" (Luke 9:35). Jesus took time to think, reflect, and decide. He was convinced of what he was doing, and he spoke with authority unlike the scribes and Pharisees. He didn't simply repeat what others told him. His words came from his heart. He was authentic and genuine. His responses to his temptations and on other occasions speak to his discernment and decision making process. But at the same time he was not a self-driven individual caught up in his own ideas and thoughts. He did not allow his ego to dictate everything.

There were moments when Jesus was tempted to seek his own will and disengage from the dialogue. The temptations give us a good indication to attractions to a self-focused life. The devil tempted him with many desirable things that would have elevated him to high levels of self-accomplishments and glory. After he had multiplied the bread and fed the large crowd, people thought that he was going to fulfill all their expectations. They expected that the Messiah would come and defeat and destroy their political enemies like the Romans and others and establish a powerful kingdom for them. Convinced that Jesus was the awaited superhero, they went to take him forcefully to make him king. Recognizing their misguided thoughts and madness, Jesus withdrew from the scene. In the normal circumstances, anyone else would have given into that hype and hurrah and used it as a marketing strategy to promote him or herself. But Jesus did not simply fall victim to the mob frenzy.

On some occasions, he withdrew from the crowd and his disciples and stayed by himself in deserted places. There were times when the community tried to keep him out of the dialogue. The people of his hometown, Nazareth rejected him and drove him out of the town. Condemning him to death and crucifying him were signs of his community rejecting him. But Jesus did not allow these experiences to dampen his spirit and break his love and the dialogical process.

Jesus bent his will without breaking it. He tamed his mind and heart without being subdued or becoming passive. He allowed himself to be led by the Spirit and his heavenly Father, preserving the unity of the Holy Trinity. He dialogued with his community, listening to them and learning from them. He remained in communion with the whole creation preserving the oneness and unity of the whole creation. He kept the dialogue actively going and continued his journey manifesting his love to all.

24

Love that Crosses the Border

IN JESUS WE FIND a God who crosses the borders and challenges all kinds of exclusivism. As we discussed, his birth itself marked a break from all kinds of exclusive ideas of God. He was a Savior born for all.

Human beings always appear to have lived as exclusive groups and communities throughout history. In ancient times if it was tribal groups living in separate camps, in the present times their equivalent is nations or states building up borders and barricades. The threat of the other, whether it was real or imagined kept tribal groups inimical to each other. Each group watched out for danger and attack from the other. They would steal each other's livestock, occupy their territory, and take away their people and property as booty.

Things changed over the centuries, but the same story of exclusivism and inimical attitude toward each other continued in every age. Kingdoms and empires kept the story intact with the only difference of employing new tools and techniques of stealing, occupying, and overpowering others. Castes, classes, races, and ethnicities kept people separated from each other. Some of them even engaged in exterminating or subjugating others. Religions and religious communities engaged in the same kind of exclusivism and isolationism, turning out to be warring groups in the name of God. They all built up walls and borders around them.

We would think that with the passage of time and human beings moving into the post-modern era things would change for better. But it hasn't happened yet. We continue to live and relate to each other with exclusivist and isolationist attitudes and ideas. We continue to maintain our tribal or secluded mentality, seeing others as a threat or as people to be kept away or avoided. We do it as nations and communities. We do the same thing that our ancestors did, building walls and borders around us, and engaging in war with each other. We need a visa to cross over to the other side. There is no free access or movement. There is border patrol with security agencies monitoring who is crossing over from one side to the other. They don't let anyone in freely, especially if the person is perceived to be a threat.

Such monitoring and patrolling are done not only in the physical settings of our lives but also psychologically. Many of us are watchful about who we are dealing with. We don't just allow anyone to enter into our territory without that monitoring and evaluation, especially if we have some biases or prejudices about the other person or group. We like to keep to our familiar surroundings and people. Strangers and enemies are often not welcome to our territory. Sometimes the other person or group may not be an enemy and yet we may not want to do anything with them because of our fear of the other and exclusive mentality.

These behaviors and attitudes could be thought of as part of our animal nature, which relates to our basic need for survival and security. Most animals are protective of their territory. It is important for their survival. Other animals are perceived as a threat to their security and survival. Outwardly some animals might look ferocious and wild but that could be an external expression of their internal fear of danger or threat. By their ferociousness they try to scare away the threatening animal and protect themselves. Sharing in that nature, we are not much different from our fellow animals when it comes to our survival. Our group or tribal mentality could be a result of our need for survival. Anything or anyone unfamiliar could be a cause of concern and threat to our survival and security. Hence we might become ferocious and aggressive to scare away others and protect ourselves. We might remain secluded and watchful.

For most of us, it takes time to build relationships and confidence in others. Even within the same group or community, it takes time for people to trust and confide in others. We don't become friends overnight. It is a gradual process. Building relationships and trust becomes all the more difficult when it is between people belonging to different communities, races, ethnicities, nationalities, etc. Our lack of familiarity and fear of the other make it harder.

Human societies in every age appear to have experienced tensions and mistrust between people of different races, ethnicities, religions, nationalities, and other denominators. Some of the most commonly used words in such contexts are "racism," "tribalism," "nationalism," "exclusivism," "prejudice," and "bias." Lately, such words have attained much negative weight and connotations that they are used to brand and condemn people. All these may be present in many of our communities and societies, but before engaging in any name calling and condemnation, what we need to realize is that as human beings sharing in the animal nature, all of us are protective of our territory in some way or the other. We don't simply open our doors and borders to anybody just like that.

Even within a family, it takes time for the members to trust and confide in each other. A child needs many years to form attachment bonds and healthy relationships with his or her parents. When a secure attachment is developed in the family, the child maybe ready to develop such relationship bonds with others outside of the family. It takes many years and many steps to grow in that trust and confidence with others especially if others belong to a different class, race, religion, ethnicity, nationality, etc.

But many of us are not raised with such secure attachment feelings in our families. Hence our negative family backgrounds add to the difficulty in connecting with others.

We could wonder why often our first love and concern are for our immediate family members and close friends. Often we think about our family and friends first before we think about others. When these is some accident, natural calamity, terrorist attacks, or other tragedies happening in some place where a lot of people are involved and injured, our first thought is often about whether some of our family members or friends are involved and whether they are safe. Only after that we think about others. When we pray, often we first pray for our dearest and closest people, which often happen to be our family members and closest friends. Only after that we often include others in our prayer. At least, that is how many of us are taught and raised. Of course, not all people are the same. But most people have their love and concern going out to their immediate family members and friends first before it goes out to others.

Love could be thought of as the primary reason for that special concern for our family and friends. But that love seems to have some biological reasons too. Our physical and emotional connection with our loved ones is such that any harm or hurt that come upon them is a harm and hurt inflicted on us. When they are hurt and are in pain, we feel the hurt and pain. This physical and emotional connection is also significant from the perspective of our survival. In a family context, loving and caring for each other is important for our survival. It is important to remain close to our biological family because they are the first people who would help us to stay safe and alive. Parents take upon themselves the responsibility of keeping their children safe from predators, illnesses, and all other kinds of threats. Most animals do that. They care for their young. We are weak and vulnerable like other animals. Many things often threaten our survival. We need people to keep us safe. And often it is our immediate family and friends who do that for us. If anybody in our biological family or among closest friends is threatened or is in danger, it is a threat to our own safety and survival not only in the physical sense but also in the psychological sense. Any danger to them is going to negatively affect our physical and psychological survival. Hence the family members and friends try to keep themselves together, protecting and caring for each other.

Once our survival is ensured in our family and friendship circles and we have built up a sense of confidence and healthy relationship with them, we begin to do the same with others outside of our family and circle of friends. But then again our love and concern are restrictive based on our affiliations and associations. We might love and be concerned about the people of our race and community before our love goes out to others in other races and communities. Our love is restrictive and selective not because we are bad people or we have something against the people of other races, religions, or nationalities, but because our natural instinct is to associate with people who are like us since they are the first people whom we believe would ensure our physical and emotional safety and survival.

Some people, because of their life contexts may not have any interaction with anybody outside of their own tribe, community, and country. And some communities and groups have inimical feelings and fears of each other going back to several decades and centuries.

Given all these factors, we are often selective and restrictive in our love and concern. Building relationship and trust is a step-by-step process. We have to cross over many borders and territories before we become a person who embraces everyone. None of us becomes a man or woman of the universe in an instant. Because of this slow process, on many occasions and in many ways we might appear to be exclusive and territorial in our attitudes, behaviors, and relationships. To make progress in our life, we have to come out of that exclusivism. The drawbacks of protectionism and territorial mentality are stunted growth and relationships. When we remain exclusive and territorial, we live in fear of each other and never experience the larger world of freedom and fraternity. That is where Jesus dares us to be different. He invites us to break down the borders and barricades that we raise. Instead of closing our borders he asks us to cross over our borders. The love that Jesus preaches is a love that extends to all irrespective of who they are. He knows that it is not easy and quick, but he invites us to move toward it.

There are several stories in the Bible where we see Jesus trying to break down walls and cross over to the other side to embrace those who felt excluded or were left out. One of such stories is that of his encounter with the Samaritan woman (John 4:1–42). He did something that other Jews and rabbis did not usually dare to do. As the story indicates, Jews and Samaritans did not mix. Each group kept to themselves. But Jesus broke down that wall. He went into a Samaritan territory and interacted with a woman first, and then he ended up staying with the people of that city for a couple of days.

Jesus took a great risk in interacting with this woman. First of all, she was a Samaritan whom the Jews kept away. Secondly, she was a woman of bad reputation, whom no rabbis or men of great reputation wanted to be associated with. But Jesus did not run away by seeing the woman. Although she was a woman of bad reputation, he did not condemn or judge her either. He spoke to her with kindness and compassion. The narrative says that his own disciples were surprised to see him speaking with a woman. Jesus' actions often surprised many people. But that acceptance and kindness of Jesus was the beginning of conversion for the Samaritan woman and for the people of her town. For him, they were also important to be included in his ministry, because they were also his children. The love of Jesus is an all-inclusive and embracing love.

There are several other stories that depict Jesus as someone who breaks down the walls and crosses over to the other side. Jesus cleansed lepers whom no one ever dared to touch or come close to. By this action he included in his ministry the excluded and the outcasts. Jesus extended his helping hand to a centurion, a Roman official, and thus reached out to the non-Jewish world (Luke 7:1–10). Jesus dined with tax collectors and sinners who were often despised by the people, and helped them feel included in the community (Matt 9:9–13). Jesus used the parable of the Good Samaritan highlighting the need to go beyond one's religious and cultural exclusivism (Luke 10:29–37). He used the parable of the rich man and Lazarus to highlight the need for bridging the gap between the rich and the poor and addressing the economic and cultural disparity in the society (Luke 16:19–31). His encounter with Zacchaeus was a life changer for the latter demonstrating that change is possible for anyone (Luke 19:1–10). Jesus shows compassion and gives a new life to a sinner woman who was condemned by everyone else (John 8:1–11). By this act of kindness he was not agreeing with what she did or condoning her sin but rather feeling for her pain in that moment of shame and public ridicule. He was giving her another chance to choose healthy living as well as reminding the society that a woman had as much right as a man to live and receive justice.

In the gospel of Matthew, there is a story of an encounter between Jesus and a Canaanite woman, which speaks to the need for breaking down the walls and barriers between people and see everyone as God's children (Matt 15:21–28). In fact the story might give an idea that Jesus himself was exclusive, narrow, and prejudiced in his thinking and interactions. The Canaanite woman came to Jesus requesting him to heal her daughter who was tormented by a demon. With great faith and hope she came to Jesus but he seemed to ignore her. All the customs and traditions of his time must have told Jesus not to help the Canaanite woman. She was a Canaanite, and in the eyes of the Jewish people, the Canaanites were the bad people, the enemies of the Israelites. Being a Jew, the first reaction of Jesus had to be to ignore her or refuse her request, which appeared to be happening in his response "I was sent only to the lost sheep of the house of Israel" (Matt 15:24). The woman persisted and did not give up, and even appeared to be begging him for help. And Jesus goes further in his resistance to the woman's request and even seemed to be insulting her, "It is not fair to take children's food and throw it to the dogs" (Matt 15:26). The woman still didn't give up. She persisted. Jesus was amazed by her strong faith, and he extended his love and compassion to her. He went beyond the Jews-only exclusivism and broke down the barriers of enmity and ill feeling.

Given the nature of Jesus as compassionate and kind to those who came to him, it is most unlikely that he treated the woman badly as it appears. We don't find Jesus rejecting or humiliating anybody, especially the poor and simple people who came to him. But even if we want to look at the responses of Jesus as exclusive and narrow because of his background as a Jew, his encounter with the woman helped him to go beyond all such exclusive and elitist thoughts and attitudes. But the larger point in this story is the intention of the Evangelist, Matthew. In presenting this story, Matthew appears to have had a specific goal in giving a deeper message to his Christian community and the world at large. The story could be seen in two different ways. First, it could be seen as an invitation and challenge to break down the barriers of exclusivism and elite mentality and extend our love to others whom we often don't associate with. Secondly, it could be seen as a challenge to the individual, group, or community to change their ways first before they go to change others.

As the tradition holds, Matthew's gospel was addressed to his Christian community that was primarily Jewish in its cultural background. The community first consisted of Jews who converted to the Christian faith. But gradually there were also non-Jewish people who were generally referred to as the "gentiles" who started accepting Jesus and becoming part of the community. However, because of this mix of cultures, there appears to have arisen a tension in the community. The Jewish Christians appear to have discriminated against the gentile Christians. There is a reference to this tension in the Acts of the Apostles, "Now during those days, when the disciples were increasing in number, the Hellenists complained against the Hebrews because their widows were being neglected in the daily distribution of food" (Acts 6:1).

It appears that although they had accepted Jesus and the new way of life, they had not changed much in their thinking and attitude toward people of other cultures and backgrounds. The Evangelist, Matthew, seems to be addressing this problem in the community. He brings in the story of the Canaanite woman and her encounter with Jesus. In fact, he seems to be saying to his community, "Let us see what Jesus did in such a situation." All the customs and traditions of his time told Jesus not to help the Canaanite woman. Like any other Jew he first appeared to be reluctant to go beyond his cultural and territorial mentality. But the incredible courage and faith of the Canaanite woman moved Jesus into action and he looked beyond the walls and barriers human beings had built. He dismantled the dividing wall of intolerance between Jews and gentiles. It must have taken enormous courage for Jesus and the woman to face the group of people gathered around them. Most probably it was an all-Jewish and all-male gathering. But the woman's courage and faith paid off and Jesus got his people to pay attention to the message.

The story also could be seen as a challenge that Jesus places before his people to change themselves before they go to change others. When he says, "I was sent only to the lost sheep of the house of Israel" it could be indicating the necessity of converting the "chosen" people or those who claimed to be "true believers" before going to convert the so-called "pagans" and "gentiles," all of whom the Canaanite woman must have represented. Even though his own people claimed to be the chosen people of God, Jesus found that many of them had gone away from God and his ways. He had to first bring them back to God before he ventured out to those outside the community. That could be a reminder to all of us that change has to happen first with us before we try to change others. Our narrow, exclusive, and unhealthy beliefs, ideas, and thoughts have to be changed first before we try to change that of others. Today we hear about Christianizing or re-evangelizing the Christian world. The communities and societies that claim to be Christian appear to be manifesting and living a non-Christian culture and value system that they need to change themselves first before they go to change or convert others. Christ needs to be brought back to the Christian world first before he is taken to the non-Christian world.

There are other individuals in the Bible who carry this message of breaking the barriers and opening themselves up to God's ways. They had to go beyond their comfort zones and familiar grounds. We discussed about God asking Abraham to leave his country and kindred to start a new life and relationships. It is not simply about the physical movement. Leaving his country and kindred must have meant something more than leaving his physical environment. To grow and make progress in his life, God was telling him that he had to change psychologically, socially, and spiritually. He had to leave his isolated, narrow, exclusive, and unhealthy beliefs, thoughts, and practices. He had to begin to see God, others, and himself in a new way. He had to break down the barriers and walls he had built up. We can assume that it was not easy for Abraham to do that. Maybe physically moving from one place to the other is much easier than changing things in us psychologically, socially, and spiritually because often we are set in our ways of thinking and doing things. But once Abraham left his usual ways, his comfort zone, he was ushered into a larger horizon of possibilities and freedom.

Saint Paul was a zealous, devout, and law-abiding Jew and Pharisee. Out of his misplaced zeal he became a persecutor of Christians. But when he encountered Christ all those things that he boasted about in his life became worthless. Christ showed him a new horizon of space and freedom. His conversion was not just about changing his name and religion. It was about changing his heart, his thoughts, his ideas, and opinions. He had to break down the barriers that he had built up. When he did that, he found a new freedom and peace. This newfound freedom made him become a Jew to the Jews, a gentile to the gentiles, and weak to the weak, and thus finally becoming "all things to all people" (1 Cor 9:19–22). This transformation from being exclusive to becoming an inclusive and all-embracing missionary, we can assume, was not an easy transition for Paul. He had to cross over to the other side of the border many times.

Saint Peter, the most prominent of the apostles of Jesus, also seems to have gone through a personal struggle before he opened himself to others who were different from his culture and beliefs. He had to begin to see God in a new way. In the book of the Acts of the Apostles, there is an account of God revealing to Peter that he had to become more accepting and embracing of gentiles or non-Jewish believers (Acts 10). One day Peter was hungry, and in a vision, he saw a large sheet coming down from heaven and on it were animals, reptiles, and birds of all kind. A voice said to Peter to kill and eat. But being a devout Jew and having not eaten anything defiled or unclean in his life, Peter was reluctant to obey the voice. But the voice said that he should not call profane anything that God created. At that time a centurion named Cornelius from Caesarea had also seen a vision in which he was asked to send for Peter. As Peter was reflecting on his vision, the men from Caesarea came asking for him, and Peter realized that his vision was God's message to reach out to the gentiles. Until then, Peter's ministry was presumably limited to the Jewish community. He followed the men to Caesarea and preached the gospel to Cornelius and his family, and they were baptized as Christians. From then on, Peter began to open himself up to the non-Jewish world. He began to experience God and the world in yet another new way. Peter realized that although we are from different contexts and backgrounds and we may be at different levels in our spiritual life and relationship with God, God's love is extended to all of us. Until then Peter and his companions probably never thought that God would love the gentiles, the so-called pagans.

In many ways, we are products of our own culture and upbringing. Our familial, ethnic, racial, religious, linguistic, gender, national, and all other backgrounds have an impact on how we think, feel, and do things. Our beliefs, attitudes, and thoughts are often influenced by the images and ideas we develop about God, others, and ourselves over the years. There are things ingrained in our psyche that may not be easy to erase. We may have developed distorted and not so healthy attitudes about God, other people, cultures, and communities. Those attitudes and prejudices inform our reactions and relationships with God and with one another. They create walls between us and between God and us. We remain as exclusive and isolated individuals, groups, and communities. There have often been divisions and discord between Jews and gentiles, Catholics and Protestants, Christians and non-Christians, men and women, blacks and whites, higher class and lower class, high caste and low caste, conservatives and liberals, and the privileged and the less privileged. To step out of those cultural barriers and destroy and dismantle the walls that we may have created is often difficult. To try something new is often unsettling. We might resist and resent. We are reluctant to do things that risk our survival and security. It happens in our personal lives, families, and communities. In communities and societies, changes have been painful processes. Integration and interaction between different groups have been often difficult. Crossing over to the other side of our borders is not easy.

Jesus introduces a new vision of God, a new culture, and a new social order. It is a vision of seeing God bigger than what we often think of. It is a culture of inclusion and integration. It is an invitation to reform and re-create our psyche. The force that guides this reformation, inclusion, and integration is love. Love breaks down all walls and barriers. Love is God's language, and it speaks to the human person and human heart and not to the external factors such as color, caste, gender, language, religion, or nationality. We have to break down the walls that we create in our societies and world. We have to challenge the prejudices and falsity that exist in our midst. We have to stop the negativity that we engage in as individuals, communities, and nations. We need to have a love that crosses over to the other side of the border.

Pope Francis in his apostolic exhortation, *Evangelii Gaudium*, reiterates this invitation and challenge of Jesus by saying that the Lord calls all of us "to go forth from our comfort zone in order to reach all the 'peripheries' in need of the light of the gospel" (Francis, 2013). Referring to the role of the church in the world, the Pope says that the church should be a welcome place for anyone to come in as well as a missionary that goes out to bring God's love and goodness to others. As a welcome place with open doors, the church is to be a community or place where anyone can walk in and experience God's love. But that is not enough. The church has to be also a missionary that goes out. The church has to go out to those who do not come to church and those who do not belong to the community. If we expect them to come to us, they might never come. We have to go to them. And when we talk of the "church," we have to remember that we are the church. The church is the people of God. So we have to be a welcoming people to whom anyone can come and experience God's love. And we have to be missionaries who bring God's love to others. If we remain in our exclusivism and narrow mindedness, with our walls built high around us, we cannot be the true church, abodes and channels of God's grace and love.

Being abodes and channels of God's love is simply a continuation of what Jesus did. People came to him in large numbers and he had his door open for everyone. He didn't put any condition on anyone before they came to him. He didn't limit his access to only a certain kind of people. He was available and welcoming to all, both saints and sinners. But he didn't wait for them to come to him all the time. He went out to them as well. He went in search of the lost and the lonely. He went to those places and people where no one was willing or dared to go. He was a leader who went in search of people instead of waiting for them to come to him. In calling his disciples, we see him going out to their places and meeting them. Often disciples and students came to rabbis and teachers. The teachers and rabbis rarely went to where the students or disciples were. Even in this day and age, our system in most of our societies is such that students and disciples go in search of teachers or masters. The prospective candidates or followers go to the leader. They go to where the teachers or leaders are. We don't see teachers, gurus, or leaders going to their disciples or followers. Jesus was a different kind of teacher and rabbi. He met people where they were. He didn't wait for them to come to him to begin his ministry. And in going out to them, he didn't exclude anyone. He dined with tax collectors and sinners as well as with Pharisees and others whom he often chastised and criticized. He didn't limit his ministry to one location alone but went to many regions that needed him. He ministered to his people in Nazareth and Galilee, but he also went to territories that were not his home front. He said to his disciples, "Let us go on to the neighboring towns, so that I may proclaim the message there also; for that is what I came out to do" (Mark 1:38).

If we want to understand and experience God, we have to be willing to step out of our usual ways of thinking and doing things. If we have built up walls and barriers that make it hard for God to break into us we have to be willing to pull down those barriers. Exclusivism and isolation might serve certain purposes but they are not healthy when it comes to our relationship with God and life as a human community. Opening ourselves up to God and stepping out of our comfort zone is the Jesus' way. In his letter to the Philippians, Saint Paul writes, " . . . though he was in the form of God, did not regard equality with God as something to be exploited, but emptied himself, taking the form of a slave, being born in human likeness. And being found in human form, he humbled himself and became obedient to the point of death—even death on a cross" (Phil 2:6–8). The God whom we experience in Jesus is a God who comes down to our level. He meets us where we are. He doesn't wait for us to come to him, but rather he comes to us. The incarnational love of God challenges all kinds of exclusivism, elitism, and narrow-mindedness in beliefs and practices.

25

Jesus in Time and on the Move

WE SAW THAT THE God who has revealed himself in the Judeo-Christian traditions is a God of the temple and the tent. He was with his people in their particular historical contexts but he was also on the move. That dimension of God was powerfully manifested in the life and ministry of Jesus. He was with us in a unique way in our history, but he also moves with us through times and seasons. Jesus was born in Bethlehem, and lived with his people in Nazareth, Galilee, and the surrounding areas. People experienced God's personal love for them through his presence and ministry. But Jesus was not going to be limited to a certain territory, group of people, or certain period of times. He was a savior for all. He was on the move. Physically, Jesus was on the move all the time. He did not have a permanent home. He was an itinerant preacher. His family wanted to take him home forcefully and make him stay put but he escaped from their plan.

It was not only the physical movement but also the psychological, social, and spiritual movement that he was involved in. Psychologically he made many decisions that took him on the journey forward. There were many attractions and temptations that came on his way that could have made him get stuck. But he moved on. It is no surprise that Jesus ran away and escaped when some people wanted to make him a king forcefully. He was simply reminding them that all such ideas and dreams they were entertaining were not lasting. The kingdom he wanted to build and invited everyone to build was a kingdom that would last forever. That kingdom is not of earthly origin. It is not physical in nature. We hear that in his reply to Pilate, "My kingdom is not from this world" (John 18:36). It is not a kingdom made up of money and military power. It is not a kingdom that is subject to destruction and decay. It is a kingdom built around God. It is a kingdom built around a loving relationship with our fellow human beings. It is a non-physical kingdom. It is built on the power of love and healthy relationships. It is built around the dialogical triangle. Realizing that many of the ideas and concepts they had developed about God and themselves were distorted, Jesus again reminded them, "Heaven and earth will pass away, but my words will not pass away" (Matt 24:35). The only thing that lasts is our life united with the Lord and one another. All the structures, ideas, opinions, beliefs, and other things that we might be holding on to as permanent and sacrosanct are going to come to an end one day.

It is also no surprise why Jesus was not interested in fighting or overthrowing Herod, the Romans, or others who occupied and ruled over his people. Many Jews, especially those with radical ideologies, wanted to fight the Romans and overthrow their government. And they expected their Messiah as someone who would do that for them and establish a kingdom for them. Even some of his own disciples held on to that idea. When Jesus did not seem to be fitting into that concept of Messiah, many of them had difficulty in accepting him. But Jesus was consistently telling them that all such powers and kingdoms of this world were passing realities. They would come and go. If it is not Romans, it would be somebody else. But none of them would last forever. Even their own kings and rulers were bad and exploitative.

Of course for our social functioning and life as a community we need some of those structures and systems. We need governments and leaders. They are important for our individual growth and development. Without those structures and systems, life becomes hard. If everybody is going to do what he or she wants, family life, community life, or societal life is going to be hard. If everybody wants to be leaders, that is also not going to work. Hence some sort of systems and structures of governance are important and necessary in any situation of life. And God wishes that those systems and structures are good and godly, helping us to live healthy and holy lives. But those systems and structures are not permanent. It doesn't matter who is occupying the seat of power; they are all going to go eventually. In the long run, none of them is permanent. They all disintegrate and disappear.

It happens in the small circle of our families too. In some families, three or four generations stay together, but then gradually they take new forms and shapes. After a few decades, they are not connected with their distant cousins anymore. That is the nature of families. They get splintered and distanced. If we go back to a few generations, we would realize that we are related to many other families, but because we have become so large and splintered, we don't think of them as our relatives. When we think of our relatives, we only think of our immediate family members in three or four generations. And if we go back to the origin of our human communities and human race, we should be saying that we are all relatives. But we got splintered and distanced from each other so much that we don't often think that way. Only when we rise to the spiritual realm of our life, we begin to think of all of us as God's children and as one family. But in our day-to-day life, we don't think of people in another community or culture as our relatives.

Our families have some sort of permanence in the immediate context, and we need that to grow and develop. They are important for our survival and growth. But those arrangements and groupings are not permanent. They change. After some five hundred years, not many in our family tree would even know that we were their ancestors. Jesus was constantly trying to tell his people that all these connections and relationships in families and communities are temporary. What we need to grow into is the larger relationship with God and the whole humanity, seeing everyone as our family. We have to keep moving psychologically and spiritually to get to that sense of the universal family of God.

The same thing applies to our communities, nations, and the world. The nations and kingdoms we have today were not the nations and kingdoms we had some five hundred years back. They changed. They were not permanent. The nations and kingdoms we have today may not be around after five hundred years from now. Maybe many kingdoms and nations would come together to become empires again. Many present day kingdoms and nations might split and give shape to newer and smaller nations and kingdoms. Of course, we will not be around to see those changes, but that is how our history has been.

Structures, systems, kingdoms, and nations are important for our life and growth, but at the same time, they are not permanent. The only thing that would last is the kingdom we build around God and others, which is more relational than physical. This is what Jesus was trying to inculcate in his people. But they couldn't buy into that. They wanted to build their kingdom and ensure stability and security on this earth. They wanted to overpower other kingdoms and empires and establish supremacy over them because they have been overpowered and dominated over several times in their life. They and others still focus on building such earthly kingdoms and empires soon to realize that they don't last.

Indicating that nothing was going to stop Jesus from continuing his journey, the gospel of Luke says that he resolutely set out toward Jerusalem (Luke 9:51). There were many pleasurable and attractive temptations presented to him. But he did not get stuck; he was on the move. Even though there were people in Jerusalem plotting to kill him he was not going to run away out of fear. He was going to face the cross that was going to come on his way. As he was moving ahead, he sent his disciples ahead of him and they wanted him to stop at a Samaritan village (Luke 9:52–56). But the villagers did not want to have him there. They rejected him. The disciples were furious and wanted to call down fire from heaven on them. But Jesus was not discouraged. He rebuked his disciples for their anger. He told them to cool down and not get too emotional. He knew that such things would happen. He did not allow rejection or cold responses of people to discourage him. He continued his journey.

Luke suggests that people rejected him because his face was turned toward Jerusalem. Jerusalem is not necessarily referring to the actual city of Jerusalem but the heavenly Jerusalem, heaven, or fullness of life with God. On that road to heaven or fullness of life, Jesus knew that he had to face many hardships. But he was determined to keep moving forward in spite of those discouraging elements. As we follow Jesus and move forward in our journey toward our eternal Jerusalem, heaven, or lasting relationship with God and one another, there will be many temptations and pleasurable things presented to us. There may be many people who might want to offer us this or that and we may be tempted to go after them. There will be many discouraging elements that we come across on our way. Rejections, disappointments, and unexpected turn of events might happen, but we keep on marching ahead. We don't allow ourselves to get stuck. We don't allow our anger, discouragement, and other negative emotions to take over us. We don't allow temptations to distract us. We continue with courage and confidence in the Lord who is leading us.

In the gospel of Luke, we hear about three people who wanted to follow Jesus and his response to them is very telling about what it involves to really follow him (Luke 9:57–62). It might look like he was discouraging them from following him and was turning them away. The first one said, "I will follow you wherever you go" (Luke 9:57). Jesus seemed to be reminding him that he appeared to be very unrealistic and unaware of the implications of what he was saying. He probably didn't know what it meant to follow Jesus wherever he went. Even his closest followers, the apostles did not follow him wherever he went. They did not follow him to Calvary and the cross; most of them ran away from him. This man did not seem to really understand the full implications of what he was saying. Jesus replied to him, "Foxes have holes, and birds of the air have nests; but the Son of Man has nowhere to lay his head" (Luke 9:58). Even the animals and birds may have some permanence and security in this world, but following Jesus does not assure any such things. Following Jesus would mean that we would be on a journey. We wouldn't have a permanent place here; we are not going to settle down and be stuck in our own world. We will have to give up or let go off many things. We have to be on the go, being ready to go anywhere and do anything, even to the point of laying down our lives for the sake of love as Jesus did.

Many of us could relate to what this man in the gospel said. We make promises and commitments to Jesus and we realize that sometimes it is not easy. We might say that we would go wherever Jesus wants us to go and do whatever he wants us to do. But when it comes to really going where Jesus asks us to go or do what he asks us to do, we find that we are often not ready for that. Sometimes we want to stay where we are comfortable. We might go to some place physically as a missionary, but psychologically and spiritually we may be still stuck in our ways. Sometimes we don't want to leave our familiar territories. We don't want to change our thinking and ways of doing things. We don't want to do things that are difficult or those that we don't like.

In a marriage, for example, the spouses say to each other at their wedding, "I will be with you in good times and in bad times." But when it really gets to some bad times some realize how difficult it is to keep that commitment and promise. It could be a similar experience for people in other vocations of life. Many of us might have said to Jesus like the man in the gospel, "I will follow you wherever you go." It is not that we cannot do it. It is doable. With his help and with courage and determination we can do it. But Jesus says that we have to be prepared for it. Simply saying, "I will follow you" is not enough. That doesn't do it. Jesus wants us to know that following him is to be on the road with him. We should be willing to change many things. It is challenging.

That road has twists and turns. That road does not halt permanently anywhere on this earth. We are in a tent and we keep moving. That journey asks us to leave all the defenses and debilitating elements in our life.

The second person whom Jesus invited to follow him said, "Lord, first let me go and bury my father" (Luke 9:59). And the third person who wanted to follow Jesus said, "I will follow you, Lord; but let me first say farewell to those at my home" (Luke 9:61). Jesus seemed to be turning both of them away as well. In the normal circumstances, nobody would think that there is anything wrong in burying one's father and saying good-bye to one's family. They are good things to do. It will be unchristian and uncharitable to neglect burying one's father and unkind or rude to avoid saying good-bye to one's family. But that's not exactly the point. It is about following Jesus and being on the road right now. The two men were still stuck in their world and were not ready yet to enter into the world of Jesus. Following Jesus is about being on the journey with him now. There is no place for demands and delay. If we put it off for tomorrow, tomorrow might never come.

Jesus warns us about getting stuck. When we follow him, we don't say "Lord, I will follow you after a while, or I will follow you, but I am not ready yet." Jesus calls us now and the journey begins now. When God calls us, it is about being fully available to him without allowing anything to hold us back. He wants us to keep moving, especially in the psychological and spiritual sense. God told Abraham to leave his country and kindred, and the story says that Abraham immediately responded to God's call (Gen 12). But Abraham did not leave his family completely. He had his wife, his nephew, and many others who continued to be with him. When Jesus called his first four disciples, Peter, Andrew, James, and John, the gospel says that they immediately left everything and followed him (Matt 4:18–22). It doesn't mean that they left their families and work forever, because we hear about Jesus and the disciples going back to their families and doing the same work. Peter must have continued to stay with his family for a long time and at the same time he must have spent a lot of time with Jesus and the other disciples as well. We hear about Jesus visiting Peter's family and curing his mother-in-law (Matt 8:14–15).

Although the gospels say that the disciples left their boats and nets and followed Jesus immediately, we know that they continued their profession of fishing. The gospels tell us that they were in the boats and on the lakes on several occasions. Fishing probably continued to be their main way to support themselves and their families financially. So following Jesus without delay and conditions is not simply about leaving families and commitments in the usual sense or physical sense. It is more about a psychological and spiritual journey that involves constant transformation. It is about leaving things that hold us back from being on the journey with the Lord. It is an invitation to leave unhealthy life and sinful behaviors. It is about recognizing our fantasies of building a permanent home on this earth and rejecting the temptation to live in our own worlds. It is about being on the road with Jesus. The freer we are from all that is enslaving us the more available we can be to Jesus and his mission.

In his Sermon on the Mount, Jesus reminds us that it is futile to store up treasures on this earth because they don't last (Matt 6:19–21). They rust and rot. But many people develop and live with the fantasy that this world is going to be their permanent home. They get stuck with many things.

Jesus uses the parable of the rich fool who stored up wealth and possessions thinking that they were going to keep him on this earth forever (Luke 12:13–21). We know that none of us is going to carry anything from this world when we die. But that doesn't seem to stop many of us from accumulating things in our life. Like the rich fool many of us could be building castles and kingdoms as if they are going to keep us here forever. Greed becomes part of our life, and we keep feeding our greed. Sometimes some societies and cultures promote extreme narcissism and feed into the greed of their members. The rich fool may be an extreme case of narcissism. He talks to himself. And he congratulates himself. We may not be doing all that, but if we are not watchful, we could be sucked into greed and extreme narcissism.

The rich man had to leave everything behind and leave this world. He had to be on the journey. Some ancient people like the Egyptians are believed to have loved their earthly life so much that they entertained a false hope that they could go on with that life unendingly. Even mummifying their bodies seems to have risen out of their hope that they would come back to life to live the same or better life again. Many of us may not be much different from those ancient people. Our advancement in science and technology may have given us a false hope that we would live on this earth forever.

Jesus wants us to be free from such distorted ideas and false hopes. We may be able to prolong it a little longer, but this earthly life is going to be limited. No matter what fantasy we entertain, however much we acquire and accumulate, or however much we advance in science and technology, there is a limit to our physical life on this earth. Jesus reminds us that our life does not end with this earthly life and death is not something to be feared. Of course, death could be something scary for many of us. All of us are not prepared for death. Many of us may not have the courage and strength to face death as many heroic men and women did in our faith history. We might choose to stay alive if we had a choice. But we also want to live with the awareness that death is part of our journey. It is not the end but only a pause. If we are afraid of facing it, we keep praying for strength and courage. We also want to live with the awareness that our journey of life continues into eternity, and death simply moves us from the physical realm of this world to a limitless and eternal realm with God.

Jesus manifests that truth by his own death and resurrection. The events of Good Friday appear to be sad and scary. It seemed to be a victory for the powers of evil and sin. As he approached the impending suffering and death, even Jesus was troubled and anxious. He prayed to the father that the cup would pass from him. But he once again surrendered himself to the Father, and the Father sent him an angel to strengthen him.

With that strength he courageously faced the agony, and he knew that death was not the end. Good Friday was not the end of the story or the final chapter of his life. Cross and death did not have the final victory. He rose from death. He was victorious over suffering, sin, and death. Love was stronger than death. Mary Magdalene and some of the apostles went to the tomb looking for him. They all went to the tomb looking for a dead Jesus. They found that the stone that covered the tomb was rolled away. They gradually realized that Jesus was too big and too great to be contained by a tomb. No stone or cave could block him. He was on the journey.

The resurrection of Jesus proved to his disciples and others that death and this world were not the end. Life continued into eternity. But to enter into that realm of limitlessness and eternity he had to pass from the physical realm of this earthly life. That was a life changing experience for the apostles and other disciples of Jesus. When Jesus was crucified and killed they all ran away, scared, dejected, and disappointed. But the resurrection experience changed all that and brought them back. They were empowered by the Holy Spirit. The scared and disappointed apostles became bold preachers and missionaries. They were willing to do anything for Jesus. They were no more afraid of suffering and death. They realized that death was not the end, and it was not to be feared. The victory was with Jesus and not with death and suffering. Hence Saint Paul would ask, "Where, O death, is your victory? Where, O death, is your sting?" (1 Cor 15:55).

Like the events of Good Friday, there may be many things in our life that try to scare us. Illness, sufferings, loss, problems and worries, loneliness and sadness, betrayal and denial, and all such things might make us experience the darkness of Good Friday and the tomb. There may be many powers of evil that try to discourage us and silence us. There may be many personal crosses we have to bear and Calvaries that we have to mount. Death may be right before us staring at our face. But Jesus assures us that the darkness of Good Friday will move into the light of Easter and resurrection. Jesus by his own resurrections shows us that there is something beyond this world of sufferings and death. There is new life and eternity. The journey of our life continues. We are not to get stuck anywhere or with anything. To move into the realm of eternity and limitlessness we have to keep moving with Jesus and let go off many things, including our physical life. Jesus lived in history, but he was destined for something bigger. Hence he kept moving without getting stuck anywhere or with anything. That is another reason why he incarnated. It is to reveal to us the bigger picture of our lives and invite us to be on the journey with him.

26

Moving Past the Temptations and the Tomb

THE GOSPELS RELATE THAT Jesus faced many situations that came as stumbling blocks in his journey forward. They came in the form of temptations and trials leading all the way up to the tomb. But Jesus moved past all of them. Nothing could make him get stuck or shut him out.

We hear about the three prominent temptations in the gospel of Luke (Luke 4:1–13). They came in the form of physical delight, psychological satisfaction, and spiritual arrogance and isolation. Luke presents them as temptations that came to him before he began his public ministry, which might indicate that they were placed before him to make him stay and settle down, and stop him from being on the journey. They were all attractive and delightful, and anyone would have easily fallen for them. He was caught in the middle of moving on in his journey of fulfilling his Father's will and at the same time being tempted to stay and get stuck with these desirable and delightful offers.

The first temptation Jesus faced was in terms of satisfying his hunger. He was fasting for forty days and he was hungry. The devil said to him, "If you are the Son of God, command this stone to become a loaf of bread" (Luke 4:3). Jesus was the Son of God and he had the power to do anything. So the Devil most assuredly used that as an avenue to allure him. In other words, the Devil was saying, use your power and do whatever you can to satisfy your hunger. We know that is a very strong temptation that anybody could feel. It doesn't have to refer only to satisfying physical hunger. We experience all kinds of hunger, cravings, and desires. Our craving and desire may be for wealth, power, sex, domination, revenge, retaliation, and all such things. Our temptation may be to do whatever we can to satisfy that hunger. And many of us do many things to satisfy such hungers we carry. The question is whether all those hungers and desires are good and healthy. Just because we have certain kinds of hunger or cravings, and just because we have the power and resources to satisfy them, do we really have to do it? Do we have to get stuck with those hungers and cravings or can we move on?

Jesus countered the Devil by saying, "It is written, 'One does not live by bread alone'" (Luke 4:4). It is not only by bread that man lives. Jesus was not going to just focus on the immediate satisfaction of his desires and cravings. His focus was on the journey ahead, fulfilling his Father's will. He rejected that temptation to get stuck.

Desire or hunger for food is a rich and significant symbol in the scriptures. It could stand for our desires and cravings that are unhealthy and destructive. Once we give into that desire, we lose our freedom, dignity, honor, peace, and joy. We become slaves of that hunger or desire. We end up in sad situations. Adam and Eve gave into their hunger and desire for the forbidden fruit and sabotaged their growth and development (Gen 3). They were stuck. They were not walking with God anymore. They were not comfortable with each other any longer. Esau sold his birthright to his brother, Jacob for food (Gen 25:29–34). It might look like Jacob was cunning and cruel in taking away the birthright from his elder brother in the name of some bread and stew. But the story is much more than that. It could be pointing to what people do to throw away their birthright, their salvation, their peace and joy for some immediate satisfaction of their desires. They get stuck. The younger son in the parable of the prodigal son hungered for food and ended up with the pigs, the dirtiest animals (Luke 15). He lost his freedom and family, and he was stuck. After Jesus multiplied bread and fed the large crowd, people again came to him looking for more bread. And Jesus tells them not to look for bread that perishes, but for the bread that lasts for all eternity, which Jesus offers (John 6:27).

In all of these stories, bread or food stands for things and desires that are immediate, short-lived, unhealthy, and destructive. This temptation of Jesus to turn stones into bread could be seen as a warning against making choices that make us get stuck. It is about doing things against a true love of self. We will truly love ourselves when we try to nourish us with things that are really good. That would mean that we make choices that are healthy and good, choices and behaviors that take us forward in the journey of life. People make bad choices and become slaves of unhealthy and dangerous things and behaviors. They sabotage their own growth and development by giving into unhealthy cravings and desires. They get stuck. Although in many of the biblical stories bread or food represented things that were unhealthy and transient, it is important to note that Jesus used the same element of bread or food for his Eucharistic presence with us and nourishment for us. He becomes the new bread that gives the fullness of life and eternity. Instead of focusing on things that perish he wants us to focus on things that last, which basically involves a life in union with him.

The second temptation Jesus faced was to acquire power and riches of the world. He was presented with the kingdoms of the world, and the Devil said to him, "To you I will give their glory and all this authority; for it has been given over to me, and I give it to anyone I please. If you, then, will worship me, it will all be yours" (Luke 4:6–7). The whole focus is on increasing one's possessions and positions, seeking one's own needs and desires, and putting oneself above others. It is a temptation to become extremely narcissistic and seek one's physical and psychological satisfaction through unhealthy means. Jesus was not going to bow down before the devil to build up such a kingdom.

That is not the kind of kingdom that he was going to build. He was going to build a kingdom of love. He was not going to make it all about himself. It was about fulfilling his Father's will and manifesting his love in the world. He was engaged in the dialogical triangle rather than making it all about himself.

This is another strong temptation that we might experience in our life. The whole focus in our life could be about what we can accumulate and gather and how we can dominate over others. It becomes all about us. When we speak, it is all about us. When we do something, it's all about what we can gain from that. Our whole focus becomes establishing our kingdom or empire.

This temptation could be seen as a warning against selfishness and a call to true love of neighbor. It is about making space for others rather than building up one's own kingdom. People bow down before all kinds of things and worship the Devil. They separate themselves from others and create their own little world. Instead of bossing over others or turning against each other we are called to love and care for each other. We are called to be on the journey together.

The third temptation of Jesus was to jump down from the pinnacle of the temple. The Devil said to him, "If you are the Son of God, throw yourself down from here, for it is written, 'He will command his angels concerning you, to protect you,' and 'On their hands they will bear you up, so that you will not dash your foot against a stone'" (Luke 4:9–11). This was a temptation to show off and engage in some spiritual arrogance and exclusivism. He was tempted to show his super human powers and seek self-glorification. By doing that he could gather a crowd around him and establish his kingdom or group. This was a temptation to doubt and test his Father's love and work independent of him. Again it was a temptation to distract him from his mission of fulfilling his father's will and stop him from moving forward in his journey.

This could be a strong temptation for many of us. We may find ourselves on the pinnacle of the temple, that is—pride and self-glory, spiritual arrogance and exclusivism. It could come out through our words or actions. There may be moments when we act like God, forgetting that we are human beings with our own limitations and imperfections. We may be tempted to test and question God's love for us. We may be tempted to show off and work independent of God. All these block us from moving forward in our journey of life.

It appears that Jesus really struggled hard before he made some fundamental choices regarding what direction he should take in his life. Even the whole context of the temptations that the Evangelist Luke presents is very significant. Jesus was tested while praying and fasting in the desert for forty days before he began his public ministry (Luke 4:1–2). Desert is a place of extreme temperatures. During the day it could get extremely hot and dry. During the night, it could get extremely cold. It is a place of loneliness with nobody around. It is a place that could evoke scary feelings. It is a place deprived of nourishment and strength. The desert experience of Jesus could point to a very difficult time that he went through in his journey of life. Maybe sometimes he felt his life as dry as a desert. The questions might have been about whether he should stay, go backward, or move forward.

Forty days in the desert could mean a long time of difficulties and struggles. The number forty could be referring to the forty long years the Israelites travelled to move from Egypt to the Promised Land, from slavery to freedom. They struggled hard on the way. Many times they were tempted to go back to Egypt. Many times they were tempted to stay put. They found their forward movement hard and cumbersome. Prophet Elijah traveled for forty days and forty nights as he was escaping from King Ahab and Queen Jezebel who were trying to kill him (1 Kgs 19:8). He went through a very difficult time in his journey of life. Being exhausted and broken he even prayed to God that he would take his life. Forty days and forty nights could be referring to a long time of distress that he went through.

At the end of the story Luke says, "When the devil had finished every test, he departed from him until an opportune time (Luke 4:13). It seems like tests and temptations never left Jesus. They continued until the end. Even his crucifixion and death were ways to silence him. But he was victorious over all of them. When the women returned to the place where he was buried, they found that the stone was rolled away from the tomb (Luke 24:2). He was risen. Jesus proved to everyone that neither the temptations nor the tomb could shut him out. He was on the journey and nothing could make him get stuck.

The struggles, tests, and temptations of Jesus are only pointers to our own experiences in life. If Jesus was tempted and tested, we can be sure that we will not be spared from them. We experience deserts and temptations of many kinds in our lives. We experience times of extreme difficulties, doubts, disappointments, loneliness, fear, emotional and spiritual emptiness, sadness, and pain. Jesus overcame those temptations, but some of us may not find the same amount of strength and conviction in resisting them.

In Cognitive Processing Therapy (CPT), a treatment model that is widely used to treat posttraumatic stress disorder (PTSD), patients are often helped to identify, challenge, and change their "stuck points." Stuck points are defined as "conflicting beliefs or strong negative beliefs that create unpleasant emotions and problematic or unhealthy behaviors" (Resick, Monson, & Chard, 2014, p.41). To move into healthy living, patients have to get unstuck from their stuck points or inaccurate and unhelpful thoughts and feelings. There may be many things that make us get stuck in our life. We succumb to many temptations, defenses, and destructive desires, attitudes, and behaviors. We hold on to negative and distorted viewpoints, thoughts, and ideas. Many of these things make us get stuck and stop us from being on the journey with Jesus. It is important that we recognize and identify our stuck points so that we can get ourselves unstuck and be back on the journey with Jesus again. If we have fumbled and fallen Jesus wants us to lift ourselves up and keep moving. In Jesus we find a God who chooses and encourages us to choose good over evil, growth over stagnation, and life over death.

Part V

Living the Mystery

27

The Divine Dance

WE HAVE DISCUSSED IN some detail how God has been revealing himself or how we have been experiencing the mystery of God in our human and faith history. The Judeo-Christian traditions show us some very unique dimensions of this God. He created us out of love and continues to share that love with us at all times. In Jesus we see what that love means. This God whom we have known and experienced doesn't seem to be one who wants to be confined only to some structures and systems or theological concepts and theoretical discussions. He is one who is and who wants to be intimately close to us. He loves us and he desires that we reciprocate his love. Being created in his image and likeness means that we are created to be loving and loveable like him. God is not some impersonal object or mystery that dictates things to us. He is someone in whom we live, move, and have our being (Acts 17:28). Hence it is not enough to unravel and understand the mystery of God, it is also important to live that mystery in our lives. The revelation needs a response.

True love involves a "personal signature" on the covenant and commitment that is established between two parties. When someone says, "I love you," we reciprocate that sentiment by saying, "I love you too." When our love is true and strong we not only feel and express it in words but also translate it into action. Love seeks reciprocity and union. When two people intensely love each other, they long to be together as much as and as frequently as possible. Our God longs to be with us, and he desires that we long to be with him. He is not simply a mystery that reveals and remains on the intellectual level.

It is like a dance, a dance between two partners or lovers. Both dance to the tune of love, and they dance until they are in each other's arms. We are engaged in a dance with the divine. Our God, the divine dancer has entered into an eternal dance with us, human beings. He desires that we partner with him in that dance, beginning with our physical life on this earth and continuing it into our life in eternity.

Partnering with the divine dancer in the reciprocation of his love would mean what I called in my previous book, *The Accent*, "surviving and thriving well." I talked about two motivating instincts that we, human beings, have—the "Drive to Survive

(DTS)" and the "Drive to Thrive (DTT)." These two instincts are very important to consider when it comes to living our lives well. The drive to survive (DTS), I said, is a basic need of all living organisms, including human beings. We want to survive or stay alive. To accomplish whatever it is meant to accomplish, an organism first needs to stay alive. But survival is not easy for anyone. There are many challenges that come on our way physically and psychologically that threaten our survival. Each organism employs all the resources available to it to fight all the odds and stay afloat. Some succeed and some fail. However, everyone is driven by this need for survival. Until death puts a natural end to that need, each of us fights to stay alive.

The Drive to Thrive (DTT) on the other hand is the phenomenon that facilitates our growth and development. It is a phenomenon that helps us to bring the best out of ourselves and live well. It helps us to blossom to our highest potential, bringing honor and glory to our creator. When it comes to the drive to survive, it applies to all living organisms. Every organism needs and tries hard to stay alive. But when it comes to the drive to thrive, there is a difference between human beings and other organisms. Simply as a movement towards higher levels of growth and development, the drive to thrive might look common to all organisms. But as a phenomenon open to one's conscious awareness, I suggested that it pertains only to human beings. Or we could say that the way God wants us to thrive is different from how other beings are called to thrive. Only we, the human beings can think of bringing the best out of ourselves in the physical, spiritual, intellectual, emotional, and all other realms that apply to our lives. As far as we know, no other organism possesses constructs and faculties like will, intellect, emotions, intuition, imagination, reason, and memory as we do. No other organism can think about their thinking, feel about their feelings, and imagine about their imaginations. No other organism is capable of accomplishing all that we have accomplished, whether it is in the field of music, art, architecture, science, technology, philosophy, theology, or any other area of ingenuity and excellence. We are uniquely gifted, and when rightly channeled these gifts take us to the best of our being.

Although these two phenomena of DTS and DTT are meant to help us to bring the best out of ourselves, I also mentioned that sometimes we engage in negative survival and thriving. Some of us also may be just surviving and not thriving well. When we do that we neither bring the best out of ourselves nor allow anyone else to do the same. When we take the negative route we will not be much concerned about the higher levels of healthy growth and development or bringing the best out of ourselves. We will be caught up in a negative survival and thriving mode, bringing the worst out of ourselves. We will become aggressive, manipulative, destructive, deceptive, and evil. We will be on a path of self-destruction and doing harm to others. When we do that we are not engaged in the dance with our divine dancer but rather in a solo dance of our own. We will be like those that Saint Paul refers to in his letter to the Philippians, "Their end is destruction; their god is the belly; and their glory is in their shame; their minds are set on earthly things" (Phil 3:19).

All of us are driven by the two phenomena of DTS and DTT. We all want to and need to survive and thrive. But the question is whether we are just surviving or we are also thriving? And if we are thriving, are we thriving well or are we engaging in negative and unhealthy thriving? What we need is to engage in positive survival and thriving. And positive survival and thriving are about partnering with our divine dancer and dancing to the tune of love.

Saint Francis de Sales, the Bishop of Geneva, who lived in the late sixteenth and early seventeenth century in France, is known for a famous saying, "Be who you are and be that well." Besides his episcopal responsibilities, Francis was a greatly sought after spiritual director. One of the women who sought his guidance was Madame Brulart, the wife of Nocolas Brulart, president of the Burgundian Parliament. In one of the letters that Francis wrote to Madame Brulart, he said, "It seems to me that white is not the color proper to roses, for red roses are more beautiful and more fragrant; however, white is the distinctive characteristic of lilies. *Let us be what we are and be that well,* in order to bring honor to the Master Craftsman whose handiwork we are" (De Sales & De Chantal, 1988).

All of us are called to dance to the tune of divine love, but all of are not called to do that in the exact same way. Just as roses and lilies have characteristics unique to each of them and they are beautiful in their own distinctive ways, all of us are unique in our own ways, and we are called to bring out our beauty and best in our own distinctive ways. Saint Paul speaks of this distinctiveness in each of us, "Now there are varieties of gifts, but the same Spirit; and there are varieties of services, but the same Lord; and there are varieties of activities, but it is the same God who activates all of them in everyone . . . " (1 Cor 12:5–10). Each one of us is gifted, and recognizing what we are good at, each one of us is called to bring out the best in us. Paul then uses the example of human body to demonstrate how each organ of the body has a specific function and how the body maintains its health only when each organ does its work well (1 Cor 12:14–26).

God does not ask all of us to do the same thing, but he desires that all of us give our best in what we are good at. Jesus highlights this idea of giving our best in the parable of the talents (Matt 25:14–30). Three persons were given talents according to each one's ability, and they were asked to trade and multiply them. The servants who received five and two talents took personal responsibility to fulfill the intentions of the master. They invested well, worked hard, and brought out rich results. They were not just surviving; they were thriving well. They partnered with the master and his will. But one servant was too narrow minded, lazy, and wicked. Instead of taking the responsibility of doing something with what he received, he began to scrutinize the intentions of the master and wasted his time and talent. He was just surviving and failed to thrive well. He was dancing to his own tune rather than joining with the master.

Some of us may be like the first two servants. We may have partnered well with God and given our best or are trying to give our best in what we are good at. We may be not only surviving but also thriving well. We may be good dance partners with our divine dancer. If we find ourselves doing well, our call is to keep growing and doing our best. The two servants in the parable brought to the master the fruit of their labor. They did not keep it for themselves. When we survive and thrive well, we are reciprocating God's love. God gives us his best and we give our best to him. We don't live for ourselves. When roses bloom, they look beautiful and many people delight in them. But they also bring joy and fragrance to others. Similarly when we do well with our life bringing the best out of ourselves, we might receive accolades and appreciation. But more than all the appreciation and adulation we receive, we become a blessing to others and bring glory to God.

We could wonder why God needs all glory and honor or why we need to dance to his tune. Sometimes there is a lot of emphasis given to giving glory to God or God is presented as someone who deserves our praise and thanksgiving. In the book of Isaiah, we read that God created us for his glory (Isa 43:7). Hearing such things we might wonder whether he is narcissistic and self-obsessed. Does his existence depend on all the glory and honor he receives from us? I don't think so. It is not about God seeking glory, honor, and praise. It is about God glorying in our glory and honor. The glory and honor that God receives is similar to the glory and honor that parents receive when their children do well or are honored and glorified for something. It is similar to the glory and honor a friend receives when his or her friend does well or is honored and glorified.

The parents rejoice in the glory and honor bestowed on their children or a friend rejoices when his or her friend is bestowed with some honor and glory. Sometimes the children or friends might bestow glory and praise on their parents or friends out of love and respect but that doesn't mean that the latter are looking and living for it. Some parents might see their children as extensions of their narcissistic self and expect their children to praise and glorify them but that is not something usual of loving parents. If they feel honored and glorified, it is something that they experience as a result of what is bestowed upon their loved ones.

Our God is not a God who seeks honor and glory as it is often depicted. Of course, as our creator and divine lover, he deserves our honor, love, and praise. Taking into consideration all that God has done for us, we cannot but praise and glorify him. But he is not a bully who scares us with things and gets what he wants or forces us to praise and honor him. He is a God who has loved us into being and who continues to love us no matter what. His glory is in our glory. As his beloved children, he wants to see us living well. When we live well, he is honored and glorified just as parents or friends feel honored and glorified when their children or loved ones live and do well.

Roses and lilies do not resent their flowers. God does not resent us. He rather rejoices in us. He delights and rejoices when we join him in the dance of love just as a lover rejoices when his beloved dances with him. He is glorified when we shine forth in love and bring the best out of ourselves. A saying that is often attributed to Saint Irenaeus of Lyons is "The glory of God is the human person fully alive." When we reciprocate God's love and bring the best out of ourselves, we become fully alive. And when we become fully alive, God is glorified. God knows that we experience the fullness of life only when we are united with him. Cut away from him, our life is incomplete. Hence he wants us to be with him. Although parents need to respect and value the independence of their children, we could also think that most parents expect their children to be united with them. They rejoice when the whole family is together. A family is a family only when everyone loves each other and stays united. God's family is fractured and incomplete when we stay away from him or do not survive and thrive well.

The master rejoiced and was honored when the two servants did well with their talents. And because they did well, the two servants were given more responsibilities. We never stop growing. There is always something that we can do to become better and better. We have to keep thriving in the best way we can. When we live well and shine forth in love, God is going to take us to higher levels of growth and development. And when we do well again, God is going to be honored and glorified again.

Some of us may have turned out to be like the last servant who buried the talent. We may not have done well with our life and with what God has given us. We may have spent our time and energy on useless and meaningless things. We may have made bad choices and engaged in bad and unhealthy behaviors. We may have scrutinized the intentions of God and others and blamed them for everything that has gone bad in our life as the lazy servant did. We may have engaged in our own solo dance or gone out of tune in our steps. We may be caught up in negativity and narrow-mindedness. We may be just surviving rather than thriving well. If we find ourselves in that category, we can always start anew. We all start somewhere.

The dance is on, and the divine dancer wants us to partner with him. We discussed about many individuals in our human and faith history who partnered with God in the dance of divine love. Today, at this particular time in our human history, it is our turn to enter into that dance. The dancers on the stage are the same—God and human beings. And the tune or melody is the same—love. But the way we dance to that tune with our divine lover is unique and different for each one of us. Maybe some of us are called like Abraham to leave our country and kindred and go to a place that he is going to show—that is, entering into a new horizon of physical, psychological, and spiritual renewal and transformation.

God may be asking us to leave our "Egypts" that are keeping us in slavery and follow him into the Promised Land of freedom and holiness as he did with the Israelites. Maybe he is calling some of us to be a prophetic voice in today's world as he called Prophets Elijah, Isaiah, Jeremiah, and others. He may be calling us to be like Mary and Joseph to cooperate with him to make his love and presence come alive in the particular contexts of our lives. God may be wishing that we come to our senses, turn away from our sins, and return back home as the younger son in the parable of the prodigal son did. It could be that he is calling us to get up from our tax booths of sins and evils and follow him as Matthew, the tax collector did. He could be asking us to leave our boats and nets, leave everything that is holding us back from Jesus and follow him as Peter, Andrew, James, and John did. He may be telling us to sell and let go off things that are holding us slaves as he told the rich young man. Maybe he is asking us to let go off some of our distorted images and ideas of him and rise up to a new understanding as he asked Mary Magdalene and other disciples to do. There may be all kinds of ways in which God is calling each one of us to respond to him and participate in his divine dance of love. The mystery of God that has been revealed and continues to reveal to us needs a response from us.

28

The Christological Model

MANY COMPANIES AND ORGANIZATIONS have what they call the Standard Operating Procedures or SOPs. The SOPs are put in place to ensure efficiency, quality of service or product, and reduction of attrition, failure, mismanagement, wastage, and mis-communication. When I think of our participation in the divine dance of love or our response to the mystery of God, the Standard Operating Procedure that comes to my mind is one based on the life of Christ. It is Christological. There is none other than Christ himself who can show us best how to partner with God in the dance of love. He said, "I am the way, and the truth, and the life" (John 14:6). He didn't say, "I will show you the way, the truth, and the life" but instead, "I am the way, the truth, and the life."

Living in him and allowing him to live in us is what helps us to experience the fullness of life. And that essentially means living a Christological life, which is to be in a triangular dialogical relationship involving God, self, and others or the community. If we build and live our lives after this Christological Model, we will be partnering with God in the divine dance of love and bringing the best out of ourselves. I shall once again provide here the pictorial illustration of the triangular dialogical relationship or the Christological model of life.

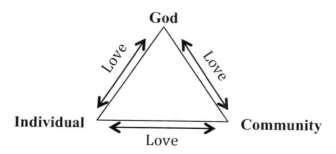

The Christological Model

There are three dimensions to the Christological model. First, the Christological model is Trinitarian in its nature, which is represented by the triangle in the illustration. The three parts or players in the relationship are God, the individual, and the community. If we want to respond to the mystery of God and reciprocate his love, we need to participate in the life of the Holy Trinity and live a Trinitarian life. Just as the three persons of the Holy Trinity, the Father, the Son, and the Holy Spirit are unique in themselves but are inseparably united with each other, we need to enter into a dialogue and discernment with God and one another. In this model, there is a place for God, a place for others or the community, and a place for ourselves. The relationship between the three components is dialogical. The arrows in the illustration represent this dialogical relationship. It is neither a top-down nor a bottom-up spirituality or relationship. It is dialogical. Each of the components is dynamically and positively present to each other and is in dialogue with each other. All the three components together make up one family. With God and others we are one family like the Holy Trinity.

The component of the community or others includes everything and everyone other than God and the individual. If I am the individual in the dialogical triangle, then my community includes you because you are part of my life. I am not an isolated individual. So we could say that the dialogical triangle is made up of you, God, and I. But when I think of my community, it is more than one person. It also includes my family, my faith community, my colleagues at work, my neighbors, my social and friendship groups, the society in which I live, my country or nation, the world at large, and the rest of the creation. All these are part of my community and part of my life, some having immediate and significant impact on my life and others remotely connected to me.

The second dimension of the Christological model is that it is all about love. God is love, and the glue that keeps the Holy Trinity united with each other is love. The way God has revealed himself to us, particularly through the person of Jesus is as love. That same love becomes the glue that facilitates our dialogue or relationship with God and others. If we want to partner with God in the dance of love, we need to remain united with him and one another in love. Just as Jesus incarnated as love, we as individuals and communities need to incarnate ourselves as love wherever we are. We need to manifest the mystery of God and the mystery of our lives by living loving lives. This love is not anything mysterious. God has gifted us with his love. There is love in all of us. Because of many reasons, we may not be manifesting that love. But if we permit, it can come alive again.

The third dimension of the Christological model is that it is a journey, a journey with God and others, which begins here on earth and continues into eternity. The double-headed arrows between the three components in the illustration represent the uninterrupted and constant movement in our relationships and journey of life. If we want to partner with God in the dance of love, we have to be on the journey with him. Our God is a God of the temple and the tent. He is a God who is uniquely present to each one of us, but he is also universally present to all creation. He lives with us and moves with us. Our life is also a journey with others. We are fellow travelers. To journey with God and others, we need to make effort to pluck ourselves out of all our physical, psychological, and spiritual stuck points. We need to keep moving forward with faith and confidence in the Lord who is leading and journeying with us.

This moving forward has to happen more in the psychological and spiritual sense than in the physical sense. Physically we don't need to move all the time or frequently unless we are called to such ways that necessitates frequent movement. But psychologically and spiritually all of us need to keep moving and changing all the time. Everyday we have to grow in love. Everyday we have to dialogue with God and others. Everyday we have to be in harmony with our creator and the whole creation. Everyday we have to remain open to new ways in which God reveals himself. Everyday we have to be willing to change and transform our distorted ideas and images that we have of God, others, and ourselves. Physical movement may not be too hard. What is more important and difficult is psychological and spiritual movement. Physically we may be moving around frequently, but if we don't allow the Lord to transform us and move forward psychologically and spiritually, we will not be living the Christological model in our lives and participating in the divine dance of love.

In the Christological model of life, God is the center that holds everything together. Both the individual and the community are to be participants in the mission of God, which is to participate in the divine dance and manifest his love in this world. Hence, we as individuals and communities need to be in dialogue with God. As one family and one community, the whole creation needs to be united with the creator. We do not thrive well without God. Our mission is God's mission.

In the Christological model, the individual is an inevitable part. A family or community is made up of individuals. In the family of God, every individual person has a place. Both saints and sinners are part of the family. As individuals, each one of us is uniquely gifted and blessed, and God values our uniqueness. God sees each one of us as a special person. We have our God-given gifts and talents that God wants us to develop and excel in to make our lives better and make this world a better place. The community and the world thrive only when its individual members thrive. The divine dancer needs each one of us to partner with him to keep the dance of love going.

Just as the individual person and God are important parts in the dialogical triangle, so is the community or others. An individual cannot survive and thrive well without the community or others. The community or others need to be an integral part of the person's growth and development. We are not created to be isolated individuals. We are a community of persons. If the individual members of the family do not care about the family, the family does not stay together. It will break apart. And when the family is broken apart, it negatively affects the growth and development of the individual members. To survive and thrive well, we need others and the creation. God calls us into the divine dance not only as individuals but also as communities.

Just as it is in the Holy Trinity, none of the components of the triangle is kept out of the dialogue, and none of them dominates. All the three components are constantly in dialogue with each other. They develop a loving relationship between them. Even though our mission is God's mission, even God does not dominate. He instead remains as the servant. The dialogue is not simply about talking but rather about developing a loving and supportive relationship where due respect and value is given to the uniqueness of each of the components and at the same time they preserve the unity between all three of them. They are actively, lovingly, and mindfully present to each other. They journey together. If any of these components is excluded or if there is any interruption or imbalance in the dialogue between the three components, the actualization of the Christological model is going to be highly compromised. To participate in the divine dance of love, we have to ensure a healthy balance between the three components in the dialogical triangle. A Well-balanced loving relationship between God, the individual, and the community or others leads to the fulfillment of the two commandments that Jesus placed before us, loving God and loving our neighbor as ourselves. In the next few chapters we shall discuss the first dimension of the Christological model of life, its Trinitarian nature.

29

Make Disciples of All Nations

As his disciples and children, Jesus invites us to partner with him in the divine dance by living a Trinitarian life. If we want to be Christ-like and live the dialogical triangle, our participation in the life of the Holy Trinity is inevitable. To his disciples, it was given as a commandment and not an option. He told them, "Go therefore and make disciples of all nations, baptizing them in the name of the Father and of the Son and of the Holy Spirit, and teaching them to obey everything that I have commanded you. And remember, I am with you always, to the end of the age" (Matt 28:19–20).

We need to understand what this command really means. It has been often mis-conceived and misinterpreted as a command to go to different parts of the world to conquer and forcibly convert people into Christianity. Changing people's names and religion by force is not what Jesus commanded. We can forcibly change people's names and religions, but that is not going to change their hearts and lives. That is not going to make them Christ-like or help them to become partners in the divine dance. What Jesus desired is a change of heart and lives, a participation of every individual person in the divine dance of love. And that becomes possible only when we are truly baptized into the Trinitarian life, which essentially involves actualizing the dialogical triangle in our lives. We have to be in communion with God and others. Our lives have to be ruled by the law of love. That is the message and mission that Jesus desired his disciple to take to the ends of the earth.

Desiring that a dialogical triangle of relationships after the example of the Holy Trinity exist in our lives and relationships, Jesus prayed, " . . . that they may all be one. As you, Father, are in me and I am in you, may they also be in us" (John 17:21). In the prayer that Jesus taught his disciples, he desired that we seek God's will and live in harmony with one another. Jesus also desires that we live a life in communion with God and with one another because we are created in the image and likeness of the Trinitarian God.

Actualizing the dialogical triangle and being baptized into the Trinitarian life first of all involves an awareness of the presence of God or the Holy Trinity in our lives. We need to believe that our heavenly Father who created us deeply loves us and cares about us. He knows our struggles and trials. As he walked with our ancestors and helped them to move on in their life journey, he walks with us today in our present times and helps us to keep moving forward. He is who he is at all times. His love and concern for us never diminish. As we realize this everlasting love and abiding presence of the Father, we are to take that message to the ends of the earth, starting with our immediate family and friends and then extending to others outside of our familiar territories. We need to let everyone know that this heavenly Father is the Father of us all. We are all his children, and he loves us and cares about us irrespective of what culture or community we belong to, what language we speak, how we look, and what we do. We have to help people know that this loving Father knows them, especially their sufferings and struggles and that he would give them strength and grace to keep moving forward.

We need to know and believe that Jesus walks with us in our life journey as our Savior and friend. He is with us to save us from all that is evil and unhealthy and we don't need to be afraid of the terrors of evil. He comes to lift us up when we fail and fall or when we feel weak, lost, and lonely. He is a loving and merciful Savior. He is united with us. When we are in agony and pain, he is in agony and pain. When we are on the cross, he is on the cross. He would do anything for us to show us how much he loves us. Following him is following the path of health and wholeness, life in communion with God and one another. We need to take this message to the ends of the earth, starting with our immediate family and friends and then extending it to others outside of our familiar surroundings. We need to let everyone know about this redeeming love of God in Jesus who laid down his life for us. We need to let everyone know that Jesus died for all and not for just one group or class of people. He is a Savior and friend to all. When it comes to Jesus' love for us, there is no discrimination. He loves us all.

We need to know and believe that we are the temples of the Holy Spirit and that the Spirit continues to be with us as a loving companion to guide us and strengthen us. The same Spirit who led our ancestors, the same Spirit who strengthened and transformed the timid and fearful disciples, and the same Spirit who has been actively present in our world from the beginning of creation until now lives with us today in our present times. That Spirit can strengthen and transform us today. The Spirit can lead us from darkness to light and unhealthy situations to healthy lives. We need to remain open to the voice and guidance of the Spirit. We need to take this message of the ever-abiding presence of the Holy Spirit to the ends of the earth, starting with our immediate family and friends and then extending it to others who are not in our circle of friends and familiar surroundings. We need to let everyone know that they are the temples of the Holy Spirit, the dwelling places of God. We need to let everyone know that they need to remain open to the voice and guidance of the Holy Spirit to live healthy and holy lives. We need to remind them that with the Holy Spirit walking with them they should not be afraid of the evils, sufferings, and turmoil that life brings. Instead of surrendering to the demons within us and outside of us, we need to surrender to the Spirit of God who empowers us.

This is how we participate in the dialogical triangle and the divine dance of love. We are called to be aware of and experience the presence of the Holy Trinity in our own lives and we are commissioned to take that message to the ends of the earth. If we are the temples of the Holy Spirit, God dwells in us. The Father, Jesus, and the Holy Spirit are present in us at all times, in our joys and sorrows, in our darkness and pain. Everyone needs to know that they live, move, and have their being in this ever-loving and eternal God (Acts 17:28). Simply giving people Christian names or forcing them to convert to Christianity is not what Jesus meant by missionary work or baptizing in the name of the Holy Trinity.

Actualizing the dialogical triangle in our life and participating in the divine dance of love involve not only being aware of the presence of the Holy Trinity in our lives but also building our lives after the model of the Holy Trinity. It is in the image and likeness of the Trinitarian God that we are created. We are created as unique individuals with no other person in this world like us whatsoever. As unique individuals, we differ in many ways. We belong to different cultures and communities. We look and think different. We speak different languages. We differ in our age, gender, race, and nationality. We understand and perceive things differently. We feel and act differently. We differ in our family backgrounds and upbringing. We differ in our beliefs and practices, and customs and traditions. But with all these differences and uniqueness, we are still a family or community as children of God. We are all brothers and sisters created by the same God. We are like the Holy Trinity, unique as individual persons, but united as one family or community. We are one with God and others.

When Jesus asked his disciples to go to all corners of the earth and baptize everyone in the name of the Father, and of the Son, and of the Holy Spirit, it is this message of the Trinitarian life that he asked them to spread. Everyone is to be made aware of this identity they have. They are unique individuals but they are also a brother or sister to everyone else in the world. We are fellow creatures or beings to the rest of the creation. We are one family. All of us are to live our lives with this awareness. We have to respect each other's uniqueness, respect every being in this creation, and at the same time, we have to maintain our unity as one family. We are a universal family united with God and one another.

Love is the force that connects us and helps us to respect each other and maintain our unity. When we love each other as God loves us we will be able to maintain our unity as one family. It may be impossible to obtain that perfect love and perfect unity in this world, but perfection is a work in progress. It is dynamic rather than static. We are not looking to be finished products but to be clay in the potter's hand (Jer 18:4).

Jesus reminds us of this idea of the universal family of God when someone reported to him about his mother and brothers waiting to see him, "Your mother and your brothers are standing outside, wanting to speak to you" (Matt 12:47). The occasion was a public speaking event of Jesus. He was speaking to the crowds teaching them many things when his mother and relatives came to see him. We don't know what the purpose of their visit was. The gospel simply says that they wanted to speak to him. Maybe his family was upset and angry with him for all the unrest and turmoil he was causing in the community by his teaching and preaching. There were occasions when his family went to take him home forcefully because the people were saying that he was mad. They might have forced Mary to go with them thinking that he would listen to her and stop his wayward lifestyle. It could have been also because Mary wanted to see him. It could be that he was away from home for a long time and she was missing him. But because he was wandering from place to place, Mary probably needed the help of some of her relatives to take her to where he was. It could have been also because she was a woman and it was not safe and against the societal expectations for women to go to places alone, especially where big crowds gathered.

Whatever must have been the reason for their presence there, Jesus uses the occasion to teach the crowd a greater lesson. To the one who reported about his mother and brothers, "Jesus replied, 'Who is my mother, and who are my brothers?' And pointing to his disciples, he said, 'Here are my mother and my brothers! For whoever does the will of my Father in heaven is my brother and sister and mother'" (Matt 12:48–50). It might sound like Jesus was insulting or ignoring his mother and relatives. That doesn't seem to be the case. The gospels tell us that Jesus spent time in Nazareth with his family and acquaintances. He must have spent a lot of time with Mary at home. He doesn't appear to be someone who would disrespect his mother or family. But this particular occasion was used to teach the crowd a greater lesson. Jesus was reminding them that when it comes to his love, everyone was important. He did not exclude anyone from his love. His love goes beyond the immediate family and blood relations. His love was not limited to one class or group of people. Everyone who did the will of his heavenly father or participated in the divine dance of love was going to be his family. And there was none better than Mary who did that. She was one who did the will of God in the most faithful way. So when Jesus said that those who did the will of his father were his family, it definitely applied to her first before anybody else. He was in fact acknowledging her rather than ignoring her.

To live the Christological model in our life, we need to gradually rise above our small families and immediate relationships and see everyone as our family. We are all brothers and sisters united in the Lord. When we are united with God and one another in love, we become the family of Jesus. Then we become baptized into the life of the Holy Trinity.

This life modeled after the Holy Trinity has much to teach us for our everyday life. In a family, for example, each member is unique but everyone together makes up the family. They live and function as one unit. If each one begins to do what he or she wants then there is no sense of family, there is no unity. If the family does not value and acknowledge the uniqueness and giftedness of each member then the members do not receive the love and support they need to grow and develop. For the family to be Trinitarian and participate in the dance of divine love, every member of the family has to be accepted and loved for his or her uniqueness and at the same time every member has to work hard to maintain the unity of the family. They need to build their lives on love. They need to have an uninterrupted dialogue. God and love become the guiding force in their discernment and decision-making process. Everyone has a different role to play, but no one dominates. They seek what is good for each one and for the family. In such a family, there is no place for abuse, aggression, or exclusion.

The same principle applies to a community, group, nation, and the world. Every one of our relationship settings needs to have its life modeled on the Holy Trinity and the dialogical triangle. We respect the uniqueness of each individual promoting everyone's growth and development and at the same time we work hard to preserve the unity of the group, community, nation, or the world.

To make disciples of all nations, Christians need to model for others the Trinitarian way of life. Just as the three persons of the Holy Trinity value each other's uniqueness, a disciple of Jesus needs to acknowledge and value the uniqueness and giftedness of the people he or she serves, whether it is in a family, community, or the larger society. If a Christian denigrates, devalues, and disrespects other people, their culture, and their uniqueness and tries to impose his or her ideas, beliefs, and practices he or she goes against the spirit of the command of Jesus. Similarly just as the three persons of the Holy Trinity are inseparably united, a Christian or disciple of Jesus needs to be one who brings unity and peace wherever he or she is. If the disciple becomes a cause of division rather than the glue that unites people or community then he or she goes against the spirit of the command of Jesus.

The missionary work of baptizing people into the Trinitarian life and the divine dance of love has to continue until it reaches to the ends of the earth. All people of all nations have to come to know the love of the Trinitarian God and be united as they are. Unfortunately that is not how the message of Jesus has been taken to many parts of the world. The Christian missionaries have done incredible amount of good all around the world. But in many places many missionaries have been seen as associates or agents of suppressive and subjugating powers and divisive ideologies. In many places, Christianity has been perceived as a religion concerned more about increasing the membership than as a way of life that brings people closer to God and one another. In many cultures and societies, Christians have lived as exclusive groups and engaged in hatred, violence, and discriminations based on race, ethnicity, caste, language, and denominations. In many Christian communities, undue emphasis has been given to external appearances and rubrics that the importance of the internal dynamic of living as a loving community has been sidetracked. In many Christian communities, the members get sucked into and profess their allegiance to certain political and other types of ideologies, and they not only end up in rival camps but also make Jesus as their patron. Jesus thus becomes a communist, capitalist, conservative, liberal, moderate, and all such things. All such distorted presentations of Jesus and divisions in the community need to stop. Jesus is not a communist or capitalist, conservative or liberal. Jesus is Jesus, and we are all brothers and sisters in him. We are to live as a loving and unified family. Any temptation to move away from this ideal is contrary to our Christological and Trinitarian identity.

The dialogical triangle or Trinitarian model of life needs to be extended to the world outside of the human circle. We need to build a life in harmony with the rest of the creation. We are one with the whole creation. God is the author of all that is, and we are fellow creatures with the rest of the creation. As our creator is in the dance of love with the whole creation, we need to be in that dance of love with the rest of the creation. We are not licensed to abuse or disrespect other beings. Given the special status as children of God created in his image and likeness does not mean that we can be dominating and exploitative. Instead we have a special charge to be good and responsible stewards. Referring to this special status and stewardship, I wrote in my previous book, *The Accent*, "God wills that we care for the rest of the creation as he himself does. Our intelligence is not given for self-aggrandizement or exploitation but rather for making this world a wonderful place for everyone to live in. We become cocreators with God to add to the beauty and blessings of this world" (p. 156). Pope Francis has a whole encyclical letter on care for the creation, particularly our earth, titled, *Laudato Si*.

Going to the whole world and baptizing people in the name of the Holy Trinity is thus about all of us participating in the divine dance of love and helping others to do the same. It is about living and helping others to live the Christological model of life. It is about spreading the message of our uniqueness and unity by our very life and presence. We have to be loving and caring like God the Father to those whom we serve. We need to be forgiving and compassionate like Jesus to those who walk with us and we come across in our life journey. We need to be a comforting and guiding companion like the Holy Spirit to those entrusted to our care. We need to be the glue that unites people with our love. We need to keep the dialogical triangle going uninterrupted.

To live the Christological model and participate in the divine dance of love is often a challenge because there are so many things in our lives that divide and disunite us. There are many things that we do to cause harm and hurt to each other. Sometimes love is not the guiding force in our life. Dialogues are either interrupted or non-existent. There are tendencies in many of us to isolate ourselves from others and live in our own world.

However, there is also a lot of goodness in each one of us. When we recognize that, we can always strive to work toward making our lives better. If we stay inside a room and close all our doors and windows, the sun will not have much effect on us. We will not see the light of the sun, and we will not experience the warmth of the sun. To see the sun, to see its light, and experience its warmth, we have to go out of our room or house. Staying inside will keep us in cold and darkness. Closed up in ourselves, we will remain in darkness and cold. Without God and others, we are incomplete. To be true to ourselves, we need to preserve our unity as one family. This Trinitarian dimension of the Christological model is a commandment for Christians to live it in their own lives and teach others to do the same. Christians cannot afford to be agents of division and exclusion and still claim to be Christians. If we become agents of division and exclusion, we will be wrongly representing Jesus and doing a great disservice to his command of making disciples of all nations. We are called to be the salt of the earth and the light of the world (Matt 5:13–16), and for that we first need to be Trinitarian in our life and relationships.

30

The Triangular Dialogue

LIVING A TRINITARIAN LIFE is all about ensuring and maintaining a healthy balance in the triangular relationship between God, others, and ourselves. If any of the components is excluded or stays away, the dialogue is interrupted and the relationship is compromised. There needs to be a due place for God, a due place for us, and a due place for others or the rest of the creation in our lives. All the three components have to be actively engaged in a loving relationship all the time. Many of the problems in our life are due to the imbalance in the dialogical triangle because of the exclusion or withdrawal of one or two of the components. When there is an exclusion or imbalance in the dialogical relationship, our lives are no more Christological or patterned after the life of the Holy Trinity. We shall look at why the dialogue between God, the individual, and the community is important for our life and relationships.

Dialogue with God

If we want to respond to the mystery of God and be active participants in the divine dance of love, God needs to be the first and foremost on our list of priorities. Excluding God from our life or keeping ourselves away from God is going to be self-destructive because as individuals and communities we have our existence in and through him. He brought us into being out of his love. Keeping him away from our life would mean keeping ourselves away from the circle of life and love.

God is constantly in dialogue with us. He knocks on our door inviting us to respond to his love. To live healthy lives we need to respond to that invitation and reciprocate his love. We need to be in constant dialogue with him as Jesus was dialoging with the heavenly Father and the Holy Spirit. That is what we essentially mean by prayer. Prayer is a dialogue between God and us. God dialogues with us and we dialogue with him. We listen to him as he listens to us. We clear our minds and hearts from all distractions so that we can listen and be attuned to the voice of God. The dialogue is in view of growing in communion with God so as to reach a point where we can say like Jesus, "I and the Father are one" (John 10:30) and "My food is to do the will of the Father" (John 4:34). Prayer or dialogue with God is to be a process through which we ensure that we are in tune with God's will.

There are many stories and instances in the Bible where Jesus exhorts his people to get their priorities straight by putting God first in their life and growing in communion with him. One of those occasions was when some of the Pharisees and Herodians in an attempt to trap Jesus asked him whether it was lawful to pay taxes to the Roman emperor (Mark 12:13–17). If he said that it was not lawful to pay taxes to the emperor, they could say that he was a rebel and enemy of Rome and get him into trouble with the Roman authorities. If he said that it was lawful to pay taxes to the emperor, they could accuse him of being a supporter of pagans and foreign rulers and an enemy of the Jews. But Jesus knew their evil thoughts. He was much smarter than they thought. His answer silenced them. He told them to give to the emperor what belonged to the emperor and to God what belonged to God.

We belong to a certain country, state, and community. There are certain responsibilities that come with that affiliation and membership. We fulfill those responsibilities for the good of the community or nation. The leader or ruler of the community or nation may be a tyrant like many of the Roman emperors were. But that doesn't mean that we can avoid our responsibilities to the community or nation. Rulers and those who govern will come and go. Some of them may be good, and some of them may be bad. We still haven't found a perfect system of governance or a perfect ruler anywhere in the world. And sometimes we don't have much choice in who governs or how we are governed. But irrespective of who they are or what kind of government we are presented with, we are going to be part of a nation, kingdom, or system of governance. If it is an unjust and tyrannical system or government, we can protest or fight to change it, but still we are going to be part of the nation or kingdom. The government or the head of the government might change, but we continue to be part of the kingdom or nation. And sometimes our citizenship itself changes when we move to another country or kingdom. But wherever we may be, we would belong to some country, kingdom, and community, and we have responsibilities as citizens or members. Our responsibility is more to the community or nation than to a particular individual or government.

A disciple of Jesus has to be a good citizen, a good member of the community wherever he or she may be. Jesus was not going to contest that. But Jesus was also reminding us that we have another citizenship. We belong to a larger kingdom, God's kingdom. That is where our primary citizenship is. We belong to God. And that is never going to change. God is the source of our life and we continue to belong to him even after this earthly life. When Jesus said to the Pharisees and Herodians to give to God what belonged to God, it simply meant giving ourselves completely to God. Our primary loyalty is to God, because we belong to him. He needs to be our life-center. We should not allow emperors, kings, governments, or any of such things to distract us from our primary focus of being united with God. Jesus did not allow any of such things to distract him from his focus on fulfilling his father's will. Without God our life is incomplete because we have our existence in and through him. We have to be in constant dialogue with him as he is in constant dialogue with us. We have to be fully present to him as he is fully present to us. We have to tune our hearts and minds to listen to his voice.

But we know that sometimes we don't give that first place to God. Many other things in our life get the priority. Many other things influence us and we get distracted. Our relationship with God is often difficult and ruptured. We sometimes make decisions and engage in actions that are contrary to God's ways. We distance ourselves from God or keep God away from the dialogical triangle. Influenced by certain value systems and ideologies prevalent in the society, we might sometimes think that we can do without God or God is not relevant. Carrying the distorted ideas and images of God that we have been presented with or we have developed over the years, we might relate to God in ways that are unhealthy and unhelpful. All these are possible. But the truth is that when God is kept away or he is not involved in the dialogical process, our life is incomplete.

Jesus used the parable of a wedding feast (Matt 22:1–14) to speak about the importance of responding back to God's invitation to participate in his dance of love. The parable is about a king who gave a wedding banquet for his son. The invited guests refused to come to the banquet. They made excuses and stayed away. The king was angry and disappointed. He sent his servants to bring in anyone whom they could find in the streets so that the wedding feast could go on. Jesus indicated that that is how we sometimes do in our relationship with God. God keeps reaching out to us, but we stay away from him. We often are not actively engaged in the dialogical process, communion with God and others.

It is not difficult for many of us to relate the parable to our own experiences. We know how it feels like if we prepared a good dinner and invited some special friends but they all stayed away making excuses. We feel discouraged and upset, and even insulted. All our hard work and the hope of being with our friends would be in vain. But our anger, disappointment, and the feeling of being insulted are only one side of the story. Think about what the invited guests are missing. They are missing a delicious dinner and they have no idea how good it is. They have no idea about what they are missing. That is what the parable of the wedding feast presents. Often we think of the disappointment and anger of the king. But that is only one side of the story. It is important to think about what the invited guests were missing. They missed a great banquet. And they missed the chance to be with the king and his royal court. Everybody doesn't get to see the king or to be with the king all the time. It is a selected few that gets to enjoy that. But they threw away that golden opportunity.

That is what happens when we stay away from God or keep God out of our life. God invites us to be united with him but sometimes we stay away. We engage in sinful and unhealthy activities. We make bad choices. We refuse to love. Sometimes we don't realize what we are missing. When we live in sin or refuse to partner with God in his dance of love, we lose our peace and joy in life. We feel burdened by guilt and become restless. We feel broken and weak. We sometime hate ourselves for what we do. We feel ashamed. When we stay away from God we lose all good things. When talking of sins, the Catholic Church often gives a lot of emphasis to mortal sins. Mortal sins refer to those of our actions that are mortal or deadly. They deprive us of life not in the physical sense but in the psychological and spiritual sense. They take away our peace and joy. The question is, "Is it worth doing all that?" When we break our relationship with God or keep God away from the dialogical triangle, God is of course sad and distressed as the king was sad or the father of the prodigal sons was sad and distressed. But it is also important to think about what it does to us. It makes our life miserable.

In the parable, we also hear about one man who came to the wedding banquet without a wedding garment. He was thrown out. It sounds strange. The king had allowed the servants to bring in anybody, both good and bad. So why was the man without the wedding garment thrown out? It seems to be indicating that even after being given a chance to join the banquet he was still holding on to his old ways. It appears that everyone else had changed into the wedding garment except that man. He was still in his old or usual garments. He did not change. Of course, it is not referring to the garments or clothes in the physical sense. It is about being there fully present psychologically and spiritually. It was like he was there, but he was not there. His body was there, but his heart was somewhere else.

Some of us may be like this man in our relationship with God. We may be present to God or in dialogue with God partially but not completely. We respond to God's invitation partially but not fully. We may be still holding on to our old self, our unhealthy habits and sins, and our hatred and hurtful feelings. When we continue to hold on to them, we continue to torment ourselves and are not able to enjoy the joy and peace that God offers. We are with him, but we are not fully with him. We pray that his will may be done in our lives, but often we want our will and desires to be fulfilled. We want to love and serve God, but we also want to go after sinful and unhealthy things. We want to be attached to God, but we don't want to be detached from ungodly things and desires. We want to be saints but we also want to enjoy the sensations and pleasures experienced by sinners. We want to follow God's ways but we try to make God agree with our ways. We are like people with their legs in two boats. We are half here and half there. With our legs in two boats, we cannot row or move forward much. Being in dialogue with God means we remain fully open to him and give ourselves completely to him. Jesus said that no one could serve two masters (Matt 6:24). When we serve two masters, our loyalty is divided.

The purpose of our life is to participate in the divine dance of love and manifest God's love in this world. That was the focus of Jesus' life and ministry. He was focused on doing the will of his Father and manifesting his love. When we do the same, our life becomes Christological. We are not following our agenda but God's agenda. The first commandment that Jesus placed before us is to love God more than anything else. It is to put God first in our life. It is not because God is narcissistic and need all our attention but because we experience the fullness of life only when we remain united with him.

Keeping God out of the dialogical process can lead to all kinds of misguided decisions based on our wishes and desires, which sometimes are not so healthy and in tune with God's ways. Being in dialogue and communion with God helps us to rise above all self-focused motives. God helps us to see the bigger picture of our lives and our world.

When God is kept out of the dialogical triangle and decision-making process, individuals and communities might become autocratic and dictatorial. Some individuals become autocratic and dictatorial and impose their desires and decisions on others. They follow their agenda and not God's agenda. It could happen in a family, group, or society at large. In a family, for example, the father or mother can become very dictatorial imposing his or her decisions on everyone else. He or she might want the rest of the family to be passive recipients and mere executors of their decisions. There is no dialogue in such families. God or love is not the guiding force in such families. Even if they claim to have God's blessings, their actions and behaviors would negate such claims because God is not autocratic and dictatorial. The life in such families is often ruled by fear and hatred rather than love. Such imposition of the individual's decisions happens in groups and societies as well. Some individuals turn out to be dictators and unquestionable authority figures. They don't engage in any healthy dialogue with the rest of the community or group.

Autocrats or dictators who claim God's blessings may have a distorted idea of God, very different from the God Jesus presents. The God Jesus presents is not a dictatorial and self-imposing God who works in isolation. He is a God of love, a God who works with us respecting our freedom. Autocrats and dictators who claim God's blessings could also cause a conflict in theology and spirituality. If the rest of the community believes in a God of love and dialogue and if the self-imposing person claims to have God's blessings, then they will have to think that they are led by different kinds of spirits and not the same Holy Spirit. The God the self-imposing person believes in and the God the community believes in would turn out to be different.

Sometimes it could be a group or section in the community that becomes autocratic and dictatorial. They might want everyone else to be passive recipients and executors of their decisions rather than being active participants in the dialogue and decision-making process. They might also claim to have God's blessings in what they do, but that is not the God that Jesus presents to us. Such theologies and spirituality lead to splits and disunity in the community.

Whether we are individuals or communities, it is very essential that we remain united with God. The dialogical triangle will not be complete and our lives will not be Christological without God.

Dialoguing with God does not mean that we remain passive or we leave everything to God. Jesus was not a passive executor and follower of the will of his Father and the Holy Spirit. He was actively engaged with the Father and the Spirit in the fulfillment of the mission. God wants us as individuals and communities to partner with him in fulfilling his mission in this world. He wants us to be cocreators and coworkers with him in making our lives better and making this world better. He has given us intelligence and wisdom to discern and make decisions. Saying, "Lord, let your will be done" isn't about shying away from taking personal responsibility. It is about making decisions with the ultimate desire of seeking God's will rather than our own selfish motives.

Dialogue with Individual

Just as God is an essential component of the dialogical triangle, all of us as individuals are essential parts of the triangle. A community or society is not healthy if some of its members or a section of the community is kept out of the dialogical triangle. For a community to thrive well, every one of its members needs to thrive well. The community needs to recognize and value the immense possibilities and potentialities present in its members and help them to bring the best out of themselves. Whether we operate as families, communities, groups, societies, or nations, every individual member needs to be intimately connected with God and the rest of the group. But sometimes, that is not how our families, communities, and societies operate. Many members are excluded from the mainstream of life and pushed to the fringes. Many members remain indifferent or decide to stay away because they feel left out or unwanted. In some societies or communities, it is not a few members but a whole section or segment of the community that is kept out of the dialogical triangle.

At the time of Jesus, many people were excluded from the community and society, and they were often grouped into the category of "tax collectors and sinners." They included the lepers, prostitutes, people with disabilities, tax collectors, and several others. They were kept out of the community with the belief that their presence would defile or contaminate the rest of the community. But as Jesus entered the scene, things began to change. He began to include the excluded. He kept reminding people that we were all God's children and we were one family. Without everybody being together, a community is not a community. We all have to be part of the divine dance. But some people were not happy with that kind of inclusive language. The Pharisees asked his disciples, "Why does your teacher eat with tax collectors and sinners?" (Matt 9:11). Jesus replied, "It is not the healthy who need a doctor, but the sick. But go and learn what this means: 'I desire mercy, not sacrifice.' For I have not come to call the righteous, but sinners" (Matt 9:12–13). Many people tried to keep Jesus also away from the community. But he did not simply withdraw and stay away. He didn't surrender to those discouraging elements. He continued to be an integral part of the community.

It is not only at the time of Jesus but also down through the centuries before and after him that we see that such exclusions and withdrawals of individuals or sections of the society from God and the community have happened. There were communities and societies that discriminated and kept away people because of their race or ethnicity. They dominated over others. Many people owned people as slaves. Even some of the patriarchs in our faith history owned slaves. Abraham and his wife Sarai owned an Egyptian slave girl named Hagar through whom Abraham had his first son, Ishmael. Abraham's descendants, the Israelites then become slaves in Egypt after a few centuries. It then becomes the enslavement of not just one individual but also a whole ethnic group. They were excluded from the mainstream life of the Egyptians and forced into slavery. Slavery based on race and ethnicity continued in many societies even until recently. In some cultures and societies different forms of slavery still continue. Upset with and discouraged by such racial discriminations some people might stay away from the community and the dialogical triangle, and the faulty system continues its course.

In some societies like India, it was the caste system that discriminated people and excluded them from the rest of the community or society. People belonging to low castes were treated as less than human. Even within low castes, there were sub-castes that were discriminated and kept out of the dialogical process. Those belonging to the low castes had no rights but only duties. Those who belonged to the category of "untouchables" were not even permitted to appear in the sight of the people of high caste lest they pollute and defile the latter. Frustrated and angry with such unjust and exploitative systems, some people might become passive and withdraw from the dialogical triangle.

Whether it is by race, caste, or any other classification, no one has a right to dominate over others. As children of God we all are equal in dignity and honor and we are equal partners in the divine dance of love. We all need to be part of the dialogical triangle living as a loving community.

In many cultures and communities, women have been and continue to be discriminated and excluded from the mainstream of life. They are not considered equal in rights and dignity to men. They are often expected to be servants and obedient followers of men. In some communities men dominate so much that women are treated as their property. What those communities and societies don't realize is that by doing that the gifts and talents of half of the humanity is wasted or not made use of for the betterment of this world. It is erroneous to think that only half of the humanity (men) is capable of running the world. If God is the creator of men, he is also the creator of women. If men are gifted, women are gifted too. If men are called by God to be partners in the divine dance to manifest his love and make this world a better place, the same God calls women to do the same. What would men do without their mothers, wives, and daughters? Of course, men and sons would not even be around without their mothers just as women or daughters would not be around without their fathers.

We need both men and women, but some communities and societies don't think that it is important. When it comes to domination, both men and women are susceptible to it. Uncontrolled power given to men or women can be a bad news for any society or community, and it is against God's will. Keeping women away from the mainstream of the life of the community or society is a loss rather than gain. God wants all of us to work together to make this world a better place. It is not just one section or segment, but every segment and every individual that needs to be part of the dialogical triangle. In this respect, many tribal groups seem to be much more civilized and egalitarian than the so-called civilized and postmodern societies. In many tribal communities, women are given utmost respect and are valued as equal to men. They value and live in harmony with everyone and everything in the creation.

In many communities and societies people have been excluded because of their religious beliefs and practices. They have beliefs and practices that are different from what others hold. Sometimes bitter rivalry grows between communities because of their religious or denominational affiliations. Christians have been persecuted and discriminated against in many places. The Roman emperors hunted for Christian believers and subjected them to brutal persecutions and gruesome death. Christians continue to experience persecutions and discriminations in many places today. Christians themselves have excluded and persecuted each other on many occasions. Catholics and Protestants have fought bitter wars. They have hated and continue to hate each other in many places. There are animosities and bitterness between different groups within the Catholic Church. Many people have been persecuted and excluded from the church because of their differing voices. We find similar exclusions and rivalries among other religions and communities. Either they fight with other religious groups or within their group. We might differ in the beliefs and practices that we are raised in or have developed, but we all are children of God and we are a family. We cannot keep anyone out of that dialogical triangle.

In some cultures and societies people have been discriminated against and excluded because of their ethnicity or language. Ethnic cleansing and genocides still continue in many places. The tribal mentality of one group decimating or subjugating the other has not ended even in this day and age.

In some countries and societies, people are excluded or isolated because of their differences in political ideologies and opinions. It is not uncommon to hear news about governments trying to suppress or silence opposition members or opposition members trying to topple the government. Guerrilla movements and militant groups threatening the existing systems of government has been a constant irritant in many countries for decades and centuries. Political and ideological differences make some keep their rivals out of the discussion table or the dialogical triangle.

And then there are other individuals who are kept out of the mainstream of life because they are a threat to the community or society. Some people are mentally or psychologically sick and are a threat to others. Others are driven by their destructive and negative passions and emotions and end up hurting themselves or others. They are triggered by something in their life that they end up harming people. They are on a path of violence, abuse, and destruction. They sometimes turn out to be the incarnation of evil. They are not people anyone would normally include in their company. The community or society might be justified in keeping such people out of the mainstream to some extent, but even they need to be included in some way in the dialogical triangle because however bad they may be they are still part of our human family and God's creation.

Dealing with such individuals, it is important to focus on the whole picture rather than just what appears to us. In the case of a person who engages in criminal acts, for example, many people often see only the crime and not what led the person to his or her crime. It is also important to understand what and who made them criminals or what makes them do bad things. Is it their family and parents who may have taught and modeled for them unhealthy lives and behaviors? Were they taught or indoctrinated into an idea or belief that such acts were a virtue rather than a vice? Is it the unhealthy and unjust societal systems and structures they grew up in or had a hangover effect that made them like that? Is it something in their gene that they inherited that causes them to be mentally unstable and destructive? Is it some negative and traumatic experiences in their life that made them do criminal acts as a way to avenge the crimes done to them? Or is it a combination of all these that led them to the criminal act? Often we don't have sufficient knowledge and information about all these, and we don't make an attempt to understand them. The crime of the person startles and overwhelms us so much that we don't have time or patience to look for the virtues in the person. But when we look deeper into the history of the criminal, we might see the troubled person within. Vices grow in all of us and in our world because of various reasons. The justice system and mental health treatments are inadequate and highly flawed in many of our societies. We don't have adequate arrangements and resources to find out what makes people do bad things and help people with deranged personalities and backgrounds to receive help so that they don't end up in criminal and unhealthy activities.

When it comes to human life, none of us has a complete picture of any one person, including ourselves. Only God knows everything about us. Only God can make the judgment. We cannot. Every judgment we make is going to be partial because we don't see the whole truth. Just because we see the vices, it doesn't mean that there is no good in the person. All of us have a lot of good in us. We have love in us. We have God in us. Jesus wants us to let love grow and God shine in us. Even though we are unhappy and concerned about the vices, we want to keep nurturing the good in us. We do the same with others. We need to see the good in others and try to nurture it. For those who are given into violence and destructive behaviors, we need to restrict them from causing any further damage or harm but at the same time help them to change what needs to be changed. Their unhealthy and criminal acts will have to be discouraged and corrected. They need to be provided with adequate help and treatment to recognize and rectify the vices in them as much as they can. But that doesn't mean that we condemn and reject the person for all eternity.

Exclusions and discriminations of people happen in communities and societies in many ways for good and bad reasons. The community or society might feel that it would be better for the community if some individuals or some segments of the community are kept out. And some individuals and segments within the community or society might feel that they are going to be better off if they kept away from the community and God. But in the long run all these have proved to be faulty thinking. By such exclusions and withdrawals those communities, societies, individuals, and segments were hurting themselves. If some individuals or some segments are ignored or excluded, it is going to cause more problems for the community or society. Either the individuals or segments could get discouraged and disappointed with the way they are taken for granted or could be angry and upset with the way they are treated. Being ignored and excluded, they might withdraw and isolate. They might become totally disengaged with the rest of the community or world. The attitude could be, "If they don't care, I don't care." If they are angry and upset because of exclusion they might hold it in for a while but then blow up some day. If they are going to withdraw and keep away, it is going to isolate them and cause them further problems in life. Either way it is not going to be good for them and the community.

Any community, society, or group that takes for granted, ignores, or excludes some of its members or segments of people from the dialogical triangle is going to sabotage its own growth and well-being. The community, society, or group should always remember that it is made up of individual members. The whole does not exist without its parts. The whole should have the capacity and generosity to absorb even the parts that might seem to be problematic and irksome.

Some members or segments of the community or society may be happy if other members and segments are kept out or excluded. But in the long run it is not good for the community because the community remains splintered and fractured. Besides, the members or segments that are kept out will continue to be a problem.

These days when we see some news reports we are informed that they are not reports that were freely available to the journalists or the general public but that the journalist had to find some ways to get it. Often we see the reporter adding a line about the source of the report, something like, "this information was disclosed by someone who is not authorized to speak on this matter" or "this information was leaked to the press by someone on the condition of anonymity." The question then would be if nobody was authorized to give out the news how did the news get out? The journalists seem to have a way of getting news out of places and situations that often seem to be impossible for others to break into. Although the journalistic integrity and professionalism are called into question in such contexts, the fact is that there sure are people ready to divulge the information. Some people might think that they can keep things hushed up and sealed away from others, but that is simply a fantasy. When something is hushed up, especially if it is something sneaky, dishonest, and against the basic human values of justice and truth, there will always be somebody within that system who will rise up against that. Systems, organizations, and communities might succeed in keeping people and information locked up or excluded for some time, but they can't do it forever. The very information and people they lock up or shut out are going to haunt them sooner or later. Jesus rightly said, "For there is nothing hidden that will not be disclosed, and nothing concealed that will not be known or brought out into the open" (Luke 8:17).

This truth about the impossibility of keeping things hidden or excluded applies to people as well. Fear and hatred of someone whom we dislike or who disagrees with us might make us think of shutting them out of our life or community. But that is not what helps our forward movement as individuals and communities. Instead of avoiding or shutting them out what we need is to befriend them, befriend the very things and persons that we dislike or cause us trouble. Being aware of what is hurtful and hurting we can try to change what we are able to change and learn to live with what we can't. Excluding them or avoiding them is not healthy and helpful. Excluding them will not only make them a continued problem for the community but also leave the community splintered and shattered. In the Christological model, everyone has a place in the dialogical triangle.

In doing trauma treatment for children or others who have had a traumatic history, one of the things that often stands as a strong hurdle against their recovery is avoidance. Many of the patients push down or store away their traumatic experience and the feelings and thoughts associated with it into their unconscious, not wanting to have it on their everyday conscious level lest it keeps bothering them and makes them relive their traumatic experience. They develop a belief or idea that keeping the memory, thoughts, and feelings about it out of their conscious self will help them get over it. But often it does not. As long as it is repressed and shut out it will keep coming back bothering them every now and then if not every day. One of the goals in treatment is to help the patient become aware of this avoidance strategy they have developed and understand its futility. Instead of avoiding, what would help them is to learn to befriend it. Befriending it would involve being able to talk about it, being not afraid of it anymore, finding ways to change their distorted thoughts and beliefs and negative feelings, and learning to live with it without allowing it to control their life and actions thenceforward. They would recognize that the trauma has happened and it is not something that is going to be undone. What can be undone or reduced are the negative reactions and repercussions arising out of it. They would find ways to move forward accepting the traumatic experience as something that has had a negative impact on their life but not allowing it to control their life any further.

Like the trauma in a person, a family, community, group, or society might try to avoid and keep some of their difficult and disliked members out of their system and everyday life thinking that it would help them. But keeping them out might hurt the community or group more than it does when they are within the system. The community hast to find ways to befriend and include those individuals or segments in the dialogical triangle.

Jesus used a parable of wheat and weeds growing together (Matt 13:24–30). Worried about the weeds choking the wheat, the laborers wanted to pluck out the weeds, but the master forbid them from doing that. He wanted them to allow the wheat and weeds grow together until the harvest time. The weeds might continue to grow or they might die before the harvest time. But the final decision is to be left to the master.

Of course, in the normal farming situations, allowing the weeds to grow along with the wheat or any other crop may be imprudent. But Jesus is not talking about our farming or harvesting in the normal sense. It is about our life as individuals and communities. When it comes to our life on this earth, there is always going to be a mix of likeable and unlikeable people, saints and sinners in our world. We find that combination of wheat and weeds within us too. Whether it is about us or others, we have to be patient and hopeful of change. The weeds might gradually die or can be rooted out. Instead of rejecting and condemning the sinner, we have to help the person change and transform. Sometimes we may not get all the weeds out. We may have to learn to live with it without allowing it to take control of our lives. Leaving all judgment to God, we need to continue as one family, everyone having a place in the dialogical triangle. As communities and societies we need to find ways to help those who are on the fringes to come to the mainstream of the community or society's life. We need to keep including them in the dialogical triangle. That is Jesus' way.

Dialogue with Community

Just as God and the individual members are essential parts of the dialogical triangle, the community as a whole is also an inevitable component. As mentioned before, the community could mean everything and everyone that is part of the individual's life. It could be a family, group, a specific community or organization, the society, a nation, the world, or the creation at large. All these together make up our community. Our life is incomplete without them. We are not meant to be isolated individuals. In reality, we cannot live without others. We are so dependent on others and the creation that completely cut off from them, we will cease to exist. But at the same time, we could be living as isolated individuals in many ways. Our ego can have a fantasy of a "self-only" world. We are created to be Trinitarian, to be in communion with God and others. Sometimes it could be a section of the community or society that keeps away from the rest of the community or society. Isolating ourselves as individuals or groups is not healthy.

To be Trinitarian and live our lives well, we need to be in dialogue with others as we do with God. We have to live in harmony with the whole creation. It is to live with the idea and attitude that everything is sacred. And because everything is sacred, we deal with them with respect and love. Accordingly, when I relate to another person, I would see that person as God's creation in whom God is present. If God is present in me, God is also present in the other person. If I am sacred, the other person also is sacred. The other person may be engaging in evils and unhealthy behaviors, but that does not cancel out the presence of God in that person. Our effort should be to help that person to recognize the evil he or she is involved in and change it rather than avoiding that person. If all of us begin to avoid each other because of each other's flaws and faults, we will not be able to live our lives well. Instead if all of us see each other as sacred and God's temples and help each other to reduce the evils and sins in our lives, there will be much more respect and love in our human communities. This sense of the sacred needs to be extended to the rest of the creation, as everything is part of God's creation. God is present in everything and everyone.

As individuals, we have to realize that we are not the center of the universe. If everything is left to us, it can become a one-man show, and we can terribly go wrong. We can become dictatorial and autocratic. In the dialogical triangle none of the components dominates. We have to be always in dialogue with God and others. If our discernment and decisions happen without including others or the community, then the dialogical triangle is not complete. It becomes egocentric or self-focused. We become our own self-appointed authority. Some people don't care about others or the community. They do things as it pleases them. They make decisions that are self-focused and they cause discomfort and problems in the family, community, or society.

Jesus teaches us that we are a community of persons united with God and one another. He uses the parable of a rich man and a poor man named, Lazarus to drive home the message that we are not to live as isolated persons concerned only about our life and well being (Luke 16:19–31). Our life on this earth as well as in eternity is to be a life of communion with God and others. The rich man in the parable does not have a name, but the poor man does. People who live a self-only life might think that they have built up a name for themselves, but in God's sight, that doesn't count. What actually counts is whether they have made an effort to find out the names of others—that is, whether they have taken time and made effort to connect with others. If they do that, it will continue into eternity.

Sometimes some people dialogue with God in their discernment and decision-making process but they exclude others or the community. If my discernment and decisions involve God but excludes others or the community, there is no way to authenticate the veracity of this dialogue. If the community or others are not involved, then, any or all of my personal presumptions might be claimed as authorized by God, but it is difficult to authenticate such claims. Although the community could mean different things depending on the context, in our immediate contexts, it could mean our family, or the group, organization, neighborhood community, faith community, or other associations that we are part of. Since all the major decisions we make have an impact on these people in our immediate contexts, it is important to engage them in the dialogical process.

The dialogical triangle that involves God, the individual, and the community is our model of life. A balance between all these three components is very essential in our deliberations, decisions, and relationships. The divine dance of love is not complete when it is solo or dyadic. The dance is triangular. With God and others we are one family, and our life decisions have to be made in communion rather than in isolation. This has to be our model of life. This applies to every situation of life and relationships, whether it is in an individual's life or in the family, community, groups, or organizations. Exclusion or withdrawal of any of the components in the dialogical triangle leads to an imbalance in the relationship and unhealthy directions in life. Of course, there are certain individuals or groups that are incapable of participating in such decision-making processes because of their mental or psychological conditions or other reasons. But that is an exception rather than the norm.

31

Dynamic and Positive Engagement

Two things that block us from living a Trinitarian life and cause ruptures in the dialogical triangle are ignoring people and focusing excessively on their weakness and failures. Research shows that ignoring others and focusing on their weaknesses lead to gradual disengagement and dissatisfaction. Tom Rath, the author of *StrengthsFinder* 2.0, and his team at Gallup, the research and consulting company, found that managers who ignored their employees or focused on their weaknesses received a very low percentage of productivity and engagement from the latter. According to the survey, if the managers ignored their employees, there was a 40 percent chance for those employees to be actively disengaged. If the managers focused on the weaknesses of their employees, there was a 22 percent chance for those employees to be actively disengaged. But if the managers focused on the strengths of their employees, there was only a 1 percent chance for those employees to be actively disengaged.

These research findings, I believe, apply not only to people's engagement or satisfaction in the corporate world but also to all relationships. Sometimes people wonder why they are not able to make any headway in their relationship with others. It could be because they are consistently ignoring the other person or focusing on their weaknesses.

If we consistently ignore somebody—their needs, views, presence, and even grievances and complaints—the relationship is going to grow cold or negative. Some people get tired of trying to get their ideas, views, needs, and grievances across to others. The ignoring parties may be consciously or unconsciously putting up a wall against them by constantly ignoring them or taking them for granted. Being tired of trying, the other party gives up. It happens in families, communities, and societies. Sometimes certain members feel ignored or feel that their weaknesses are overly highlighted. Sometimes it is a whole section of the group or community that feels ignored or disparaged. Such acts of ignoring or focusing too much on the weaknesses of the other do not help the dialogical process. When ignored or found fault with, some people might stay disengaged from the dialogical process. They take an approach of indifference and disinterestedness in the relationship.

For some people, experiences of being ignored and weaknesses being excessively highlighted begin from their childhood. Many children disengage and isolate themselves when their parents or caregivers ignore them or focus on their weaknesses. Attachment theorists such as John Bowlby and Mary Ainsworth speak of the need for a healthy home environment for a child to develop a healthy attachment experience. Parents or caregivers who are physically and emotionally available, responsive, and helpful provide the child with a sense of safety and security, love and affection. Unfortunately many children in this world are deprived of such healthy environments. Their parents or caregivers are often unavailable, unresponsive, and unhelpful to them in their physical and emotional needs. Children depend on their parents or caregivers for support and safety. They look for the emotional and physical presence and attention of their parents and other caregivers, especially when they have emotional experiences that are too overwhelming. They look to the parents or caregivers for an affirmation that they are loveable and likeable. But instead they are ignored and found fault with. Some parents and caregivers are not attuned to their children adequately. They may be emotionally distant because of their psychological problems. They may be physically absent because they are sick or they are too busy and preoccupied with other things. Such children are very vulnerable and can easily feel ignored or unwanted. They would try all kinds of things to get the attention of the parents or caregivers. They might engage in behaviors such as whining, drooling, rolling on the floor, throwing a temper tantrum, and acting out behaviorally in different ways. But some parents and caregivers still remain with flat affect or distant and disconnected from their children emotionally and physically. And the children again feel ignored.

It may be appropriate to ignore the behaviors of older kids if they engage in negative behaviors, provided that parents and other caregivers are emotionally and physically present to them appropriately at other times. But for babies and younger children, it is too overwhelming to be consistently ignored or deprived of connectedness with the mother and caregivers for a long time. The child needs to be soothed and comforted. The child does not have the capacity to do that by him or herself.

If ignoring and deprivation of emotional and physical support or attunement continue and become consistent or habitual, the child might give up expecting the parent or caregiver to provide that sense of support and safety. The child might slowly withdraw from the parent and caregiver and begin to find other ways to comfort or soothe itself. The child might find some comfort in sucking his or her fingers, holding on to a blanket or toy, or developing some attachment to some other objects, all of which Donald Winnicott and others often refer to as "transitional objects" (Winnicott, 1953). The physically and emotionally absent parents and caregivers cause a great amount of damage to the child's self-image. The child might develop negative feelings about him or herself such as, "I am unlovable," "I am unlikeable," etc. The child also may have difficulties in developing attachment to the parents.

In some families, children isolate and withdraw because their parents and other caregivers focus only on the negative things or problem behaviors of their children and do not say anything good or positive about them. The children get tired of hearing it and they gradually withdraw or remain with an attitude of "whatever." Everyone has weaknesses but if someone focuses only on our weaknesses, the relationship becomes a platform for discouragement and regress rather than progress and growth. Hearing only the negative things, the child slowly gets disinterested in the relationship and withdraws or remains passive.

It is not only with babies and little children but also with adults that this disruption in relationship that can occur. People ignore and focus on the weaknesses of each other, and they either withdraw or remain passive in the relationship. When such things happen, the dialogical triangle remains stagnant. The context may be a family, marriage, or community. In a family, when the members neglect, ignore, and become emotionally unavailable to each other, the dialogue process gets disrupted. Some may be ignoring others because the latter are too overwhelming, narcissistic, or dominating. Even if they have such negative traits in their personalities, they need to be kept in the dialogue. Ignoring them is not healthy and helpful. Similarly if some of the family members begin to focus mostly on the weaknesses of other members, the latter may not be interested in being engaged with the former. They might isolate themselves into their own world. The ignoring and critical members of the family might claim that they are spiritual and are in dialogue with God, but their indifference and negative attitudes and comments leave the family divided. Their idea of God might be that of one who loves them and hates the other, but that is not the God whom Jesus presented. To be Christological, the family needs to have all the members engaged in a positive and dynamic relationship with each other and be willing to accommodate and absorb even those whom they find distasteful and difficult.

Sometimes partners in marital relationships or friendships ignore each other or they move into negative interactions. They engage in pointing out each other's weaknesses and drawbacks, and ignore all the positive things they have about themselves. They blame, condemn, and shame each other. They become passive or take the other for granted. They both know in their heart that there are positive things, which brought them together in their relationship or marriage, unless they were forced marriages or relationships. But as they engage in more and more negative interactions they begin to forget or ignore each other's positive qualities. The more they ignore and disparage each other the more isolated and disengaged they become. Gradually the relationship gets to a point where dialogue is almost non-existent. Referring to marriages that grow cold and dead, Marissa Gold quotes Michael McNulty, a marriage and couples therapist, who said, "Relationships die by ice rather than fire." When partners begin to ignore and withdraw from each other the dialogue begins to fade, and the forward movement or progress begins to slow down. The partners might claim to have dialogue with God, but since there is no dialogue with each other, their relationship is not Christological.

Similar dynamics play out in other relationship settings too. In certain communities, people who are ignored and who have been deprived of affirmation and acknowledgement might find it hard to stay connected with the community. They feel unjustly judged and found fault with. Either they withdraw completely or remain passive and disengaged. Many communities and organizations slowly become inefficient and dead because those in the leadership positions often ignore their members or vice versa. If the leaders ignore or focus only on the weaknesses of the members, they are causing a rupture in the dialogical triangle. Some leaders may be ignoring some of their members because of the latter's dissenting voices or because they do not belong to the leaders' support groups. A leader proves to be a true leader only when he or she can absorb and include in the dialogical process even the dissenting voices and rival groups. The leader needs to look for and include the "lost sheep." If the members ignore their leaders or focus only on their weaknesses, they are also causing a rupture in the dialogical triangle. Both parties might claim that they are in dialogue with God, but it is not Christological. The dialogical triangle remains ruptured when there is no active engagement between both parties.

Some people might say that they can directly pray to or dialogue with God and that they don't need the community. And some communities might think that they can do without some of their individual members or sections within the community. In both cases it goes against the Christological model of life. That is not the kind of God and life that Jesus presents before us. We have to be in dialogue with God and one another. The individual members may be praying to God directly but they are missing the community in their life. They may not feel the need of the community, but the community needs them. The community is not a community without them. It is not complete without them just like the family in the parable of the prodigal son was not complete when the prodigal son and the elder son stayed away. The father needed them home. The community also might feel that it can do without certain members, but the community is not a community without all its members. The elder son in the parable of the prodigal son felt that he and his father did not need his younger brother. But the family was not complete without the younger son. God wants all of us home. Because many people stay disengaged when they feel ignored or judged, special attention and support need to be given to members who are weak, vulnerable, rejected, and excluded in our families, communities, and societies so that they can return back to the dialogical triangle.

Among the myriad of strengths we find in Jesus, two of them are his ability to give personal attention to everyone who came to him and focusing on the strengths of people rather than on their weaknesses. All who came to Jesus felt valued irrespective of who they were, where they came from, and what they did. He talked and dealt with each person as if he or she was the only person who mattered and existed in the world. Jesus listened to the cry of a leper whom no one else would have ordinarily cared about. Jesus heard the cry of an official, a centurion, who was a pagan to others. Jesus saw the distress of a man whose son was tormented by a demonic spirit. Jesus took time to be with the sick mother-in-law of Peter and many others who came to their house. Jesus spent time with a Pharisee, Nicodemus and engaged in a detailed discussion about his mission. Jesus found time to stop and comfort the widow of Nain. Jesus was personally and lovingly present to the tax collectors and sinners whom nobody else cared about. Every individual person was made to feel special when they came to Jesus or when Jesus met them. He did not ignore anybody, and he did not disparage anybody. Even if he disagreed with some people or people disagreed with him, we don't see Jesus ignoring anybody.

Jesus also focused on the strengths of each of those individuals he dealt with rather than focusing on their weaknesses. The twelve apostles Jesus chose were not the promising and talented group of men in the eyes of the world. They were tax collectors, fishermen, and men with militant and extremist attitudes and ideals. But that is not what Jesus focused on. He focused on their strengths. Even the scribes and Pharisees whom he criticized knew that he valued them for who they were. He criticized their hypocrisy, but he did not question their authority or role in the community. He wanted them to purify their intentions and deeds so that they could be better leaders in the community. He asked people to follow what they taught but not follow what they did, "The scribes and the Pharisees sit on Moses' seat; therefore, do whatever they teach you and follow it; but do not do as they do, for they do not practice what they teach" (Matt 23:2–3).

Jesus looks at what is good in us rather than focusing on all our weaknesses. He does not look at us as a crowd. He sees each one of us as unique persons and values us for who we are. Every one of us is important and precious to him. He wants us to make better choices and stay away from sins and evils, but he does not beat us up, torment us, or put us down by focusing only on our weaknesses and failures. Just as God values us as unique and special individuals with our own strengths, and includes and counts on us as his partners in making this world a better place, we need to value each other's dignity and strengths and work together as a family or community with one mission. This has to happen in every situation of life and relationships whether it is in the family, work place, faith community, groups and organizations, or the larger society. Looking at our own lives and experiences, we know that it is those who encouraged us, recognized our strengths and abilities, and valued our presence that helped us to grow and remain engaged rather than those who discouraged us, ignored us, and focused on our weaknesses and limitations.

In the dialogical triangle, God may be the only person that does not ignore us, disparage us, and give up on us at all. No matter how many times we ignore or reject his invitations to healthy living, he still waits for our return. He is still waiting for us to join the dance. In our human relationships it is possible that individuals and communities ignore, judge, and give up on each other. But to remain true to our identity as children of God and make God alive in our lives and in our world we need to be positively engaged with God and one another. The dialogue between God, others, and us has to be kept active and alive all the time. The dance and dialogue need to go on uninterrupted.

32

Call to Communion

To be Christological or Trinitarian means living in communion with God and others. In the Christian tradition, especially in the Catholic tradition, the importance of our communion with God and one another is emphasized throughout one's life. One of the ways in which this aspect of communion is given emphasis is through the sacraments. In the Catholic Church, there are seven sacraments that the community celebrates: baptism, confirmation, Holy Eucharist, reconciliation, matrimony, holy orders, and anointing of the sick. A person's life and spirituality are intermingled with these sacraments, and they are neatly spread out throughout one's life. It begins with baptism, which often takes place at the beginning of one's life as an infant, and ends with the anointing of the sick, which often happens at the end of one's life. All the other sacraments are neatly interspersed in between.

The focus of all the sacraments is this call to communion, communion with God and one another. This communion is what ultimately makes a person holy. We are called to be with God, to be in an uninterrupted and loving relationship or dialogue with God. This communion with God should help us to be in communion with others because we are one family with God. The communion with others is what we often refer to as our call to mission. Our mission is to go out to others to bring them God's love and presence. Thus the sacraments embody the triangular dialogical relationship between God, others, and us. They help us to participate in the divine dance of love.

Just to bring home how this idea of communion, holiness, and mission is richly ingrained in sacraments, I shall talk about one of them, the sacrament of Baptism. At baptism, a child or candidate is baptized into the life of the Holy Trinity and the Christian community. The ceremony of baptism usually begins at the entrance of the church, near the front door. The sense of the candidate's communion with God and the community is very profoundly and powerfully brought out through this simple act of starting the ceremony at the entrance of the church.

First, the candidate is made aware that he or she is entering into the holy presence of God, which speaks of God's place in his or her life. It is a call to holiness or communion with God. The physical structure of the church is a reminder of the presenc of God in our lives and in our world. The church is not simply any kind of building. It is a special place dedicated to God and filled with God's presence. It reminds us that God is in our midst. It is a place of prayer. It is a place where God and human beings dialogue and unite. So when we enter a church, we enter with devotion and faith. We enter with the faith that God is waiting for us, he is welcoming us, and we belong to him. To be baptized means to be united with God. It is a call to the individual to have God come first, above all else in his or her life.

To be a Christian is to keep oneself close to God or to have his or her life centered on God, which is basically what we mean by holiness. The candidate is to keep that basic tenet of faith ever alive and live it until the end of his or her life. In other words, the sacrament of baptism is to be lived throughout one's life. It is not simply a ceremony done and finished once and for all in the church. It is a sacrament to be lived and celebrated throughout one's live, and that is true of all the sacraments.

Baptism tells the candidate that he or she belongs to God. God is the author of our lives and hence the candidate is a child of God. Just as God is present in the church, God is present in the candidate. It is an awareness of one's own uniqueness and individual self. God is welcoming and receiving the candidate as a unique person with dignity and honor. God says to the child or the candidate the same thing that he said to his people through the Prophet Isaiah, "You are mine" (Isa 43:1). You are mine; you belong to me; come to me and stay with me. To be baptized means to live with the awareness that he or she is a child of God. The candidate is to live with that awareness until the end of his or her life. If the candidate is an infant, the parents and the godparents take the responsibility of raising the child with this awareness. Everyday the parents and other family members have to communicate to the child that God loves him or her, and that he or she is a precious child of God.

When parents, family members, and the community fail to communicate this message to the child and fail to give to the child a sense that he or she is special and deeply loved, they are already causing damage to the child's sense of identity and worth. When children or people in general have a feeling that they are neither loved by God nor by anyone else, their sense of self and identity are damaged and blurred. They don't know who they are and they don't know whether anyone cares about them or whether they belong to anyone. Such damaged self and blurred identity can cause enormous problems in their personal, social, and spiritual lives later. For a person to bring the best out of his or her life, he or she needs to know always that he or she is a child of God and that God deeply loves him or her.

Second, starting the ceremony at the entrance of the church also reminds the candidate that he or she is entering into the community. The physical structure of the church represents the community. It is in the church that the community gathers. When the child or candidate enters the church it is symbolic of he or she entering into the community or being part of the community. It is true that the child or the candidate belongs to a particular family, but the family is the basic unit of the larger community of the Church and the world. Hence the child or candidate is a member of a larger community. When the child or the candidate is baptized, the community says to the individual, "You belong to us." The community is welcoming the child or candidate and God is calling the child or candidate to stay united with the community. It is a reminder that we are not meant to live as isolated and individualistic individuals but rather as a community united with God and one another.

The Christian community in the church is representative of the larger community of the world that includes both Christians and non-Christians. Essentially what the sacrament is communicating to the child or the candidate is that we are all part of a big community, the larger family of God. Hence the person has to be united with the community, and be at the service of the community. The sacrament of baptism reminds the candidate that the purpose of his or her life in this world is to partner with God and others in the dance of love. That communion with God and others in love is what is meant by holiness and grace. Loving and serving God are intertwined with loving and serving others. If it is an infant who is being baptized, the parents and the rest of the family take the responsibility of raising the child with this awareness. They have to constantly communicate to the child that he or she is not an isolated individual, but part of the community. The child has to experience that he or she is deeply loved by the community.

When parents, family members, and the community fail in this duty to communicate this truth to the child, it can cause enormous problems in his or her personal, social, and spiritual life later in life. If the parents and community do not give to the child a sense of belonging and fail to teach the child about the need to be part of the community, the child's future is open to confused and convoluted ideas about his or her place and purpose in the world. If the child grows up with the idea that the purpose of his or her life is individual survival and thriving without any regard for the community or the rest of the world, it is going to create a narcissistic and negative life. The fraternal and communal aspect of our life cannot be ignored if we want to live well. The sacrament of baptism commissions us and empowers us to be missionaries, and our mission is to bring God's love to others. Highlighting the importance of our call to service in the community, Jesus said, "In truth I tell you, in so far as you did this to one of the least of these brothers of mine, you did it to me" (Matt 25:40). The sacrament of baptism brings us the awareness that we belong to God and to the community. We are not meant to live as isolated and disconnected individuals.

At baptism, the candidate is also made aware that the union he or she enters into with God and the community is not only meant for this earthly life but also the life in eternity. As children of God we are destined for eternal life. Baptism lays the foundation for that journey into eternal life. Jesus said to Nicodemus, "In all truth I tell you, no one can enter the kingdom of God without being born from above . . . without being born through water and the Spirit" (John 3:3–5). The road that leads to eternal life is a life of holiness and grace, a life in union with God and others. If it is an infant that is being baptized, the family and the community has to constantly bring this awareness to the child that he or she is destined for eternal life, and that this world is not the end. When the family and the community fail in this duty to communicate this truth to the child, it does great damage to the child's sense of his or her destiny. Being unaware of the real destiny, the individual might live as if this world is everything. And when this world is taken as the be-all and end-all of one's life, the person might live without any regard for God or others. And that could easily lead him or her to narcissism, negativity, and unhealthy life and relationships.

Conveying these truths about our life, the sacrament of baptism is filled with rich symbols and meanings. The elements of water, white cloth, lighted candle, and holy oils are used during baptism to bring home the message about our Trinitarian life and call to communion. The water that is used to baptize the child or the candidate symbolizes cleansing and purification, renewal and refreshment. Immersing oneself into the water and coming out of it is symbolic of a new creation. As water cleanses, purifies, renews, and refreshes, the child or the candidate is cleansed, purified, renewed, and refreshed by the power of the Holy Spirit. The person becomes a new creation. God claims the person as his own. Baptism sets the person on the path of holiness and grace. This process of cleansing and renewal has to go on throughout one's life. The person has to remain open to God's grace and transformative power throughout his or her life.

The child or the candidate is anointed with holy oils, which symbolize strengthening and empowering of the person by God and sharing in the life of Christ. The child or the candidate is anointed to share in the priesthood, prophetic role, and kingship of Christ. A priest is a servant to God and the people, after the example of Christ. He is a connecting link between God and the community as Christ himself was. His mission is to unite his people with God as Christ did. The child or candidate who is being baptized is anointed to share in that priesthood of Christ to become a servant to God and the community, a connecting link between God and the community, and an instrument of unity. A prophet is one who stands in the place of God and speaks or proclaims God's message. Christ was not just standing in the place of God but was God himself. The message he proclaimed was the message of love, inviting the people to be united with God and others by participating in the dance of love. A child or candidate who is baptized is anointed to be a prophet, sharing in that prophetic life of Christ, to proclaim and live the message of love.

A king is one who stands on behalf of God to govern his people with love. He governs with justice and righteousness. Christ is the king of all kings inviting all of us into his kingdom of love. A child or candidate who is baptized shares in this kingship of Christ and takes upon him or herself the mantle of governing or caring for others with love. The anointing with the holy oils reminds the person that he or she is set apart for holy and grace-filled life, which is to live a life in communion with God and others. God empowers the individual to remain unmoved in the face of trials and temptations. The individual is vested with the power of God to fight all evils and remain united with God and others.

At baptism the child or the candidate is clothed with a white garment, which symbolizes purity and holiness. Clothed in the white garment, the person is reminded that he or she is a new creation. The person is called to live a life of holiness and grace, which essentially involves being in communion with God and others.

The child or the candidate is presented with a lighted candle, which symbolizes Christ or God himself and the call to become a light in the world. The individual is reminded that he or she should always walk in the light of Christ, allowing God to shine in and through him or her. The person has to radiate the divine light through his or her life and actions so that others may come to know and love God. The person becomes a light for the community, leading others to God, once again becoming a channel of God's grace and communion.

Thus the whole sacrament is a graceful experience of an encounter between God, self, and the community. This communion between God, self, and community is to be preserved and lived throughout one's life.

Most people start well with these ideals. But as time goes by, things change. Either they distance themselves from God and others or they are pushed away by others as unlovable and unwanted. Problems begin to pop up in their personal lives and relationships as a result of these. When people move away from God or the community, they end up in problems and become a problem for others. They might begin to act like God and forget that they are children of God. They might do things that are against the spirit of the community. They might create their own world and isolate themselves from others. To participate in the divine dance of love and live the Christological model in our lives, we need to live our lives in communion with God and others. Anything that separates us from that communion is unhealthy and against our very being.

In most churches, there is a font, stoup, or bowl with holy water at the door or entrance. As people enter the church, they dip their fingers in the holy water and bless themselves with the sign of the cross. When it becomes a routine, it is possible that people forget why they do it or they might think that it is simply a ritual to bless themselves. In actuality, it is a reminder of their own baptism. When they enter the church they once again remind themselves of who they are and what they are meant to be. They belong to God and need to remain united with God, and they belong to the community and need to be united with the community. We know how often and how easily we get distracted and distanced from God and others. Coming to the church once again helps us to "reboot" and reunite with God and others. Hence the more frequently we come to the church the better it is for us to return to our ideals.

33

Coming Home

THROUGHOUT THE HUMAN AND salvation history God has been calling his people back to healthy living, to be in right relationship with him and with one another, which essentially meant living a Trinitarian life and being part of the dialogical triangle. People keep going away from God and from one another, and God keeps calling them back "home." In the book of Genesis we hear of Adam and Eve going against God's commandment. They hid from God and they blamed each other. They were not "at home" with God and each other anymore. But God came in search of them. They had two sons, Cain and Abel. Cain murdered his brother, Abel, and caused a rift in his relationship with God and with his family. At the time of Seth and his children, it appears that people began to return back to God. And then at the time of Noah, people had again gone away from God and engaged in evils and sins. The flood at the time of Noah could be seen as human beings going through a destructive phase because of their unhealthy living. They had turned away from God and failed to live as a loving and healthy community. Through Noah, God again tries to bring back his people into right living and relationship, building up a new community.

Abraham becomes another prominent figure through whom God is trying to build a new community that lives in right relationship with God and with one another. God enters into a covenant with Abraham promising to make him a great nation. The promise and covenant were God's way of calling people back to healthy living and relationships. People again go away from God and fail to live as a loving and healthy community. We hear God warning Isaac's wife, Rebekah that her children and their descendants would fight and fail to live as a loving community. Many generations came and went with this story of people going away from God and one another, and God calling them back.

Then comes the great story of slavery in Egypt and the freedom through Moses. God commissioned Moses to go and free his people from slavery in Egypt. The story of the Israelites' slavery in Egypt and their freedom are not necessarily about physical slavery and physical freedom alone. Egypt and Canaan or the Promised Land don't need to be seen only in terms of their geography and physical settings. It could be seen as a story with much wider implications.

The story could be seen as a call for a new relationship with God and a return back to healthy living as a community. People had become slaves of many things and God was again trying to free them from all that and build them up as a loving community, united with God and one another. Being in Egypt for four or more centuries many elements of the Egyptian culture and religions must have influenced the faith and religion of the Israelites. It is possible that many of the Israelites abandoned God and started worshipping the deities of the Egyptians. Many Israelites must have felt that their God had abandoned and forgotten them leaving them to live in slavery. They must have been angry and disappointed with God for leaving them in slavery. Many of them must have felt that their God was not powerful enough to save them from their misery. They must have turned to the Egyptian deities looking upon them as more powerful than their own God.

Their life and slavery in Egypt also could be pointing to their struggle in living as a loving community. The Egyptians making the Israelites slaves speaks to the tension between two races or ethnic groups. They could not get along with each other and live as a loving community. One started dominating over and subjugating the other. Maybe the Israelites themselves lived as an isolated and exclusive community without getting integrated into the larger Egyptian society. There must have been many mixed marriages between the Israelites and the Egyptians, but other Israelites and Egyptians must have frowned upon them for doing that. The Egyptian society, which consisted of the Egyptians, the Israelites, and maybe many other ethnic or racial groups was disunited and disintegrated.

Egypt could be seen as a place or society that made the people lose their sense of God and sense of community. It is not that Egypt as a place was bad or Canaan as a place was better. It is more about the society losing their sense of God and community. Egypt represented such a society. And the Promised Land or Canaan was supposed to be a new society where people returned back to God and a sense of community. God was asking Moses to save his people from false religions and spirituality and disintegration as a community. It was a call to correct their wrong and unhealthy images of God. And it was a call to be united as a community once again. Egypt represented a distorted faith and a disintegrated community. They were not meant to stay in that. Moses and the people marching to the Promised Land represents the birth of a new community. When we are disconnected from God and disconnected from one another, we are not "home;" we are in "Egypt."

Many generations passed by again with this drama of going away and returning home being played out on and off. God called and appointed many prophets to lead their people back to God and back to community living. God called Prophet Isaiah to free his people from ungodliness and unhealthy living. Prophet Jeremiah was called to tear down and uproot the powers and systems of evil and rebuild a community that lived a healthy life. Prophet Hosea had a hard mission to fulfill. God asked him to marry a prostitute. Who would want to marry a prostitute? By making Hosea do that, God was making him a sign to his people. God was telling his people that they had become unfaithful like a prostitute, going after false gods and living unhealthy lives. They had gone after man-made gods and goddesses like a prostitute goes after men or women without any commitment or faithfulness. They had disintegrated as a people, failing to live as a loving community. God was reminding them that even though they had become unfaithful he was continuing to be faithful to them.

God called Prophet Ezekiel and told him that he was sending him to his people who had rebelled and transgressed against God. God shows him a valley filled with dry bones representing the dead and disintegrated community. They had become lifeless like dry bones. They had turned away from God and failed to live as a loving and united community. But God was going to raise them up as a God-centered and lively community again.

There were many other individuals whom God called as leaders in the Old Testament times whose mission was to bring people back to God and a healthy life as a community. The call to Trinitarian life continued throughout the faith history.

In the New Testament times we see God repeating the same story again, calling people back to him and to a healthy community life. John the Baptist is one of the prominent figures in this salvific plan of God. The events connected with his birth itself were very significant. His parents, Elizabeth and Zechariah were advanced in age and did not have children, which could indicate that God could bring life out of barrenness and hopelessness. Through a special intervention of God, the elderly couple conceived their son, John the Baptist. His name itself was very significant. The family wanted to name him Zachariah after his father, but Elizabeth and Zechariah told them that it was not to be so. God had told them that his name would be John. John meant, "God is gracious" or "God shows his favor." John was going to be a sign and symbol of God's graciousness and favor over his people. God was going to show his favor to his people by sending them a Savior. The Savior, Jesus was going to bring them back to God and bring them together as a community. And John was going to be the one heralding that good news. The whole preaching and ministry of John were focused on this mission of preparing the way for the Lord.

And as promised, God himself comes to live among us through the person of Jesus, trying to bring us back to him and gather us together as one community. The whole mission and ministry of Jesus were centered on this call to Trinitarian life and participation in the divine dance of love. People had turned away from God and they were anything but a loving community. He denounced ungodly ways and unjust structures and systems that divided the community. He used great stories like that of the prodigal sons, lost sheep, and lost coin to tell his people how they needed to return back to healthy relationship with God and one another. When the prodigal sons were disconnected from their father and distanced from each other, they were not "home."

They were living unhealthy lives. The father wanted them to come home. When the sheep was cut off from the shepherd and the flock it was not safe and happy. It was living a lonely and insecure life. The shepherd waned it to be "home." When the coin was lost and was left alone somewhere, the woman was not happy. The coin must have "felt" forgotten and abandoned. The coin had to return back to the woman to recognize how much it was valued.

Jesus spent a great amount of time and energy for teaching, coaching, forgiving, and healing, all with the intention of bringing people back to God and healthy living as a community. And finally by his death on the cross he demonstrated that he would make any sacrifice for the sake of bringing us back to him and uniting us together as a community. When he was crucified and killed, even his own disciples had abandoned him and run away from him. They were afraid and suspicious. But he gathered them back again and commissioned them to continue the mission of bringing people back to God and uniting them as one community. People needed to be home and the divine dance had to continue.

God keeps inviting us back to him and back to community. He wants us back home. We keep going away, but he keeps calling us back. Sometimes we abandon God and his ways and fail to live as a loving community. Values, beliefs, and practices that are not godly and healthy influence us. Sometimes some of us feel abandoned and forgotten by God. Sometimes some of us are angry and disappointed with God. Even Jesus felt abandoned by his heavenly Father. Sometimes we get used to living in "Egypt" that we forget that we actually belong to the "Promised Land." We are not meant to live in godlessness and unhealthy ways of living. We are to be united with God and one another as a loving family and community. That is our Promised Land, the land of freedom and peace, health and wholeness.

Sometimes we get addicted to or used to unhealthy ways of life and godlessness that we think that that is what is normal and that is how we are meant to be. We could wonder why the Israelites never went back to Canaan even after four hundred years. The famine in Canaan must have ended after a while, but they didn't go back to Canaan. Going back to the Promised Land, their home did not seem to be an urgent need for most of them. Historically, there must have been many reasons for the Israelites to stay put in Egypt and why it was difficult for them to go back to Canaan. However, looking at this story as God's call to come home psychologically, spiritually, and relationally, it could be seen as a phenomenon that happens in anyone's life. Once we get used to certain ways of thinking and doing, even if it is unhealthy, it sometimes becomes difficult to break out of it. Addictions and attachment to unhealthy ways of life take us away from our Promised Land, healthy living and relationships. By using our freedom we get into such things, but then those things take away our freedom. We become slaves to them and find it hard to break free from them. We get stuck in our "Egypts." By ourselves, sometimes we find it hard to leave those Egypts. We need God to send us a "Moses" as in the case of the Israelites who would make us recognize what we need to leave and where we need to be. The Moses in our life could be a friend, a spiritual guide, a teacher, a parent, a coworker, a stranger, so on and so forth.

Many things may have happened in our life that keeps us away from God and others. We may have become bitter and angry with God and others. We may be cunning and deceitful, trying to take advantage of others. Narcissism and selfishness may have become part of our personality. We may have become a racist, nationalist, religious fanatic, or someone with extremist ideas and behaviors. We may have harmed and hurt people by our words and actions. We may have become arrogant and proud religiously and culturally, looking down upon others. We may have used our power and position to dominate over others. Maybe we are stuck with certain unhealthy and negative images of God. We may have created God in "our own image and likeness." There may be so many things that make us get stuck in Egypt. God calls us once again to a life of freedom and health, right relationship with him and with one another. We need to ask God to help us to go beyond our distorted ideas and destructive behaviors. The God who has revealed himself to us in our faith and human history, particularly through the person of Jesus is a God of love and compassion. He is a God who knows us more than anyone else. He is a God who walks with us at all times. He is a God who is not only concerned about our life on this earth but also our life hereafter.

We need to think of God and us in a new way. We need to give God a chance to renew and reshape our lives. There is nothing in our life that is too big for God that he cannot change or forgive. In the book of Isaiah, we hear God saying, "Though your sins are like scarlet, they shall be like snow; though they are red like crimson, they shall become like wool" (Isa 1:18). Change and transformation are possible even for the worst sinner. The examples of King David, Saint Peter, Saint Paul, and many others should give us hope and confidence that when God is on our side or intervenes in our life, anything becomes possible. God is willing to do anything for us. What he needs is our desire and willingness to reciprocate his love. We need to return home, return to the Trinitarian life by being in communion with God and others. We need to be active participants in the dialogical triangle and the divine dance of love.

34

Loving as He Loves

THE SECOND DIMENSION OF the Christological model of life is love. We shall discuss about this dimension in this and the next chapter. The great "I AM" who has been revealing himself in our human history is all about love. It is love that unites this Trinitarian God. It is his love that led to our creation. And it is this love that incarnated in Jesus. The dialogical triangle that involves God, the individual, and the community is to be glued together by love. And the kind of love that should animate this relationship is what we see in Jesus.

People experienced Jesus as someone very different from the usual kind of leaders or rabbis in the community or society. The gospels say that people were amazed by his teaching and words because " . . . he taught them as one having authority, and not as their scribes" (Matt 7:29). He was not simply preaching something or passing on some message from somebody. He himself was the message. His life communicated more than all the words and preaching he used. He not only preached about love but he himself was the embodiment of love. He was the incarnation of love.

Commandment of Love

Among the many things that Jesus asked his disciples to do, two of the prominent ones that stand out are his commandment to them to love one another as he loved them and asking them to be different from the rest of the world. The commandment to love one another as he loved them is given in the context of Jesus washing his disciple's feet and asking them to abide in him (John 13). The exhortation to be different from the rest of the world was given immediately after two of the disciples, James and John asked for positions in his kingdom (Mark 10). In fact both these commandments go together. If they loved and served one another as Jesus loved and served them, they would be different from the rest of the world because that is not the kind of love that is often seen in the world.

It is good for us to take some time to understand what these commandments mean. When Jesus says, love one another as I have loved you, we have to first understand whom he loved and how he loved. If we want to look at it as addressed to the twelve apostles, we would realize that this commandment has some deep implications. Jesus and his disciples were one of the most difficult groups of people who ever got together to live as a community. It is amazing how Jesus could keep this group together. There was nothing much common between them. Usually when leaders or people form a team they often select like-minded people. The team that Jesus formed was strange.

From the gospels we get some idea about who the twelve apostles were. All of them had their own peculiar personalities and traits. They fought among themselves to see who was the greatest. A few of them were fishermen whom others must have considered uneducated and belonging to low class. There was Judas Iscariot who loved money. He is referred to as a thief who used to steal money from the common purse, which means his companions may not have trusted him. And he would betray his master later. There was another disciple, Simon the Zealot, whose background is sometimes disputed among scholars, but many think that he was a member of a radical group, which later came to be known as the Zealots. It is possible that by the time the gospels were written this group attained the name, the Zealots, and the evangelists must have added that title to this apostle. If he was a member of that group it could mean that he was someone with some fanatic or militant ideologies and belief systems, probably wanting to overthrow the Romans. Many of his companions must have been leery of him, not agreeing with his extremist views. Then there was someone on the opposite side of the spectrum, Matthew, tax collector, an associate of the Romans, whom everybody else must have hated. There were James and John who were called sons of thunder due to their short-tempered nature and anger. When the Samaritan village rejected Jesus they were angry and upset and wanted to call down fire from heaven to destroy the villagers. The same duo, James and John tried to bribe Jesus and asked for positions in his kingdom, that one would sit at his right and the other would sit at his left. Simon Peter who is often considered the right-hand man of Jesus was going to deny him. Most of these disciples were going to run away from him and abandon him when he needed them most. And all of them would doubt his resurrection. They tested his patience and love throughout his life. But he loved them to the very end.

In the ordinary sense, it was not easy to love any one of them. They were not so loveable. But Jesus loved them. He loved them without any reservation, without any limit, and without any condition. The love of Jesus was not just a nice sentiment. It was sacrificial and self-giving. Even though it was difficult, he loved them. He had to put up with them many times; he had to be patient with them over and over again; he had to forgive them not once or twice but unendingly. He had to forget and forgive many things they did. And he had to love them even though they did not love him in return. It was a sacrificial love.

He loved them not because they were loveable, but because that was the only way to change them and show them what it really means to love. His love was transforming. And that transforming love melted their hearts and they changed gradually. Jesus was inviting them to do the same for each other and teach the rest of the world what it means to truly love. Given the kind of personalities and natures these men had, we can assume that it was not easy for them to love each other. But the love of Jesus that each of them experienced in their lives transformed them and that helped them to do the same for one another.

We could wonder why Jesus chose such a diverse group of people to be his closest companions. The reason I believe is that these apostles represent the rest of us. The gospels state that Jesus chose these twelve from his large number of disciples, which means that these twelve were representative of the larger group of disciples. In that larger group of disciples all of us are included, and hence the twelve apostles represent all of us. Our stories may not be very different from that of these apostles. We might see in us many of those characteristics that we see in them. We bribe and cheat, we fight for positions and power, we try to outdo each other, we get worked up by our anger and other negative emotions, we become greedy for money and steal, we deny, we betray, we abandon, we become militant, fanatic, and rigid in our beliefs and ideologies, and we do all kinds of other things that we find the disciples doing. We belong to different classes and categories in our communities and societies. But with all that, God still loves us. He is patient with us. He forgives us over and over again. He waits for our return to healthy life and relationships. He loves us unconditionally. We may have messed up our life, committed sins, and made bad choices, but God still loves us. He loves us in spite of our limitations and imperfections.

Jesus loved not only those who were closest to him but also those who were far away. He loved those were in the community and outside the community. He loved everyone irrespective of who they were. He loved even those who hated him and killed him. He forgave and prayed for those who persecuted him. It was a love without any reservation or limit. It was a love that was totally giving, patient, and forgiving. It was a love that was gentle and kind and yet challenging and tough. It was a love that was agonizingly painful.

That is the kind of love that Jesus is asking us to put into practice. He asks us to love those who are closest to us and are known to us. He asks us to love those who may be far away. And he asks us to love even those who hate us and hurt us.

We know sometimes it is not easy when it comes to loving those who are closest to us and are known to us. That involves a daily dose of love. People with whom we live and work may not be so loveable. Either they find us difficult or we find them difficult. Our family members, colleagues, neighbors, and others may not be people that we really feel like loving. They might deny us, betray us, become greedy, fight for positions and power at our expense, and do all kinds of things that hurt us, but Jesus wants us to still love them. It is a real challenge to love them. We may have to be patient with them over and over again. We may have to forgive them many times. We may have to forget many things they do. We may have to be kind and compassionate even when they are rude and hurtful. In his first letter to the Corinthians, Saint Paul has a whole chapter dedicated to the theme of love that tells us what it means to love somebody on a daily basis (1 Cor 13). Commenting on this Pauline text, Pope Francis says that in Paul's understanding, "love is more than a mere feeling" (Francis, 2016). In his prayer for the Ephesians, Saint Paul says that they may be "rooted and established in love" so that "Christ may dwell in their hearts" (Eph 3:17). It takes a tremendous amount of patience and courage to love consistently those whom we may not feel like loving.

Loving those who are not known to us or far away is not usually easy because often we tend to love those who like us and are like us. Those who do not belong to our group, class, race, community, nationality, and all such variations usually do not fall on our radar of love. It takes tremendous amount of courage and generosity to cross over the walls and fences and love those who are different from us. But that is what Jesus invites us to do. To live as a family and bring into fruition Jesus's dream of establishing God's kingdom on earth, we have to cross over our walls and barriers and love those who are different and unknown to us. Otherwise we will continue to live in our small worlds excluded and isolated from everyone else. And that is not Christian and Christological.

The most difficult of all loves may be loving those who hurt and harm us, especially those who inflict brutal physical injury and pain. Both psychological and physical pains are difficult to bear when they are intense. And both of them could have lasting negative effects on us. Sometimes psychological pain caused by somebody is as bad as physical pain, and sometimes it could be worse. However, physical pain caused by somebody could have all kinds of repercussions that we are not prepared for. It has an immediate impact on us. We become a helpless victim without any defense or sense of safety. That is what Jesus faced. Throughout his public ministry Jesus experienced psychological pain. People judged him, isolated him, criticized him, spread all kinds of calumny against him, and tried to break his spirit. But he was still "unharmed." He could escape from many situations. If people didn't like him or accept him in one place, he could go to another. If some people judged him, there were other people who loved him. He was still "safe." But when he faced his final moments of agony and pain in the physical sense, he was no more safe. There was nobody to help him.

He was totally helpless and defenseless before those wretched and ruthless men. He was dragged, scourged, kicked, spat upon, punched, whipped, and beaten. A crown of thorns was pressed deep into his skull. A heavy cross was laid on his shoulders and he was made to walk quite a long distance. He fell and was probably pushed to the ground several times. Nails pierced into his raw flesh on his hands and feet as he was nailed to the cross. He was lifted up on the cross and was left hanging for some hours. A spear pierced into his raw flesh again as a soldier wanted to inflict the last act of brutality on him. Even thinking about those gruesome acts of those evil men would give us chills and make us tremble with fear. Jesus knew the heaviness and hardness of this physical pain and agony. There is no wonder why he sweated blood in Gethsemane, on the Mount of Olives.

Given into the hands of those brutish men, Jesus was totally helpless. Of course we can think that Jesus being God had some extra energy or strength to bear all those agonies and pains. Or we might think that he could have escaped if he wanted. But that is not the kind of person that we see in Jesus. Jesus was totally human like us, feeling pain and agony like any one of us, being defenseless and helpless like any one of us. If and when we are faced with such agonies and pains, the normal emotions and feelings that could come up in us could be rage, hatred, extreme sadness and grief, revenge, discouragement, and all kinds of distress and negativity. But that is not what we see in Jesus. We see only love. We see only compassion. And we see a prayer on his lips for his persecutors.

We experience psychological pain because of what people do to us. When they criticize us, judge us, isolate us, spread all kinds of calumny against us, humiliate us, and put us down, we experience a lot of agony and pain. But even with all that we are still "safe" in some way. We may have some people who care about us, love us, and encourage us. Or at least we can seek healing and help from somebody for all those psychological wounds that are inflicted on us. But when we are faced with some real physical injury and harm because of the violence and brutality of someone, our pain and agony might be indescribable.

We have many examples of extreme violence and harm done to people in the past as well as in our contemporary world. If a frenzied mob comes pouncing on us wanting to harm or kill us and takes pleasure in what they do to us, the feelings and emotions we go through may be indescribable. We become totally helpless before them. When a person takes us hostage and threatens and begins to slit our throat or chop off our heads we have absolutely no way to defend ourselves. When a shooter with a gun or pistol appears in front of us all of a sudden and starts shooting at us, we are not prepared for such an eventuality. When our tormentor does brutal things like peeling away our skin, dismembering our body, sticking sharp objects through our body, locking us up in gas chambers and suffocating us, and beating us to death, we are totally helpless and defenseless. On a larger scale, in the context of wars and ethnic conflicts, indescribable harm and pain are caused to people. In many of these situations we are totally defenseless, helpless, and at the mercy of the tormentor. There is no way to escape. In such situations, to love those tormentors is anything but human. But that is the extent to which Jesus is asking us to take our love. Of course, in many of those situations, even before we have a moment to think about forgiving or loving we may be killed. But if we do have a moment before we die, the question is whether we would continue to love or give into anger and hatred.

Loving one another as Jesus loved is going to be truly sacrificial. It is going to demand a great amount of courage, commitment, and determination. Jesus knows that it is difficult. It was difficult for him too. But he chose that path rather than the path of violence, revenge, hatred, and anger. It is doable, but it is not going to be easy. We need a great amount of grace from God. Our own effort and determination alone will not do it. We need God to send us an angel to assist and strengthen us as he sent an angel to strengthen Jesus in his agony in Gethsemane.

Reasons for Loving as Jesus Loves

The first reason for us to love as Jesus loves is that only by doing that we can be his disciples. As disciples of Christ or Christians, Jesus is very clear about what the foundation of our life should be. It is love. Our lives have to be based on love. It is a commandment and not a choice or option. If we really want to be Christians or children of God, we have to be loving people. There is no option there. Saint John says that if we really want to know God we have to love, "Everyone who loves has been born of God and knows God. Whoever does not love does not know God, because God is love" (1 John 4:7–8).

Simply calling ourselves Christians or children of God does not make us disciples of Christ or God's children. We have to live a life of love. We have to live our lives modeled after the life of Christ, the life of the Holy Trinity, which is all about love. As Jesus was the incarnation of love we have to incarnate as love wherever we are. There is no other commandment that Jesus places before us than this commandment of love. This love is not anything mysterious. It is something that is planted in us. Created in the image and likeness of God who is love itself, there is love in all of us. God has planted that in our heart.

We know that we are all on different levels in our spiritual life and in our relationship with God. Some of us may be very intimate with him, some of us may not be so close and intimate, and some of us may be very lukewarm and indifferent. But all of us are called to keep growing into the person of Christ. Everyday we have to pray to God that it is "more of him and less of us." We have to desire and pray for that love to grow in our heart. We know that even then we might live selfishly. But we can hope that some day we will come to a point when it will be truly more of God and less of us. Until we get to that point we need to keep praying and striving for that.

Saint Francis de Sales is someone who had a deep sense of this love of God and loving as God loves. Taking into account his writings on the theme of love, he is often referred to as the "Doctor of love." The maxim he suggests in regard to loving, as God loves is "Live Jesus." To love as God loves is to live Jesus at every moment of our life. It is to make Jesus come alive in our life. It is to allow our whole self to be directed and guided by Jesus. It is to become what Jesus said of his relationship with his father, "The Father and I are one" (John 10:30). To live Jesus is to be able to say, "Jesus and I are one." We know communities and organizations have code of conduct, mission statements, logos, dress codes, and values they live by. That is how they want to be known. For the disciples of Christ, it is the commandment of love by which they have to be known.

The second reason for loving as Jesus loves is that it is such love that brings us joy in life. Jesus said, "If you keep my commandments, you will abide in my love, just as I have kept my Father's commandments and abide in his love. I have said these things to you so that my joy may be in you, and that your joy may be complete" (John 15:10–11). Jesus wants us to be joyful. And to be joyful we have to have love in our heart; we have to love one another. No one can be really joyful when they have hatred in their heart, when they are full of rage and anger, when they don't forgive, when they wait to take revenge, when they are jealous and greedy, when they engage in violence and destruction, when they isolate themselves into their own world, and when they harbor all kinds of negative feelings and thoughts in their heart and mind. These things simply take away our joy. We are disturbed and troubled. Most people who engage in such things go to bed with a heavy heart. They don't have peace. They don't sleep well. They are worried about the enemy, either worried about when the enemy is going to attack or about when they should attack the enemy. When we engage in such negative and unhealthy things we may have a sense of pleasure and satisfaction, but that is not real joy. We may feel that we got even with the other person, but that doesn't make us any better. Jesus wants us to experience real joy in our life. For that we need to be freed from all unhealthy elements in our life and be filled with God's love. Life becomes really burdensome when there is no joy in life.

The third reason for loving as Jesus loves is that only such love can transform human hearts and transform this world. Jesus said, "By this everyone will know that you are my disciples, if you have love for one another" (John 13:35). The one word that has changed people throughout human history is "love." And this is a word that all of us understand. No matter in what century we live, what community we belong to, and what culture we have inherited, love is a universal theme. Love is a language that everyone understands. Love is the force that connects us—connects us with God and with each other. You and I know what it means to love. And you and I know how to love. If anything has helped us to make changes in our lives, it is the love of someone who cared about us. Because there was somebody or there were people who loved and cared about us, we were able to grow and develop. Their love transformed us. If somebody hated us, disliked us, or harmed us that did not help us to grow, and that did not make us feel good about ourselves or the other person. It is only love that changes human hearts and lives.

We know that Jesus did not give sight to all the blind people who lived in Palestine, Galilee, or Jerusalem. He did not heal all the lepers or sick people who were living in those territories. He did not raise all the people who died in those days. And he did not preach the good news to all the poor and afflicted people or forgive all the sinners in those areas. What he did was inaugurating a new era of God's love and inviting his disciples to spread that love to the ends of the earth. The twelve disciples whom he chose, formed, and loved represented the rest of the humanity. The few people whom he touched and healed or showed compassion to represented the larger humanity that is seeking love, healing, and compassion. Today it is our turn to be the disciples of Jesus, to be formed and loved by him first, and then to be sent out to bring his love to others. Today we become Jesus to the broken hearted, to the sick and the suffering, to the lost and the forsaken, and to the stubborn and the sinful. Jesus keeps reminding us that only love can change our world. There are many things in us and in our world that divide us and keep us apart from God and one another. Hatred, anger, ill feelings, jealousy, lack of forgiveness, narrow mindedness, exclusivist mentality, and all such things make our lives and relationships difficult. But there is also the strong force of love that God has planted in each one of us that can keep us as one family. And that is what we want to focus on. We are one family, and we have love in our hearts. We are created in the image and likeness of the Holy Trinity, which means that like the Holy Trinity we are unique individuals but we are united as one family.

Our normal human tendency is to love those who love us in return. We don't usually think of loving someone who does not love us. But that is the challenge Jesus puts before us. He wants us to be different from the usual ways of the world. We have to love even those who may not love us in return. We have to bring the glue of love to those situations and relationships where bitterness and divisions exist. We have to continue to love even when we know that people might turn against us, deny us, betray us, and do all kinds of evil against us.

Our love has to be such that we see the sufferings and agony of others and we reach out to them even when we ourselves are going through agonies and pains. That is what Jesus did. His heart went out to the women of Jerusalem who were following him on the way to Calvary, to his beloved mother and disciple who stood at the foot of the cross, and to the thief who was hanging on the cross alongside with him. Our love has to sometimes take the form of silent suffering in the face of mockery and shame as Jesus did around his persecutors. Judas Iscariot was going to betray him, but still Jesus washed his feet. Peter was going to deny him, but still he washed his feet. All the disciples were going to run away from him and abandon him, but still he washed their feet. Usually the disciples bend down before the master. But with Jesus the roles were reversed; the master bends down before the disciples. He was willing to go to any extent for the sake of love.

Abraham was asked to sacrifice his only son, Isaac. We might wonder what kind of God it is that he demands Abraham to kill his only son after granting him that son in his old age. He might look like a cruel and heartless God. But it is not so much about the sacrifice itself but about love. The question was, "To what extent Abraham was willing to go for the sake of love." It probably was the most difficult moment in Abraham's life. He had to let go even the dearest possession of his life, his only son. Of course, Abraham didn't have to sacrifice his son. God stopped him from doing that. But in Jesus, that is what God did. He gave himself up for us to show us how much he loves us.

The love of Jesus is sometimes unfathomable and even scary. It really calls us to get out of our usual ways, and often we are not prepared for that. But Jesus says that that is the only way to change human hearts and change our world. If we don't do that then we are not going to be any different from those who engage in things that are against love. As disciples of Christ we are called to be different. And the way to be different according to Jesus is to love as he loved.

A saying that is often attributed to Saint Teresa of Kolkata is "love until it hurts." And she seems to have added that if we love until it hurts, there can be no more hurt but only more love. The love of Jesus calls us to love not only until it hurts but also even after it hurts. In other words, no hurts or harms are going to detract us from loving. We remain ready to bear anything for the sake of love. Loving as Jesus loves is what makes our lives truly Christological.

35

Forgiving Love

LOVING AS JESUS LOVES is a forgiving love. Forgiveness may be one of the most difficult things in our life. Jesus was not only teaching about forgiveness but also demonstrating it through his own life. He forgave people not once or twice but without limit. He forgave the people who judged him, criticized him, made fun of him, and spread all kinds of calumny against him. He forgave his disciples over and over again even after they denied him, betrayed him, and abandoned him. He forgave the hateful men who persecuted and killed him. The forgiving love was Jesus' way to win human hearts. If he kept anger, resentment, and hatred in his heart, he would not have been any different from others. If he avoided, rejected, and ill-treated those who hurt him, he would not have fulfilled his mission of bringing back the lost and the sinful.

Jesus wants us to be forgiving. If we do not forgive, we are not going to be well. If we do not forgive, we cannot move forward in our growth and development. If we do not forgive families and communities cannot get along with each other. Parents are worried and sad when their children are seriously sick. Their hearts go out to the sick child. They give special care, love, and attention to the sick child so that he or she can recover fast. And when the child gets well, the parents are relieved and happy.

It is not only about the physical illness of their children that parents are worried about. They are sad and worried when their children don't talk to each other. They are sad and worried when their children take to drugs and substances. They are sad and worried when their children are engaged in destructive behaviors. They are sad and worried when their children are sad, lonely, and psychologically sick. When those children get well and come back to healthy life, parents are happy and relieved. Sometimes those parents are angry at the behaviors of those children. But that anger is not destructive. It is an anger that desires the good of their children. Destructive anger desires and wills the destruction of the other. It makes the person do things to hurt and harm others. Loving parents may be angry with their children because they want them to realize the destructiveness in their behavior. They wish to see their children living well. Even the worst criminal has loved ones who care about him or her. They may not condone or agree with what he or she does, but they are concerned about the person.

Our God is worried, concerned, sad, and even angry when we are sick and live unhealthy lives. He is sad and worried when we live with destructive anger, resentment, and other destructive behaviors. He is sad and worried when we stay away from him and others. God's anger is not destructive. Jesus was angry in the temple when he saw people turning the temple into a market place. God does not desire the destruction of anyone, because we are all his children, and he wants to see all of us living well. In the book of Ezekiel we hear God saying, "Have I any pleasure in the death of the wicked, says the Lord God, and not rather that they should turn from their ways and live?" (Ezek 18:23). In the parables of the prodigal sons, lost sheep, and lost coin, Jesus shows us how much God is concerned about us when we are lost in sins and evils.

But human beings do develop destructive anger. Human beings desire and will the destruction of others. We intend hurt and harm toward others. Hurts and harms create resentment and destructive anger in us. In the story of Cain and Abel, God asked Cain, "Why are you angry, and why has your countenance fallen?" (Gen 4:6). Cain's destructive anger led to his murdering of his brother. In the story of the prodigal son, the elder son was angry with his father and brother. He did not wish that his brother should come back home.

Negative experiences are part of our life. It is a near impossibility to live without getting hurt, offended, misunderstood, blamed, shamed, rejected, lied to, etc. It is also most unlikely that we will live a life totally free from anger, ill feelings, and misunderstandings. We get angry and upset with others and with ourselves. Sometimes we may be even angry with God. But God wants us to be free from all those negative experiences, thoughts, and emotions that keep us enslaved or keep us away from God and others. He wants us to experience life in its fullness. He wants us to move on with our life and not allow the negative experiences and feelings to control our lives. To the paralytic, Jesus said, "Son, your sins are forgiven" (Mark 2:5). Sins and evils, especially destructive anger, hatred, and resentment can paralyze us.

God wants us to experience a new life. In the book of Isaiah, we hear God saying, "I am about to create new heavens and a new earth" (Isa 65:17). God wants to start anew. We often dwell on the past, but God does not. When we dwell on the past, we miss the present. It is not that we are going to say to others or ourselves that everything that they did or we did was fine and good. Forgiveness is not denying the seriousness of the offense or condoning it. Forgiveness is not excusing the person from taking responsibility for the offense. When things have not been done well, they and we know that they were not fine and good. But today we are different or we can be different. Today we can learn from our past and make new decisions for our present and future.

Forgiveness is a decision to let go off the anger, resentment, hatred, and other negative feelings and thoughts that we may have against others, God, or ourselves. Forgiveness is the process of entering into the troubled inner life of the offender and being able to say that the offender does not know what he or she is doing. It is the willingness to give the person another chance. Forgiveness is a gift rather than a right. Sometimes some people may not deserve our forgiveness for the hurt or harm they have caused us. But we give it as a gift. We let the anger and resentment go, so that we can keep moving forward and they can keep moving forward.

Forgiveness includes seeking and offering forgiveness. First, we seek forgiveness from God. There is nothing in our life that God cannot forgive. He wants us to get healed. The Psalmist sings that God is kind and merciful, slow to anger and steadfast in love (Ps 103:8). God knows our struggles and troubles. Sometimes we are burdened by sins and spiritual darkness. But God's love transforms all these. God comes to save us and give us life in abundance. Through Prophet Ezekiel, God says to us, "I will sprinkle clean water upon you, and you shall be clean from all your uncleannesses . . . A new heart I will give you, and a new spirit I will put within you; and I will remove from your body the heart of stone and give you a heart of flesh" (Ezek 36:25–26). The God who has revealed himself to us is a forgiving God. People experienced that forgiving love of God in Jesus. Inviting us to give to him the burdens of our sins and evils, he says, "Come to me, all you that are weary and are carrying heavy burdens, and I will give you rest" (Matt 11:28). There was nothing too big for him that he could not forgive.

Although it might sound strange, we also need to "forgive" God. Because of many reasons, we may have developed wrong ideas and images of God and we may be angry with him. We may have had times or situations when we felt that God didn't care. We may have had times when we prayed and didn't get a favorable answer from God. We may have felt angry with God when our loved ones were taken away or we were pushed into difficult situations. The elder son in the parable of the prodigal son was angry with his father. We need to release those negative feelings and thoughts we have developed about God. We need to enter into a new relationship with God. We need to give God another chance to show us how much he loves us.

Second, we need to forgive ourselves and seek forgiveness from our own self. We may not often think about that, but sometimes we are mad at ourselves for all the mess we create in our life. We make bad choices and end up in difficult situations. Many a time we are unhappy and angry with ourselves. We are disappointed and disgusted with ourselves. We are ashamed of ourselves. We blame ourselves. The prodigal son was disgusted with himself. Peter was probably disappointed and angry with himself after denying his master. Judas was angry and upset with himself after betraying Jesus. There are moments when we are not happy with what we do. We say and do things that hurt and harm people. We make decisions that we regret later. Disappointed and angry with ourselves, and feeling guilty we sometimes beat ourselves up. We need to forgive ourselves and seek forgiveness from our self for all those bad moments and situations. We need to release those negative thoughts and feelings we have built up about ourselves. It is not that we are congratulating ourselves for all the bad things we have done or saying that they were all appropriate but that we are giving ourselves a chance to change and do better.

We can do better. We don't need to continue to be self-destructive. Judas went and hanged himself after betraying Jesus. It appears that he could not forgive himself and he did not think that God would forgive him. God is merciful, and others are merciful. We need to be merciful to ourselves too. If we could have done differently in the past, we would have done it. We did what we did because of many reasons, especially our blindness to the truth and ignorance. But today we can learn from our past and make new decisions for what is healthy and loving. We need to give ourselves another chance. If we have been doing harm to others we start doing good. If we have been speaking badly about others we start saying something good about people. If we have been making bad choices, we start making good choices. If we tend to get worked up emotionally and make decisions without thinking well, we begin to balance our emotions and reason. We need to think, reflect, and pray well before we jump into actions or decisions. For all these, we need to start with forgiving ourselves and giving ourselves another chance.

Third, we need to seek forgiveness from others and offer them forgiveness. This may be the most difficult part of forgiveness. There may be people and situations in our life that we do not want to forgive. There may be people and situations that we think we have forgiven, but they still hurt us and bring back hurtful and painful memories. We may have to forgive a second, a third, and a fourth time, and those memories and feelings may not still go away. It takes several positive experiences to get over one negative experience. It takes several attempts and instances of forgiveness to be healed from one negative experience.

Peter asked Jesus how many times he should forgive his brother (Matt 18:21–22). It appears that in those days, people were taught in the Synagogues that they had a duty to forgive others three times. When Peter asked if it was enough to forgive seven times, he must have been thinking that he was going way more than the expected norms. But Jesus responded to him that forgiveness should be practically limitless. Sometimes an offense requires repeated forgiveness, and it might still bother us. Sometimes we have to apply a balm or ointment over a wound over and over again. It takes time to heal. Until it is healed we have to keep applying that ointment. Forgiving others is similar. Until the wound or the hurt is healed, we have to keep forgiving.

There may be also people from whom we have to seek forgiveness. We make mistakes. We say and do things that hurt and harm people. And we need to seek their forgiveness. This is also difficult because we may be afraid that they may not forgive us. We may be also ashamed of asking for forgiveness. But however difficult it may be, it is important to ask for forgiveness because only by doing that we can move on in our life.

Reasons for Seeking and Offering Forgiveness

There are many reasons why we need to seek and offer forgiveness from others. I shall list a few of them here below.

Recipients of Mercy and Forgiveness

One reason why we need to seek and offer forgiveness to others is that we all have been recipients of God's unconditional forgiveness and mercy. God has forgiven our many sins. If God were to punish us for all that we did, we would not have grown and moved ahead in our life. We have also experienced abundance of forgiveness from others. Our parents, families, friends, teachers, colleagues, and many others have been generous in forgiving. If they were to keep an account of all our wrong doings, and if they were to retaliate and punish us for everything, we would not have grown and moved ahead in life. Jesus wants us to be aware of that and show similar mercy and compassion to those who offend us and seek mercy from those whom we offend. Jesus speaks of the necessity of that mutual love and mercy, "Be merciful, just as your Father is merciful. Do not judge, and you will not be judged; do not condemn, and you will not be condemned. Forgive, and you will be forgiven" (Luke 6:36–37). In the prayer that Jesus taught his disciples, forgiving others was emphasized as important as receiving God's forgiveness.

The same message is conveyed in the parable of the unforgiving servant (Matt 18:21). The king forgave all the debts of the unforgiving servant. But the servant did not show compassion to his fellow servant who owed him much less than what he himself owed to the king.

Important for Personal Healing

Forgiveness is often more for our personal healing than for anyone else. Research shows that forgiveness is important for our own self-healing. When we don't forgive the flow of life is cut. There is no more connection or relationship with the other or it is strained. We become burdened and enslaved by hatred and ill feeling. Sometimes resentment and hatred hurt us more than it hurts the offender. It creates in us negative feelings such as anger, hatred, sadness, and vengeance. Holding on to grudges and being angry and revengeful lead into resentment and hostility. It affects us physically, emotionally, and spiritually. Dwelling on grudges spike blood pressure and heart rate, which are often signs of stress. Holding grudges compromises our immune system, making us less resistant to illnesses. Keeping hatred and anger in our heart is emotionally draining. Forgiveness frees us from those burdens that we carry. Forgiveness has power to heal. It heals wounds. Lack of forgiveness has power to hold. It holds us enslaved. Forgiveness makes us happier. It improves our health. It restores the broken relationships. Forgiveness brings the forgiver peace of mind and frees him or her from destructive anger. It helps the person let go off deeply held negative feelings and thoughts.

Refusing to Repeat the Offense and be like the Offender

Another reason why we forgive is because we refuse to repeat the offense and become like the offender or add on to the sins in the world. When we act with vengeance and hatred, we fall into the same level of the offender. We are called to be different. In one of his exhortations, Jesus says, "For if you love those who love you, what reward do you have? Do not even the tax collectors do the same? And if you greet only your brothers and sisters, what more are you doing than others? Do not even the Gentiles do the same?'" (Matt 5:46–47). Again in the same chapter we read, "For I tell you, unless your righteousness exceeds that of the scribes and Pharisees, you will never enter the kingdom of heaven" (Matt 5:20).

Yes, forgiveness is hard. When somebody inflicts pain on us, or when our children, parents, family members, or friends are abused and brutally killed in front of our eyes, it is not forgiveness that comes first into our mind. What we experience is vengeance, anger, and desire to pay back in the same measure or even more gruesomely. The blood boils within us seeking retaliation. When Cain murdered his brother, Abel, God said to him, "Your brother's blood is crying out to me from the ground" (Gen 4:10). When the blood of our loved ones cries out, forgiveness and love may not be on our radar. We may be justified in our retaliation and anger in some way, but our offense in return does not make us any different from the offender. The love and forgiveness that Jesus presents before us is to refuse to be like the offender. Forgiveness is essential to rise to a higher level than that of the offender. When sin makes us go down low, forgiveness makes us go up high. Sin pushes us down to hell while forgiveness pushes us up into heaven. If we sink into the level of the offender, we are not making much difference in our personal lives and in the world.

Not Allowing the Past to Determine the Present and Future

Another reason why forgiveness is important is that we don't want the negativity and evils of our past to determine our present and future. The negative and evil experiences already make us feel burdened and enslaved, but we don't want them to hold us hostage for the rest of our life. We need to move on.

We forgive not because we are weak, but because we are strong. Jesus shows us that the real power is in love and forgiveness. We forgive because we don't want sin or the sinful person to break our spirit and control the rest of our life. We want God or Jesus to control our life. We don't want to get stuck with our past. We want to live in the present. Today is another day, and we want to enjoy this day and live our lives to the full. People may do many things to break our spirit, to defeat us, and to dishearten us. Many people tried to silence and defeat Jesus. They thought they could break his spirit, but they failed miserably. He did not allow sin and evils to stop him. Instead, he defeated sin, suffering, and death. That Jesus is our strength, and he encourages us to forgive and let go off the enslaving powers of hated, anger, and evil.

An Enemy is Bad News

Another reason why forgiveness is important is that an enemy out there is not good news for anybody. The person who is avoided or kept out because of hatred or anger is going to do us more harm than good. The enemy might continue to hurt or attack us physically and psychologically. And if we have others whom we dislike or keep away, they might join hands to hurt us. When we have an enemy, we are forced to be always on the watch for the attack of the enemy with fear and vigilance. And that is going to demand a lot of energy and resources from us. If we didn't have the enemy, that energy and resources could be invested in other areas where we could grow and make progress. An enemy is always an unnecessary burden on our lives. It is a situation where no one wins. Either the enemy will win this time and we will suffer the loss, or we win this time and the enemy suffers loss. But the enemy is not gone. The enemy will come back more furious and upset because of the loss and will fight back. And we will be again at war with each other. The battle will go on unendingly.

Given this prospect of no one winning and everyone unnecessarily burdening themselves, Jesus rightly said, "You have heard that it was said, 'You shall love your neighbor and hate your enemy.' But I say to you, Love your enemies and pray for those who persecute you" (Matt 5:43–44). If the enemy can be befriended, he or she will be less likely to cause us harm and trouble. We may not become best friends, but we will have the enemy turned into someone we can work with or tolerate.

Rising to the Level of God

Forgiveness takes us to the level of God. When we forgive, we begin to see the offender as God sees. If God loves me with all my frailties, he cannot but love my offender with his or her frailties because we all are his children. As God desires our good, he desires the good of our offenders. Just as he weeps when we are far away from home or healthy living, he weeps when our offender is far away from home. Hence forgiveness helps us not only to take the offender to God in our prayer but also to pray for the good of that person. Since God desires that person to live healthy and happy life we also want to desire a healthy and happy life for that person.

Jesus in his prayer on the cross shows us how we can rise up to the level of God, "Father, forgive them; for they do not know what they are doing" (Luke 23:34). We might say that certain people know what they are doing. It will be illogical to think that the men who persecuted, crucified, and killed Jesus didn't know what they were doing. It would be strange to think that Judas or Peter did not know what they were doing. But on a deeper level, Jesus knew that they didn't know what they were doing. They were ignorant. They were blinded by their anger, fear, hatred, resentment, and all such negative elements.

It would be great if we can get into the offender's mind and see what makes him or her to think, feel, and do things that are bad. But we don't have such access to people's minds. Only God knows the person completely. We only see the consequences or expressions of what is going on in them. Something blinded them from doing what is good. If they could have done anything different they would have done it. Forgiveness allows a space for human frailty and weakness. It is not that we desire or promote mistakes and wrong doings, but knowing that other people are weak and limited as we are, we remain prepared for the possibility that they would make mistakes. If we accept that we are imperfect, it might become easier to accept others with their imperfections.

Not Necessarily Becoming Best Friends

Forgiving doesn't mean that we are going to be best friends with the offender. If we become best friends, that will be wonderful news. But that is most unlikely to happen. We can't be best friends with everybody. Even Jesus couldn't do that. To be best friends with somebody, there should be many things that we would be able to share with one another. There are people with whom we don't find too much in common. They might find some things in common with others, but that doesn't mean that it works for everybody. Forgiving is not about becoming best friends. It is about not allowing hatred, hurt, and past injuries to hold us slaves, exhaust us, and keep tormenting us. It is about getting rid of the destructive anger. It is about not wanting to desire or direct harm or hurt toward the other person, which once again takes us to the level of God who does not desire the destruction of anyone.

Having said all these, we still know that forgiveness is not easy. It is harder for some people than for others. It takes a tremendous amount of courage and inner strength to forgive. Some people try very hard to forgive, but they do not seem to succeed. Every time they remember the injury or harm done to them, anger and hatred build up in them. Sometimes it appears to be humanly impossible to forgive. Hence we continue to seek God's grace and strength. We continue to take to prayer the person and the situation that have hurt us. We have to do the same if we find it hard to ask someone for forgiveness. We may be afraid and ashamed of asking for forgiveness. So we ask the Lord for strength and courage to seek healing and forgiveness. Some injuries and memories may have to be placed before the Lord over and over again. Gradually the Lord will bring the healing. To be Christological, we need to seek and offer forgiveness.

36

Pilgrims on a Journey

THE THIRD DIMENSION OF the Christological model of life is that it is a journey, a journey with God and others. In the remaining part of this book we shall discuss this dimension.

Saint Luke presents Jesus as resolutely moving toward Jerusalem (Luke 9:51). If we look at this journey of Jesus toward Jerusalem without understanding its deeper meaning we might be deceived to think that he was careless and suicidal. Jerusalem is where he got crucified and killed. So resolutely moving toward Jerusalem could mean that he was going there to get killed. We could think that he didn't have to do that and that he had many ways to escape that. But I don't believe that that is what the evangelist is intending by this passage. It has a deeper meaning. Resolutely moving toward Jerusalem could mean that he was going to go to any extent to manifest his love for the humanity. If it meant giving up his life, he was not going to shy away from that. There were many things that came as stumbling blocks on his way, but he was determined to keep moving toward Jerusalem. Nothing and nobody was going to break his spirit and change his mind from reaching that goal because he knew that love was the only thing that could change our hearts and win us back.

Moving toward Jerusalem also could be seen as his goal of completing the mission of his heavenly Father. And the mission of the heavenly Father was to gather all of us as one family in love. Jerusalem was the heart of the Jewish religion. That is where the temple or the holy of holies stood. They had many synagogues but only one temple. Having only one temple for the whole nation or community meant that the Jerusalem temple was the unifying factor for the community. That is where God and his people would be united. That is where the community would be united. Hence Jerusalem symbolized the presence of God and the coming together of the community. The mission of Jesus was to be the presence of God among his people and to be the unifying factor for the whole humanity. He came to gather us all as one community united in love. He is the divine dancer who came to invite us to join him in the dance of love. It is not the actual city of Jerusalem but the heavenly Jerusalem or heaven where we are united with God and others that he is marching toward and inviting us to join him. Jesus would not rest until that goal is achieved. This is not a goal that is achieved and wrapped up at a particular time in history. It is a dynamic goal that continues for all eternity. Jesus continues to be with us and continues to be on that journey toward Jerusalem. His redemptive work continues. He would not rest until he gathers us all together.

His movement toward the eternal Jerusalem or heaven is in view of having all of us being on the journey with him. We are to focus on being united with God and others in love. Saint Paul reminds us, "our citizenship is in heaven" (Phil 3:20). When the goal of our life is heaven or union with God and others we are not to get stuck with things that are transient and passing, whether they are physical or psychological. We need to keep moving as Jesus did. As he did not allow anything or anybody to hold him back from that goal, we are to resist all temptations that would take our attention away from that goal. It is possible that we are held back from that goal by many things during our earthly life. We may be afraid of truly loving God and others because of the sacrifices involved in it. We may be reluctant to let go off many things, as they are often attractive and pleasurable. We may not want to be on the road to Jerusalem.

In the gospel of Matthew there is a story of a rich young man who comes to Jesus and asks him what he needed to do to attain eternal life (Matt 19:16–26). Knowing that he had followed all the commandments in the traditional sense, Jesus asks him to sell all his possessions, distribute the money to the poor, and then come and follow him. The story says that the young man went away very sad because he did not want to give up his possessions. He did not want to be on the road with Jesus. He did not want to make sacrifices. If he sold everything, what would happen? He would become dependent and insecure. He was afraid to lose his independence and security. He didn't want to be on the road like Jesus. But what did his possessions do to him? They got him stuck. Maybe there are many of us who are afraid of giving up things and possessions in our life and being on the road with Jesus. We often want to stay; we want independence and security; we want to be attached to things and people; we want to hold on to our ideas and opinions; and it is hard to move from all that and be on the road with Jesus.

We could wonder what the rich young man envisaged as eternal life. Maybe he thought that eternal life was going to be an extension of what he had on this earth— that is, having many possessions and wealth for all eternity. If that is how he thought of it then it did not make sense to him to leave everything. Jesus attempted to correct the young man's distorted idea of eternal life and wanted him to be free from things that were holding him back. But the young man was not ready for that yet.

The richness of the young man doesn't have to be seen only from the physical and material perspective. He could be standing for anyone who is afraid of giving up independence and security that this world offers or anyone who is unwilling to leave their unhealthy ideas, ideologies, thoughts, beliefs, values, and behaviors.

Jesus used the parable of a rich fool who thought that his possessions were going to save him and keep him permanently in this world (Luke 12:16–21). God reminded him that he had to move on, and that this world was not the end. On another occasion Jesus said that we couldn't serve both God and wealth (Luke 16:13). If we have to be on the journey with Jesus, we have to be willing to leave many things. We cannot hang on to the things of this world and at the same time have things of heaven or be united with God and others.

Some of us might think that this world is the be all and end all of everything, and that we are going to be here permanently. With that idea we might try to hold on to our possessions and positions. But God reminds us that we are not citizens or permanent residents on this earth. In many countries people belong to different categories such as citizens, green card holders or permanent residents, visa holders or visitors, and illegal immigrants. When it comes to our life on this earth, we are almost like "visa" holders or visitors. We stay here for a short stint and then move on. We are on the road with Jesus.

In the story of the blind beggar, Bartimaeus, we have a man who first sits by the wayside blind and begging. When Jesus came by, things changed for him. After he was healed, he was no more blind and begging. And he was no more sitting by the wayside. He was on the road with Jesus, following him. His blindness doesn't have to be seen only from the physical perspective. It could be referring to all kinds of things that were keeping him away from God and others. When he allowed Jesus to touch his life, he was no more blinded by those things. He was freer to be available to God and others.

After the resurrection, Jesus appeared to the women who had gone to the tomb and told them to be on the road, being missionaries, announcing the good news about his resurrection. He did not want them to be stuck in their grief and sadness. He wanted them to keep moving. He didn't want them to be afraid of death and the tomb. He wanted the women to tell his disciples that he still loved them even though they had abandoned him. They didn't have to get stuck in their guilt and shame. He wanted them to keep moving. And that is the good news that God has been telling his people throughout the salvation history, that he still loved them even though they had abandoned him. They didn't have to be stuck in their fear and shame. He wanted his disciples to move on and go to Galilee. Asking them to go to Galilee could mean that he wanted them to come out of their rooms, come out of their fear, and keep moving. After Jesus was killed, the disciple retreated to a room for fear of the Jews. They were stuck. But Jesus comes to them, telling them not to be afraid and calling them to be on the road again.

When Jesus appeared to Mary Magdalene, he asked her to go and tell his disciples about the good news about his resurrection. He wanted her to be on the road, moving forward with him and being a missionary. He didn't want her to be stuck in her sorrow and pain. We find Jesus walking with the two disciples who went to Emmaus, being on the journey with them. They were sad and downcast. He walked with them, listened to their story, and gave them a new strength and vigor. He wanted them to keep moving and tell the other disciples about the resurrection. Jesus sent his disciples to the ends of the earth, "Go therefore and make disciples of all nations" (Matt 28:19). He encouraged them to keep moving.

In all the post-resurrection narratives, we find Jesus encouraging his disciples to keep moving and not to be stuck in their sadness and sorrow. Discouragement and disappointments were part of their life, but Jesus did not want them to get stuck with that. He wanted them to be on the journey. And he was accompanying them or walking with them through all of that.

Jesus sent seventy or seventy-two disciples on a mission. The mission was to go and preach, teach, heal, and drive out demons. These were the things done by Jesus himself and now he was commissioning them to do the same. It is interesting to note how Jesus instructs them about how they should go about on their mission. He told them not to take too many things—no purse, no bag, and no sandals. Why so frugal, we might wonder. They were on a journey and they had to go light. They were not to be too concerned about all kinds of possessions and things. Otherwise their comfort and possessions would have become the focus. That was not the focus. The focus was about bringing God's good news to others. They were told to stay in one house and not move around from house to house. They were to eat what was set before them. Again the message was that they were on a journey and they were not to get stuck with food and comfortable stay. They needed food and other basic things, and Jesus did not forbid them from having that. He said, "the laborer deserves to be paid" (Luke 10:7). But they were not to be going around looking for the most delicious food and the most convenient place to stay. They were on the journey.

Sometimes the number seventy or seventy-two is interpreted as referring to the whole world, indicating that the disciples were asked to go to the ends of the earth taking the good news of God's love. The disciples must have gone to different towns and villages. It doesn't say that they all went to the same place. The story also doesn't say that they all did the same thing. Maybe some of them peached, others healed the sick, while still others listened to people's agonies and pains and brought them peace. They must have included both men and women. We don't have any of those details. But they were all sent on the mission. They were asked to be out there being on the journey for and with the Lord rather than getting stuck in their own world.

What all of these stories tell us is that as individuals and communities God is calling us to be travelers on the road with him. We are pilgrims on the road, marching forward with the Lord and others. This journey that we are on began with God himself. The God who has revealed himself is a God who is on the journey. In fact our journey of life is modeled after his journey. He is the first pilgrim. He is the one who put in motion the whole creation. And he has been with his creation in its journey ever since. In the journey of humanity, he has been with us through all the twists and turns of our life. He has been living with our ancestors in their unique and particula historical contexts, but he has been also moving with different generations, times, and seasons. Jesus modeled this journey of life by his own life. He was born and he lived in a particular place at a particular time in our history, but he was also on the move. He lived with his people but he did not have a permanent abode anywhere. He was a pilgrim who kept moving throughout his physical life on earth and then through his resurrection he moved into the realm of eternity making himself once again present to all people at all times. The difference between God and us in our pilgrim journey is that he can be everywhere at all times, whereas we are limited to certain places and times during our earthly life. We cannot be everywhere at all times, at least during our earthly life. We are limited by space and time.

Our call to be pilgrims on the journey with the Lord is a challenge as well as a blessing. It is a challenge because many of us may not want to be on this journey. The lack of security, stability, independence, and permanence could make us scared, upset, and bitter. The unknown part of what is coming could make us afraid. We might want to stay with the familiar, our comfort zones. We may not like any change. We may not want all the hurdles and hardships, the twists and turns that come on our way. We want to hold on to something that gives us some sort of stability, safety, and security. We may not be prepared to make all the sacrifices he is calling us to for the sake of love.

We want to be renewed but often we are afraid of facing anything new. We want to attain heaven and eternity but we are afraid to leave this world and the physical realm of our life. We don't want to leave and break out of our structures and systems; we want to maintain and make stronger the systems we have built up. We don't want to break down the walls and fences we create around us; we want to stay with our familiar territories and environments. We don't want to venture into the unknown; we want to remain within our familiar surroundings. The future scares us; we want to hold on to our past and present. Anything that does not provide us with a sense of space and time scares us. Space and time give us a feeling of belonging somewhere and to something. Going beyond space and time is throwing us into a world of unknown, and we are often not prepared for that. We want to be grounded somewhere. To be on the road with Jesus, we have to leave behind many things, step out of our usual ways, and move ahead with courage and confidence.

But if we look at our human history we find that even physically and geographically, people have always been facing the unknown and yet moving forward with faith and courage. As individuals and communities, people migrated from place to place. If we look at any major country today, we see a mixed population inhabiting the land. They or their forefathers came from somewhere, sometimes from very distant lands.

⸱ ⸳⸳ immigrating to other places all the time. In the past people moved
ımunities, and today they move as individuals and families. Today
ɛek asylum in distant lands. Their life is unstable, but they are on the
ɩead with faith in God and trusting in the goodness of humanity. A

thousand years from now, their descendants may not even know that their forefathers were refugees and where they came from.

If we trace back the history of our families to ten thousand years back, all of us will see that our families or some parts of our families came from somewhere and got settled somewhere. We will also realize that many mixes have happened in the races, ethnicities, languages and other specificities that we have inherited. We have always been on the move and we will always be on the move. We all are refugees in essence. We seek refuge somewhere all the time, and we keep seeking better places of refuge. But all these places of refuge on this earth are temporary. We need to keep moving toward our permanent refuge, the eternal Jerusalem, our union with God and others in eternity. But sometimes we desire to settle down and make these temporary places of refuge our permanent homes.

The resistance to be on the road with the Lord is often not because people are bad. It is often because of fear and anxiety about the unknown that is ahead of us. It is because we like to stay with the familiar. There may be a fear in leaving our familiar grounds. The resistance may be because of the fear that if we did anything different or started thinking in new ways, the structures and systems that we have built up for centuries would crumble and fall and we would be decimated. But such fears would leave us with putting out trust and security in the structures and systems rather than in the Lord. Our security is the Lord. Our permanence is in the Lord. And the Lord is always on the move. Everyday he is calling us to love more and better. If we don't move with the Lord, we are going to rust and rot like a ship that is docked and abandoned at a port.

This is the challenge about the Christological Model. God is constantly inviting us to be on the road with him. He is constantly inviting us to leave our familiar territories and surroundings, our usual ways of thinking, feeling, and doing things, and our fears and anxieties. He is constantly inviting us to break out of the structures and systems, and walls and fences we have built up. He is inviting us to learn from the past, live in the present, and look forward to the future with hope. He is constantly inviting us to take the risk of leaving our comfort zones and facing the unknown. He is always inviting us to die to sin so that we can rise to new life.

This journey with God is not only a challenge but also a blessing, because when we move forward, we experience newness of life. If we don't break out of our structures and systems we will not grow and develop. If we do not break down the walls and fences, we will not experience the larger world of freedom and newness out there. If we do not leave our past and present, we are going to be stuck without any forward movement. If we do not change our ways of thinking, feeling, and doing things, we become static, boring, and monotonous. If we do not leave the realm of space and time, we cannot enter into the unlimited and eternal realm of God. If a child wants to stay as a five-year-old his or her whole life, no growth and development is possible.

The struggle of leaving our familiar grounds and moving or walking with the Lord is highlighted in the story of Peter and his companions experiencing a rough night while they were in their boat on the sea (Matt 14:22–33). Their boat was being tossed and turned by heavy winds and waves and Jesus was not with them that night. The story says that Jesus had made them go on ahead while he remained back and dismissed the crowd. As they were caught in the stormy waters and were far from the coast, they were, no doubt, scared and worried. Even with many years of experience as fishermen fighting winds and waves, they must have held on to their boat fearing for their dear life. But Jesus comes to their rescue walking on the water. Although the disciples were first scared thinking that it was a ghost, they were relieved that it was Jesus. He calmed their fears and brought them peace. Then we find Simon Peter wanting to step out of the boat and walk on the sea as Jesus did. And Jesus invited him to do that. Peter stepped out of the boat and started walking on the water toward Jesus. But when he noticed the strong wind he began to be frightened and started to sink. He cried out to the Lord, and the Lord rescued him, asking him why he doubted.

This is a beautiful story with many layers of meaning. It could be seen as something that really happened to Jesus and the disciples. It could be seen from the context of the struggles and problems of the evangelist, Matthew's community. It could be seen from the context of Peter's struggle in venturing out into the non-Jewish or gentile world and his fears about that. It could be also seen from the perspective of our life as a journey in general.

Jesus and his disciples were on the lakes and seas on many occasions and they must have experienced rough weathers and waves quite frequently. The story could be referring to something that really happened.

The story could be seen as a tool that Matthew uses to teach us something greater. Matthew's community, as the history of the early church shows, had many struggles and problems as they were trying to build their community and grow in faith. Matthew's community is believed to have been primarily a community of Jewish people who became Christians. They must have had many oppositions, persecutions, and problems to face from the Jewish leaders and others who persecuted and killed Jesus himself. Besides, gradually there were non-Jewish people joining the community and that appears to have created a lot of tension due to cultural differences. They must have also had issues regarding their theology and beliefs as they were still trying to make sense of who Jesus was and how they were different from the rest of the world including the Jewish community itself.

When Matthew describes the story of the boat in which Peter and his companions were traveling being tossed and turned by winds and waves, it could be refer-~y and tumultuous situations the early Christian community faced h. Their feeling must have been something like being far away : in stormy waters and feeling the absence of Jesus. Being far away ould mean being plunged into an unfamiliar territory or a scary and challenging situation. The early Christian community had many such situations. At times they must have felt like Jesus had left them in the dark without much help and support. But Matthew tells the readers that Jesus is not unaware of their struggles and troubles. He did not allow the disciples to be left defenseless.

On many occasions in our life we could identify with this experience of the disciples of the early Christian community. We are tossed and turned by the storms of life that come to us in many ways. We are terrified by illnesses, conflicts, failures, negative experiences, financial crisis, and other struggles of life, and we might feel that we are perishing. We cry out to the Lord in fear. But Jesus wants us to remember that we are not alone. He comes to calm our fears and bring us peace. He says to us the same thing that he said to the disciples, "Do not be afraid" (Matt 14:27).

When Matthew presents the story of Jesus sending the disciples ahead of him or Peter stepping out of the boat it could be pointing to some significant changes and new directions that the church or the early Christian community made or took. It could mean that Jesus was daring them to confront their fears and face the challenging situations. At first they didn't want to go out of the Jewish world. But then they had to step out of that little world to take the message of Jesus to the ends of the earth. There were people who resisted any change. The early Christians in Jerusalem and other places seem to have continued many of the customs and traditions of the Jewish community. And there were disputes and debates among the apostles and others regarding the imposition of practices such as circumcision on non-Jewish Christians.

Matthew presenting the story of Peter stepping out of the boat and Jesus inviting him to do that could be indicating that sometimes we as individuals and communities have to step out of some of our conventional ways so that we could experience new life. We have to dare to do the improbable and seemingly impossible. Not only in the early Christian community but also throughout the history of the church there have been times when people resisted any change or newness. In the Catholic Church, it is no secret that the institutional Church has been resistant to changes or newness on many occasions. But the Church grew only when it broke out of its narrow thinking and unhealthy structures and systems. We should not look at the institutional Church as some sort of an impersonal monster that is out there. It is made up of people like you and me. We are the Church. So it is basically the resistance of people themselves. Just like the people of Israel who were resistant to go forward with the Lord, just like the people who refused to be open to the message of Jesus, and just like some of the early Christians who were reluctant to go out of the Jewish territory or embrace the gentile Christians, some of us may be very resistant to leave our familiar grounds and embrace the new ways in which the Lord is revealing himself to us.

But to be on the journey with Jesus sometimes we have to step out of the boat. That boat could be our unhealthy and negative racial, cultural, and caste feelings, our rigid and fanatic religious attitudes and beliefs, our exclusive and discriminatory mentality, our arrogant and judgmental approach to other people, the positions and powers that make us pompous and proud, our fears and anxieties about the future, our addictive and destructive behaviors, so on and so forth. We have to leave our boats and familiar grounds and not be afraid to do that. Worrying about the possible impact and implications, we might feel that we are sinking or going downhill like Peter felt. We might fear that changes would decimate our community or destroy our personal lives. But we need to always remember that it is Jesus who is inviting us to step out of the boat and he is there to hold our hands when we falter or sink.

This truth about resistance to be on the road with Jesus or step out of the boat is true not only of the Catholic Church. It applies to any individual, family, community, group, or society.

As we move forward in our journey of life what we need to remember is that we are not alone. God is our traveling companion. God is our leader and guide. It is him that we are following. It is his mission that we are focusing on. It is his dance of love that we are participating in. He invites us to be on the journey with him, a journey that goes beyond the earthly life. He is not only our leader and guide but also our friend and traveling companion. He is the Emmanuel, the God with us. He is always with us. When we feel tired and exhausted, he is with us to hold our hands. When we find the journey hard and difficult, he is by our side to strengthen us and encourage us.

Often when we think of traveling somewhere we think of one person as the driver and all others as passengers. We don't think of two people driving the vehicle at the same time. But in the journey of our life, I would think of God and us as co-drivers, co-pilots, and co-travellers. God does not do it all by himself. He wants us also to be at the wheel. And God does not leave it all to ourselves either. He is with us to help and guide as a true friend and father. We do it together.

Of course, we can try to drive our bus or car all by ourselves without including God in the journey. But that is going to take us to accidents and problems. We might go too fast or too slow. We want to stay with the Lord at all times so that we keep the balance.

Our pilgrim journey also includes our fellow human beings and the rest of the creation. We travel together as one community. We are not isolated travellers. We are a pilgrim community. We need each other. We need other human beings to be our companions on the journey. We cannot journey alone. A loving marriage, for example, is a journey of two people traveling together committed to each other's welfare and growth. In that journey every day is a new day. They live their marriage in a new way every day. The same thing applies to those who follow other vocations. When it comes to our life as a pilgrim community, it is the same. We travel together supporting and caring for each other.

When Jesus sent his disciples on the mission, he sent them two by two. We could wonder, why. Why didn't he send them one by one? Is it because they would not have been able to do well if they went by themselves? That doesn't seem to be the reason. The reason seems to be that we are to be on our journey as co-travelers. We are not isolated individuals traveling alone. To live our lives and engage in God's mission, we need support from each other. Life has many twists and turns. We encounter many things. Many things surprise us.

Jesus said that he was sending them like lambs among wolves. Life is not easy, especially when we try to live the mission of the Lord. There will be fears, anxieties, sufferings, disappointments, sorrows, rejections, persecutions, and unexpected events coming on our way. We need support from others so that we don't get discouraged and overwhelmed. We might also get exhausted because of the volume of work. We need somebody to help us. So another person or a community is important in that regard. Lonesome work gets tiring after sometime. As fellow travellers, we need to care for and support each other. Our journey becomes easier when we hold each other's hands like a father holds the hand of a child or friends hold each other's hands.

There is also a danger in being on the mission alone. When we go on our own, it might become a one-man show. We might do things as we like. We might get disoriented. There will be no one to guide us, correct us, and tell us whether we are on the right track. We become our own masters. We might lose our path. And that is very dangerous, because then no one can question or correct us. It might become all about us and we might end up building our own world rather than being on the road with the Lord.

Although sometimes we might feel that we don't need anybody else, the reality is that we cannot live without others. We need others for our journey. We also need the rest of the creation for our journey. We need the nature, the animals, the birds, the plants, the stars, the planets, the winds, the seas, and everything in this creation. With some of them we are immediately connected, and with others our connection is remote. But they are all part of our life, and we need them.

As travelers with the Lord and fellow travelers with one another, we keep moving forward with faith and confidence. We don't wait for everything to be perfect to begin our life. Our life is a journey on the road of perfection. Every day we perfect it. We never step into the same moment twice. It is always a new moment, a new experience, and a new step forward.

37

The Paradox

ALTHOUGH WE ARE CALLED to be on the journey, often we find it difficult to do that because of the paradoxical situation that we are caught up in. Human life is filled with many paradoxical situations. One of them is the paradox of wanting to stay and needing to move. On the one hand as individuals and communities we like to stay and settle down but on the other hand we have to keep moving. As much as we seek permanence and stability in life we know that there is so much of instability and impermanence in this earthly life. We have to find a balance between stability and movement.

We do many things to ensure some sort of permanence and stability in our life. Most of us get educated and get a degree. Then we look for a job, build or rent a house, find a partner and get married or find another life vocation, have children and grandchildren, ensure a stable financial situation, and make sure that we are healthy physically and psychologically. To make our life more solid and secure we might find membership in a faith community and build up friendship circles and social relationships. Many of these things might happen as we plan and dream, and they make us feel that we can settle down and have some permanence.

But life shows us that we cannot really stay and settle down completely. The moment we think that we have settled down and have everything secure and stable, something shakes us up. We are faced with a new situation or new phase of life into which we have to move. It could be the loss of our job, some financial crisis, some illness, the death of our spouse, one of our children, or a family member, some family crisis or issues in marriage, some psychological problems, some debilitating accidents, our children getting into destructive behaviors and addictions, some troublesome happenings in the community or society that personally affects us, or some other tragedy. Many of those things come without any warning and we are least prepared for them. When they occur we are shaken up and we are not settled and secure anymore. But we have to face them and keep moving. Otherwise we will get stuck and stagnated. In the case of a sudden illness, for example, we have to go to a doctor, get treated, and be well again. We may refuse or may be afraid to go to the doctor or get treated. But then we are faced with the possibility of getting worse, getting incapacitated, or dying.

If we want to get well and keep moving, we have to go to the doctor and get treated. In some cases, there is no guarantee that we would get well at all. But if we do get well, we would again try to settle down and make our life secure. But again some other situation might arise that would make us unsettled and insecure. We need to face it and keep moving again.

Even for those who have committed themselves to a life of transitions and movements such as priests, the religious, and missionaries, there is this longing to settle down, have a steady ministry, have good health, and find some permanence. But they also experience things that shake them up. It may be some crisis in their vocation, some unpleasant transfers and appointments, some fights, disagreements, and power struggle between the members and superiors, some addictions and relationship problems, some health problems, or other issues. These happenings put them in a new phase of life, and they need to keep moving. If they don't face it and keep moving, they get stuck and stagnated.

We see this paradox of wanting to stay and needing to move happening in the life of communities, groups, and nations as well. A community, group, society, or nation may be going through a phase where they think they have peace and harmony, but then something happens that shakes them up and makes them unsettled. It could be a fight between two races, ethnic groups, languages, or some other groups within the society. Racial, ethnic, and language-based tensions are not uncommon in many societies. It could be a fight between two ideological groups like the conservatives and liberals. It could be a tension within a group that leads to a split. It could be a war between two nations. All these make communities, groups, and nations unsettled. They need to face the new reality and keep moving. If they don't move, they get stuck and stagnated.

This is the paradox, the paradox of wanting to stay and needing to move. We have some sort of stability and permanence but it is not really permanent and stable. It is short-lived. We may not like these movements and transitions. We might like to stay and settle down, but life does not guarantee such permanence and security in this world. We have to keep transitioning and moving from one thing to the other, one situation to the next. If we don't keep moving, we don't grow and make progress. Our struggle is in finding the balance between stability and growth, stillness and movement.

But this paradox of wanting to stay and having to move is not just about our physical life alone. It applies to our psychological and spiritual life too. Spiritually, we may have developed our own spirituality and religiosity based on our understanding or images of God and the world. We develop certain beliefs, practices, routines, and ways of doing things based on what we have been taught, what we have read, and what we have learned and experienced. But often we are challenged to review and renew those beliefs and practices. Religion and spirituality never remain the same because our God is always revealing himself in new and numerous ways. Our understanding and experience of God keeps growing and changing or we are unraveling the mystery of God throughout our life. But at the same time we know that we cannot and should not throw away everything that we have learned or been presented with. It is about finding the balance between keeping what is healthy and discarding what is unhealthy. Some of our beliefs and practices may be distorted, and we may have to change them. Changing or leaving some of them may be difficult. We become people of habits and routines and we may not want to change anything. But refusing to change our distorted ideas of God can be detrimental to our spiritual growth and development. We will get stuck and stagnated. If we refuse to be open to the new ways in which he reveals himself to us, God may not be able to bring about much change in our lives.

Psychologically and relationally also we experience the paradox of needing to move and wanting to stay. All of us are born into a particular family, community, culture, and country. Based on our particular background and experiences, we develop certain ideas, beliefs, and thoughts about others, about the world, and about ourselves. To grow and develop, we have to go beyond these immediate relationships, ideas, and thoughts. But at the same time we know that we cannot throw away everything of our culture and history. What is important is to find the balance in keeping the healthy elements and being willing to discard the unhealthy. We need to find a balance between being local and being global. It is about staying grounded and at the same time launching out into the larger horizons of growth and development.

Being limited to our own small worlds, some of our thoughts, feelings, and ideas could be small and limited. Some of them may be distorted and detrimental to our growth and development. To grow and make progress in life, we have to move out of our small worlds and narrow thoughts and experience the larger world out there. We have to be willing to change or refine some of our ideas, beliefs, and opinions. We have to be willing to see others, the world, and ourselves in new ways. When we open ourselves up, we always discover something new about others, the world, and ourselves. The way we see or perceive things as a little child is not the same as how we see or perceive as an adult. If we refuse to leave the childish ways, we will never grow to be an adult.

Wanting to stay and settle down is something basic to our nature as human beings. But moving forward and being on the journey is also basic to our nature. The struggle of finding a balance between these two paradoxical ends will continue as long us we live on this earth. But then again we realize that the journey continues in one way or the other. Even physically our life shows us that throughout our life we are on a journey. We keep moving from place to place. When we reach the school age, we separate from our parents and the immediate family and begin to connect with a larger world. We move out of our biological families when we become adults or go to college. When we get married, we separate from our parents and immediate family members again and begin our own family. We move to other cities and towns for the sake of jobs. We move to other places when we buy or build a new house. We move to different countries and regions as immigrants and refugees. When we get old and sick we move to nursing homes, hospitals, or other facilities of care. And finally, when we die, we have to move out of this physical world.

The journey of our life never stops. It does not end with this world. It continues into eternity, beyond space and time. Death takes us to another phase of life, life in eternity. When it comes to the last moment of our life on this earth, we may not want to let go off our life and die. We might want to stay. We may be afraid to die. But if we don't die, we don't enter into life in eternity. We would remain in the limited realm of space and time. Of course, when it comes to death, we don't have a choice. It is part of our journey.

We are pilgrims on this earth. Whether it is about the physical, psychological, or spiritual dimension of our life, we don't stay in one place or with one thing forever. As pilgrims we stop in certain places or stages of life briefly but we keep moving. We need a certain amount of stability and structure but we also need a great amount of openness to the new avenues and horizons of growth and development that God opens up for us.

38

Biblical Stories on the Paradox

THE BIBLE PRESENTS US with many stories that highlight the paradoxical situation, where people had to find a balance between their desire to stay with the familiar and at the same time being open to the new ways in which God was calling them to grow and become a blessing for others. We shall look at a few of those stories both in the Old Testament and New Testament times.

The Old Testament Times

Abraham

We discussed about the call of Abraham and the journey that he was asked to embark on. He experienced the paradoxical situation of wanting to stay and needing to move in many ways in his life. He had to leave his familiar territories and surroundings and start a journey into the unknown. He was on the move all the time. As we discussed, asking Abraham to leave his country and kindred could be understood as an invitation to enter into a larger world of freedom and growth physically, psychologically, and spiritually. We also discussed that it was not just Abraham alone who was on the journey. There were a lot of people going with him including his wife and nephew. Abraham simply stands for anyone whom God calls to a new way of life.

Physically, Abraham moved from place to place navigating through unknown territories and situations. God took him through various experiences, opening up a larger world to him. But Abraham's call was also about the psychological and spiritual movement and growth. He had to change his image of God as a tribal God to a God of the universe. He changed from being a tribal man to becoming man of the universe. He learned to live with people outside of his tribe. He lived with the Egyptians and people of many other lands and territories. He became a man of peace and justice. He refined his ideas, thoughts, and beliefs about God, others, and himself.

There are a few significant stories in his life that speak to his psychological and spiritual journey. It appears that when Abraham and his people ended up in Egypt because of the famine in the places where they were living before, Abraham wanted to stay and settle down in Egypt. But he got into trouble because of lying about Sarah. He told the Egyptians that Sarah was his sister and hid the fact that she was his wife for fear of being killed. Thinking that she was Abraham's sister, the Pharaoh took her as his concubine. When he came to know that Sarah was Abraham's wife the Pharaoh expelled Abraham from the land. He had to be on the journey again.

Later Abraham and his people moved to Gerar and he did the same thing there. He lied about Sarah, and King Abimelech of Gerar decided to keep Sarah as his concubine. God was going to punish Abimelech for keeping Sarah. When Abimelech heard from God that Sarah was Abraham's wife he was shocked and upset. When he questioned Abraham about his lie, Abraham said that he was not actually lying because Sarah was in fact his sister. And she was; she was his half-sister (Gen 20:12). But at the same time she was also his wife. In those days consanguineous marriages (marrying a blood relative or cross-cousin, cross-uncle/niece marriages) were common in certain tribes and communities. Such marital contracts happen even today in many places.

When Abraham told the Egyptians and the people of Gerar that Sarah was his sister, we could say that he was lying because she was also his wife. He kept that truth hidden. But at the same time what he said was not a complete lie. She was his sister too. He did not say the complete truth for the fear of getting killed.

We hear about people lying and not being honest. Sometimes we also hear people making references to "little lies" or "white lies," meaning that they are not completely lying and yet not being completely truthful either. Abraham's lying could be referring to the fact that he had to keep growing psychologically and spiritually before he became a completely honest and holy man. Holiness or growing closer to God was a gradual process for him. It took time for him to trust and love God. It took time for him to trust and love people of other cultures and backgrounds. It took time for him to make internal changes and become a holy man.

We see the same thing getting repeated in the life of Abraham's son, Isaac. Isaac also lied to the people of Gerar about his wife, Rebekah. He told them that she was his sister. And she indeed was his sister, a cousin of his whom Abraham's servant went and brought from Abraham's tribe to be Isaac's wife. It once again points to the practice of consanguineous and arranged marriages in certain tribes and communities. But Isaac hid from the people of Gerar the truth of Rebekah being his wife. Like his father, Abraham, he was also afraid of getting killed because of Rebekah. But both Abraham and Isaac got better and better as they moved along in their journey of life. They didn't have to be afraid and lying anymore. But it took time for those changes to happen. We could see similar journeys of faith with many other individuals in our faith history. They did not become saints or holy people overnight. They had to be on the journey going through struggles and difficulties.

Like Abraham, Isaac, and others in our faith history, we all have to go through that journey of psychological and spiritual growth. We don't attain holiness or fraternal love overnight. There may be many real lies and many white lies that we tell before we become completely honest and truthful. Abraham and Isaac lied because they were afraid that they would be killed. People often lie because of different kinds of fears. As God took Abraham through that journey of faith where he got rid of his lies, fears, and small thinking, God desires to take all of us through a journey of faith where we can get rid of all that is keeping us away from truly loving God and others. He wants us to grow in holiness and grace every day. Abraham is simply a model person whom God calls to a life of holiness. But that call to holiness and grace is extended to all human beings in all ages. As Abraham was called all of us are called to be on that journey.

Abraham's experience of dealing with the conflict between Sarah and Hagar was another instance in which he had to move into another phase in his psychological and spiritual growth. He was not settled again. He had to keep moving. He had to love his wife and at the same time care for Hagar and Ishmael. He had to become the peacemaker in the midst of family conflict. He had to become the defender of Hagar and Ishmael in the event of Sarah ill treating them. Abraham had to become a man of peace, justice, and healing in the context of injustice and injury. That was another step of growth that Abraham was achieving in his journey of life. Although it was hard, God was opening a new door of growth for Abraham. Sometimes God allows us to go through tough and difficult situations in our journey of life. We may feel that we are never settled or we are stuck. But many of those experiences help us to grow psychologically and spiritually. When they happen they might seem to be big tragedies impossible to overcome. But when they are over, we come out as changed people with new strength, wisdom, and gratitude. We may not like those tragedies and difficulties. We might like to stay secure and undisturbed, but sometimes we have no choice. The journey of life could be full of such bumps in the road.

Abraham's call was an invitation to enter into a new way of thinking, feeling, and doing things. He had to come out of his small mind and small thinking and start thinking and seeing things in a larger way. He had to learn to live with people outside of his tribe. We can think about how many cultures and peoples Abraham must have come into contact with. He lived with the Canaanites, the Egyptians, people of Gerar, and people of many other lands and territories as he moved on in his journey. How many new things must he have learned from those encounters? We can assume that he had to change and refine many of his ideas, thoughts, and beliefs throughout his journey. He had to break free from his unhealthy and narrow attitudes and ungodly beliefs. It was an invitation to not get stuck with negativity and unhealthy systems and structures. It was a call to break down the barriers of biases and prejudices he must have had about other tribes and peoples. It was an invitation to see God, others, and himself in a new way. God calls us from being people of small families and groups to becoming people of the universe. He takes us through new experiences. We encounter new people, cultures, and situations. We encounter God in new ways. Like Abraham, we are nomads physically, psychologically, and spiritually. We keep moving, and wherever we go, God goes with us.

To be on that journey, Abraham had to leave behind many things, change many things, and remain open to God's transforming power. Yes, there were hardships and uncertainties all through his life. But God was journeying with him in all those moments. His real permanence was in the Lord. Many times Abraham must have thought that he was getting settled down and making his life secure but then again some significant things happened and his life was shaken up. He had to face the new situation and keep moving forward.

When Abraham was willing to enter into the unknown territory with faith and confidence in God, he not only flourished and grew personally but also became a blessing for generations to come. If he never heeded to the voice of God and continued to stay where he was, he would have become stagnant and stifled. He would have never experienced a larger world.

Like Abraham, if we are willing to be on the move, to journey with God, we will not only experience a new world of freedom and newness but also become a blessing for others. Caught up in our own little worlds, we neither grow nor we do anything good for anybody else. To partner with God in the divine dance of love and match his steps and tunes, we may have to go through a long period of changes, transformation, and renewal. But God is our guide and traveling companion. We keep moving ahead with courage and faith.

Moses

Another prominent character in the Old Testament that we discussed who also experienced this paradoxical situation of wanting to stay and needing to move is Moses. Moses had many situations in life where he seemed to want to stay and settle down, but God was taking him through a journey of life. The circumstance of his birth itself indicates that he was not going to stay in one place or have a permanent home. The new Pharaoh had begun to oppress the Israelites and subject them to slavery. He commanded that all the male children born to the Hebrews be killed. When Moses was born, his mother hid him for a while and then she put him in a basket and placed it among the reeds on the banks of the river, Nile. Pharaoh's daughter who saw him took pity on him and adopted him. The enemy becomes Moses' savior, which once again speaks about how God works in our life in mysterious ways.

Moses thus grew up with his biological family as well as Pharaoh's daughter. Both experiences must have opened up a larger world to Moses. God was preparing him for a larger mission where he could be a man of the universe as his ancestor, Abraham was. Living in the palace of Pharaoh, Moses must have thought that he was having a secure and well-settled life, but that security was shaken up when Pharaoh sought to kill him on account of the Egyptian whom Moses had murdered. He was not settled anymore physically, psychologically, and spiritually. He was on the run. He ends up in Midian and started living with Jethro, the priest of Midian. Being married to one of Jethro's daughters and helping Jethro in his farming and other works, Moses was probably planning to settle down and make his life secure there. But God had other plans for him. God wanted Moses to keep moving.

One day, as he was taking care of the flock of his father-in-law, Moses had an extraordinary experience of God in the burning bush. God tells Moses that he had chosen him to be the rescuer of his people living in slavery in Egypt. It appears that through all the twists and turns of his life, God was preparing Moses to be a leader for his community and enter into a larger world of mission and ministry. Moses had already proved to be a defender of the defenseless and the weak when he came to the rescue of the Hebrew who was attacked by an aggressive Egyptian and when he came to the rescue of Jethro's daughters when the shepherds were trying to bully them at the well. God probably saw Moses as the right person to rescue the defenseless and enslaved Israelites from Egypt. But we can assume that Moses was not ready for any such big mission. After fleeing from Pharaoh he was settling down in Midian and building up a life for himself. He probably was scared of going back to Egypt and did not want to go back to Pharaoh. So we see Moses being reluctant to accept the mission and he makes excuses to escape from the task. Besides feeling scared and inadequate for the mission, Moses probably did not want to go anywhere from Midian. But God was not going to allow Moses to do that. He was reminding Moses that he had to be moving forward and not get stuck with his present life and way of being.

After the encounter with God, Moses must have realized something new about himself. It was another step of growth in his psychological and spiritual development. He was not meant to be a man living a secluded life in a small place. He was meant to be a man with a larger mission and vision. His mission was not just about himself and his immediate family. He had to become a man of the universe, a man for a larger community. To do that, he had to come out of his fears, wrong ideas, and narrow thinking. He had to break with what he was doing and thinking and keep moving. He was a pilgrim on the journey with God.

Moses accepts God's commission and does as he commanded. After going to Egypt with God's mission, he had hard times dealing with Pharaoh. Many times it appeared that he was stuck, but he had to keep trusting and keep moving. After he managed to get his people out of Egypt, he had hard times convincing his people that they had to be on the journey with God. He and his people traveled all the time, occasionally pitching their tent here and there. People complained and grumbled against him and God. There were many difficult situations that Moses had to face. Maybe there were moments when he thought of giving up and withdrawing into his own little world. But he had to leave behind all such thoughts and ideas and pick himself up from where he found himself and keep moving. It was a hard journey, but the Lord went with him.

Moses who had an unstable family of origin, raised partly by his mother and partly by Pharaoh's daughter, raised a family of his own and matured as the leader of a great community. Moses who fled from Egypt out of fear went back to Egypt and faced Pharaoh courageously. Moses who was living an unknown life in Midian became the liberator of a large community of people. He encountered many cultures and peoples, which must have broadened his mind and heart. He faced many turbulent situations, but he grew stronger in faith and courage. Moses who did not know who God was became a friend of God. Moses was a changed man. He was no more a timid and secluded shepherd. He was a mighty leader, a friend of God, and a man of the universe. If Moses refused to leave his small world, his small thinking, his fears and anxieties, and refused to be on the journey with the Lord, he would not have become what he became. He left behind many things to move ahead. He was never settled anywhere permanently. There were times when he seemed like being stuck or going backward, but God was always taking him forward. Walking with God, Moses was growing in holiness and grace.

Elisha

Looking at the stories of the prophets of ancient Israel, we see that all of them in some way struggled with the paradoxical situation of wanting to stay and needing to move. They had to break with their past, leave what they were engaged in, and move forward with a new vision and mission. They had to refine and reform their images of God, images of themselves, and images of the world. They were on the journey with God. One of the prophets who had a dramatic break with his past and present life was Elisha. Being inspired by God, Prophet Elijah goes to Elisha and throws his cloak over the latter symbolizing God's call of Elisha to prophetic life (1 Kgs 19:19–21). At that point, it is interesting to note what Elisha does. He was a farmer and was plowing the field. The story says that he had twelve yoke of oxen and he was plowing with the twelfth. Usually a yoke is fitted to a pair of oxen or other animals so that they can pull together although some yokes could be fitted to individual oxen or animals. In the normal sense, Elisha plowing with twelve yoke of oxen would mean that he was plowing with twelve pairs of oxen. After receiving God's call, Elisha slaughtered his oxen, and using the yoke and other plowing equipment he cooked the meat and gave to his people. After they all had eaten Elisha leaves the place and follows Elijah to become his disciple and succeeding prophet.

Everything in this story is very significant. Cooking the flesh of twenty-four oxen is a lot of meat. It was a feast. And he gave it to his people. The people could have been his workers, fellow farmers, his family, or other people in the neighborhood. The large amount of meat could mean abundance and generosity, which could indicate that when God gives he gives in abundance, and he is generous. Killing the oxen and giving a great meal to his people could also mean that he was forgiving all their debts and doings, and wanted to start his new life on a good note. When God calls us to be on the journey with him, he is going to start with a clean slate. He is going to wipe off our past mistakes and sins and start with us all over again. Saint Paul would reiterate this point in his letter to the Galatians saying that since Christ has set us free we should not submit to the yoke of slavery again (Gal 5:1). Many things enslave us, but God frees us from all that, and he wants us to keep moving forward in our journey.

Killing all the oxen and using the plowing equipment for fuel could mean that Elisha was not going to be a farmer anymore. He was starting something totally new. He was going to break with his past and the present and move into a new future. He is saying good-bye to the old and starting a new phase in his journey. As a farmer he was localized and limited in his work and life. Now he is going to be a wandering prophet, becoming available to a larger number of people and places. He is becoming available to God's mission in a larger way. He is going to allow God to take him wherever he wanted. He was becoming a man of the universe. The journey continued.

Wisdom Literature

The wisdom literature in the Bible which consists of the Book of Job, Psalms, Proverbs, Ecclesiastes, Song of Songs, the Book of Wisdom, and Sirach powerfully bring out the theme of the paradoxical predicament of wanting to stay and needing to move ahead. All these books talk about the human temptation and tendency to stay with what is convenient, comfortable, and pleasurable physically, psychologically, and spiritually. But they also remind the readers that life is a journey with the Lord and others. They remind us about the futility of putting our trust in things that are perishable and transitory. The only thing that lasts is a life with God and others in love. It is about partnering with God and others in the dance of love. I shall comment briefly on a few of these books.

The Song of Songs is a love song between a lover and his beloved. It is passionate and intimate. It is romantic. The lover and the beloved are seeking to be in each other's arms. There are references to hugs, kisses, and the desire for intimate and passionate union between the lover and the beloved. When they are separated from each other, the lover and the beloved experience an indescribable amount of emotional pain. They spend lonely days and nights waiting for each other. They search for their loved one everywhere and at all times. We might wonder how this book got into the Bible. In a spirituality where sex or romantic relationships are considered an anathema, this book might be seen as an anomaly in the Bible.

But the whole book of Song of Songs is about the journey of love that God and human beings are involved in. Like a lover, God longs for us, his children, and we long for him, our divine lover. God desires that we live in him, participating in the divine dance of love. But there are moments in our life when God and love are not our focus. Many other things take away our attention. Our journey sometimes takes us on routes that are away from God, and we get stuck with unhealthy things. God knows that when we are separated from him or stop journeying with him, we are not happy and living well. When we are lost in evils and unhealthy ways of living, God frantically searches for us as a lover searches for his beloved. He wants us to be free from those things that are keeping us stuck. He wants us to return back to the dance of love and be on the journey with him.

It could be also seen as the longing of the human soul. We long for the Lord and his love. The Lord is with us at all times. But there are moments when we feel dry and drained out because of the burdens of our life. We feel that we are stuck and not moving. We feel that God is away from us, just like the prodigal son felt that he was far away from his home. In those moments more than other times, we look for God, our divine lover. We seek his comfort, peace, and consolation. But there are also moments when we feel very close to God. We experience his loving presence. This is a two-way longing and desire, God seeking and desiring for us and we seeking and desiring for God. Our journey of life is a chain of such longings, break-ups, and union with God. We never stay in one state of being. Psychologically and spiritually we keep moving, and the journey of our life continues.

The Book of Job is a book of deep insights about human life. Job was a good man living an honest and holy life. He had riches and prosperity and he was blessed with good health and happy life. But all of a sudden everything started crumbling down. All his wealth and prosperity started disappearing. All his family and friends started disappearing or turning against him. And finally his own health started deteriorating. He was a man of misery. Job who thought that he was secure and well settled in life was faced with a new situation of indescribable misery and suffering. Nothing was secure and sure anymore. He had to continue to trust in the Lord, face the new situation of life, and keep moving forward with courage and faith. Although even his wife told him to curse God and die, Job did not give up on God or on life. He had to let go off many things, but he did not leave God or stop his journey. There were many moments when it seemed like he was stuck, but he continued his journey.

Job's story is often used in the context of struggling with the question about why innocents suffer. When it is seen only from the context of suffering, what happened to Job may not make much sense and might be seen as a cruel joke between God and Satan. But when this book is seen as a peek into the mystery of our life, it shows us that it is about the journey of our life. Everything that happened to Job makes sense. In our journey of life, we experience what he experienced. The book tells us that things that we often consider as permanent and secure are not permanent and secure. There is nothing permanent in this world. Our life is a journey and we continue from one stage to the other as pilgrims. We see Job as a pilgrim who does not get too attached to the passing things of this world. He enjoyed the blessings and good things he had but more than anything else he enjoyed his union with God. Yes, when the misery and suffering struck him, he was not happy. He grieved and even wished that he would die.

And yet, he stayed close to the Lord. He did not stop the dance of love. In good times and in bad times, he was traveling with God. Maybe he also thought on many occasions that he was secure and he could settle down permanently. But that was not to be. He had to keep moving. His fortunes came back to him again. God blessed him again and restored back to him his lost glory and prosperity. But that doesn't mean that they stayed permanently. Job had to let go off those things again, including his physical life on earth. He had to leave everything behind and die one day. Job is simply the protagonist in the drama of human life. He stands for all of us. He stands for someone who is on a journey with the Lord in all circumstances of life.

The Book of Ecclesiastes is another text that takes a hard look at life and tells us some deep truths about the paradoxical predicament that we struggle with. If we read this book without understanding the deeper truths it is trying to communicate it can feel depressing. But if we understand the deeper insights and truths contained in it, this book is a treasure trove. The book is about living our lives with the right perspective. Many people live in this world as if this physical life on earth is going to be permanent. They do many things to make their life safe and secure. They accumulate and achieve many things. But they all soon come to realize that none of these last forever. Everything is vanity. They will have to say good-bye to all these. The young people will grow old and sick and will eventually die. Everything that they accumulate will have to be left behind. They don't take away anything when they leave this world. All their labor and hard work come to nothing. Even those who think that they are wise and are saying or coming up with something new will soon realize that there is nothing new that has not already been said or discovered.

Hearing such a message can be depressing and discouraging. If we are told that there is no meaning in what we do and all our hard work is going to come to nothing, then we could wonder why we should work hard at all. If we are told that there is nothing new in what we are saying or doing then even this book that I am writing might appear to be a waste of time. But that is not what the Book of Ecclesiastes is saying. The book is talking about the journey of life. We are pilgrims. It is talking about the futility of putting all our trust in things that are temporary and passing. It is about building our relationship with God and others as our first priority. When that becomes our priority, everything that we do makes sense and has meaning. So it is not about avoiding hard work or remaining depressed. It is about working hard and taking our responsibilities seriously. We do everything out of love for God and others. We do everything with the focus of building our relationship with God and others because that is what is lasting and takes us to eternity. If we don't work hard, then we will be living at the expense of others who work hard. And that will be taking advantage of other people. If we don't bring the best out of ourselves, then we don't partner with God in the divine dance of love. We need to bring the best out of ourselves and be a blessing for others. What we need is a balanced approach. We need to plan well, work hard, and take care of our needs and responsibilities. We need to excel in what we are, bringing to perfection the gifts and talents God has bestowed upon us. But we also need to live with the awareness that we don't have our permanent home here on earth. We are pilgrims on a journey. So we travel as light as possible, not getting too attached to anything.

New Testament Times

The paradoxical struggle between wanting to stay and needing to be on the road with God is emphasized in the New Testament times too. It is given much more focus with the life and ministry of Jesus. It is not only that Jesus himself was on the journey but he also called his disciples to be like him, to be on the move. Peter, Andrew, James, and John were fishermen, making a living for themselves and their families by fishing. Jesus called them from there to be with him on the journey. He said to them, "Follow me" (Matt 4:19). They had to leave behind many things to follow him. They had to grow in their understanding of God and themselves. They were going to be "fishers of men," no more living in their own little worlds with their own ideas and beliefs but becoming men of the universe, allowing the Lord to change and transform them psychologically and spiritually.

Matthew was a tax collector, enjoying his life and making a lot of money. Probably he wanted to stay and continue to enjoy what he was doing. He was called to leave all that behind and be on the journey with Jesus. All the other disciples were called from various other situations of life to be on the journey with Jesus. They had boats and nets, tax booths, relationships, craving for power and positions, extremist ideas, and many other things that they had to leave behind. It was a reminder to them that everything that we have in this world is temporary. They had their own ideas and images of God and the messiah. Gradually they had to refine and change their distorted ideas and thoughts. Jesus was inviting them to a new understanding of God and spirituality. Although we could look at the life of each of these disciples, we shall just look at two individuals who struggled with the paradoxical predicament and yet moved on in the journey with God.

Mary

Besides Jesus, Mary is probably the most significant person in the New Testament times who experienced this paradoxical struggle of wanting to stay and needing to move ahead. She was called for an exceptional mission, to be the mother of God's Son (Luke 1). As a young girl in Nazareth, she was probably dreaming of settling down and living a secure and quiet life with her betrothed, Joseph. But God had other plans. She was going to begin a new phase in her journey of life. Angel Gabriel announced to her that she was going to be the mother of the Savior. Think of the consequences it could have had for her. She was going to have a child through the special intervention of God, but who would believe her? People would say that she cheated on Joseph. She could have been stoned to death according to the law of that time, for being pregnant out of wedlock, for being unfaithful to Joseph. And when she was pregnant, we can imagine about all the nasty things that must have been said about her. We can think about all the nasty looks that she had to endure and all the hushed whisperings that she knew were about her. Mary knew that from the human point of view she would not have been able to bring her pregnancy to its full term because she would be stoned to death. But she had faith to believe that what is impossible for us is possible for God. And so with that faith she said yes to God's plan. She was willing even to risk death for the sake of partnering with God in his dance of love.

After she responded to God's call, she must have thought that she could settle down in Nazareth with her husband and child. But that was not meant to be. She and Joseph had to go to Bethlehem for the census, and she gave birth to Jesus there in a stable. We can assume that that is not what Mary had hoped for. She must have at least hoped for giving birth to her child in her house surrounded by her parents or others. But that is not what she got. She had to give birth to her child in a manger surrounded by animals with the stench and smell of the stable. It must have been dark and cold. They were there, staying close to the fragile child bathed in tears and trembling with cold. That is where their journey took them.

We might like to have everything cozy and comfortable, but sometimes that is not what life presents to us. Sometimes we have dark and cold nights, uncertain future, and many questions and fears in our heart and mind. We may have to be constantly open to the mystery of God and mystery of life unfolding before us. We have to continue to stay with Jesus even in those dark and cold moments of life and continue our journey with courage and faith.

Mary had to face the new situation and keep moving. She had many more dark nights coming on her way. Her life was shaken up again. She could not settle down. She and Joseph had to flee to Egypt because King Herod was seeking to kill baby Jesus. She had to live in Egypt as a refugee. It may not have been an easy transition because Egypt was where their ancestors were subjected to slavery and badly treated. But she was not going to settle down there either. She had to return back to Nazareth again. Then there is a period of quiet until Jesus begins his public ministry. It appears to be a quiet time and we assume that Jesus spent most of his time at home with Mary and Joseph. But who knows what was going on in their life during all those years? Who knows what all struggles Mary was going through in all those years, trying to understand her son, Jesus?

Mary's struggles continued and even got worse after Jesus began his public ministry. He was not home much. Mary must have missed him a lot. He lived a nomad's life. Most parents would like to see their children getting settled and living happy lives. But Mary did not see her son doing that. She must have been anxious on many occasions, worrying about her son. The angel told her that her son was God's son and he would save the world. But the angel did not say how he was going to do it. Mary was not told that her son would leave home and be a nomad. As Jesus began his public ministry, there were many complaints arising about him. People were complaining that he was blaspheming and misleading people. People, including his family members were saying that he was mad. Many people were trying to harm him. Many people, including the religious leaders must have blamed Mary for many of the things that they were accusing him of. They must have said that she did not raise him well, that she was a bad mother. Maybe she was ridiculed and chastised many times. Mary was not living a secure and happy life. She was not settled and comfortable. She had to face several difficult situations and yet keep moving.

The most unsettling moments in her life must have been the last hours of Jesus' life. We don't hear anything about Joseph. So she must have been already widowed and alone. She had to suffer all of it alone. Her son was being condemned to death. He was falsely accused of crimes he did not commit. He was treated as the worst criminal. The community forgave even the worst criminal, Barabbas, but they condemned her son for no reason. He was wounded, ridiculed, scourged, and finally put to a barbarous death. Her heart was pierced and broken as Prophet Simeon had predicted. The agony of her son was her agony, and his rejection was her rejection. She had to stand at the foot of the cross and watch her son dying an agonizing death. When he was on the cross, we can assume that she was on the cross with him. She then had to receive the body of her son in her arms and witness him being buried. No mother would want to be part of such scary and agonizing moments.

Mary had gone through everything that a woman could have gone through. We hear only once about the angel appearing to her and announcing the good news. After that there is no angel, no vision, and no messages. It's all bad news one after another. But Mary had to keep saying yes to the Lord. She was on the journey. She couldn't get stuck. She had to keep moving.

Mary had to have a tremendous amount of faith and courage to go through what she went through. She had many uncertainties. Her life was never safe and secure. The Mary that we see in pictures with blue eyes, blonde hair, a glow behind her, and clothed in beautiful garments is not the Mary of Nazareth. The Mary of the gospels is a simple woman who had a tough life. She was a real mother who knew the pains and agonies of life but probably nobody except Jesus knew her agonies. There was nobody to sing her praises or glorify her while she was alive. When she was alive, nobody called her mother of God. She didn't have titles and honors. Of course, she must have had some happy moments when Jesus was around or when people were saying good things about him. But by and large, she was a woman of sorrows. She had her questions, doubts, and anxieties. But she trusted in God and did her best. Maybe sometimes she felt like she was dragging; maybe sometimes she felt she was stuck or going backward. But with all that she still moved on with courage and faith in the Lord.

In all of these experiences of her life, God was with Mary. He was the one leading and guiding her. Even though she had difficulties and uncertainties one after another, God gave her strength to face them and continue her journey. In a quick reading of the story, we may see only the sorrows, uncertainties, and agonizing moments of Mary, but a close look at everything that happened would tell us that God's protective presence was enveloping her. After Mary said yes to God's plan and conceived her son, the gospel tells us that she went to visit her aunt and uncle, Elizabeth and Zechariah. Although it could be looked at as Mary going to serve or visit Elizabeth who was also expecting, we could think of this travel of Mary to the hill country of Judea in haste as part of God's plan to protect her from the nasty comments and looks of her people in Nazareth and even the prospects of getting stoned to death. Although Joseph had taken her in as his wife, there was no guarantee that the general public would stop their curious questions and inquiries about her pregnancy. The home of Elizabeth and Zechariah must have been a place of refuge that God prepared for her.

When she completed her term of pregnancy and was about to give birth to her son, Mary and Joseph had to travel to Bethlehem for the census. Although we could think of this travel as an inconvenience for Joseph and Mary, we could think that this was also part of God's protective plan to save them from the unkind comments, gossips, and curiosity of their people in Nazareth about the child. And then they had to flee to Egypt to escape from the murderous king, Herod. This travel to Egypt also was a great inconvenience, but it could be also seen as part of God's plan to keep them safe not only from Herod but also from the curious questions and gossips of the people of Bethlehem. They were strangers there and people would have been curious to know who they were.

Mary experienced inconveniences and paradoxes of life throughout her life, but she was not alone in her journey. God was with her as her guide and traveling companion.

The gospels tell us that Mary kept everything in her heart and pondered over them. She loved her son and sought to understand him. She sought to understand God and the journey that he was taking her through. This is what we all do, we love and seek to understand God and the journey that he is taking us through. We love and seek to understand our parents, our children, our friends, our colleagues, our community, and our world. Everyday we learn something new, or everyday they surprise us with something. We keep pondering and try to understand the mystery of God and the mysteries of life. Sometimes we may feel that we are dragging. Sometimes it might feel like we are stuck or going backward. But with all that, we still keep moving with courage and faith in the Lord.

We have many great personalities in our human and faith history who have been on the journey with God and gave themselves to God. But Mary stands out as someone special among all of them primarily because she is the one who held together the divine and the human, protecting that mystery as a fragile and yet awesome treasure.

She balances both ends of the spectrum. She was the loftiest as the mother of God and yet she was the lowliest. She was the most favored by God but probably she was the most misunderstood among human beings. She is the mother of God and mother of man. Mary is a mother who can understand the contradictions and struggles of human life. She teaches us that real love as it matures will take the form of sorrow in many ways. She teaches us that love is painful. She teaches us that we may have to let go off many things and let God. She invites us to give our best, our best to God and others in love. Mary might have shed many tears, but those tears were beads of love.

We couldn't probably think of a better person who experienced the paradoxes of life so intensely as Mary did. Her life was never settled and calm. She constantly had to keep moving. She had to keep growing in her understanding of God and her mission. She learned many things about the world and herself. She had to grow psychologically and spiritually in many ways. The young girl of the little town of Nazareth became the mother of God and the mother of humanity. She was and she is on the journey with the Lord and with her people all the time.

Saint Paul

Saint Paul is another great personality that we see in the New Testament who also experienced the paradoxical situation of wanting to stay and needing to move in his life. He was a leading Pharisee and a persecutor of Christians. He boasted about his Jewish faith and believed that he was doing a favor to God by getting rid of the infidels, the Christians. And so he was totally taken aback when his life was shaken and the Lord asked him to begin a new phase in his journey of life. He was not to be a persecutor anymore but a missionary for the same cause against which he fought. He probably never imagined that he had to leave his life as a Pharisee and fanatic law enforcer. But he had to leave all that behind and begin a new chapter in his journey of life. He had to swallow his pride and humble himself before the Lord. His life was not settled and secure anymore. The many letters of Paul that we have in the Bible speak to the constant movements, struggles, and uncertainties that he had to face in his missionary journeys. He didn't have a permanent place. He was journeying with God. There were many situations when it seemed like he was getting stuck, but he had to keep moving. Psychologically and spiritually, he kept growing. The man who was so fanatic about his community and religion became a man of the universe. He became all things to all people (1 Cor 9:22). The man who hated Jesus and persecuted Christians became the greatest missionary for Jesus and his gospel. He had to learn many things. He encountered many cultures and people and realized that God loved them all.

In his second letter to the Corinthians, Paul uses the metaphor of a tent and reminds us of our life on this earth as a journey, "For we know that if the earthly tent we live in is destroyed, we have a building from God, a house not made with hands, eternal in the heavens. For in this tent we groan, longing to be clothed with our heavenly dwelling (2 Cor 5:1–2). Paul worked as a tent maker for sometime, and he knew what it meant to live in a tent. His own life taught him that life was never settled and permanent in this world. He realized that it was a journey with the Lord. In his prayer for his disciples, Jesus had already said it, " . . . they are in the world . . . They do not belong to the world, just as I do not belong to the world" (John 17:11, 16). We don't have a permanent place in this world. There is nothing permanent about our ideas, opinions, and thoughts. If the Lord is inviting us to see things in a new way, we need to be willing to let go off some of our strongly held views, ideas, beliefs, and thoughts so that he can take us to healthier life and relationships.

We need a certain amount of physical, psychological, and spiritual stability that helps our growth and development, but the Lord reminds us that we are pilgrims on a journey. As pilgrims we stop briefly in some places to rest, recuperate, and renew ourselves. But our journey continues. We don't get stuck anywhere permanently. Our permanence and stability is in the Lord and in our relationship with others. As followers and fellow travelers we are living and moving forward with the Lord and others. We have to courageously face the rough moments and situations and prudently maneuver the twists and turns that come on our way. Jesus wants us to ascend to higher and newer ways of living.

Moving on with our journey includes leaving behind and letting go off many things. Being on the road with Jesus involves picking ourselves up from where we find ourselves and moving ahead with courage and confidence. And finally, being on the journey involves having the faith and courage to leave this world behind and move past our physical life on this earth.

If we are afraid of moving on in our journey, we cannot grow and develop. Growth and development come only with that forward movement. If a child refuses to grow up, he or she will always stay as a child. Of course, in terms of physical development, we cannot make such a choice. But in many other dimensions of our life, we can refuse to move forward. We can make choices that would determine whether we want to grow or not. People can force me to move physically, and I might oblige. If I refuse to move, there may be negative consequences. But when it comes to non-physical dimensions of life, especially, the psychological and spiritual dimensions, it is difficult for others to force us into something. Generally, nobody can force us to change what we think and believe. Even God doesn't force us. He desires that we change and transform and keep growing but he respects our will and freedom. He invites us to partner with him in the dance of love but he does not force us to dance. It is more up to us than God or others to bring about changes and forward movement in our life. We can stay with our thoughts, ideas, and beliefs all life long, but the quality of our life may be highly compromised with that stagnated state.

39

From Slaves to Sojourners

THE EXODUS OF THE Israelites from Egypt to Canaan, the Promised Land is a powerful story that highlights the pilgrim dimension and paradoxical situations of our life. It is not just one individual but a whole community that is echoing this idea of life as journey with God and others. It is a story with many meanings and implications.

As the Israelites were preparing to depart from Egypt through a special intervention of God, they were instructed to have a Passover meal signifying the Passover of the Lord. It is important to pay attention to the instructions given to the Israelites about how they should eat the meal. Their meal had to have lamb, unleavened bread, and bitter herbs. I would like to focus on the instruction given to them about how they should eat their meal. They were told: "This is how you shall eat it: your loins girded, your sandals on your feet, and your staff in your hand; and you shall eat it hurriedly" (Exod 12:11).

What does that look like? It looks like they are ready to travel at any moment. They are in a hurry. But that is not how to enjoy a meal. To enjoy a meal we sit down and take time. We relax and eat slow. But here, they had to eat as though they had to leave at any moment. What does that mean? They were going to the Promised Land; they were going to be liberated. So they had to be ready to leave Egypt any time. Maybe some of them did not want to leave Egypt. There must have been many things that they had in Egypt that would have kept them back. Over the years, even as slaves, they must have had a lot of things and property accumulated. They might have had many relationships and associations that they had built up with the natives. Since the Israelites were in Egypt for more than four centuries, it is possible that many of them did not know anything about Canaan or too much about the history of their ancestors. The only world and territory they knew about was Egypt. That was their home. We can relate to that in our own life. If somebody asks us to move from our current country of citizenship or residence because our ancestors came from somewhere else and that is where we belong, it may be very hard to make that move even if we are living in very difficult situations currently.

Hence we can imagine that leaving that familiar home of Egypt was probably not easy for many Israelites. But if they did not leave Egypt what would happen? They would be in slavery forever. They would never be free. They would never get to the Promised Land. They would be stuck in Egypt for the rest of their life.

This story tells us something more than the physical aspect of travels and slavery. It speaks about how our life is meant to be. We are on a journey and we are pilgrims on this earth. Our God is a God who lives with us and intervenes in our life as our Father, redeemer, and traveling companion. And we are on the journey with him. That journey does not end in this world. It continues into eternity. And to be on that journey we have to leave many things behind. We have to be ever ready to say yes to Jesus. We have to be ready to let go off many things. To get attached to Jesus means getting detached from many things. To be united with God and move ahead as a community, we have to be disconnected from everything that is enslaving us physically, psychologically, and spiritually. Moving physically from one place to another may be easy, but what is more demanded of us is moving psychologically and spiritually. We could be slaves to many psychological and spiritual ailments. We need to be freed from that and keep moving forward into healthy lives and relationships.

We have to move from being slaves to becoming sojourners with God. But sometimes it is hard to do that. We may not want to be on the journey. We may not want to get detached from certain things. We may not want to leave Egypt. We may not want to leave our slavery, our evil habits, sinful tendencies, unhealthy thoughts, feelings, and behaviors, unhealthy structures and systems, the hurts and wounds of the past and present, our biases and prejudices, our anger and hatred, and all such things that keep us in slavery. Maybe we have gotten used to many of those things that we don't want to leave them. A heavy smoker may know that smoking is harmful to his or her health, but the pleasure derived from smoking and the addiction to it may be so much that he or she may not want to leave it. We sometimes like our "Egypts."

Sometimes it is not because we don't want to leave our Egypts or enslaving elements in our life but rather because we don't realize what they are doing to us. Our slavery to certain things becomes so much part of us that we begin to think that that is what is normal. When we are so soaked and sunk in certain unhealthy things or ways of living, they might appear to be healthy. It is also possible that we are staying in our Egypts or unhealthy ways because we don't know how to get out of them. We feel weak and helpless. These are all possible in our life. But we need to leave them if we want to make progress in our life. If we don't leave those Egypts or enslaving elements we don't experience the larger world of freedom and opportunity for growth and development. God did not allow his people to get stuck in slavery. He took them out of there and encouraged them to keep moving forward. We need to keep moving and be back in the dialogical triangle and the divine dance of love.

Many patients who come to treatment for their mental health issues present themselves as very defended or with many defense mechanisms. Over the years they have developed these defense mechanisms by which they have learned to protect their self from excessive anxiety or psychic distress. When the self feels attacked by someone or something it immediately finds ways to defend itself. According to Salman Akhtar, a psychoanalyst, theorists and therapists have identified one hundred and one defense mechanisms that people employ or engage in. Some of the common defense mechanisms are regression, repression, reaction formation, denial, undoing, isolation, projection, introjection, sublimation, identification with the aggressor, acting out, dissociation, and compartmentalization. Even if they don't think of these terms, once they come to know what they are, many people would realize that they employ these defenses in their daily lives. These defenses work in the person unconsciously.

Although the defense mechanisms could be beneficial in the immediate circumstances or temporarily, they are unhealthy and detrimental to the person's growth and relationships in the long run. For example, a person who is addicted to alcohol could use the defense mechanism of "denial" by denying that he or she is an addict by saying, "I am just a social drinker." Such denial might help the person avoid the shame and embarrassment of being branded as an addict in the immediate context but in the long run the denial is not going to help the person get any better. He or she will continue to be an addict and not seek help or treatment. We even hear people commenting about this defense mechanism when they talk about others, "He is in denial" or "She is in denial."

Most of the time, the person is not aware that he or she is using some defense mechanisms. The person might think that what he or she does is normal. Therapy helps the patient to recognize some of the defense mechanisms and work on them. But dismantling those defenses are a threat to the self. The patient would make all effort to protect and put up those defenses lest he or she becomes vulnerable. They defend their defenses. Again, it is an unconscious process that goes on in the person. Often we need those defenses to survive in the immediate context. They are like guards or shields we put up to protect ourselves. But if we really want to thrive, we have to befriend and confront them. Only when we become less and less defensive and learn to hold together our vulnerabilities and strengths we can be on the forward movement. Otherwise the defenses would keep us stuck and stifled.

Even after they left Egypt, the Israelites found it difficult to move forward. During their sojourn through the desert, they found life very hard. They were faced with hunger and thirst, and they longed for things they had in Egypt. They grumbled and complained against Moses and God. They longed for the meat and potatoes of Egypt and wanted to go back there. They said, "If only we had died by the hand of the Lord in the land of Egypt, when we sat by the fleshpots and ate our fill of bread" (Exod 16:3). They did not want to go forward. The Israelites wanting to stay or go back to Egypt could be referring to our human tendency to stay stuck with or go back to our defenses. The desert could be referring to a dry and difficult moment in life.

Even after we make some forward movement, we might go through some "desert" experience like the Israelites did. And then again we might feel like going back to our old ways or defenses, going back to Egypt. We might return back to our hatred, anger, fears, frustrations, shame, disappointment, laziness, greed, pride, depression, and all such things. All these things could function as our defenses. They give us a certain amount of power and protection. My hatred or anger can keep my enemy or the one I dislike away from me. My hatred or anger stand as a wall or guard against that person. My laziness could be a defense that I employ to keep away from hard work. My fear could be keeping me away from what I am afraid of. As long as I keep away I don't need to confront what I fear. All these things might be seen as sins or evils in spiritual terminology, but they also could be seen as defenses that we employ to protect ourselves from anxiety and stress. They give us a certain amount of power and protection against our enemy whoever or whatever the enemy may be. And sometimes some of these defenses and sins are pleasurable, and hence we hold on to them. There may be all kinds of reasons why we develop these defenses or sins. For each person it may be different and we may not be even aware what causes these defenses and sins in us. What is needed is to recognize them, find out their causes, and work on reducing their impact on our daily life and functioning so that we can be on the path of growth and development.

The exodus story also tells us that the Israelites not only resisted to be on the journey themselves but also attempted to contain and stop God from being on the move as well. They made a golden calf to represent God (Exod 32:1–6). Probably they built an altar for it and wanted to stay there. Although Canaan was their destination, it probably seemed to many of them as a never reachable place. They probably didn't like God's idea of being on the move constantly. Maybe they wanted to settle down and stay, but God made them to keep moving forward.

Forward movement or attaining holiness is often tiresome and difficult, and so we might want to stay put. But as long as we hold on to our defenses, sins, and other enslaving elements, we will never get to the Promised Land, healthy living, union with God and others. We will never experience the freedom that God offers us. If the younger son in the parable of the prodigal son was going to stay with the pigs forever he would have never gotten home and experienced freedom and new life. If the elder son was going to get stuck with his anger and stubbornness he was never going to be home and experience joy in his life.

The Israelites' resistance to the constant forward movement and unsettled lifestyle continued even after they reached Canaan. They wanted to be like everybody else in the world, settled down, structured, and secure. They wanted to build up their own kingdom. They went to Samuel and demanded a king so that they could be like other nations (1 Sam 8:5). God said to Samuel that their demand for an earthly king was an indication that they didn't want God to be their king anymore (1 Sam 8:7). Not wanting to have God as their king anymore could mean that they had refused to be on the journey with God and slowly moved into unholy and unhealthy life. They were chosen to be different, to live a holy life, but they seem to have abandoned that call and wanted to be like everybody else. Jesus wanted his disciples to live a life different from the ways of the world, but on many occasions, we realize that we abandon that call and follow what everybody else in the world is doing.

God warned the Israelites about having a king, "He will take your sons and appoint them to his chariots and to be his horsemen, and to run before his chariots . . . He will take your daughters to be perfumers and cooks and bakers. He will take the best of your fields and vineyards and olive orchards and give them to his courtiers . . . He will take one-tenth of your flocks, and you shall be his slaves" (1 Sam 8:11–17). God warned them about the dangers of stopping their journey and getting stuck. But they did not listen to God.

God's warning about the dangers of building up the kingdom and having an earthly king could also mean that he wanted them to focus on something more than the immediate satisfaction and what this world offers. In God's salvific plan, our life continues into eternity. Building our kingdoms in this world and getting too much settled here might make us think that this is all what matters in our life. We can be so caught up in the things of this world or the immediate pleasures and needs that we forget that there is something more to life than these. We might want to stay here forever with all that we build up. But fortunately or unfortunately, these are all passing.

God's invitation to his people to be on the journey also needs to be seen as an invitation to focus more on building their relationship as a community than on building structures and systems as nations and kingdoms often do. To build their relationship and grow as a community, they had to focus more on the psychological and spiritual aspects than on the physical aspects. The real movement has to happen internally more than in the external sense. The Ten Commandments God gave them were more about making internal changes rather than external changes. Externally, they could build a kingdom with all the structures and systems, but that was not necessarily going to make them a good and loving community. Of course, families, communities, and nations need some sort of structures and stability to function and live together. They don't need to be moving all the time in the external or physical sense. What is more important is the internal transformation.

God's invitation to the Israelites was more about the psychological and spiritual journey without which they were not going to make progress. When God says to Samuel that the people had rejected him as their king, it might be indicating that people had begun to focus more on their external life than internal transformation. They were not following God's ways but their own desires and plans. When God warned them about what an earthly king would do to them, he was indicating how they would stop being a loving community. They were going to be divided as the rulers and the ruled, the privileged and the neglected, and the powerful and the powerless.

But the Israelites did not listen to God's voice and warning. They insisted on having an earthly king and they got what they wanted. They had a king and a kingdom was established. But they got stuck. Their king, Saul proved to be a bad king. Their community life was in bad shape.

The story of the Israelites is our story. God keeps reminding us that we are pilgrims on a journey. We are not slaves; we are sojourners. If we don't keep moving, we get stuck. There will be many unhealthy things that come into our life as "Egypts," that make us enslaved and get stuck, but God wants us to leave them and keep moving. To experience freedom, peace, and joy, we have to be willing to leave behind many things. Our true joy is in being united with God and others in love.

40

A Species Hard to Tame

THE JOURNEY WITH JESUS and living the Christological model of life are more about an internal transformation than external changes. Jesus denounced the hypocrisy of the scribes and Pharisees because they were more concerned about the external appearance than the internal transformation. To reciprocate God's love, we have to focus on cleaning ourselves up internally. We have to allow Jesus to transform us psychologically and spiritually everyday. It is a gradual process and lifelong journey. Changes don't happen overnight.

Of all the species that roam this earth, human beings, we could say, are the kindest, most compassionate, and most loving. But the same human beings seem to be the wildest, most cruel, and most difficult-to-tame of all creatures on this planet earth as well. Sometimes we bring the best out of ourselves, and sometimes we bring out the worst. We can be the most loving persons at one moment and yet the most hateful people in the next. The world around us can be very loving today, but the same world can be very mean and ugly tomorrow. Sometimes we choose to be nice, but at other times we choose to be nasty.

We might wonder why it has to be that way. Why can't people always be loving, kind, and compassionate? Why can't we learn to behave better and live in a healthy way at or after a certain age? Why can't we always remain in the dialogical triangle and be partners in the divine dance of love? Why can't we be united with God and others all the time? The answer doesn't seem to come by easily. The only thing we can say is that we still have a lot more to learn and grow. From the time we are born to the last breath of our life on this earth, we seem to be in a constant need to be told, taught, and even forced to do certain things in certain ways. Physically, when we are born, we are one of the most fragile of all creatures. We need constant help and support from our parents and others before we can stand on our feet and do something on our own.

Although gaining physical stability and strength takes a long time, what takes us more time is gaining psychological and spiritual stability. The road to our psychological and spiritual health is long and cumbersome. As we grow and develop, we make great strides and do a lot of good things. But even after we turn ninety, we might need to be coaxed, coached, and contained in many ways. Every stage of our life challenges us with new tasks and tricks to learn. Sometimes we succeed, but sometimes we fail. If we succeed, we have new tasks awaiting us. If we fail, we try again. It is a chain of rising and falling, and rising again and falling again. The hardest part is to accept and hold together these dichotomous dimensions about us.

Various psychologists have theorized about the different tasks associated with each of the stages of human development. They postulate that each of our developmental stages has certain tasks associated with it. A healthy personality and human development require a satisfactory accomplishment of those tasks.

In early childhood, for example, one of the main tasks for children is potty or toilet training. At this stage, children develop more control over their sphincter muscles that allow them to eliminate their body waste in a more controlled way. In infancy, they don't possess such control over their body muscles and functions. Infants urinate and defecate at will. They don't have the capacity and control to tell their parents or other caregivers that they "want to go" to toilet or urinate and defecate. Even before they give any indication, the parents or caregivers would realize that "they already went!" During that stage, parents or caregivers assist children with diapers and other holding and protective materials so that the deposits they make do not make a mess and spread a bad odor around. But after a while, as they grow older, most children gain control over their body muscles and functioning and don't seem to need the assistance of diapers or their parents.

However, even after we grow older, there are other areas of our lives that sometimes seem to be going out of control. Our thoughts, emotions, imaginations, and behaviors seem to spill and spread all kinds of bad tastes and odors everywhere, making our lives and the lives of others difficult. We experience both the positive and the negative dimensions of all these faculties. We have positive and negative thoughts, good and bad feelings, healthy and unhealthy imaginations, and constructive and destructive behaviors. Our mind and spirit take us through all these, and sometimes the greatest of all our tasks in life seems to be gaining control over them.

Certain children, we have heard, are "strong willed." But we hear the same thing about an adolescent, a young adult, and an elderly person. Strong willed persons could be found across all age groups. Similarly, a young kid, a college student, and an old man or woman can be found rebellious and hard to handle. Toddlers and older kids sometimes throw a temper tantrum and withdraw from their parents when they are upset or when the parents are not emotionally attuned to them. It might take a while for the parents to cajole and coax the kid to come out of the upsetting and withdrawn mood. But such behaviors and emotional reactions are not peculiar to children alone. Adults do the same. They throw a temper tantrum and stay away from the person who offends them or is emotionally unavailable to them. Some people stay withdrawn and isolated from their offenders for several years. People don't get over certain issues just because they have grown older or bigger. Some adults behave like little kids or adolescents, and some kids and adolescents act like grown up adults.

When it comes to knowing the working of our mind and taming our human will and spirit, we have a hard job to accomplish. We have learned many things about the functioning of our body and mind, but we are still baffled and amazed by many things that are going on in us, and they have no easy explanations. Understanding and taming a ferocious animal from the wild seems to be much easier than comprehending the working of our human psyche and taming our human will or spirit. Our mind doesn't ask our permission before it processes and comes up with the million thoughts that take us to realms that we never knew we were going. In fact it doesn't make sense to even think about that because it is the mind, which asks and gives the permission, and questions why it is not asking for permission.

How would it be if the thief, the victim, the police, the prosecutor, the judge, and the jailor were all one and the same person? Our mind or human psyche is something like that. It makes us question things, and it also makes us question our questions. It helps us to be conscious about things, and it also helps us to be conscious about our consciousness. It makes us imagine things, and it also makes us imagine about our imaginations. It makes us reason and rationalize, and it also makes us wonder about the rationality of our rationalization. It makes us judge things, but it also makes us judge our judgments. It makes us think about things, but it also makes us think about our thoughts. It makes us feel, but it also makes us feel about our feelings. It takes our thoughts into all kinds of directions and distracts us, but it also makes us keep away the distractions and concentrate. It is difficult to understand fully the working of our mind, and it is hard to predict where our mind is going to take us in the next moment.

Try, if you can, to follow the movements of your mind for half an hour. Pay attention to everything that your mind takes you to, including the awareness of your mind paying attention to your mind. This is not about looking at the movements of the mind when someone is engaged in an intensely focused meditation. Those who practice meditation may be able to focus their mind on a single thing. And that is what we do when we want to direct our mind onto something specific. It is not just in meditation, but we are constantly trying to focus or redirect our mind into certain realms that we want to concentrate on. But again we realize that it is our mind that is helping us to direct or redirect our mind. In that sense, in our wakeful or conscious state of being, we cannot escape or avoid our mind in any way. And when we are not awake, it works in us through our dreams. Even when we try to pay attention to the thousand things that the mind takes us to, our mind is in fact directing our mind in that direction. Don't freak out, but the question will be: what is your mind telling your mind about your mind? Or what are you telling you about you? We may not be aware of it, but we often engage in it. We engage in self-talks about our self-talks.

That's the story of our mind and life. The moment we think we have a grasp of it, our mind will have taken us elsewhere. Our mind takes us to directions we may not have even imagined. It protests, rebels, and questions. It is constantly engaged in thoughts, feelings, imaginations, rationalizations, evaluations, so on and so forth. It is said that in a given day there are fifty to sixty thousand thoughts going through our mind. Do we have track of or control over all of them? No. But at the same time, we are constantly at work to tame ourselves.

If we look at the different areas of our life and relationships we will notice that most of our energy and resources are spent on this need for constant taming of others or ourselves.

In our social lives, the society is constantly at work, trying to coach and teach us about living as a cohesive and healthy community. Rules and regulations, and policies and procedures are not simply for nothing. They are tools the society is using to regulate everyone's thoughts, emotions, and actions and hold everybody together. Good manners and etiquette are not just about people trying to control us. They are necessary ingredients for civility and a healthy community living. When we say "thank you," "please," or "excuse me," it makes our interactions and communications much smoother. When we try to be on time, let others go first, do not interrupt, and make room for others or respect their personal space we enter into a respectful accommodation of one another. Learning social behaviors takes a lot of practice and regulation of our minds. Like a mother, the society has to prod, placate, and punish to get us pay attention. It has to constantly remind us how we need to act and why we need to act in such stipulated ways. Civilization is not just about building structures and systems in the external sense, it is also about building internal structures and systems that help us interact and deal with each other better. It is about developing a more civil and respectful culture and relationship with one another. The societal taming of our minds and lives go on until the end of our lives.

In religious circles, the story is pretty much the same. Much of the effort and energy in religious groups and communities are spent on "straightening up" their members. Some do it with threats of hell and punishments, while others do it with a promise of heaven and paradise. How many thousands of sermons and spiritual talks are given everyday all over the world? Morality and discipline are constantly emphasized upon. The Ten Commandments were a set of ideals and framework of life that God presented to his people through Moses for them to live a healthy life as individuals, families, and a community. Every community and society around the world lays down commandments and laws likewise to tame and guide their people into healthy ways of living.

In Catholic religious communities, consecrated men and women take a vow of obedience. Although it is essentially about becoming a Christ-like servant to God and the church, in reality, it is also the religious community's way to make its members bend their wills and tame themselves. Members with unbendable wills and uncontrollable personalities are not going to be easy for the community to handle. The vow is a requirement that the community puts on the individual for membership and continuity. Dying to self or mortification of self is presented as a virtue as well as a requirement for such ways of life. Although some use this vow to silence and suppress others and make their authority felt, obedience in the true sense is a necessary component in community living. It is not simply obedience to one person or authority figure but rather obedience to God and obedience to the whole community that is required of the person. And in that respect, even those in authority need to be obedient to God and the community. No one is exempt from this requirement of bending their wills and taming their minds.

The story is not much different in family life or a marriage. The spouses are required to make a vow to each other to bend their wills and die to their self in many ways so that they can function as one unit. They have to constantly tame their minds and wills to respect each other's individuality and at the same time keep their unity as a couple. In the words of Pope Francis, marriage is a "friendship marked by passion, but a passion always directed to an ever more stable and intense union" (Francis, 2016). If each of the spouses begins to do things as he or she wills, the relationship is not going to grow into that stable and intense union. They might stay together but they will live as two railroad tracks that never meet. The same principle applies to the context of a family. Each member of the family has to tame him or herself so that everyone has a revered place in the family and at the same time they maintain a strong sense of love and unity.

In politics, we are constantly trying to refine our governance and decision-making processes so that our individual and communal lives become healthy and happy. We have tried many systems of government and ideologies, and we are still looking for the perfect one. One party or government gives way to another, but almost every politician and political system disappoints those whom they govern. The gap between the government and the governed keeps growing. Taming of the minds and wills of those who occupy the seats of power seems to be a herculean task for every nation and society.

In all of these, it is not only the individuals who are found to be difficult to tame but also certain groups and their associated institutions in certain communities. Certain groups and institutions become like monsters that no one can approach or tame. They have a life of their own. They do a lot of harm to their communities and the rest of the world by their unhealthy ideas, ideologies, actions, hard-heartedness, and lack of openness and tolerance. The communities and societies have to constantly rein in and tame such groups to keep themselves from tilting to one extreme or the other. Whether it is as individuals or communities, we need to constantly tame our minds and wills to live healthy lives and be in communion with God and others. We need to ensure that we are journeying with Jesus at all times, following his footsteps. We need to make his values our values. Following our own path can lead us to unhealthy choices and actions.

Referring to the necessity of remaining close to God at all times, Saint Francis de Sales uses the metaphor of a father and child going for a walk. As they walk the child holds on to the hand of the father or the father holds the hand of the child so that the child does not stumble and fall. With one hand tightly held on to the father's hand, the child might use the other hand to collect berries from the hedges or vines as they walk by. The child needs to make sure that he or she does not leave both hands from the father. Otherwise the child would fall and hurt him or herself. Similarly, the saint says, as we engage in the affairs of our daily life and affairs of the world, we should make sure that we hold tightly to the Lord in our heart and mind. If we completely leave the Lord, we might stumble and fall, and end up in dangers and difficulties. We have to also stay united with others. If we completely withdraw or isolate from others, it becomes a lonely journey. To stay united with others, we have to constantly remain open to them and be willing to adjust and accommodate. For both these, to remain united with God and to live in communion with others, we will have to tame our hearts and minds, our decisions and desires, our ideas and opinions, and our thoughts and feelings. Advancing in psychological and spiritual growth and growing in the love of God and others may be a hard and slow process, but with Jesus as our guide and traveling companion we can do it.

41

Tilting to the Extremes

JOURNEYING AND REMAINING UNITED with Jesus and others are difficult processes because as individuals, families, communities, and societies we sometimes get tilted from one extreme to the other. Either we become too rigid and restrictive or uncontrollably loose and lax. In either case we end up in unhealthy situations of life. And both these extremes may have something to do with our image of God and spirituality.

We may have an image of God as a strict and no-nonsense judge, who would determine our future based on the number of good deeds we do. Such an image could make us lean toward an extremely rigid and ultraconservative mode of life making us to do things with fear and extreme care so that we would be found pleasing in his eyes and we would find a place in heaven. Some of us, on the other hand, may have an image of God as someone for whom "anything is fine" because he loves us no matter what. He is full of mercy and compassion, and hence we don't need to care about how we live and worry about getting by.

Both these extremes have problems because they are not looking at our life as a journey with God and others participating in the divine dance of love. In those images of God and modes of life, we are not seeing ourselves as partners with God and others in the dialogical triangle. In the dialogical triangle and dance of love, there is no place for fear and disregard for God or others. It has to be based on love, and love alone.

The extreme positions that we take or develop don't have to be arising out of image of God and spirituality alone. It could be also because of the social and psychological elements existing in our particular families and societies. But whatever may be the cause, what is important and desirable is that we return back to our dialogical relationship with God and others. We shall look at these two extremes in a little more detail.

Having been presented with or having developed an ultraconservative mode of life and being concerned about losing control of our behaviors and interactions sometimes we set for ourselves rigid rules and regulations that sometimes take away all flexibility and openness. Some individuals and families are extremely hard on themselves. They appear to be too tight and rigid. It will be rare to see them smiling or exhibiting a pleasant or happy countenance. They view this world as totally evil and hostile, and turn their face against the wonders and beauties of the earth for fear of inviting God's wrath and losing heaven. They are given into extreme austerity and renunciation. They are hard on themselves and hard on others. In their dictionary, the word "mistake" does not appear. They are strict law abiders and they stick to the rulebook. They set strict boundaries, and there is no room for anything out of the ordinary in their lives. If anything happens out of the ordinary, they are extremely upset and agitated. They are less tolerant of mistakes and failures. It will not be a surprise if they are hoping to "impress" God by their piety and looking forward to their long awaited reward in heaven.

It is not that people with extremely rigid and conservative personalities don't have their flaws and fears, but they are often afraid of letting anyone know of their fears and failures. They are afraid of spilling some of their undesired emotions and behaviors before others. They dread being vulnerable. It will not be a surprise if many of them develop an obsessive-compulsive personality. Their personality style gets exhibited in different areas of their lives. They might be extremely conservative in their religious views, practices, and observances. They are extremely close-fisted and miserly in their financial dealings with others except when it advances or promotes their interests. They can be arbitrary and authoritarian in their familial, societal, and legal dealings and relationships. Some of them become cruel taskmasters, tyrants, and fanatics. Some of them take on God as their ally and present him as a taskmaster and a no-nonsense strict judge.

People with such rigid personalities are painfully stiff and hard to change. They are less open to alternative ideas and opinions. They might consider those who differ from them as contaminators and destroyers of the world and culture. Sometimes these individuals form themselves as groups and communities and become a powerful force in the society. They are on a mission to cleanse the world of all its ills and contamination. Their extremist and rigid views and ways of living create a rather uncomfortable environment for the rest of the society. Such people are found in every community and society. They might be like the elder son in the parable of the prodigal son. They do and follow what is expected of them, but they suppress and repress all their feelings of dissatisfaction and discontentment. They might look perfectly fine externally but internally they are seldom happy and at peace. They are afraid and angry within. They might blow up one day or live unhappily forever.

This is the kind of personality that many of the scribes and Pharisees had, and Jesus had hard time convincing them about the unhealthy positions they were in. They often found Jesus as the rule breaker and renegade. They called him a glutton and drunkard, and a friend of tax collectors and sinners. They criticized him when his disciples ate the grains of wheat on the Sabbath. They called him blasphemous and irreverent when he healed people on the Sabbath or did not follow the customs of washing hands and ritual cleansing. They had developed a distorted idea of God. They considered themselves better than others. Their spirituality was not modeled after the triangular dialogical relationship. Jesus wanted them to leave their extreme ideas and beliefs and join him in the dance of love, to be in communion with God and others. Some of them, like Nicodemus, responded to his invitation, but others appear to have remained in their rigidity.

And then there are others who are on the opposite side of the spectrum. They care less about rules and regulations of their families, communities, or society. They take the word "freedom" to all its extreme interpretations. They shun all societal structures and systems. They are not concerned about spilling their undesirable feelings and behaviors anywhere and everywhere. They set no boundaries for themselves and try to break all boundaries that others or the society set. They make unhealthy decisions and engage in self-destructive and harmful behaviors. They also end up hurting other people by what they say and do. It will be no surprise if such individuals become extremely narcissistic. Everything turns out to be about them. Even the apparent good they do to others are done with the intention of satisfying their ego. They give no heed to those who try to rein in on them to bring them back to healthy living. They eschew and disregard directions and guidance. They are a hard group to tame. Some of these individuals also get together and form themselves into groups and become a force in the community or society. They are on a mission to challenge and pull down the existing structures and systems of the society. With their extreme views and ideals they also create an uncomfortable environment for the rest of the society. They may be likened to the younger son in the parable of the prodigal son. They cause ruptures and divisions in their families, communities, and society by their life and behaviors.

There are many psychological reasons as to why we become what we become. People become rigid and tight-fisted if they had negative, cold, and insecure attachment experiences from their parents or caregivers in their childhood. Some of them grow up with dominant, authoritarian, and over-controlling parenting experiences or live in rigid and overly strict home environment. A child who has had an insecure attachment experience where the parents or caregivers were not emotionally and physically available and attuned adequately could develop a personality that is cold, rigid, and withdrawn in later years. Some families that are ultra orthodox and conservative in their presentation and practice of religion and spirituality could produce members who become overly rigid and restrictive. People who experience abuses and other kinds of traumas could develop a personality that is painfully rigid. People who come from hierarchical and closed familial and social systems and settings could be very closed and restrictive in their thinking and behaviors. A child who grows up in a hierarchical and closed system of familial and social interactions might become the new patriarch who transmits the same pattern of behavior and relationships in his or her family and social settings. People who have been recipients of intergenerational transmission of negativity, distress, and various kinds of mental disorders could develop personalities and behaviors that are unhealthily narrow and rigid. They could also become the opposite. Because they had a very rigid and strict upbringing, they might discard all rules and regulations and become overly lax and liberal when grown up.

Those who develop a personality that breaks all healthy boundaries and expectations might have had unhealthy and insecure parenting experiences, abandonment and profound neglect, various kinds of traumatic abuses, a home environment without boundaries or rules, intergenerational transmission of certain kinds of mental distress or disorders, and prenatal and postnatal exposure to drugs and alcohol. A child, who has been abused sexually or physically, for example, experiences boundary violation and breaking of social contracts in a profound way. According to the unwritten social contracts, a family or society is expected to protect the child from all harm. When someone abuses a child that contract is broken, and the child's faith and confidence in the family or society weakens. When such abuses happen, the abuser breaks all boundaries. The abuser breaks into the private space of the child and violates his or her protective boundary and safe space that everyone is expected to respect and keep as a sacred space. The experience highly compromises or challenges the child's trust and confidence about the rest of the world. When the child grows up, it is possible that he or she has absolutely no regard for the boundaries and safe spaces of other people because the society or responsible people in their own life never gave it to them. They would break every boundary that is set by the society or family because their boundary has been broken when they were growing up. They don't feel the need to respect and keep the social contracts because they were never given such privileges. Thus the abused become abusers. Many of these behaviors in later life could be happening unconsciously. The person may not even be aware that he or she is doing anything bad. The person could also become the opposite. He or she could also become overly rigid. Since the boundaries and social contracts were broken, the person could become overly cautious, rigid, and strict with everyone in the future so that no one dares to repeat the same offense again.

It is not necessary that all the children who experience such negativity and trauma should turn out to be rigid and hard or uncontrollably loose and lax, but these are possible contributors to the development of such personalities. Sometimes children with the same or similar experiences develop opposite kinds of personalities. Children growing up in the same family develop different personalities as they differ in how their genetic coding is structured and how their minds process all the experiences they are exposed to. Our personalities consist of inherited and learned traits. Although some children inherit unhealthy elements from their parent generations and are exposed to unhealthy experiences and environments, they can still turn out to be healthy and good and do not have to necessarily continue the chain of unhealthy behaviors and lives of the past generations. It is not only our childhood experiences but also the experiences in later stages of life that influence the formation of our personalities. We often are unaware of what contributes to the shaping of our attitudes, ideas, thoughts, feelings, and behaviors.

When generally it is hard for all of us to tame our minds and direct our wills toward healthy decisions or choices, it will be harder for people with extremely negative behaviors and problematic personalities to do that. People who have been abused, exposed to unhealthy lives and environments, inherited unhealthy traits from the past generations, or developed destructive and unhealthy behaviors and personalities might find it very difficult to change their thoughts and feelings and do something different. They have a greater chance to repeat the unhealthy trends and behaviors of the past generations. They might need professional help and treatment to address their issues and problems before they can tame their minds and wills on their own. It is possible that because of various reasons we have fallen into one or the other extreme. Sometimes we may not be in either of the extreme positions but vacillating between the two. If we are caught up in some unhealthy and extreme ways of living and doing things, we need to lift ourselves up from there and keep moving. Our minds and wills may not cooperate all the time. They might go wild and wayward. But we can try to redirect them to healthy decisions and choices. Whether we are like the elder son or the younger son in the parable of the prodigal sons, we need to come home. We need to return back to healthy living where we are united with our Father and brother, with God and one another.

We know change is not easy. We can talk for hours about changing, but to make any simple change in our life, it is not easy. We are often comfortable with the way we are. We are used to certain ways of doing and behaving and that is what is "normal" for us. Certain things have become a habit. Sometimes our experiences in life turn us into what we become. And given their experience in life, sometimes what we see in certain people is the best that they can do. It is amazing and even miraculous that some people turn out to be healthy and happy even after they experience horrible traumas and negative experiences in their lives.

Change is not a uniform thing that we can demand of everyone in the same way. Change requires different things for different people. And change is hard work. But to live healthy lives personally and interpersonally all of us need to be in a dynamic process of change and transformation, both internally and externally. We need to keep moving forward. If we don't keep moving forward and change, we will either go backward or stay stagnant. In either case it is going to stifle our growth and development. The Christological model of life is about being on a journey with God and others. Holding on to our extreme positions and refusing to be open to change and transformation denies God the freedom to work with us. Fears and Pharisaic attitudes make us get stuck. Instead of giving into those debilitating elements, what is needed is to be on the road with Jesus, to be the clay that the divine potter can shape into something beautiful.

42

Heaven, Hell, and Purgatory

THE DISCUSSION ON THE journey with Jesus and living the Christological model will be incomplete without some discussion on the three topics of heaven, hell, and purgatory. These topics have been matters of great interest for most Christians and people of other religious traditions. People are curious to know what happens after they die or depart from the physical life of this earth. Even those without any religious affiliation or spirituality might engage in some conversations about these topics. The topic of purgatory is often a point of discussion mainly for Catholics. All the three topics are often like hot potatoes that people pass from one to the other because they are too "hot" to handle or hold. Nobody seems to know completely what they are but at the same time they have their ideas and beliefs.

Being aware of the delicateness of these topics I shall dwell on them for a while. But even while attempting to discuss these topics, I admit that I don't have any absolute idea about what they are because only an absolute being can have an absolutely accurate idea about anything. And I am not an absolute being. Only God is absolute. Like any other human being, I am limited in what and how much I can comprehend. It is also important to note that many of the thoughts and reflections I present on these topics here are not doctrinal or definitive. They are personal reflections intended for discussions and dialogue. Having said that, let us discuss how they are important in our journey of life.

I don't think it will be a strange idea if I say that people are very selective and decisive when it comes to their sense of who goes to heaven and hell. After I came to the United States I learned that there were some Christian denominations or groups that believed that all Catholics were going to go to hell. That came to me as a great surprise and it was somewhat off-putting, because I was raised with the opposite belief. In India, we were raised with the idea that all Protestants were bad and they were probably on their way to hell, unless they became Catholics. The Catholics were thought to be the good guys, destined for heaven. But now after hearing about these groups in the United States who believed that the Catholics were going to hell, I was not sure about my free ticket to heaven based on my Catholic identity. The information also made me confront my own biases and judgments about other groups and denominations. And I wondered whether some Christian groups in India itself consider the Catholics as destined for hell. Maybe they do, and I didn't know that. Our interactions often being limited to our own quarters, we seldom hear what other Christian denominations think about us. I believe many of us take on the role of God and make judgments on others. I don't think we were too sure about the non-Christians, whether they went to heaven or hell. But there are some Catholics and other Christians who believe that all non-Christians are going to go to hell. In that case, the vast majority of the people living in this world now and who went before us are already condemned because all of them are not or were not Christians or Catholics. I dread all these conclusions and judgments we make about each other because that will leave heaven with no occupants whatsoever, and hell will be overcrowded. In fact, hell will have a hell of a time to accommodate all those people! Besides, if everyone is going to end up in hell, God is going to be a lonely figure abiding in heaven all alone. People often leave out of the discussion the topic of purgatory since it is mostly a topic only for the Catholics, and even for them it is more vague than the topics of heaven and hell.

Before we go any further into our discussion on these topics, it is good to pay attention to what Saint James has to say to all those who make judgments on others, "There is only one Lawgiver and Judge, the one who is able to save and destroy. But you—who are you to judge your neighbor? (Jas 4:12). Since judgment is reserved only to God, I dare not decide and judge who qualifies for heaven, hell, or purgatory. And I dare not condemn anybody. Jesus also has some good reminders for those who think that they are among the "chosen" few. He says that those who claim to be among the chosen might be disappointed because they might see themselves thrown out while people from the east and west, and north and south who are not among the chosen few will find a place in the kingdom of God (Luke 13:27–29). Reserving the judgment to God about who gets to be in heaven, hell, or purgatory, let us look at what we believe and what new insights we could have.

Conventional Beliefs

There are some people who think of heaven, hell, and purgatory as an extension of this earth in terms of its physical features in space and time. They think of heaven as a real physical place or space with all kinds of attractive and desirable things. They imagine of having varieties of wines and spirits, delicious food, air-conditioned and spacious rooms and mansions, separate quarters or sections for each ethnic, religious, or racial groups, gardens of beautiful flowers and fruits, blue and open skies, twinkling stars, and feathery clouds to surround them.

They expect their best friends and closest family members to meet them at the pearly gates. They think of it as a place free from sufferings and pains. Heaven is often visualized as a place somewhere up in the sky or above the sky. They imagine of meeting God, the Supreme Being, judge, and ruler of heaven who might be seated like an emperor or king on a golden throne wearing golden robes and a crown of glowing jewels in a spacious and majestic room. If God moves or stands up, there will be great thunder, lighting, and roaring of wild animals. Angels will be singing and dancing, floating in the air moving from one end of the room to the other. Other heavenly beings will be positioned as sentries or soldiers guarding the house. The saints and angels will be escorting the new entrants into heaven.

Saint Peter will be standing at the gate with a book of accounts regarding each person's doings, to assign appropriate quarters or cells. Heaven, in their imagination, is the perfect place that gives them everything that they did not have in this world or an extension or unlimited supply of what they had. It is a place of unlimited bliss as well as awesome power and might. It is visualized as something that happens after we leave this earthly life. It is a place of eternal bliss.

These are beautiful and very tempting imageries of heaven. And there are some biblical passages that would make anyone think that this is how it is going to be. In the book of Isaiah, there is a passage that is sometimes taken as a reference to heaven, "On this mountain the Lord Almighty will prepare a feast of rich food for all peoples, a banquet of aged wine—the best of meats and the finest of wines. On this mountain he will destroy the shroud that enfolds all peoples, the sheet that covers all nations; he will swallow up death forever. The Sovereign Lord will wipe away the tears from all faces; he will remove his people's disgrace from all the earth" (Isa 25:6–8).

In the book of Revelations we read, " . . . they are before the throne of God and serve him day and night in his temple; and he who sits on the throne will shelter them with his presence. 'Never again will they hunger; never again will they thirst'" (Rev 7:15–16). In another chapter of this book, Saint John describes the physical look of heaven that he sees in his vision, "The wall was made of jasper, and the city of pure gold, as pure as glass. The foundations of the city walls were decorated with every kind of precious stone. The first foundation was jasper, the second sapphire, the third agate, the fourth emerald, the fifth onyx, the sixth ruby, the seventh chrysolite, the eighth beryl, the ninth topaz, the tenth turquoise, the eleventh jacinth, and the twelfth amethyst. The twelve gates were twelve pearls, each gate made of a single pearl. The great street of the city was of gold, as pure as transparent glass" (Rev 21:18–21).

Besides the scriptural passages, there are paintings and other art forms that capture the imagination of the artists about heaven. We see them on the ceilings and windows of many churches and art galleries. They are also similar in their depiction of heaven as a place of pomp and glory.

Of course, most scriptural scholars would not interpret these passages in the Bible in the literal sense but it is easy to fall into the temptation of creating earth-like images of heaven based on these passages and artists' imaginations.

On the opposite side of the spectrum is hell, similarly thought of as a physical place in space and time. People who visualize hell in such terms think of it as a place of all the bad stuff. It is a place filled with fire and brimstone. It is a place of excessive heat and suffocation. It is dark and dreary. There is constant fight between the inhabitants of hell. There is no food to eat and drink to quench people's thirst. It is visualized as a place somewhere below, under the earth. The ruler of hell is Satan or devil with his associates who are little devils or demons. They have scary looks and curvy tails. They make creepy noises and movements. Hell is visualized as something that happens after our life on earth. It is a place of eternal damnation.

There are many scriptural passages that allude to hell and life in hell. Sometimes hell is referred to as "Hades," "Sheol," and "Valley of death." In the book of Revelation, we read, "But the cowardly, the unbelieving, the vile, the murderers, the sexually immoral, those who practice magic arts, the idolaters and all liars—they will be consigned to the fiery lake of burning sulfur" (Rev 21:8). Speaking about who does and does not belong to the kingdom of God, Jesus says, "The angels will come and separate the wicked from the righteous and throw them into the blazing furnace, where there will be weeping and gnashing of teeth" (Matt 13:49–50). In the story of the rich man and Lazarus, the rich man is pictured as condemned to hell from where he cries out for help, "So he called to him, 'Father Abraham, have pity on me and send Lazarus to dip the tip of his finger in water and cool my tongue, because I am in agony in this fire" (Luke 16:24). Speaking of the last judgment, Jesus says, "Then he will say to those on his left, 'Depart from me, you who are cursed, into the eternal fire prepared for the devil and his angels" (Matt 25:41).

There are also paintings and other forms of art that depict hell similarly, as a place of death, decay, and devils. Again, most scripture scholars would not interpret these passages in the Bible in the literal sense, but we can see how easy it is to fall into the temptation of developing all kinds of images and ideas of hell in the physical sense based on these biblical passages or arts.

Purgatory is understood as an "in-between" time where the person or soul is neither in heaven nor in hell. It is a time or state of purification with the hope of being in heaven. There are some scriptural passages, such as the one in the Book of Maccabees (2 Macc 12:45) that are taken as references for purgatory. Purgatory is also often understood as something that happens after a person dies. And some people think of it as a place in terms of space and time, but they are not sure what kind of place it is. It is conceived as an in-between place where there is some food and drink but not enough; maybe there is some fire and brimstone, but not enough to burn us; maybe there is a glimpse of God and heaven but not long enough to enjoy all the good stuff; and maybe there is a glimpse of hell and devils just enough to scare us, but we are not condemned to go there yet.

These are the beliefs that many people carry. But these beliefs are not convincing for everybody. So how do we understand or make sense of these topics of heaven, hell, and purgatory? Are they real or are they simply imaginations? If they are real, what are they and what do they mean for us in our daily life?

A New Understanding

Since people have all kinds of ideas and imaginations about the realities of heaven, hell, and purgatory, it is important to understand them as healthily and realistically as possible.

There are three reasons why I believe that heaven, hell, and purgatory are real and not simply an imagination or fantasy. The first reason is that they fit well with my understanding of life as a journey with God and others. Our journey of life is all about being with or separated from God and others, and heaven, hell, and purgatory are all about that. The second reason is that they are realities that we experience in our daily lives, which means they are not completely mysterious. Thirdly, the God who has revealed himself to us in our human and faith history whom we have been discussing so far has unequivocally referred to them as part of our journey of life. Given all these reasons and admitting that they are real, let us now look at each of them and see how they play out in our daily lives and in eternity.

What do we understand by heaven and hell? In simple language, I would say heaven is where God is present, and hell is where God is absent. Heaven is a loving communion or relationship with God and others, and hell is the absence or refusal of it. Heaven is partnering with God and others in the divine dance of love, and hell is the refusal to be in that dance. Heaven begins or happens when we remain actively engaged in the dialogical triangle, and hell begins or happens when we refuse to be part of it. Heaven is an experience of joy, love, and peace that we experience in our union with God and others. Anything that detaches us from this union with God and others is the experience of hell. Such a life will leave us in distress. It takes away our peace and joy. It deprives us of real life that Jesus promised us.

What is purgatory then? Purgatory, I believe, is an in-between experience between heaven and hell. We are not completely detached from God and others, but we are not completely united with them either. We experience joy and peace when we are united with God and others, but that union is short-lived, because we separate from them, and consequently we experience anguish and distress.

To use certain examples from our everyday life, heaven is something similar to the joy and love a child experiences when he or she is with his mother or father and siblings, and that experience continues everyday and lasts forever. And hell is something similar to the great distress and pain that the child feels when he or she is taken away, kidnapped, or disconnected from that family forever. Purgatory is the in-between experience of the child being separated from his or her parents and family for a short period but hopes to be reunited with them.

Heaven is like two intimate friends enjoying each other's love and presence and wanting to spend all their time together. They cherish each other so much that when they are together hours pass by like seconds. Hell is like the two friends being separated from each other without the hope of being together again, causing them great anguish and pain. They are in great distress, and a second or minute without the other feels like eternity. Purgatory is the in-between experience of separated from each other for a short stint, but they have the hope of seeing and being with each other soon. They don't see each other but they know that they love each other and can't wait to get reunited with each other again. The longer it takes to see the other, the greater the anguish. That waiting also makes seconds and minutes feel like eternity. Again, these are examples from our everyday life and they can give us some idea about what these realities are like, but they cannot capture the reality as they truly are since they apply not only to our life on earth but also in eternity.

Jesus gives us many indications about what happens after we die. In his conversations with Martha, after the death of her brother, Lazarus, Jesus said, "I am the resurrection and the life. The one who believes in me will live, even though they die; and whoever lives by believing in me will never die" (John 11:25–26). Lazarus, Martha, and Mary were united with Jesus in their friendship. They had a deep loving relationship. And when Lazarus died, Jesus assured Martha and Mary that the union and friendship they had developed would continue into eternity. He assured them that our physical death does not end our life. Our journey continues into eternity. If we are united with him while we live on this earth he will raise us up to new life with him after we die, because he is the resurrection and life. On another occasion, he had said, "I am the way, and the truth, and the life" (John 14:6). Being united with the Father and the Holy Spirit, he is the source of our life both here on earth and in eternity.

When the good thief who was hanging on the cross alongside him prayed to him to remember him when he came into his kingdom, Jesus promised him a life with him in eternity, "Truly I tell you, today you will be with me in paradise" (Luke 23:43). In his conversation with the Samaritan woman, Jesus indicates that heaven or life with God begins here on earth and then continues into eternity, " . . . whoever drinks the water I give them will never thirst. Indeed, the water I give them will become in them a spring of water welling up to eternal life" (John 4:14).

In the parable of the rich man and the beggar named Lazarus, Jesus indicates that heaven and hell are for real and that their foundation is laid during our earthly life (Luke 16:19–31). These realities have a physical or earthly dimension as well as a non-physical or non-earthly dimension. We will experience their fullness in eternity after we die. The rich man is presented as living a luxurious life and dining sumptuously while the beggar, Lazarus lay at his gate longing for some food. The rich man did not even seem to notice Lazarus. He was blessed with wealth and prosperity but he did not care about anybody else except himself. Both the rich man and Lazarus died, and according to the parable, the former ended up in hell and the latter ended up in heaven.

In his discourse on the judgment of nations, Jesus speaks about who would end up in heaven and hell, again indicating that the foundation for these realities is laid during our earthly life. Turning to those who choose heaven, God would say, "Come, you who are blessed by my Father; take your inheritance, the kingdom prepared for you since the creation of the world. For I was hungry and you gave me something to eat, I was thirsty and you gave me something to drink, I was a stranger and you invited me in, I needed clothes and you clothed me, I was sick and you looked after me, I was in prison and you came to visit me" (Matt 25:34–36). But to those who choose hell, he would say, "Depart from me, you who are cursed, into the eternal fire prepared for the devil and his angels. For I was hungry and you gave me nothing to eat, I was thirsty and you gave me nothing to drink, I was a stranger and you did not invite me in, I needed clothes and you did not clothe me, I was sick and in prison and you did not look after me" (Matt 25:41–43).

Jesus predicted his own resurrection, "He then began to teach them that the Son of Man must suffer many things and be rejected by the elders, the chief priests and the teachers of the law, and that he must be killed and after three days rise again" (Mark 8:31). In the gospel of Luke again we find Jesus predicting his resurrection, " . . . everything that is written by the prophets about the Son of Man will be fulfilled . . . On the third day he will rise again" (Luke 18:31–32). And then as he promised and predicted he was risen. The disciples experienced the risen Christ on many occasions. The women who went to the tomb to pay homage to Jesus had an extraordinary experience of the angel first and then the risen Christ himself, "The angel said to the women, 'Do not be afraid, for I know that you are looking for Jesus, who was crucified. He is not here; he has risen, just as he said' . . . So the women hurried away from the tomb, afraid yet filled with joy, and ran to tell his disciples. Suddenly Jesus met them. 'Greetings,' he said" (Matt 28:5–9). Some of his disciples did not believe what the women reported. He then appeared to his eleven apostles, "While they were still talking about this, Jesus himself stood among them and said to them, 'Peace be with you'" (Luke 24:36).

The resurrection experience of Jesus was a life changing experience for the disciples. They were no more afraid of sufferings, persecutions, or death because they knew that as long as they were united with Jesus none of those things were going to stop their life. He was going to raise them up because he is the resurrection and life. So we hear Saint Peter speaking of the eternal life and heaven that we would experience because of our union with Christ, "In his great mercy he has given us new birth into a living hope through the resurrection of Jesus Christ from the dead, and into an inheritance that can never perish, spoil or fade. This inheritance is kept in heaven for you" (1 Pet 1:3–4). Having experienced the risen Christ himself, Saint Paul also speaks of our resurrection and entrance into new life, "For if we have been united with him in a death like his, we will certainly also be united with him in a resurrection like his" (Rom 6:5).

All these references in the Bible speak of our life as a journey during which we are either united with God and others or disconnected from them. The choices that we make while we live on earth have a great part to play in determining whether we will be in the realm of heaven, hell, or purgatory during and after our earthly life. What we experience during our earthly life is only a glimpse of what is coming.

The irony of the journey of our life is that it begins with God but does not necessarily end with God. We might wonder why? If we begin our life in God and we are eternal like him, we would ordinarily think that we should be with him in eternity. Why should there be a discussion about heaven, hell, and purgatory at all? Shouldn't it be only heaven? Shouldn't we be living with God all the time—before we are born, during our earthly life, and after our earthly life?

To answer these questions, we could look at a child's life in a family and see what that tells us. Although a father and mother love their child into being and desire that the child reciprocate that love and remain united with them, it is not necessary that the child should love them in return and stay united with them. The child might turn against them and disconnect from them like the younger son in the parable of the prodigal sons did. The child receives the life from the parents, but that doesn't mean that he or she is going to necessarily pledge his or her love and life to them. Sometimes the child might remain in an in-between state where he or she does not completely disconnect nor stay completely united with his or her parents. These are all different possibilities in how the child would relate to the parents after it is born. That is where the free will comes in. The parents desire the union and love in return but they respect the freedom of the child. They do not force the child to love them or stay united with them. If they force, then it is no more love because genuine love does not force somebody into doing something.

Hence although the child begins his or her life with the parents, it is not necessary that the child should remain with the parents for the rest of his or her life. But at the same time, just because the child is not united with the parents or refuses to love the parents in return, his or her life does not end. The child's life continues. The child remaining distanced and disconnected also doesn't mean that the parents have stopped loving or rejected him or her.

Similarly, although God loves us into being and desires that we remain united with him and others, we might stay away from God and others and go on our own way. Having our origin in God is no guarantee that we are going to be in the realm of heaven or we will be eternally united with him and others. But just because we stay away, our life does not end. It continues because we are eternal. Being separated from God also does not mean that God stops loving us or rejects us. God desires that we reciprocate his love and remain as active partners in the dialogical triangle so that we can be eternally in the state of heaven, being united with him and others.

43

On Earth as It is in Heaven

ALTHOUGH WE OFTEN THINK of heaven, hell, and purgatory as after-death realities, our everyday experience shows that they also have a physical and earthly dimension. They are not completely otherworldly and mysterious. We know what it means to be in a loving relationship with God and others and how that makes a difference in our life qualitatively. We know what it means to live separated from God and others and go through hellish moments, and how that makes our life miserable and sad. We know what it means to be separated from God and others in a limited way and how we long to get back to healthy and happy living and relationships. All these are things that we experience in our daily life. They are not totally unknown or mysterious. Let us look at what it means to experience each of these in our daily life.

Heaven on Earth

To those who expected the kingdom of God to be something eschatological or future reality, Jesus said, " . . . the kingdom of God is among you" (Luke 17:21). Our life with God or heaven is not only something that we are looking forward to in eternity but also something that we begin here on earth. God is not someone that we are going to experience only in the future. He is here and now. He is in our midst. He is our Emmanuel, God with us. Saint John, in his vision of heaven and earth, sees God dwelling with human beings, "See, the home of God is among mortals. He will dwell with them; they will be his peoples, and God himself will be with them" (Rev 21:3). Jesus prayed that we remain united with God and one another not only after our death but also during our earthly life (John 17:11). The prayer, "Our Father" echoes that desire of Jesus (Matt 6:10). He wishes that everything might be on earth as it is in heaven. While we are on this earth, God calls us to be holy as he is holy (Lev 20:26). In his letter to the Ephesians, Saint Paul says that God has chosen us "before the foundation of the world to be holy and blameless before him in love" (Eph 1:4). All these scriptural passages make it amply clear that heaven is not some mysterious thing that we are waiting for after death. It is a reality that needs to begin here on earth. God dwells in and with us, and he desires that we dwell in and with him. What we are going to experience after death will be a continuation and completion of this union with God on earth. If we are united with God and others in love while we live on this earth, we begin heaven on earth.

In the previous chapters we discussed what it means to be united with God and others. It is participating in the divine dance of love and being actively engaged in the dialogical triangle. Heaven on earth becomes a reality when we become Christ-like. And becoming Christ-like is to incarnate as love wherever we are.

For some people love might sound very vague and philosophical, but God does not leave it vague at all. For God, real love is incarnational and experiential. It has to be visible through our lives and everyday actions. If we think of the different levels of growing in love, we could group them into feelings and thoughts about love, a desire to love, and expressions or acts of love. It is not just enough to have feelings and thoughts about love. And it is not enough to talk about love. We have to take it to deeper levels. We have to desire it in our own lives and in the lives of others. We have to desire to be loving and loveable. But that desire is not enough either. We have to go to yet another level. We have to live it or do it, which is basically engaging in expressions or acts of love in our everyday life. What we feel, what we think, what we talk about, and what we desire need to be translated into action. Love needs to be the guiding force behind all our thoughts, words, and actions. Love needs to be manifested as God manifested his love in Jesus. In other words, as Saint Francis de Sales says, real love would be to "live Jesus."

In translating our love into action, we have to again think about what that means. Jesus clearly reminds us that it is not about doing some extraordinary things. In Chapter 7 of the gospel of Matthew, Jesus warns us about self-deception. He says that if we think that we are going to be counted as loving and worthy of his kingdom because we have been engaging in great acts like prophesying or driving out demons, then we are deceiving ourselves. He says, "On that day many will say to me, 'Lord, Lord, did we not prophesy in your name, and cast out demons in your name, and do many deeds of power in your name?' Then I will declare to them, 'I never knew you; go away from me, you evildoers'" (Matt 7:22–23).

Normally, anyone would think that prophesying or driving out demons is a great act and it is done for the Lord. But that may not be the case. The one who does prophesy or drive out demons may be drawing all attention to him or herself rather than bringing people closer to God. It may not be an act of charity but self-glory. The one who prophesies and drives out demons may be uncharitable on other occasions. Saint Paul in his chapter on love in his first letter to the Corinthians reiterates this point. He says, "If I speak in the tongues of mortals and of angels, but do not have love, I am a noisy gong or a clanging cymbal. And if I have prophetic powers, and understand all mysteries and all knowledge, and if I have all faith, so as to remove mountains, but do not have love, I am nothing. If I give away all my possessions, and if I hand over my body so that I may boast, but do not have love, I gain nothing" (1 Cor 13:1–3).

Extraordinary actions or having great talents are not necessarily signs of being a loving and loveable person. They could be signs and expressions of one's own pomp and glory. Then Saint Paul goes on to say what real love in action would look like, "Love is patient; love is kind; love is not envious or boastful or arrogant or rude. It does not insist on its own way; it is not irritable or resentful; it does not rejoice in wrongdoing, but rejoices in the truth. It bears all things, believes all things, hopes all things, endures all things" (1 Cor 13:4–7). This is what real love in action involves. It is incarnating ourselves in a loving way in our own specific life contexts. That is what creates heaven on earth.

Thus in my everyday life, when I use words that are respectful, positive, kind, compassionate, and forgiving in my communication with my spouse, my children, my parents, my friends, my coworkers, my neighbors, or even strangers, then I am manifesting my love and allowing heaven on earth. Instead, if I am contemptuous, humiliating, threatening, unkind, abusive, and harsh, then I know I am allowing hell in my life and relationships. When I am dialogical and accommodative instead of being bossy, authoritarian, and over-controlling, I am growing in love and promoting heaven on earth. When I am humble and gentle like Christ, allowing God to shine forth through my words and actions rather than being boastful, arrogant, haughty, and proud, trying to project myself as somebody great, then the love of God is my focus and I am allowing heaven on earth. When I am positive and respectful in my comments and conversations about others instead of gossiping and creating disunity and ill feelings, then I am trying to live heaven in my daily life.

When I choose the path of peace, reconciliation, and non-violence, I am choosing heaven on earth. On the other hand, if I cause injury or harm to somebody or even myself by aggression, violence, and other destructive behaviors, then I am not being very loving and heavenly. When I remain honest and truthful in my business dealings and transactions instead of cheating and becoming greedy, taking advantage of people and situations, then I am promoting heaven in my life and in the world. When I am merciful and forgiving rather than engaging in hateful feelings and actions, and judgments and condemnation, then I reflect God's love and heaven on earth. When I see myself as part of the dialogical triangle and see others as my brothers and sisters no matter how they look, where they come from, and what they do, then I am living heaven on earth. But if I exclude and discriminate people because they belong to a different religion, class, caste, race, nationality, and all such specificities, then I am not being very loving and heavenly.

Love that is divine helps us to live heaven on earth. When we truly love we will stay away from everything that is selfish and evil. We will avoid words and actions that hurt and harm people. We will not entertain thoughts that are negative and destructive. We will not wish anything bad for anybody, even those who hate or do harm to us. We will befriend our enemies instead of avoiding them or excluding them. We will see the needs of others and reach out to help them. We will not dominate in conversations and claim to have all knowledge and wisdom under heaven. We will not seek to accumulate wealth and possessions more than what we need to take care of ourselves and those entrusted to our care. Even if we don't have enough and sometimes will have to live in poverty, we will continue to work hard and trust in the Lord who provides for us all the time.

When we are united with God and others, we will gladly share with others what we have and be companions and co-travelers with them in the journey of life. We will find ways to regulate our emotions and feelings in such a way that they direct us to healthy living and interactions. We will not look at others or this creation as objects for our pleasure but rather as God's blessings to be hallowed, respected, and loved. We will become a channel of God's grace and love and be a healing force and uniting bridge. We will be God's presence wherever we are. When people come to us, they will see God in us, and they will go back refreshed and rejuvenated. Heaven on earth, in short, is living a life free from sin and evils and embracing God and others in love. It is living a life of love. Heaven is making the Holy Trinity come alive in our lives and relationships. As the Father, the Son, and the Holy Spirit are united in love, we unite ourselves with God and others in love.

Incarnational love or heaven on earth in our everyday life comes down to the simple, monotonous, and ordinary matters of our life. It is not vague or mysterious. Love has to exist and grow in the ordinary situations of our life. That is where Christ needs to be born and heaven needs to start. Saint Paul concludes his chapter on love by saying that only love lasts; everything else disappears. Love lasts because love is of God or God is love, and God never ends. And because heaven is our union with God and others in love here on earth and in eternity, love needs to be the focus of our everyday life.

All these might appear to be unrealistic and lofty ideals, and we might wonder who can attain heaven or live heaven on earth. This is not what we often experience in our life. Our life is often a mixture of lofty ideals and broken promises. We sometime fail miserably. We stumble and fall over and over again. God and others are often not on our radar. Our life is a hell on many occasions. We follow our wishes and desires and we engage in things that are against God's will. We sometimes become self-destructive. Heaven sometimes feels like a far away reality. But at the same time, there are moments in our life when we are very much focused on God and others. Sometimes we are the kindest and most loving people. Sometimes we seek others' good before we think of ourselves. We are in harmony and peace with God and others on many occasions. We have glimpses of heaven. That is why we have to think that heaven is not something like a finished product but rather a journey with the Lord. In that journey, sometimes it is possible that we go off the road because of many reasons. But then we try again to get on track, to be with the Lord. Because of those interruptions and instances of going off track, our journey with the Lord and the experience of heaven on this earth is imperfect. It is something that we begin here on earth. The question is whether or not we want to make this experience of heaven permanent and consistent. To make it permanent and consistent, our focus needs to be on growing in that love and staying close to the Lord and others during our journey so that we can continue that union in eternity.

Jesus desired and prayed that we grow in that union. Using the parable of the vine and the branches (John 15:1), he exhorts his disciples to stay connected to him and one another. Just as the branches draw strength and nourishment form the vine, we draw our strength and nourishment from God when we remain united with him. Cut off from the tree a branch withers and dies. When we are separated from God and others, we wither and die. We become lonesome and isolated. We live in our own world. But that goes against our very nature, because we are created in the image and likeness of the Holy Trinity and we are meant to be a community of persons united with God and others. There may be temptations to stay away from God and others but that is going to hurt us.

There is also another reason why the branches need to stay connected with the vine. It is through the branches that the vine fulfills its mission. It is the branches that bring out leaves, buds, flowers, and fruits. Without the branches the vine's mission remains unfulfilled. God needs us to fulfill his mission of bringing his love into this world. He needs our cooperation. We have to be the hands of Jesus that touch and heal, the mouth of Jesus that speaks the good news, the ears of Jesus that hear the cry of the needy, the feet of Jesus that reach out to people in need, and the heart of Jesus that longs for even the worst sinner. Without us, the mission of God in this world remains incomplete.

Heaven on earth is a work in progress. Everyday we strive for it. Everyday we grow closer to God and others in love. Everyday we pray, "May it be more of you and less of me, Lord."

Hell on Earth

Hell on earth is just the opposite of all the ideals that I listed above. Hell is a refusal to remain united with God and others. It is a refusal to love. It is seeking one's own will rather than the will of God. It is choosing the path of evil rather than good. It is discriminating and excluding others. It is seeking one's own satisfaction and interests rather than being a companion in journey with others. It is looking at others and the creation as objects for pleasure and exploitation rather than as God's gifts and blessings to be hallowed and treated with respect and dignity. It is dominating over others and failing to regulate one's destructive emotions and feelings. It is causing harm and hurt to others. It is seeking one's own good and neglecting the needs of others. It is causing divisions and disunity in families, communities, and societies, going against the very essence and nature of the Holy Trinity. It is allowing the forces of evil to con-trol us rather than allowing God to guide and direct us. Hell on earth is the absence of God and absence of love. Hell takes away our joy and peace.

We know that there are moments in our life when we engage in such hellish behaviors and relationships. We live in darkness and sin. We cut ourselves off from God and others. The question is whether or not we want to make this experience of hell permanent. Our effort is to be on reducing those hellish moments and increasing the heavenly moments.

Jesus used the parable of the rich man and Lazarus to show us how we might be allowing hell to grow in our daily life. In the parable, it is important to pay attention to the conversation between the rich man in hell and Abraham in heaven. Hell being presented as a place of extreme heat and fire, the rich man calls out to Abraham ask-ing him to send Lazarus to dip his finger in water to cool the rich man's tongue. But Abraham responds by saying, " . . . between us and you a great chasm has been set in place, so that those who want to go from here to you cannot, nor can anyone cross over from there to us" (Luke 16:26).

Abraham's reference to the great chasm between them is an important factor to consider when it comes to heaven and hell. It is important to think about who cre-ated that chasm and when that chasm was created. The chasm was created when they were living on earth. The rich man created that chasm by not connecting with the poor Lazarus who lay at his gate. He had already separated himself from Lazarus on this earth, and Abraham was reminding the rich man that the chasm was continuing in eternity. He had chosen the path of creating the chasm or separation rather than reaching out to Lazarus and connecting with him. He had become the branch that separated from the vine and other branches. He had lived in his own world not caring about God and others. He had already chosen hell while living on earth.

If we look at the rich man's life on earth in terms of prosperity and wealth his life on earth was not hell at all. It was heaven, some might say. For those who think of heaven as a place of physical pleasures and prosperity, the rich man had a perfect start to heaven. But if we think of heaven as a relationship with God and others united in love, then he had already begun his hell because he was not concerned about being united with God and others. He had created a chasm instead of building a bridge.

The rich man's story is a warning to all of us about what it means to experience hell. As individuals, families, communities, groups, and societies, we create all kinds of chasms culturally, economically, linguistically, physically, politically, psychologi-cally, religiously, and socially. When we choose the path of sin and evil we create a chasm, breaking the relationship with God and others. When we turn a blind eye to the needs of others around us or exclude them from our dialogical triangle we are cre-ating a chasm. When we keep hatred and ill feelings in our heart against other family members or others we create a physical and psychological chasm. When we become a cause of division and disunity in our families, communities, and society, we cause a chasm. When we build up our own world and accumulate more than what we need, we create an economic chasm. When we discriminate people based on their color, race, caste, ethnicity, language, religion, sex, and all other specificities, we are creating a cultural chasm. When we dominate and become intimidating and dictatorial especially to people who are poor and weak, we create a chasm. When we neglect, ignore, or abuse children, the old, the sick, and the defenseless, we create a chasm. When we engage in violence and destructive behaviors we create a chasm. When religions and denominations fight with each other, there is a religious chasm that we are creating.

We see chasms created in the political field when different political and ideological groups engage in acrimonious accusations and fights. We see chasms created in the international field when nations and kingdoms engage in bitter fights and wars. We see some as "insiders" and others as "outsiders." We see ourselves as pitted against each other as "us" versus "them." We have built up walls and fences around us making us unable to cross over to others and not letting others to cross over to our territory. These chasms that we create are hell on earth. There may be many "Lazaruses" laying at our gate begging for mercy, compassion, and love. If we ignore them and fail to connect with them, we are already causing chasms and beginning our hell here.

In the parable of the unforgiving servant (Matt 18:21–35), Jesus brings home the message that we have to be united not only with God but also with our fellow human beings. In the prayer that Jesus taught his disciples, God's forgiveness of our sins and our forgiveness of each other's sins were equally emphasized (Matt 6:9–15). If we really want to experience heaven, we need to live in love and union with God and one another.

In Jesus's conversation about the judgment of nations (Matt 25:34–43), those who chose heaven didn't even know that they were choosing heaven. They just focused on living a life united with God and others, which resulted in them reaching out to those in need. But those who chose hell lived selfish lives, not concerned about building their relationship with God and others.

That takes us to the question whether it is we who choose heaven, hell, and purgatory or it is God's decision. I would think it is a combination of both. God is the ultimate judge, but we have a part to play in determining whether we experience heaven, hell, or purgatory. Miracles often happen when God and we work together. We know that we are weak and limited. We need God's grace. It is God's grace and human effort working together that makes heaven possible. Even when we see some things as impossible, everything is possible for God. When the angel, Gabriel announced to Mary God's plan of choosing her as the mother of his Son, Mary asked, "How can this be?" (Luke 1:34). And the Angel replied her, "Nothing is impossible with God" (Luke 1:37).

But at the same time God does not impose things on us. He respects our freedom and will. Although in the story of the judgment of nations it sounds like God is acting like an unmerciful and strict judge, it is not God who chose the path of heaven or hell. It is the people themselves who chose it. In the gospel of John, Jesus says that it is not

God who actually judges or condemns people to hell but rather the people by their own choice condemn themselves to hell (John 3:16–21). Instead of choosing light, they choose darkness. Instead of choosing life, they choose death. Instead of choosing God, they choose evil and sin. Conveying the same message about how we choose heaven or hell, Paul and Barnabas respond to the Jews who rejected their preaching of the gospel, "Since you reject it and do not consider yourselves worthy of eternal life, we now turn to the Gentiles" (Acts 13:46).

In the story of the rich young man, Jesus asked the man to give up his possessions and follow him if he wanted to inherit eternal life. He had to be on the road with Jesus, leaving behind many things. But the young man went away sad because he found it hard to give up his possessions. Jesus did not force him to follow him. Jesus opened the door to him, and it was left to the man whether or not to enter. When the young man went away sad, Jesus said to his disciples, "Truly I tell you, it will be hard for a rich person to enter the kingdom of heaven. Again I tell you, it is easier for a camel to go through the eye of a needle than for someone who is rich to enter the kingdom of God" (Matt 19:23–24). We might wonder why Jesus made it look like eternal life was so hard. Yes, eternal life or life in union with God is going to be hard if we leave it all to God and do not cooperate with him. God wants us to cooperate with him. We don't find Jesus offering us a smooth sail with anything. He warns us again and again that following him is going to be hard. Our journey is going to be a rough road ahead. If we are following the crucified Christ, then we can be certain that it is not going to be easy. The only things he is assuring are his companionship and fullness of life. We will not be alone; he will be our leader and traveling companion. He will give us the needed strength for the journey. If we can endure that journey, we are going to experience unending joy. That is what he promises.

In his response to the rich young man, we might also wonder whether Jesus was against wealth and wealthy people. Not so. Jesus had many wealthy friends who provided for him and his disciples. Jesus knows that we cannot live without money and materials. But in the story of the rich young man, Jesus was warning us about the dangers of wealth. Wealth can weigh us down and hold us back from being on the road. Even though we know that we don't carry anything from this world when we die, that doesn't stop us from holding on to possessions and positions. The rich young man's possessions don't need to be referring to money and wealth alone. It could be referring to many things that he was attached to. Wealth, possessions, positions, and many other things can make us arrogant and proud. They can make us think that we are self-sufficient. They can make us forget that life continues even after this earthly life. There are people who get so enamored by their wealth, possessions, successes, and other things that they think they are unstoppable and omnipotent like God. Prophet Ezekiel reprimands the prince of Tyre who was so carried away by his wealth, wisdom, and worldly possessions that he declared himself as god (Ezek 28:1–2). Wealth and other possessions can make people forget that they are human. We are human; we are not God. We have our abilities and power, but we are not omnipotent. We are weak and limited.

God desires that we are united with him and others here on earth as well as in eternity, but he is not a God who shoves heaven down our throat or drops it like a candy into our lap. He desires that we cooperate with him to make our lives heavenly while we live on this earth so that we can continue to enjoy that in eternity. God does not desire that anyone of his children be lost (2 Pet 3:9). In the book of Ezekiel we hear God saying that he does not take pleasure in the death of a wicked person; he desires that the person turn away from his or her wicked ways (Ezek 18:23). Jesus incarnated so that he could gather all of us as one family united in love. He wants us to choose heaven and not hell. But He does not force it upon us. He respects our freedom and will, and waits for us to respond to his invitation.

Purgatory on Earth

We could also think of times in our everyday life when we are somewhere in between—that is, neither completely united with God and others nor completely disconnected from them, which we refer to as purgatory. As we discussed about heaven and hell, we could think of purgatory also as something that begins here on earth and continues into our life after. Most of us hate evil and sin, but in our weakness we stumble and fall. As soon as we realize that we have fallen, we long to get up and walk toward the Lord and others. We recognize our weaknesses and failures and feel great anguish in being disconnected from God and others. We are in a state of constant purification so that we can be united with God and others here on earth as well as in eternity.

Purgatory becomes a real experience on many occasions. There are moments when we desire a loving relationship with God and others and we obtain that somewhat, but we realize that we have not given ourselves completely to God and others. We are in the in-between times, when we are neither too far from nor too close to God and others. There are moments when we are kind and compassionate toward others, but at the same time we may realize that we are sometimes rude and unkind. We are somewhere in between the two. We reach out to others in generosity but there are times when we are selfish and look only for our own needs. We see ourselves somewhere in between. There are times when we cross over the walls and fences and connect with others, but there are also biases and prejudices that sometimes make us resist that. We may find that we are on the fence or wall itself!

We want to put God first and seek his will but at the same time we realize that sometimes we are resistant to that. We have our own will and wishes that we often want to fulfill before we can think of God's will. We have a little bit of both. We want to live with what we have and are even prepared to live in poverty, but then there are times when we have a desire to accumulate and gather more than what we need. We want to be very positive and optimistic about people and things but sometimes our negative thoughts and emotions direct our actions and behaviors. We forgive others and ourselves and let go off things, but there are times when our past haunts us and others' failures make us judge and react negatively. Our experience of purgatory is that we have not given our heart and mind to God completely. We love God and others but there are also temptations and evils that we give into. God desires that our love for him and one another is total and unconditional.

Looking at all these, it might feel a little overwhelming. We might recognize that often our life is a combination of heaven, hell, and purgatory on this earth. Often we can relate to what Saint Paul wrote about his own struggle, " I do not understand what I do. For what I want to do I do not do, but what I hate I do . . . For I have the desire to do what is good, but I cannot carry it out. For I do not do the good I want to do, but the evil I do not want to do—this I keep on doing" (Rom 7:15, 18–19). Heaven, hell, and purgatory come and go as passing phenomena in our daily lives. We get during our earthly life a glimpse of what is coming in eternity.

But we are reminded that we have an important part to play in determining whether we want heaven, hell, or purgatory, whether we want to be united with God and others on this earth as well as in eternity or we want to be separated. We can choose whether we want peace, joy, and love during this earthly life and in eternity or we want to live miserably without all that here on earth and in eternity. Of course, with all those choices and decisions we make, we still do not deny the fact that God is the final judge and he is loving and merciful. We don't decide everything. We give our best to God and others trusting in God's grace and power. In spite of our struggles and fallings, we say like Saint Paul, "I can do all things through him who strengthens me" (Phil 4:13). Being aware of our weaknesses and limitations we trust in God's mercy and goodness and remain in thanksgiving once again identifying with Saint Paul who said, "Thanks be to God, who delivers me through Jesus Christ our Lord" (Rom 7:25).

44

A New Heaven and a New Earth

ALL THE REFLECTIONS ON heaven, hell, and purgatory that we have had so far give us a sense that these realities need to be looked at in a new way. We need to look at them from the perspective of what Saint John calls in the book of Revelations as "a new heaven and a new earth" (Rev 21:1). Hence before we conclude our discussions on them and on our journey of life, we shall review some of the related questions and conceptions that people often have regarding them.

Earth as Part of Heaven

Some people tend to look at heaven and earth as dichotomous or separate categories and spaces. Even in some of our faith documents, our language is limited. In the Creed that Catholics and others recite, we refer to God as "maker of heaven and earth." It might make us think that heaven and earth are two separate spaces, realms, or categories. But the scriptural passages that we looked at and all the reflections we had on heaven, hell, and purgatory caution us about the dangers of such dichotomous ideas and seeing the earth as a place separated from God. If heaven is where God is, then our earth also should be part of heaven. If God dwells in each one of us and is present in the creation, then it is not only the earth but also the whole creation that is part of heaven, part of God. In some translations of the Nicene Creed, it is a much better expression, "maker of all that is, seen and unseen." It doesn't make any separation between heaven and earth. God is the creator of everything, and everything belongs to God.

As we have seen, heaven includes everything that is permeated by the presence of God, including our beautiful earth. Sometimes there is a tendency among some people to think of this world and our earth as a bad place. That is a misconstrued idea of our world. This world is a beautiful place that God created. This is the world that he incarnated in. This world is permeated by his presence. This is the earth on which the Lord walked. We are on holy grounds. Of course, there are bad things that we do that go against God's love and God's will. But that doesn't make this world a bad place.

Just because we, God's children, commit sin or do bad things, God doesn't become sinful or bad. Similarly, just because we do bad things, our beautiful earth or world does not become bad. What we want to strive towards is to reduce the bad in our world and increase the good. We want to increase the heavenly experience on earth. We want to be aware that God is everywhere and in everyone. That includes the earth and the whole creation. Everything and everyone belongs to him. Hence our earth is an integral part of heaven, and we begin our heavenly experience on this earth. We need to live with that sense of the sacredness of everything that God has created. As I mentioned before, sometimes when referring to the incarnation of Jesus, people use phrases such as "coming down or descending to the earth" or "leaving heaven to come to the earth," which could make us think that heaven and earth are two separate spaces meant for two separate beings, God and human beings, and that God was away from us before the incarnation. But the truth is that God was always present on the earth and in his creation. Jesus reminded us that the kingdom of God was among us (Luke 17:21). The incarnation of Jesus is a unique and specific way in which God revealed himself to us. The God who incarnated was present in our world before and after the incarnation. Hence we ought to believe that our earth or this world is also part of heaven or the realm of God.

Such an idea of heaven and earth would then raise the question whether heaven is a physical place or state of being. I would say that it is both. Heaven includes space and time because God is in space and time. But heaven is also bigger than space and time because God is bigger than space and time. Heaven is much more than what we experience in this world. When it is a state of being it does not need to be limited by space and time. Hence heaven is both physical and non-physical.

The Dead and Our Communication with Them

If the earth and the whole creation were part of heaven, then the question would be whether the departed souls or the human beings, including our family members and friends, who have already died are still present on the earth. The answer would be a qualified "yes." They are present on the earth even after death, but their state of being is different. It is no more the same physical state that they are in. They rise up to a non-physical dimension. And the realm of their presence covers a much larger realm than this physical world. Continuing to be present in our world also does not mean that they are floating around like some spirits or beings. What it means is that they have moved into a non-physical state of being with a capacity to be present in a much larger realm than our earth or world.

If the dead continue to be present on the earth, then the question would be whether we can communicate with them and they can communicate with us. Do they continue to be part of our lives? The answer to that question will be again a qualified "yes." They communicate with us and we communicate with them but not in the sense of physical communication as we do while we are all physically alive. It is a communication in spirit. We pray for the dead as we pray for each other when we are alive on this earth. Just because they are dead, we don't stop praying for them. In the Catholic prayers and celebration of the Eucharist, we pray for the dead. They are still part of our family, God's family. We wish and pray that they experience heaven or complete union with God. If we realize that they had lived not so a good life while living on this earth, then we pray for them just as a parent or friend would pray for a child or friend who is sick, estranged, or given into destructive ways. We wish and pray that the dead who may not be united with God would be forgiven and be united with God. We do that for each other when we are physically alive.

And when we pray for forgiveness and mercy for the dead, we pray not only for our near and dear ones but also for every human being, including our enemies because true love according to Jesus reaches out even to the enemies. God's desire and prayer are that we live as one family, and we desire and pray for the same. When it comes to our human family, we have to think that everyone belongs to our family. When we pray for our family members, we often remember only our immediate family members who belong to three or four generations. But they are not the only members of our family. We have great-great-great grandparents, uncles, aunts, and cousins, going back to hundreds and hundreds of generations. They are all our family members. And ultimately it all goes back to the first parents of the human family that God created. Whether we call them Adam and Eve or by some other name, they are our parent family. Because we are split and splintered into different races, ethnicities, and groups over centuries and millennia, we often do not think of all of them as part of our family. And often we don't think of all of them and pray for them. But everyone who has come from that parent family that God created is part of our family. If we are truly loving and focused on having our whole family united with God and others, then we have to pray for all of them. We don't want anyone of them to be outside the purview of heaven or God's presence.

As we pray for the dead, we believe that the dead pray for us and wish the best for us too. We sometimes hear some people saying that our near and dear ones are watching over us and praying for us from heaven. We believe that the saints pray or intercede for us. When we think of the saints praying or interceding for us, we can assume what they are praying for. Their prayer is that we become like them, living heaven on earth or being united with God and others so that we can continue that in eternity. It is not just the canonized saints who are praying for us. There are thousands and thousands of others, who are saints and who, we believe, are experiencing heaven in eternity, but they are not canonized. We can believe that they are also praying for us. We communicate with the saints through many forms of prayer. We seek their help as we seek each other's help while we live on earth.

Even those who may not be experiencing heaven in eternity, specifically, those in hell and purgatory, may be praying for us. In the parable of the rich man and Lazarus we hear the rich man pleading to Abraham to send Lazarus to his brothers who were living in sin on earth. He was experiencing hell, but he was concerned about his brothers. Our dead brothers and sisters have a greater vision of heaven, hell, and purgatory, whereas we are still limited by space and time and may not understand them well. So we can believe that they are concerned about us and they wish that we live well and live in union with God and others.

Hence, we communicate with the dead, and they communicate with us, but the communication is not in the usual physical sense. The dead and we belong to different realms of life. In the story of the rich man and Lazarus, we hear Abraham speaking about a chasm, which prevented people from one side to cross over to the other side. That chasm could be also referring to the different realms of life that we were living in, the physical and the non-physical. When it comes to our life and the life of the departed souls, we could say, there is a chasm, which prevents us from communicating with each other in the usual physical sense. While we live on earth we are limited in many ways by our physical state of being. But when we pass from this world after death, we rise to the non-physical realm, and our experience will be unlimited.

Saints of All Hues

It is difficult for us to say which of the three realms our near and dear ones might be belonging to because God alone is the judge. Just as we wish and pray for the safety and well being of our family and friends while they live on earth, we might wish and desire that our family members and friends who are dead are already experiencing heaven or are united with God. But we are not the ones deciding that. Only God knows each person's life and love completely. We are no authority to say what the quality of a dead person's love or life was. We may have some sense of what and how it was from the external things that we have experienced about that person. But that is only a partial knowledge. We don't have the full knowledge of that person's external and internal self. We don't know what the state of mind and heart of a dying person is. The good thief who was hanging on the cross alongside Jesus called out to him for mercy at the last moment of his life. None of us knows the depth of a person's conscience and closeness to God. It is between God and that person. Hence we leave all judgment to God. If we have a good sense that the person has lived a good and holy life united with God and others while living the earthly life, then we could believe that the person is continuing that experience of heaven even after death.

That is where the canonization or declaration of certain individuals as saints in the Catholic Church becomes significant. Looking at certain individuals' lives, the Church is convinced that they were already living a heavenly life or were united with God and others during their earthly life. And because of the life they have lived and what they have done for the community and the world, they can be raised to a special status as saints to be models and examples for the community and the world. They are honored and venerated as examples of great holiness and grace. But that doesn't mean that they take the place of God or they become objects of worship. We don't worship them, but rather honor them. Many non-Catholics have a misconstrued idea about Catholics honoring the Blessed Virgin Mary and other saints. They think that Catholics worship Mary and other saints, and sometimes some of the devotional practices of some Catholics would make anyone think that Mary and other saints are objects of worship. But that is a totally wrong idea. Catholics don't and should not worship Mary or any saint. Only God is worthy of all worship. Mary and other saints are honored and venerated because of the holy lives they have lived.

Saints were ordinary people like all of us, but they made a choice for heaven and lived the Christological model extraordinarily in their lives. They chose to partner with God and others in the divine dance of love. They participated in the dialogical triangle and remained united with God and others. They set an example for the rest of the world for living the Christological model or heavenly life even while we live on this earth. Hence they are honored, venerated, and raised to a special status. Given the special role she played in the salvation history, specifically, becoming the mother of the Savior, Mary has a special honor and status among the saints. But she is still a saint and not an object of worship. Saints are not God; they are human beings who, we believe, are united with God. And the Church invites her members to follow the same, living heaven on earth so that they can continue that in eternity.

Their declaration as saints also doesn't mean that they are the only people who are saints or who have lived a heavenly life on this earth. Saints are of all hues and backgrounds. Within the Christian tradition, there are thousands and thousands of people from different walks of life who have lived holy and heavenly lives, but most of them are unknown. They are unknown and undeclared saints before the world but God knows them.

There are also saints or those who have lived saintly or heavenly lives in other cultures and traditions. For the holy men and women of the Old Testament times, we don't give them the title, "Saint." We call them as Abraham, Moses, David, Ruth, Prophet Elijah, Prophet Jeremiah, etc. But we consider all of them as holy people who lived heaven on earth. Although the title "Saint" is used in some other cultures and traditions, it is often a title specific to the Christian community used for men and women who have lived holy lives in the last two thousand years, and hence it has to be seen from the community's perspective.

For those who have lived saintly or heavenly lives in other cultures and traditions, we would consider that they were living Christological lives or participating in the divine dance of love even though they were not belonging to the official Christian religion or did not know Christ as we often think of. When they lived saintly lives or living heaven on earth, they were living Christ in their lives, and Christ was living in them. In the narrative on the judgment of nations, Jesus says that those who found themselves worthy of heaven or kingdom of God were not even aware that they were serving the Lord when they lived a life of love (Matt 25:34–36). They just focused on living a loving life and in doing that they were, in fact, living Christ himself. When it comes to our life as human beings as a whole, what is important is to focus on living heaven on earth, a life in union with God and others. Titles and honors as saints or anything else are not what truly matter.

Salvation Outside the Church

The probability of having saints in other cultures and traditions would then bring up the question whether one can be a saint, be saved, or be in heaven without being a Christian or being baptized as a Christian. Traditionally, this would be referring to or related to the question regarding salvation outside the church. People wonder whether those who are outside the church can be saved. There are two things that we need to consider here—what do we mean by the church and what do we mean by salvation?

People have different ideas about what the church means. Quoting *Lumen Gentium*, one of the documents of the Second Vatican Council, the Catechism of the Catholic Church states that the church is the people of God, the Body of Christ, the temple of the Holy Spirit (781). By church, we are not simply referring to an institution or physical structure. The church is the people of God.

But even in the understanding of the church as the people of God, we could look at it at least in three different ways. First, the church could mean the whole human race, because all human beings are God's people. Since all human beings are temples of the Holy Spirit and God dwells in us, we could say that all of us together form the church or the people of God. In this sense, no one is left out of the purview of the church, whether they belong to the Christian religion or not. Second, the church could mean the Christian community. All those who are baptized as Christians are sometimes considered the new "chosen" people of God. They believe that Christians by virtue of their baptism and faith in Jesus will be saved. This is what many people think of when it comes to being the church and being saved. And they think that those who do not share in the Christian faith and are not baptized will be condemned. But there are also differing voices within the Christian community. Some denominations do not consider other denominations as the church and as worthy of salvation. Many Christians themselves have issues with such narrow and condemnatory attitudes and ideas.

The third understanding of the church, which I believe is the real meaning of the church, is that it is made up of people who respond to God's call to a life of holiness and grace. God calls everyone, both Christians and non-Christians, to a life of holiness. Jesus did not limit himself to one group or section of the society. He called everyone to follow him. Due to various reasons, many are not baptized as Christians. But all of us are called to live in communion with God and with one another. That would mean living a Christological life or being in the realm of heaven, as we have discussed. When that becomes the parameter for being the church, it is hard to say who comes under the purview of the church because God alone is the judge. It could include Christians and non-Christians. Understanding the church in this sense would then automatically tell us that salvation means being free from the powers of evils and sins and living in communion with God and others here on earth and in eternity.

If we understand the church and salvation in this sense, then there could be many "saints" and "unknown Christians" in other cultures and traditions. They may be living Christological lives even though they may not be belonging to the Catholic or Christian community. This understanding of the church and salvation would also tell us that there might be many of us in the Christian community who may not be the real church and experiencing salvation because of our failure to live Christ in our lives. Just because we were baptized as Christians, it doesn't mean that we are living a Christological life.

Jesus appears to be telling us that going through the ceremony of baptism and becoming a member of the Christian community is not a free ticket to heaven or assurance of salvation (Luke 13:27–29). Jesus warns us against such false thinking and tells us that we would be surprised when we see who actually gets to heaven. A true Christian is one who lives Christ in his or her life. The sacrament or ceremony of baptism is only the initiation into the Christological life that one is called to live. The spirit and essence of that sacrament need to be lived throughout one's life. Everyday we have to live heaven on earth, allowing God to lead us and guide us and living in harmony with our fellow human beings and the whole creation. That is what brings us salvation and makes us the real church and saints.

Heaven as a Collective Responsibility

Since the dead continue to be part of our family and we pray for them and they do the same in turn, the question that arises then is whether heaven is an individual or collective responsibility. Do I work toward only my attainment of heaven and personal salvation or am I also responsible for the salvation of others and their attainment of heaven? Am I responsible for your conscience as well as mine? I believe that it is a collective responsibility. We are responsible for each other. It is not just about my heaven and me. It is about our family. We are one family, and we journey together. In a family, all the members have to help each other so that everyone can grow well and be healthy and happy. As children of God and God's creation, we are one family. We journey together. If some are lagging behind, we have to carry them along or help them to move forward. We are responsible for each other in helping each other to live holy lives.

God helps us in many ways to remain in his love. He sends his angels to guide us, protect us, and watch over us. We hear of archangels, guardian angels, and other angels. Jesus has spoken about them, the scriptures talk about them, and our ancestors believed in them. We hear of Angel Gabriel as a messenger of God bringing God's good news to people. He brought the good news of incarnation to Mary. He announced to Zechariah that he and his wife were going to have a child in their old age. In the book of Revelation, we hear of Angel Michael presented as a warrior fighting against the evil force. In the book of Tobit, we hear of Angel Raphael as a healer and helper for Tobit and Tobias. An angel came to Jesus to comfort him in his agony in Gethsemane. God sends his angels and other heavenly beings to help us in many ways.

Some people have doubts and questions about the existence of angels and other heavenly beings because we don't see them. We don't see them with our physical eyes because they belong to a different realm of life than ours. There are many beings in God's creation that we have not seen. We have not seen even all of what we have on this earth. I have not seen even all of what is in St. Louis! When our knowledge is so limited, how can we claim to know or to have seen everything that God has created? God's creation is beyond our comprehension, but God has shown us that he does not leave us helpless and defenseless. He provides us with the assistance of angels, saints, and other heavenly beings. These agents of God are ever ready to assist us because they all desire what God desires—that is, we live in union with him and with the whole of God's creation.

God also helps us through our parents, family members, friends, and others. All these are provided to us to help us live healthy lives and remain united with him and others in love. When we are helped so much, we are also called to help others to live in communion with God and others. We have a responsibility to help our brothers and sisters to turn away from sin and the path of hell and turn toward God or choose the path of heaven. God reminded Prophet Ezekiel about his responsibility to be a sentinel for his people lest they fall into sin and evils ways (Ezek 3:17–20). After Cain killed his brother, God asked Cain, "Where is your brother Abel?" (Gen 4:9). Cain replied with a tone of anger inquiring whether he was his brother's keeper. They were supposed to be a family loving and caring for each other. In God's eyes, Cain was his brother's keeper, but Cain did not see it that way.

We don't build our heaven or salvation in isolation. Yes, each one of us has to take responsibility and cooperate with God in attaining heaven or our personal salvation. But as a family or community, we have to be also concerned about each other's salvation. We are our brother or sister's keepers. God wants us to journey together. We have to hold each other's hands and walk together in the journey of life. We need to support each other when we feel tired and exhausted, and lift each other up when we stumble and fall. He wants us to work and live as a team.

Our Identity after Death

God has created us as human beings and unique individuals, and I believe that that identity continues for all eternity. But after we die, the physical dimensions of our life change. We enter into a different realm of life. Responding to the Sadducees regarding the resurrection of the dead, Jesus said that after death the physical dimensions of our life such as marriage or other commitments and contracts that bind us here on earth do not continue (Mark 12:25). To live our lives here on earth, we need all such commitments and arrangements, but after we die, we enter into a different realm of life. Our relationship is on a larger scale. We are not limited to some particular individuals and families. We become part of the larger family of God with the whole of creation. Although we are part of that larger family of God while we live on earth, we are restricted in our relationships because of all the limitations that come with our physical life. But death opens up a larger world of love and relationship.

Jesus said that after we die we become like angels. That doesn't mean that we become angels. We are different from angels and other heavenly beings. Becoming like angels could mean that we would become free spirits like angels. We will be beyond the limitations of the physical aspects of our life. There will be no more whites, blacks, and browns, no more Catholics and Protestants, no more Christians, Muslims, Jews, Hindus, or other groupings, no more Americans, Indians, Russians, or other nationalities, no more rich and poor, no more men and women, no more father, mother, and children, and no more of any such physical categories that divide or separate us here. We will be free moving spirits loving and relating with everyone. We will enter into a non-physical, spiritual realm of life that makes us like the Holy Trinity, unique and yet united. We will be one family, with God as our father and all of us as his children.

Redemption from Hell and Purgatory

Since we are all part of God's family, we have to think that even those who are in the realm of hell and purgatory are our family. We need to continue to assist them with our prayers and wish that God forgives their sins and they choose heaven. In a family, some members may be estranged and cut off completely, but that doesn't stop them from being members of the family. The prodigal son was cut off from his father and brother, but he was still part of the family. The father was waiting for him. The father grieved for him. We can think that God grieves for his children who are in the realm of hell and purgatory not only after death but even while they live their earthly lives. If we are in the realm of hell or purgatory during our earthly life now, we can believe that God is grieving for us. He wants us to be in the realm of heaven. He wants us to be united with him and others in love. He constantly battles the evil force to redeem us from the realms of hell and purgatory. The same thing, we can assume, applies to our brothers and sisters in the realm of hell and purgatory after death. God looks at each of them and says, "That is my child; I hate seeing him or her living in misery and pain." He fights with the evil force on our behalf and says the same thing he said to Pharaoh, "Let my people go." Just as a father or mother is upset and sad when their children are sick, our God is sad and grieving when we are living in sin or sick and suffering in hell or purgatory. When we are hurt, he is hurt. He waits for our return as the father of the prodigal son waited.

If we think of the dead who are in the realm of hell and purgatory as continuing to be part of our family, maybe as estranged or lost, and if we believe that God is grieving for them and waiting for them to return to him, then the question is whether there is redemption out of hell and purgatory. If someone is in the realm of hell or purgatory at the time of death, does that person have an opportunity to get out of those realms and move into the realm of heaven? Is the person condemned to hell for all eternity or could he or she be redeemed from hell? Believing that our God grieves for us when we are in the realm of hell and purgatory and he is waiting for our return, I tend to believe that redemption out of hell and purgatory is possible. There is nothing impossible for God (Mark 10:27). And that is what we pray in our prayers, that the dead may be forgiven of their sins and given fullness of life. Here is where we think of these realms of life as dynamic rather than being static. Just as we discussed about heaven, hell, and purgatory as dynamic states of being during our earthly life, we could think of these realities as dynamic after death too. We don't need to think of them as finished products out of which there is no return. They are states of being which can alter with the choices we make for God or against God. That could happen before death and after death.

That would bring up the question whether we have free will after we die. Do we still have the capacity to choose after we die? The answer to that question is going to be somewhat speculative because it is difficult to say whether the free will of a person could be operative without his or her physical body. I tend to believe that it could be operative even after we move past the physical realm of our life. Since our life continues even after our physical death, it is appropriate to think that we would continue to have our free will. God's love for us is such that he continues to love and respect us as unique individuals with freedom to choose. Just because we passed from the physical realm of this earth, we don't need to think that we would lose our free will or God would force us into something. If he is going to force us into something then it is against love and that will not happen because that will be against his nature.

God wishes that all of us remained united with him and with one another in love. But it is possible that we have already put ourselves in the realm of hell or purgatory while living on this earth, making us remain estranged or lost from that larger family of God. However, God doesn't give up on us. He will continue to wait for us to choose him, choose love, and choose heaven. We could think that God could simply forgive us and take us out of hell or purgatory. And we don't deny that possibility. But looking at God's nature of love we know that he does not simply impose things on us or do something without our consent. If he has to wait for a long time to gain us back, he will do that. The father of the prodigal son waited for a long time. We could think that the father could have gone after his son and brought him back home by force. But we don't see the father doing that. He continued to wait.

In the story of creation in the book of Genesis, we read that God rested after he created everything and found everything good. We could assume that God does not rest when he sees some part of his creation—that is, us, not looking good or suffering in hell or purgatory. We can assume and believe that God's salvific work would continue until every one of his children is redeemed. The shepherd is not going to rest until all the sheep are together with him. We cannot say how long it is going to take. Of course, after we pass from this earthly life, the concept of time does not apply to our life. But even if it is going to take a million years for a sinner to turn around, God will wait for his or her return. The sad part about it is that for those million years, the sinner will be living in misery and God will be grieving for him or her. Another reason why it is difficult to say how long it is going to take for everyone to be saved is because human life on earth has not come to an end. And as long as human beings roam this earth, we could assume that there are going to be people who choose hell over heaven. We can hope that when they pass from this physical world to the world of eternity, they will have a greater vision of life and they will choose heaven over hell. But again it depends on how they exercise their free will and how God's grace works in their life. Considering all these, we have to again see the salvific work as an ongoing and dynamic process rather than seeing it as something that begins and ends at a particular time.

Jesus said that he had "other sheep that do not belong to this fold" (John 10:16). We don't know who this "other sheep" are. We could wonder whether he was referring to non-Christians, non-Jewish people, people who did not believe in God, people who were in the realm of hell and purgatory, or even some beings who do not belong to our human and earthly realm. The only thing we can think of is that God desires all of us and the whole creation to remain united with him so that there will be one flock and one shepherd (John 10:16). Even when we talk about the "whole creation," we don't really know what all beings are present in it. We have not seen all of them. We can only believe that God would want his whole creation to remain united with him.

When it comes to human beings, we might wonder why anyone would refuse to choose God after they depart from this world, because they would have a better vision of heaven, hell, and purgatory. What would stop them from choosing God? To answer that question we could look at our life on earth. We could wonder why we don't choose God while we live on this earth even after we know that choosing him brings us peace, love, and joy and choosing evil brings us misery and pain. Even after we have all that knowledge and experience, we sometimes end up choosing evil or hell. We stay away from God. So death or moving to the non-physical realm of our life does not guarantee that we would choose God or heaven.

In the story of the rich man and Lazarus, when the rich man asked Abraham to send Lazarus to his brothers to warn them, Abraham replied that if they did not listen to Moses and the prophets, they were not going to listen even if somebody came back from the dead. Jesus wishes that we already made that choice for heaven while we live on the earth here so that we enjoy it not only after death but also while we live on this earth. But sometimes we don't choose that. We don't journey with God and participate in his dance of love. We sometimes engage in our own dance and follow our own path.

Believing in the possibility of having free will or capacity to choose after death could make some people think that they don't need to choose God now since they can choose him after they die or that they will have plenty of time to make that choice. But again, that is no different from what we do while we live on this earth. We postpone and procrastinate in choosing God or heaven. Many of us say, "I will do it tomorrow," "I will be a good person tomorrow," "I will make healthy choices tomorrow," etc. But often, that "tomorrow" never comes. We continue to do what we do. Hence death or passing from this world is no guarantee that we are going to choose God even if we have the whole eternity to make that choice. Reciprocating God's love is to be without delay and demands. We discussed about that in reference to the two men, in the gospel of Luke, who wanted to delay their response to Jesus because one wanted to say good-bye to his family and the other wanted to bury his father. Jesus reminded them that their response to him had to be without delay and demands. Choosing heaven or God is to be here and now. Jesus wants us to choose him now and not tomorrow or after we die. The earlier we do it the better because we can enjoy God's peace, joy, and love so much more. The question would be if we already know how beautiful and wonderful it is to be with the Lord, why delay? But we know that choice does not come by easily.

Since we could think that our free will continues after death, and since we could think of heaven, hell, and purgatory as dynamic realities, we might also wonder whether a person who is already in the realm of heaven or with God could make a choice against God and leave the state of heaven and end up in hell or purgatory. I doubt it. That transition from the state of heaven to hell or purgatory could happen during our earthly life but not after our death. First of all, having experienced the joys of heaven in eternity, it is most unlikely that anyone would want to leave heaven or God. Secondly, after our death if we are in the state of heaven or united with God, then it is going to be that way for all eternity because a total union with God is a total union with God. There is no separation in God. During our earthly life we go back and forth between heaven, hell, and purgatory because our union with God is imperfect and partial.

Divine Grace

Although I suggest that we have the free will and we need to choose God or heaven whether it is before death or after death, we don't forget the truth that God is the ultimate judge and he is loving and merciful. Our choices and cooperation with God are only one side of our story. The other side of the story is God's grace. We need God's grace in everything. Too much focus on our efforts and choices can make us think that we have to earn heaven or heaven is the end-result of or reward for our hard work. Heaven is not just the result of or reward for our hard work. It is also a gift. Whatever we achieve or accomplish in our life, including heaven or our life with God, is to be seen as a gift of God. Even our desire to seek him and be with him is planted in us by God. The love in us is a gift of God. It is God who is leading us and guiding us. As the scripture says, we live, move, and have our being in him. We don't determine everything. Without God's grace, our efforts and choices come to nothing. Hence we want to see heaven or our union with God and others as the result of God's grace and our effort coming together, but God's grace is primary. As we try to do our part in making our choices for heaven, we also submit ourselves to God's mercy and love so that where we lack in love he can make up.

The Journey Continues

Looing at all these reflections on the concept of new heaven and new earth, we once again return back to the idea of our life as a journey, a journey with God and others. Particularly focusing on heaven, many of us may have conceptualized heaven as a destination, goal, or end-point where we reach and then stop. But if we think of our life as a journey with the Lord and others, then it is not an end-point where we reach and stop. It is an unending journey. We continue as pilgrims on the journey with the Lord and others for all eternity. Often when we think of our life, we think of it in terms of goals, destinations, end-points toward which we are moving. From the time we are born we are focused on reaching or accomplishing many goals in our life. A child goes through many such end-points or goals in his or her biological and physical development. A student sets many goals in attaining his or her degree. Married people set many goals in building up their family life, such as, buying or building a house, having one or more children, getting a steady job, and ensuring some financial security. A scientist, doctor, nurse, patient, teacher, engineer, businessperson, farmer, priest, and all others in other vocations and situations of life set many such goals. When people travel or drive, they have a destination.

Goals and destinations are part of our life. Some people come to a point of "retirement" when they don't focus on any major goals anymore. Retirement and restful life become their goal. Given this dimension of our life, it is possible that we think of heaven as a goal or destination that we want to reach, at the end of which we can "retire and rest." Even in our prayers and spiritual conversations, we use terms such as "eternal rest," "rest in peace," etc. But if we look at our life as a journey with the Lord and others, there is no real retirement or rest. Heaven is not a retirement home. It is an unending journey. It is a state of being in which we are united with God and others in love. It is a journey that begins here on earth and continues into eternity. If heaven is union with God and others, and if God is constantly journeying, we are going to journey with him. We often think of God as being busy, busily involved in our lives and in the creation. So we don't think of him being "retired." If God is never retired, then we are never going to be retired. If God is always at work, then we are always going to be at work with him. God is not going to leave us somewhere and go away to work somewhere. When we think of heaven, we are thinking of being with God at all times. And since he is always on the move and always at work, we are going to be as active as he is.

I believe such ideas might make many of us feel heavy again! Maybe some of us were thinking that we could finally rest and relax when we get to heaven. But now I am saying it is going to be "more work!" It is not rest and retirement. But the work I am referring to in heaven is not the kind of work we are engaged in here on earth. It is not even work. It is simply being with God as he is. Yes, the experience of heaven is going to be an experience of rest and peace. It is a rest and freedom from the cares of the physical life and sufferings of this world since such rest and freedom are limited during our earthly life. Heaven in eternity is going to be a state of unending peace and joy. However, it is not a rest or retirement in the usual sense. Since God is always active and present, we are going to be active and present like him. We are going to enjoy limitless love and peace, but we are going to be on the journey with him. It is never going to stop. Heaven never stops. God never stops. The work we are going to be involved in, I assume, is to assist God in bringing our fellow human beings into the realm of heaven. Yes, God and heaven are a goal or destination in some sense, but it is not in the usual sense of a retirement home or end-point where we reach and stop everything. We are hoping to be eternally united with God and others, since that union is limited during our earthly life.

I read somewhere about the different ways in which people plan their vacation. Some people plan their vacation well, identify their destination, and they travel to their destination to enjoy a time of rest and relaxation. But there are other people who have a different take on their vacation. They also plan well, they have a destination, but they don't just wait to get to their destination to start enjoying their vacation. They already start enjoying their vacation from the time they leave their home or from the time they plan. They make it enjoyable during their journey and after they get to their destination. Sometimes during their journey, things may not go as they plan. They may have some troubles on the way. They may get delayed. They may have to detour or reroute. But they still don't allow those things to weigh them down. Those experiences might somewhat dampen their spirit and the vacation mood. But they face it together. They stick together, support each other, and work together to overcome their problems. And they continue their journey.

When we think of the journey of our life, we want to look at it from the perspective of the second category of people who go on their vacation. We want to start working toward enjoying our communion with the Lord and others while we are here on earth and we want to hope and pray that it continues into eternity. We have our union with the Lord and others in eternity in mind, but we also want to pay attention to the here and now. In that journey, as we have seen, there will be many hurdles and problems to face. But we are not alone. We have the Lord journeying with us, and we are journeying with each other as fellow travelers. We want to be with the Lord and others here and now as much as in eternity. That is the Christological model of life, a life in union with the Lord and others here on this earth as well as in eternity.

With all these reflections on heaven, hell, and purgatory, we still know that we don't know everything about all these. Our effort was only to look at them in a new way so that we see them as part our journey of life. The Christological model of life invites us to be on the journey with the Lord not only on this earth but also in eternity. What Saint Paul said about knowing God partially now and fully in eternity (1 Cor 13:12) can be applied to the realities of heaven, hell, and purgatory. As pilgrims on the journey of life traveling with the Lord we live with the hope that we will know it all fully when we move from the realm of space and time of this earthly life to the eternal realm of God. Until then we keep moving forward with faith and courage.

Conclusion

WE DISCUSSED MANY THINGS and we have come a long way. But we have done it together, you, as the reader and I, as the writer. We traveled together. And in that journey, God was with us. This whole book is about that. You, God, and I are journeying together. We are in a dialogical process. You and I, as fellow travelers, were trying to unravel the mystery of God and the mystery of our lives. And in unraveling that mystery, God himself, I believe, was the guiding force.

Even with all these discussions and reflections, we know that we haven't understood everything about God or about our life. God is still he who is. We keep remaining open to his revelations. That is how God has been doing with our ancestors. He was traveling with them, helping them to unravel his mystery and the mystery of their lives. And this is how God is going to continue to do it in the future. In that revelation, there are some common denominators and some unique characteristics. To each of us, he reveals himself in a unique way because we are unique. The way he revealed himself to our ancestors is not how he reveals himself to us. The way he reveals himself to me is not how he reveals himself to my friend, neighbor, family member, colleague, or community member. But at the same time, he reveals himself to all of us in all ages in a way that all of us can relate to and share our beliefs and experiences.

Because we are unique and yet united as one family, God desires that we keep the dialogical triangle active and balanced. He loves all of us, and he is journeying with us. There are hurdles and hardships on our journey, but the journey continues. God's love never fails. When we fall and fail, he lifts us up. When we get stuck and stay away, he comes in search of us.

I know the personal story of a grandmother that speaks to this love of God and the journey of life that we are engaged in. This grandmother has a grandson who had made and continues to make bad choices and ends up in problems. He is in and out of jail quite frequently for various reasons. This grandmother is in tears for him everyday. She prays and prays for him to come to his senses and change his ways. She waits for him to come out of jail and sometimes bails him out hoping that that would be the last time he would be in jail. She longs to see him living a healthy life. But while he is in jail there is something amazing that this grandma does for him. Everyday she writes a "love" letter for him. One letter a day! But due to the rules and policies of the jail, she is not permitted to send letters to him everyday. The Jail officials would not give the letters to her grandson if she sends them everyday. But that doesn't stop her form writing a letter to him everyday. She collects them together, puts them in an envelope, and sends them to him once every two or three weeks. When he receives his mail, he sees that his grandma has a letter for him for each day. She has been letting him know that she has been thinking of him and sending her love to him everyday. Even if he has not been thinking of her, she has been thinking of him and waiting for him everyday.

This grandma is an example of God's unceasing love. He has been sending us his love letters everyday down through the centuries. He keeps inviting us to the dance of his love and waits for us over and over again. His love never ceases. But sometimes we are in "jail," drowning or locked up in our own self-only world, sinful habits, addictions, sadness, anger, disappointments, spiritual darkness, defenses, stuck points, sadness, grief, and all such negative and unhealthy elements. We choose the realm of hell rather than heaven. Sometimes we feel being pushed into all of these. God hopes and desires that we come out of our jails of hell. But even while we are in them, he never stops loving us. He never gives up on us. He hopes that our confinement to our jail is temporary. He sends inspirations, messages, and communications to make us return back to him. Either he helps us to come to our senses by ourselves as the prodigal son did or he sends us messengers like Moses, the prophets, John the Baptist, and Jesus himself.

We are special people deeply loved by God. We are his children, beloved sons and daughters. If it is God who created us, we must be his special and awesome creations, because he does not create junk. Many negative things may have happened in our life. Many things may have shaped us into who we are today. There may be many things in our life that we are not proud of. But because it is God who created us and we are his children, there is something special about us and something good in us. There is a divine spark in us. Because of different reasons we may not have been able to bring out that divine spark. But that doesn't mean that we don't have it within us. We may have gotten stuck. But that doesn't mean that we cannot move.

Maybe there were times in our life that were pretty bad and difficult. Maybe we were sad, angry, upset, ashamed, embarrassed, afraid, disappointed, discouraged, feeling hopeless and helpless, and dark and dreary, but God carried us through all of that. He is inviting us to give to him our burdens, sufferings, disappointments, anger, sadness, shame, doubts, questions, and all such things. God works with the available material. Sometimes, the material that we are is highly imperfect and flawed. But God will work with us if we let him. He does not wait for a perfect day or perfect situation to start his work. He is like a gentle river or creek that flows according to the lay of the land. He meets us at or picks us up from where he finds us.

Jesus went to the people of Galilee with the message, "The time is fulfilled, and the kingdom of God has come near; repent, and believe in the good news" (Mark 1:15). He worked with and walked among imperfect people. Today he works with and walks among us. He brings us the same message and wants us to believe in the good news that he loves us. We are not meant to get stuck and stay away. We are to be a family, God's family. With him as our leader and traveling companion, we can confidently march ahead with faith and courage in our heart. The Christological model that he places before us is all about being on the journey with him and with others.

At the end of his gospel, Saint John says, "But there are also many other things that Jesus did; if every one of them were written down, I suppose that the world itself could not contain the books that would be written" (John 21:25). I feel the same about this book. All what I have written is not any lofty wisdom or knowledge about God or about our life but rather some reflections and thoughts about how God has been revealing himself to us and how we have been experiencing him. If I ever think that the mystery of God can be reduced to a book or thousands of books, I will be sorely mistaken. This book was written with the simple purpose of giving ourselves yet another opportunity to realize how big our God is and how small he becomes to let us know how much he loves us.

Bibliography

Ainsworth, Mary. "Infant-Mother Attachment." *American Psychologist* 34 (1979) 932–37.

Akhtar, Salman. *Comprehensive Dictionary of Psychoanalysis*. London: Carnac, 2009.

Bowlby, John. *A Secure Base: Clinical Applications of Attachment Theory*. New York: Routledge, 2005.

———. *A Secure Base: Parent-Child Attachment and Healthy Human Development*. New York: Basic, 1988.

Catechism of the Catholic Church. New York: Doubleday, 1997.

De Sales, Francis. *Treatise on the Love of God*. Translated by Antony Mookenthottam, Armind Nazareth, and Henry J. Kodikuthiyil. Bangalore: SFS, 2009.

De Sales, Francis, and Jane De Chantal. *Letters of Spiritual Direction*. Translated by Peronne Marie Thibert. New York: Paulist, 1988.

Edathumparambil, Binu. *The Accent: Exploring the Path to a Rejuvenating Life*. Bloomington, IN: WestBow, 2015.

Francis, Pope. *Amoris Laetitia*. Vatican, 2016.

———. *Evangelii Gaudium*. Vatican, 2013.

———. *Laudato Si*. Vatican, 2015.

Gold, Marissa B. "*This Is the Number One Predictor of Divorce—and How to Fix It*" (February 2016). http://www.womansday.com.

Gorski, Eugene F. *Theology of Religions: A Sourcebook for Interreligious Study*. New York: Paulist, 2008.

Helms, Hal M., ed. Saint Augustine, *The Confessions of Saint Augustine*. Brewster, Massachusetts: Paraclete, 2010.

Jones, Jennifer L., and Shannon L. Mehr. "Foundations and Assumptions of the Scientist Practitioner Model." *The American Behavioral Scientist* 50 (2007) 766–771.

Medora, Nilufer P. "Strengths and Challenges in the Indian Family." *Marriage & Family Review* 41 (2007) 165–193.

Philips, Amali. "Gendering Color: Identity, Femininity and Marriage in Kerala. *Anthropologica* 46 (2004) 253–272.

Rath, Tom. *StrengthFinder* 2.0. Gallup, 2007.

Resick, Patricia A., et al. "*Cognitive Processing Therapy: Veteran/military Version: Therapist's Manual*." Washington, D.C.: Department of Veteran Affairs, 2014.

Wall, Mike. *A Manned Mission to Mars Is Closer to Reality Than Ever: NASA Chief* (September 2015). http://www.space.com.

BIBLIOGRAPHY

Winnicott, Donald W. "Transitional Objects and Transitional Phenomena-A Study of the First Not-Me Possession." *International Journal of Psycho-Analysis* 34 (1953) 89–97.

Wurmser, Leon. *The Mask of Shame*. Baltimore: The John Hopkins University Press, 1981.